PROGRESSIVE RECORD OF AUTOGRAPHS

THE EARLIEST ONE

(5 years)

Scott Fitzgerald. (11 years)

AUTOGRAPH AT ~~Eight~~ Seven

Scott Fitzgerald

AUTOGRAPH AT ~~Nine~~ Eight

Scott Fitzgerald

AUTOGRAPH AT ~~Ten~~ Nine

Scott Fitzgerald

AUTOGRAPH AT ~~Eleven~~ Ten

Scott Fitzgerald

AUTOGRAPH AT TWELVE

Scott Fitzgerald

AUTOGRAPH AT THIRTEEN

Scott Fitzgerald

AUTOGRAPH AT FOURTEEN

Scott Fitzgerald

F. Scott Fitzgerald

AUTOGRAPH AT FIFTEEN

Francis Scott Fitzgerald

AUTOGRAPH AT SIXTEEN

Francis Scott Fitzgerald

AUTOGRAPH AT SEVENTEEN

F. Scott Fitzgerald

AUTOGRAPH AT EIGHTEEN

Scott Fitzgerald

AUTOGRAPH AT NINETEEN

Scott Fitzgerald

AUTOGRAPH AT TWENTY

F. Scott Fitzgerald

AUTOGRAPH AT TWENTY-ONE

F. Scott Fitzgerald

F. Scott Fitzgerald

49

From Fitzgerald's baby book

FITZGERALD/HEMINGWAY
ANNUAL
1971

Edited by Matthew J. Bruccoli

University of South Carolina

C. E. Frazer Clark, Jr.

 Microcard Editions

Library of Congress Catalog Card Number 75-83781.

ISBN 0-910972-12-5

Editors: **Matthew J. Bruccoli**

Department of English
University of South Carolina
Columbia, S. C. 29208

C. E. Frazer Clark, Jr.

1490 Sodon Lake Drive
Bloomfield Hills, Michigan 48013

Assistant Editor: Jennifer McCabe Atkinson

Editorial Assistants: James L. W. West III
I. S. Skelton

Address all editorial correspondence to the editors.

Address orders and inquiries to NCR/Microcard Editions,
901 26th Street, N.W., Washington, D.C. 20037.

For Marge

Contents

PREFACE TO "THIS SIDE OF PARADISE"

never used

Two years ago, when I was a very young man indeed, I had an unmistakable urge to write a book. It was to be a picaresque novel, original in form and alternating a melancholy, naturalistic egotism with a picture of the generation then hastening to war.

It was to be naive in places, shocking in others, painful to the conventional and not without its touch of ironic sublimity. The "leading character", a loiterer on the borderland of genius, loved many women and gazed at himself in many mirrors -- in fact, women and mirrors were preponderant in all the important scenes.

I completed it during the last gasp of a last year at college, and the intricacies of a training camp. Its epigrams were all polished by the substitution of the word one for the word you; its chapter titles were phrased to sound somewhat like lines from pre-Raphaelite poems, somewhat like electric signs over musical comedies; the book itself was a tedius casserole of a dozen by McKenzie, Wells, and Robert Hugh Benson, largely flavored by the great undigested butterball of Dorian Gray.

The conservative publisher to whom I sent it kept it for several months and finally returned it with the complaint that the hero failed in the end to find himself, and that this defection would so certainly disappoint the reader as to predestine the book to failure.

He suggested that I remedy this and I pondered the difficulty for several weeks -- how I could intrigue the hero into a "philosphy of life" when my own ideas were in much the state of Alice's after the hatter's tea-party.

At length I took a tip from Schopenhauer, Hugh Walpole, and even the early Wells -- begged the question by plunging boldly into obscurity; astounded myself with an impenetrable chapter where I left the hero alone with rhapsodic winds and hyper-significant stars; gemmed the paragrpahs with neo-symbolic bits culled from my own dismantled poems -- such awe-inspiring half lines as ***the dark celibacy of greatness *** Youth, the Queen Anne Clavichord from which age wrings the symphony of art *** the tired pitying beauty of monotony that hung like summer air over the gate of his soul ***
And finding that I had merely dragged the hero from a logical muddle into an illogical one, I dispatched him to the war and callously slew him several thousand feet in the air, whence he fell "not like a dead but a splendid life-found swallow **** down **** down ****"

The book finished with four dots -- there was a fifth but I erased it.

After two months it was again refused. The conservative publisher was, however, optimistic enough to send it to a more radical competitor, who specialized in leading out the new Slavic novelists and giving free air to experiments in Celtic phrasing. This publisher did not even faintly consider it.

The war over, I slumped into a mental lethargy in the misty depths of which I searched for the causes of my book's failure, and eventually discovered the root of the trouble. All I had written of things I was interested in: THE INFLUENCE OF NIGHT, RATHER BAD WOMEN, PERSONALITY, FANATICISM, THE SUPERNATURAL, and VERY GOOD WOMEN, was quite above the average.

All I had written of subjects with which I was thoroughly cognizant:

1

THE "PREP" SCHOOL, COLLEGE, THE MIDDLE WEST, NATURE, QUAINT STUPID PEOPLE, and MYSELF was, because I was quite bored with all of them, well below average.

My course was obvious, my inspiration was immediate. Virtuously resisting the modern writer's tendency to dramatize himself, I began another novel; whether its hero really "gets anywhere" is for the reader to decide.

For bait to the hesitant I hold out the promise that the words passion, moonlight, sin and God occur many times; the words shimmer, debutante and mystic with less frequency.

Resisting a temptation to dedicate it either to a certain prelate -- who would quite possibly be exhumed and excommunicated -- or, throwing ▓▓▓▓▓▓ ▓▓▓▓▓▓▓▓▓▓▓▓▓▓▓▓▓▓▓▓▓▓▓ guile aside, to myself, with love and affection, I offer it to all those argumentative and discoursive souls who once frequented a certain inn whose doors are now dark, whose fabled walls ring no more to the melody of Chaucer's lesser known poems.

F. Scott Fitzgerald
St. Paul, Minn.
Mid-August, 1919

This Preface was not included in *This Side of Paradise*, but parts were published in Robert Sklar's *The Last Laocoön* (New York: Oxford University Press, 1967, pp. 34-35). It exists in two different typescripts: one at The Princeton University Library, and one at Harold Ober Associates—which is reproduced here. All rights to this Preface are the property of Frances Fitzgerald Smith.
—M. J. B.

Fitzgerald's Ledger

F. Scott Fitzgerald's ledger consists of three sections: a yearly accounting of his earnings through 1936; a detailed table of his writings and sales; and an autobiographical chronology. The accounting section only is printed here. We plan to publish a facsimile of the entire ledger.

What follows is an exact transcription of Fitzgerald's accounts. No attempt has been made to correct spelling or arithmetic. Material in square brackets was crossed out or erased by Fitzgerald.—*M.J.B.*

Money Earned by Writing since Leaving Army

Record for 1919

Stories

Babes in the Woods	[30 00]
The Debutante (Play)	$ 30. 00
The Four Fists	35. 00
The Cut Glass Bowl	150. 00
Porcelain & Pink (Play)	150. 00
Dalyrimple goes Wrong	35. 00
Benediction	40. 00
Head and Shoulders 400.00 Commission 10%	40. 00
A Dirge (Poem)	360. 00
Mr. Icky (Play)	4. 00
	35. 00
Total Earnings	879. 00

4

Record for 1920

Stories			
The Ice Palace	$400. 00.	Commission 10%	$360 00
Myra Meets His Family	400. 00	"	360 00
The Camels Back	500. 00	"	450 00
Bernice Bobs her Hair	500. 00	"	450 00
The Off-Shore Pirate	500. 00	"	450 00
The Smilers			35 00
May Day			200 00
Tarquin of Cheapside			50 00
The Jellybean	900. 00	"	810 00
The Russet Witch	900. 00	"	810 00
Total			3,975 00
Movies			
Head and Shoulders	2500. 00	"	2,250 00
Myra Meets His Family	1000. 00	"	900 00
The Off Shore Pirate	2250. 00	"	2,025 00
Option on my out put	3000. 00	"	2,700 00
Total			7,425 00
Other Writings			
This is a Magazine			75 00
Total			75 00
From Books			
This Side of Paradise			6,200 00
Flappers and Philosophers			500 00
Total			6,700 00
Total			$18,175 00
*Ommission----The Lees of Happiness $750.00, Com 10%			$675 00
Total			$18,850 00

Record for 1921

Stories	The Popular Girl	$1500.00	Commission 10%	$ 1,350 00
	Total			1,350 00
Serial	The Beautiful & Damned	7000.00	Commission 10%	6,300 00
	Total			6,300 00
Other Writings	Jemima			100 00
	The Baltimore Anti-Christ			13 50
	The Far-seeing Skeptics			5 00
	Brass			7 00
	Total			135 50
From Books	This Side of Paradise			5,636 68
	Flappers and Philosophers			2,730 00
	The Beautiful and Damned (advance)			2,813 19
	Total			11,179 68
English Advance	(Add *Syndication Jelly Bean* $5.00)			100 00
	Total			$19,065 18

Record for 1922

Stories

The Diamond as big as the Ritz	$300.00	Com. 10%	270. 00
Benjamin Button	1000.00	"	900. 00
Two for a Cent	900.00	"	810. 00
Winter Dreams	900.00	"	810. 00
Total			2790. 00

Movie

The Beautiful and Damned	2,500.00	"	2250. 00

Other Writings

On Being Twenty five			800. 00
{ Little Brother of the Flapper	1000.00	"	900. 00
{ The Moment of Revolt			
Canadian Winter Dreams	100.00	"	250. 00
"Love Legend" (review)			90. 00
"The Oppidan" (review)			5. 00
"Margie Wins The Game" (review)			3. 00
Movies and the Publisher			5. 00
			5. 00
Total			7,098. 00

(continued next page)

(Page 54 continued)

English Rights
From Books

Forty seven pounds	212.	00
This Side of Paradise	1,200.	00
Flappers and Philosophers	350.	00
The Beautiful and Damned	12,133.	00
Tales of the Jazz Age	3,056.	00
The Vegetable (advance)	1,236.	00
Total (all these book figures estimated)	17,775.	00
Total	$25,135.	00

Zelda's Earnings

The Super-Flapper	$500.	00
The Moment of Revolt	250.	00
Review of Beautiful & Damned	15.	00
Eulogy on the Flapper	50.	00
Total	$815.	00

Record for 1923

Stories

Option from Hearsts	$1500.00	Com. 10%	$1350.	00
"Dice, Brass Knuckles and Guitar"	1500.00	"	1350.	00
Hot and Cold Blood	1500.00	"	1350.	00
"Diamond Dick"	1500.00	"	1350.	00
"Our Own Movie Queen" (half Zelda)	1000.00	"	900.	00
Gretchen's Forty Winks	1200.00	"	1080.	00
Winter Dreams (English Rights)	125.00	"	112.	50
Total			7,492.	50

Movies

This Side of Paradise	10,000.	00
The Camel's Back	1,000.	00
Grit	2,000.	00
Titles for Glimpses of the Moon	500.	00
Total	13,500.	00

Play Advance ---------------------------- 500.00 --- Com. 10% ---- 450. 00

(continued next page)

(Page 55 continued)

Other Writings

Imagination and a few Mothers	1000.	Com 10%	900.00
The Cruise of the Rolling Junk	300.	"	270.00
Making Monagamy Work	300.	"	270.00
Our Irresponsible Rich	350.	"	315.00
The Most Disgraceful Thing I ever Did	[20.	"]	20.00
Review of Being Respectable,	[15.	"]	15.00
" " Many Marriages	[5.	"]	5.00
" " Through the Wheat	[5.	"]	5.00
Total			1,800.00
Syndicate Returns	74.75	Com 10%	67.28

Books

This Side of Paradise	880.00
Flappers and Philosophers	98.00
The Beautiful and Damned	292.00
Tales of the Jazz Age	270.43
Total (figures estimated)	1,510.00
Advance on New Novel (The Great Gatsby)	3,939.00
Total	5,450.00

Total	$28,759.78

Record for 1924

Stories

		Com. 10%	
The Baby Party	$1500.00	Com. 10%	1350 00
*The Sensible Thing	1750.00	"	1575 00
Rags Martin-Jones and the Pr-nce of W-les	1750.00	"	1575 00
The Third Casket	1750.00	"	1575 00
One of my Oldest Friends	1750.00	"	1575 00
The Pusher-in-the Face	1750.00	"	1575 00
The Unspeakable Egg	1750.00	"	1575 00
John Jackson's Arcady	1750.00	"	1575 00
Love in the Night	1750.00	"	1575 00
The Adjuster	2000.00	"	1800 00
Total			15,750 00

English Rights

The Third Casket	95.00	"	
The Sensible Thing	83.00	"	
Rags Martin-Jones and the Pr-nce of W-les	90.00	"	
Total			241 20

Articles

Wait till You Have Children of Your Own	1000.00	"	900 00
How to Live on $36,000 a Year	1000.00	"	900 00
How to Live on Practically Nothing a Year	1200.00	"	1080 00
Total			2880 00

(continued next page)

(Pages 56-57 continued)

Syndicate	115.22	"	103	52
Other Rights				
From Books	The Third Casket (German Rights)		17	50
(inc. English	This Side of Paradise		325	00
and Syndicate)	Flappers and Philosophers		16	00
	The Beautiful and Damned		527	00
	Tales of the Jazz Age		7	00
	The Great Gatsby (furthur advance)		325	00
			1,200	00
	Total		$20,192	22
	*Ommission----Absolution		118	00
	Total		$20,310	22

12

Record for 1925

Stories			
Not in the Guide Book	$1750.00	Com 10%	1575. 00
A Penny Spent	2000.00	"	1800. 00
The Rich Boy	3500.00	"	3150. 00
Presumption	2500.00	"	2250. 00
The Adolescent Marriage	2500.00	"	2250. 00
Total----------			11,025. 00

Books		
This Side of Paradise		26 24
Flappers and Philosophers		21 65
The Beautiful and Damned		144 30
Tales of the Jazz Age		20 54
The Great Gatsby		1981 85
All the Sad Young Men (advance)		2717 33
Total----------		4,906. 61

Misselaeneous			
Advance on Gatsby play	$1000.00	Com 10%	900 00
Gatsby second Serial	1000.00	"	900 00
Old New England Farmhouse	200.00	"	180 00
Syndicate	313.00	"	282 00
Gretchens Forty Winks (English)	67.00	"	60 00
Love in the Night (English)	89.00	"	80 00
Total----------			2,402 00

| Total---------- | | | $18,333 61 |

13

Record for 1926

Stories				
Your Way and Mine	$1750.00	Com 10%	1575	00
The Dance	2000.00	"	1800	00
Total			3375	00

English Rights				
Love in the Night (see previous page)	91.75	Com 15%	78	00
One of Our Oldest Friends	97.00	"	83	45
A Penny Spent	76.38	"	61	92
The Adolescent Marriage	76.23	"	64	80
Total			288	17

Syndicate ect.				
Adjuster, Pusher in the Face, Oldest Friends	239.19	Com 10% + 7.50	222	68

Article				
How to Waste Material	100.00	"	90	00

Books (inc. English)				
This Side of Paradise			44	00
Flappers and Philosophers			35	80
The Beautiful and Damned			33	10
Tales of the Jazz Age			21	20
The Great Gatsby			508	25
All the Sad Young Men			1181	05
Total			2033	20

Foreign				
Danish and Swedish Rights to Gatsby			213	00

Moving Picture Play (The Great Gatsby)				
The Great Gatsby	16,666.00	Com 10% (twice)	13500	00
New York Run (Deduct last years advance)	3907.76	Com 10%	2616	98
Chicago "	2971.07	"	2673	97
Road Run "	751.38	"	673	26
(Detroit, Brklyn, Balt, St. Louis, Chi, Denver, Phila)			5964	21
Total			$25,686	05

Love in the Night (English)—97 75

Record for 1927

Stories	Jacob's Ladder	$3000.00	Com 10%	$2,700 00
	The Love Boat	3500.00	" "	3,150 00
	A Short Trip Home	3500.00	" "	3,150 00
	The Bowl	3500.00	" "	3,150 00
	Magnetism	3500.00	" "	3,150 00
	Total			15,300 00
Movies	California work on "Lipstick"			3,500 00
	Additional Payment "Gatsby"	$3333.00 (Com 10% Lawyer $100)		2,910 00
	Total			6,410 00
Other Writings and Rights	Princeton	$500.	Com 10%	450 00
	Editorial Photoplay (Zelda)		Com 10%	450 00
	Park Avenue "			300 00
	Looking Back 8 Years "			300 00
	English "Presumption"	£15S15	Com 10%	68 98
	German "Rags Martin Jones"			25 00
	Golden Bk "Pusher in Face"	110.	Com 10%	99 00
	Anthology 'Pusher in Face"	25.	Com 10%	22 50
	Anthology "Jellybean"			26 67
	Syndicate "Your Way & Mine" ect.	153.82	Com 10%	137 44

(continued next page)

15

(Pages 61-63 continued)

German Rights to Gatsby	141	00
All English Book Royalties	95	32
Total	2096	11
Books This Side of Paradise	13	03
The Beautiful and Damned	14	80
The Great Gatsby	55	65
Flappers and Philosophers	26	70
Tales of the Jazz Age	16	35
All the Sad Young Men	43	05
Advance on New Novel Serial	5752	06
Total	5911	64
Total	29,737	87

Tax Unpaid 1926

Adolescent Marriage	$64.80
Gatsby Road	320.15
	384.95

Record for 1928

Stories

The Scandal Detectives	$3500.00	Com 10%	3150.	00
The Freshest Boy	3500.00	"	3150	00
A Night at the Fair	3500.00	"	3150	00
He Thinks he's Wonderful	3500.00	"	3150	00
The Captured Shadow	3500.00	"	3150	00
The Perfect Life	3500.00	"	3150	00
The Georgia Belle	3500.00	"	3150	00
Total			22050	00

Other Writings

Outside the Cabinet Makers	150.00	"	135	00
Who Can Fall in Love after Thirty (Zelda)	200.00	"	180	00
Syndicate (Wheeler)	13.50	"	12	15
Magnetism (English)	86.94	"	78	25
Bell Syndicate			2	23
Total			406	67

Advertisment

	1000	00

Books

This Side of Paradise	22	05
The Beautiful and Damned	22	40
Flappers & Philosophers	12	30
Tales of the Jazz Age	12	90
The Vegetable	3	60
The Great Gatsby	44	15
All the Sad Young Men	25	05
Further Advance on New Novel Serial	2129	03
Total	2272	96
Total	25,732	96

Record for 1929

Stories			
Forging Ahead	$3500.	Com 10%	$3150 00
Basil & Cleopatra	3500.	"	3150 00
Rough Crossing	3500.	"	3150 00
Majesty	3500.	"	3150 00
At Your Age	4000.	"	3600 00
The Swimmers	4000.	"	3600 00
Two Wrongs	4000.	"	3600 00
First Blood	4000.	"	3600 00
Total			27,000 00

Zelda's Sketches			
Original Follies Girl	400.	"	360 00
Poor Working Girl	500.	"	450 00
Southern Girl	500.	"	450 00
Girl the Prince Liked	500.	"	450 00
Girl with Talent	800.	"	720 00
Total			

Misselaneous			
Talkie Rights B & D.	1000.	"	2430 00
Girls Believe in Girls	1500.	"	900 00
Advertisement	500.		1350 00
			500 00

Short Autobiography	100.	"	90	00
Golden Bk. "One of my Oldest"	100.	"	90	00
English "Outside Cabinet"	40.86	"	34	56
Reprints			21	85
Total			2986	41
Books				
This Side of Paradise			4	80
Flappers & Philosophers			11	70
The Beautiful & Damned			3	60
Tales of the Jazz Age			3	00
Great Gatsby			5	10
All Sad Young Men			2	10
Vegetable			1	13
English Gatsby				34
Total			31	77
Grand Total			$32,448	18

Record for 1930

Stories	A Nice Quiet Place	$4000.	Com 10%	$3600 00
	The Bridal Party	4000.	"	3600 00
	A Woman with a Past	4000.	"	3600 00
	One Trip Abroad	4000.	"	3600 00
	A Snobbish Story	4000.	"	3600 00
	The Hotel Child	4000.	"	3600 00
	Babylon Revisited	4000.	"	3600 00
	Total--------			25,200 00
Other Items	Salesmanship in the Champs Elysee	75.	"	
	At Your Age–Modern Library	100.	"	
	Two for a Cent–Golden Book	75.	"	
	Jacobs Ladder English	121.	"	
	Reprints	8.	"	
	Total--------			341 10
Zelda's Writings	The Millionaires Girl	4000	"	3,600 00
	Miss Bessie	150	"	150 00
	Total--------			3,750 00

Books

This Side of Paradise	10	20
Flappers & Philosophers	10	05
The Beautiful & Damned	4	80
Tales of the Jazz Age	8	40
The Vegetable	1	12
The Great Gatsby	15	60
All the Sad Young Men (& Presentday Stories)	37	86
Further Advances (Serial new novel & 1583.06 against bk.)	3701	97
Total	3,800	00
Grand Total	$33,090	10

Paid tax on a miscalculation of earnings on $254. more than I should have. Will deduct from earnings of 1931.

Record for 1931

Stories

Indecision	$4000.	Com 10%	3600	00
A New Leaf	4000.	"	3600	00
Flight and Pursuit	4000.	"	3600	00
Emotional Bankrupcy	4000.	"	3600	00
Between Three and Four	4000.	"	3600	00
A Change of Class	4000.	"	3600	00
Half a Dozen of the Other	3000.	"	2700	00
A Freeze Out	4000.	"	3600	00
Diagnosis	4000.	"	3600	00
Total			31,500	00

Other Items

Treatment Metro Goldwyn Mayer	6000.	"	5400	00
Echoes of the Jazz Age	500.		500	00
Vegetable Performance	25.00	"	22	50
New Leaf (English)	£ 17	"	59	00
Flight & Pursuit (English)	Ginnies 35	"	126	00
John Jackson's Arcady	2.21	"	2	00
Total			6,109	50

(Page 67 continued)

Books

This Side of Paradise	12	90
Flappers & Philosophers	9	30
The Beautiful & Damned	4	40
Tales of the Jazz Age	3	90
The Vegetable	1	13
The Great Gatsby	17	90
All the Sad Young Men	7	90
Advance against Bk.	44	15
Total--------	100	00
Less: Not paid in 1931 by Metro 173.72 "	−155	35
Grand Total	37,554	00
New Yorker sketch 50.00	45	00
	37,599	00

Record for 1932 (writing *Tender*)

Stories					
Crazy Sunday	$ 200			$ 200	00
Family in the Wind	3500	Com 10%		3150	00
What a Hansome Pair	2500	"		2250	00
The Rubber Check	3000	"		2700	00
Interne	3500	"		3150	00
On Schedule	3000	"		2700	00
Total------				14,805	00

Other Items			
Reprint of The New Leaf	22.50	Com 10%	
Walter Baker Royalty	15.20		
Flight & Pursuit (English)	110.42		
Couple of Nuts (Zelda)	$ 150.	Com 10%	
The Gourmets (Zelda)	50.	"	
Total of all these------			313 40

Books		
All Royalties		20 00
Advance on Novel		480 00
Total------		500 00
Grand Total		15,823 40

Record for 1933 (Writing *Tender*)

Stories	More than just a House	3000	Com 10%	2700 00
	I Got Shoes	2500	"	2250 00
	The Family Bus	3000	"	2700 00
Articles	My Lost City	1000		900 00
	One Hundred False Starts	1200		1080 00
Books	*Tender* and *Taps* Advance and new advance of [2000]	[900]		4,200 00
		1,690.21		
	($1000. Commission paid Ober on serial)			
	Other Books			30
	Save me the Waltz			120 00
Sound Rights	The Great Gatsby	2500		2250 00
Other Items	Two for a Cent (English)		"	34 81
	New Leaf (Home Mag. English)		"	63 03
	John Jackson (Royalties)		"	19 00
				16,328 03

Record for 1934

Stories

	$3000	Com 10%		
No Flowers	$3000		2700	00
New Types	3000		2700	00
Her Last Case	3000		2700	00
In the Darkest Hour	1250		1125	00
The Count of Darkness	1500		1350	00
A Kingdom in the Dark	1500		1350	00
The Fiend			250	00
The Night before Chancellorsville			250	00
			12,475	00
			58	35

All Books

Misselaneous

Ring Lardner	50	00
Preface to Gatsby	50	00
Broadcast of Diamond	45	00
Family in the Wind (Swedish)	12	27
Your Age (Modern)	3	16
Show Mr & Mrs F.	200	00
Auction--Model 1934	200	00

(Page 74 continued)

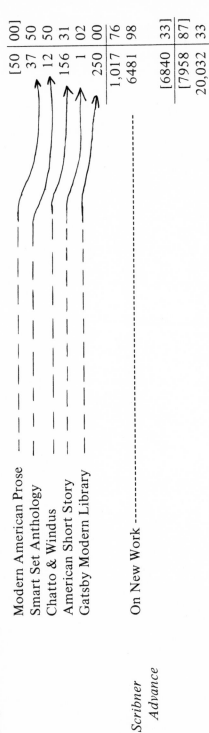

Modern American Prose		[50	00]
Smart Set Anthology		37	50
Chatto & Windus		12	50
American Short Story		156	31
Gatsby Modern Library		1	02
		250	00
		1,017	76
		6481	98
Scribner	On New Work	[6840	33]
Advance		[7958	87]
		20,032	33

May 1938

Record for 1935

Stories	The Intimate Strangers	$ 3000	2700	00
	Zone of Accident	3000	2700	00
	What you Don't know	3000	2700	00
	Too Cute for Words	3000	2700	00
	Gods of the Darkness	1500	1350	00
	The Esquimo Boy	1500	1350	00
	The Image on the Heart	1250	1125	00
			14,725	00
Misselaneous	Lamp in a Window		22	50
	Modern Library Royalty		17	89
	English Sale—The Fiend		41	93
	Columbia Broadcast "Lets go Out"	700	630	00
	Shaggy's Morning		250	00
	Same—London		31	00
	Sleeping & Waking		250	00
	Your Age		10	88
	Crack Up		250	00
	Paste Together		250	00
	Brittish Fiend		41	93
			[1,596	13]
			1796	13
All Books	and Advance	$ 342.03	[832	00]
	Total	16,845.16	[17,153	13]

May 1938

[This is evidently a grand mistake. Even if I only got $200 for Esquire articles I still underpaid by $307.97.

This again will appear in 1938 Tax. Both these errors were made during my illness.]

Again the error if any is in my favor. I have recieved less from Scribners than I have paid taxes on

Record for 1936

Stories			
	Outside the House	$3000	00
	Make Yourself at Home	2500	00
	The Pearl & the Fur	1000	00
	Trouble	2000	00
− 10%		7650	00
Esquire Pieces	Handle with Care.	250	
	Three Acts of Music	"	
	The Ants at Princeton	"	
	Author's House	"	
	Afternoon of an Author	"	
	An Author's Mother	"	
	I didn't Get Over	"	
	Please Send me in, Coach	"	
	An Alcoholic Case	"	
		2250	00
Misscelaenous	Modern Library, Brittish & Danish, John Jackson ect	199	79
All Books		81	18
Total		10,180	97

Stories

Record for 1937
The Goon
The Long Way Out
In the Holidays
Room 13
Financing Finnegan

Misselaeneous

Obit on Parnassus
Book of Ones Own
Early Success
Foriegn Sales (Gatsby)
Random House
Scribners (All Books)

Zelda's Earnings

Year	Title		
1922	Four articles (See page 54)		$ 815 00
1923	Our Own Movie Queen (Story-half mine) $1000.00 Net 500.00 Com 10%		450 00
1927	Editorial Photoplay (*unpublished*) $500.00 Com 10%		450 00
	Park Avenue		300 00
	Looking Back Eight Years		300 00
1928	Who Can Fall in Love After Thirty $200. Com 10%		180 00
1929	The Original Follies Girl $400 Com 10%		360 00
	The Poor Working Girl (*Unpublished*) $500 Com 10%		450 00
	The Southern Girl $500 Com 10%		450 00
	The Girl the Prince Liked $500 Com 10%		450 00
	The Girl with Talent $800 Com 10%		720 00
		Total---5	075 00
1930	The Millionaire's Girl	$4000. Com 10%	3 600 00
	Miss Bessie	150. Com 10%	135 00
1931	The Continental Angle		
1932	A Couple of Nuts		
1932	Save Me the Waltze		
1934	Show Mr & Mrs F to Number——		
1934	Auction Model 1934		

Lost and Unpublished Stories by F. Scott Fitzgerald

Jennifer McCabe Atkinson

A search through the Harold Ober archive for material connected with the correspondence in *As Ever, Scott Fitz*—[1] led to the discovery of unpublished Fitzgerald stories. These were not unknown stories, for there is mention and discussion of them in the correspondence. However, these were thought to be lost and unrecoverable stories, possibly destroyed by Fitzgerald because they had not been salable. Even though these were stories which had not been considered publishable by certain editors at the time they were submitted, they will offer new material for critical comparison and contrast with his successful stories and extend the Fitzgerald canon in such a way as to provide scholars with new means for studying Fitzgerald's style and creative practices. The stories even contribute to a more detailed understanding of Fitzgerald as a writer as they evidence changes in theme, subject, and attitude.

A thorough critical study of these stories in light of Fitzgerald's career as a short-story writer does not fall within the purview of this article. (Such analysis properly belongs in a study of Fitzgerald as a short-story writer.) With the publication of these lost stories, no doubt many scholars will come forward to fill the void with comparisons and contrasts, analyses and dissections which will be possible because of this new material. This article, however, is concerned essentially with Ober and Fitzgerald.

From information located in Ober's records about some stories which remain lost, from Ober's assessments and synopses of stories which have survived (some in carbon-copy typescripts, two even in manuscript), and from the correspondence pertaining to the stories,

---

the depth of Ober's commitment to and the degree of his quasi-collaborator relationship with Fitzgerald can be seen. Ober is revealed giving encouragement, reassurance, and constructive criticism in an attempt to keep a great writer working—and writing the quality of story he was capable of producing. When Fitzgerald wrote in bitterness to Ober on 19 July 1939 and 2 August 1939 about Ober's refusal to advance funds to him, he used two metaphors: one of a man lost in the Arctic being saved by his partner once but not a second time, and one of a drowning man being saved once but not a second time. These references were analogies to all Ober had done to give Fitzgerald help during the bad times between 1932 and 1937. In addition to the advancing of funds and outright loans Ober made to Fitzgerald during that time, the efforts by Ober to aid Fitzgerald with his work revealed here made up a large part of his attempts (which Fitzgerald felt had been successful) to "save" Fitzgerald.

At least nineteen stories have been located or identified, and they cover the twenty-year span of Fitzgerald's literary career. Out of the nearly 140 works that Fitzgerald submitted for Ober to market, Ober was *unsuccessful* in selling only seventeen stories. Though two stories discussed here were sold, they were never published. One story was rewritten, sold, and published.

The lost or unpublished stories are:

"The I. O. U."—1920
"Recklessness"—1922
"On Your Own" ("Home to Maryland")—1931
"In the Safety Zone"—1931—(Revised and published as "Zone of Accident," *The Saturday Evening Post*, 13 July 1935.)
"Nightmare" ("Fantasy in Black")—1932
"What to Do About It"—1933
"Daddy Was Perfect"—1934
"Travel Together"—1935
"Lo, The Poor Peacock"—1935
"I'd Die for You" ("The Legend of Lake Lure")—1935-36
"Make Yourself at Home"—1935 (Sold to *Pictorial Review* but never published.)
"The Pearl and the Fur"—1936 (Sold to *Pictorial Review* but never published.)
"Cyclone in Silent Land"—1936
"Thank You For the Light"—1936
"They Never Grow Older"—1937
"The Vanished Girl"—1937
"Offside Play" ("Athletic Interview," "Athletic Interval")—1937
"Temperature" ("The Women in the House")—1939
"The Couple"—n.d.

The I.O.U.

by

F. Scott Fitzgerald

The above is not my real name — the fellow it belongs to gave me his permission to sign it to this story. My real name I shall not divulge. I am a publisher. I accept long novels about young love written by old maids in South Dakota, detective stories concerning wealthy clubmen and female apaches with "wide dark eyes", essays about the menace of this and that and the color of the moon in Tahiti by college professors and others unemployed. I accept no novels by authors under fifteen years old. All the columnists and communists (I can never get these two words straight) abuse me because they say I want money. I do — I want it terribly. My wife needs it. My

"The I. O. U."—1920

Attached to the manuscript of this story is a short, typed synopsis by Harold Ober, which reads: "Cleverly written story. Almost a satire on publishing business. Told by a publisher. He brings out book by famous psychic research man, purporting to be communication with his nephew killed in War (WWI). Publisher goes to Ohio to visit author. The nephew who has been in prison camp arrives at same time. Girl he was engaged to also there. Both are angry at author & publisher. Book is selling at great rate. Shows nephew dancing with angels in filmy garments. Publisher offers them money to keep quiet for a while—but native of town arrives. Recognizes nephew because he owes him $3.85 lost at poker. Publisher decides to publish only love stories and mysteries. HO."

About nine months after beginning his association with the Paul Revere Reynolds agency and his relationship as a client of Harold Ober, Fitzgerald sent a manuscript with a letter to Ober. In this letter of 2 June 1920, Fitzgerald indicated that this story was "a plot that Sell[2] particularly wanted for Harps. Baz and which I promised him." Someone in the Reynolds office identified the story as "The I. O. U." There is no evidence that the story was actually offered to *Harper's Bazaar,* and that magazine published no Fitzgerald stories during his lifetime. Ober obviously offered it other places, because on 17 July 1920, Fitzgerald wrote concerning the story again: "If 'The I. O. U.' comes back from the Post[3] I wish you'd return it to me as I think I can change it so there'll be no trouble selling it." No correspondence survives indicating whether Fitzgerald resubmitted the story in a new version or with a new title. There is not even a record of what magazines Ober offered it to. However, the manuscript and a typescript survive, and a note attached to the typescript shows that at some time (probably after Fitzgerald's death) Ober reworked or considered reworking the story in an attempt to make it salable.

Unfortunately Ober's assessment of "The I. O. U." is not one of his better judgments. He seems to have read more complexity and subtlety into the story than actually exists. While it could be considered a "clever" story, and perhaps could have been worked up into a salable story, "The I. O. U." is truly one of Fitzgerald's inconsequential efforts. The characters lack the charm of his flappers and the appeal of his young men in such stories as "Head and Shoulders," "The Offshore Pirate," or "Bernice Bobs Her Hair"—all published in *The Saturady Evening Post* in the same year. No, this time the magazine editors seem to have been more perceptive than Mr. Ober.

"Recklessness"—1922

This story remains a lost story, if it were ever actually completed. There are only two references to it in the correspondence. One is in a Fitzgerald letter that Ober received on 11 December 1922, in which Fitzgerald says he is sending a story which Ober identified as "Recklessness." The other reference occurs five months later in a Fitzgerald letter received by Ober on 22 May 1923, in which Fitzgerald says he has not "done anything about 'Recklessness' " because he had been working on his play (*The Vegetable*). There is no record of which magazines Ober may have offered it to.

"On Your Own" ("Home to Maryland")—1931

Attached to a surviving typescript is a synposis by Harold Ober, which reads: "Story of a man and a girl who meet on boat coming back to New York from Europe. Girl an actress—she goes South when her father had died. The man follows her. The girl meets his mother. Girl tries to defend herself and man thinks she is rude to his mother. They quarrel but make up. H.O. This has been shortened and simplified and improved. Still it is very slight. H.O."

Because of missing letters between 1931 and 1934, the correspondence about "On Your Own" is slim. The first mention of the story occurs in an Ober letter of 19 March 1931, in which he says: "ON YOUR OWN has just come in and I have read it. I think you have improved it, especially in its construction." The only other reference to it is on 15 June 1936, in a letter to Fitzgerald from Constance Smith (Ober's assistant), when the story is listed as unsold. On the note attached to the typescript there appears a list of magazines to which it was offered: *College Humor, Collier's, Good Housekeeping, Pictorial Review, Redbook, The Saturday Evening Post,* and *Woman's Home Companion.*

"On Your Own" has promise of being a good Fitzgerald story. After the years of living abroad and writing stories about Americans either traveling to Europe or living in Europe, Fitzgerald shows in this 1931 story a shifting in emphasis to Americans living in America and how their values appear to someone who has not lived here for a number of years. The major fault with the story lies in the conflicting and ambiguous behavior of the heroine. Perhaps, like the actress, Fitzgerald had not resolved his own attitudes in 1931; if he had, he might have controlled the story better and revised it into a salable one. There is a potentially serious underlying theme concerning cultural values with which Fitzgerald has not successfully grappled.

"In the Safety Zone"—1931

A file card on this story remains and it includes Ober's synopsis, which reads: "Another Interne story. Bill Tulliver sees girl on street car—cannot forget her—later a moving picture actress has accident and is brought to hospital. She falls in love with Tulliver but he cannot forget girl on car. Actress stays in hospital longer than she needs to—Finally she leaves and agrees to judge a picture contest. The girl of the street car is a contestant and the actress chooses her to get her away from interne Tulliver. Fine for illustration. H.O."

No correspondence on this story survives, and no manuscript or typescript remains. However, according to the file card, it was twice offered to and rejected by *The Saturday Evening Post*—once in March 1931, and then in a revised version on 31 March 1933. Three copies of the story were returned to Fitzgerald from Ober on 17 April 1933. Between the Ober synopsis and the published story, it seems clear that this story was revised again by Fitzgerald and became "Zone of Accident" (*The Saturday Evening Post,* 13 July 1935).

"Nightmare" ("Fantasy in Black")—1932

Attached to the typescript of this story are two synopses—one by Constance Smith (Ober's assistant) and one by Harold Ober. Ober's reads: "Original and amusing. But slight Setting Institution for crazy people. Heroine daughter of doctor who owns institution. She acts as nurse, etc. Three rich brothers have been committed. They will their fortune to institution. Fourth brother has a breakdown and comes. Girl saves him from being kept there so Institution can get all the money. Very improbable of course but well told. H.O."

The first mention of the story is in a Fitzgerald letter received by Ober 23 April 1932. Fitzgerald bemoans the fact that "*Nightmare* will never, never sell for money, in *any* times." The only other mention of the story appears in Constance Smith's letter of 15 June 1936, where it is listed as unsold. According to the note attached to the typescript, "Nightmare" was offered to and rejected by *College Humor, Cosmopolitan, Redbook,* and *The Saturday Evening Post.*

"Nightmare" is a zany, humorous story. After his experiences with Zelda and psychiatric clinics, Fitzgerald seems to have felt the need to put the experience in perspective with a tongue-in-cheek story spoofing clinics and insanity. Although he tried to extract literary material from his experience, which was his usual creative method, Fitzgerald does not appear to have had control over his material (i.e., the experience) or the familiarity with it that he exhibits in stories based on social activities of the flapper era. Despite some good writing, the story lacks the sharp satire underlying the fantasy in a story like "The Diamond As Big As the Ritz" to save it from being inconsequential.

"What To Do About It"–1933

No Ober synopsis remains, but a typescript of the story survives. Dr. Bill Hardy, assistant to Dr. Hines, is called to see hypochondraic Mrs. Brickster. She isn't home when he arrives, but he meets her children—Miss Mason the daughter, a pretty young lady just back from Europe, and the thirteen-year-old son. When Mrs. Brickster comes home, Dr. Hardy listens to her complaints until the early hours of the morning. Finally called away, he goes to the home of Mrs. Dykes, his lover, where he is met unexpectedly by her husband. Dykes threatens him, but the little Brickster boy appears from the back seat of Hardy's car with a "gun" and frightens Dykes away. It is now daylight. Hardy takes the boy home, goes to work, and taking his lead from the little boy, stands up to Dr. Hines. Then he goes off to woo Miss Mason.

The first reference to the story occurs in the Fitzgerald letter of 12 June 1933. By this time in the Depression, Ober was faced with a magazine market which was tightening its belt, and that situation coupled with the poor quality of Fitzgerald's stories prompted Ober to write on 30 August 1933, a serious "letter of advice" to Fitzgerald. This letter is one of the first in which Ober talks not only about the marketing of Fitzgerald's story, but also suggests ways or offers criticism intended to aid Fitzgerald in improving a story.

> This letter is a letter of advice and if you don't feel like receiving advice you may throw it in the waste basket without reading further.
> I think we have made a mistake in sending your recent stories to the Post in a very hurried fashion and I think it has been a mistake to let them know that we were in such a hurry about a decision. I think perhaps we have caused the wrong psychological effect on a possible buyer. I think we have let the Post feel that you were rushing out stories in order to get some money.
> Before we show the next story to the Post I think we ought to be sure that it is just right, I think I ought to have it properly typed, and I want to try to create the impression that I am sending them a Scott Fitzgerald story, that it is a fine story and that I don't care whether they take it or not. I am sure it is a mistake for the Post to feel that you are uncertain about a story and anxious to know whether or not they like it.
> I would like to start to create this new impression with this new story you are writing. I think perhaps by trying to gain a day or two we have

lost a good deal. So I hope you will send the next story to me when you have it done. I'll read it right away and tell you frankly if I have any criticisms to make.

It is true that all the magazines have been harder to please this year than ever before. I feel sure that this last story of yours, WHAT TO DO ABOUT IT, would have been accepted a year or two ago by the Post and published and that many readers would have liked it. It is also true of course that a great deal is expected of an author who has written as many fine stories as you have written. An editor expects every story to compare favorably with some story of yours which he has considered your finest story. I believe you make a very fine story out of WHAT TO DO ABOUT IT. I think you will have to make the reader care more what happens to the girl and to the doctor. To give yourself space to do this do you think it would be possible to have the girl beg the doctor to take her with him when he goes to answer the call? The boy could be hidden in the rumble seat just as you have him. This is probably a poor suggestion but I am sure you will be able to work out some way to get some feeling between the doctor and the girl.

The gaps in the correspondence during 1933-1934 make it difficult to record the history of this story. However, the files show that the story was rejected by *The Saturday Evening Post*, *Redbook*, and *Cosmopolitan*. The last evidence concerning "What To Do About It" appears in Constance Smith's letter of 15 June 1936, in which the story is listed as still unsold.

The story is one of several (some successful, some not) attempts Fitzgerald made to write about doctors, nurses, hospitals, and medically related subjects between 1931 and 1937. Between Zelda's experiences with clinics and psychiatrists and Fitzgerald's own dealings with doctors because of his recurring tuberculosis, his alcoholism, and other physical ailments, he had a storehouse of material to draw upon. Somehow he never drew upon it in the right way—or at least in a commercially successful way. Although he had perennially popular material, subjects with great reader appeal, he could not find the framework that would set up a formula for successful stories. One problem, perhaps the key problem, is that he could not resolve the old successful formula of slick flapper stories with this new material. Ober suggests that he do more with the relationship between the doctor and the girl (a very weakly drawn relationship) in this story. One of the major flaws of the story is indefiniteness—whether the story is about the doctor and the girl, the doctor asserting his independence from his older partner, the doctor and the thirteen-year-old boy, or what. Apparently Ober felt that to make it more commercially successful, Fitzgerald needed to elaborate on the love interest thread of the story and thus focus on one appealing aspect of the story.

"Daddy Was Perfect"—1934

This is a lost story. No mention of the title occurs in the remaining correspondence, and no typescript has been located. The file card on the story includes a synopsis by Constance Smith: "Little girl goes opening playwright father's new play. Adores him. He is top of wave. Woman accuses him of plagiarism. Starts suit lasting five years. Girl grows up, father's money all used up by suit. She falls in love with woman's son. Manager dies—admits he gave woman's idea to playwright not telling him source. Woman loses case but she and man make up, split what profits are left from play. Poor story. C.S."

The story was offered to and rejected by *Ladies Home Journal, Redbook, The Saturday Evening Post;* it was returned to Fitzgerald on 29 October 1934.

"Travel Together"—1935

No Ober synopsis remains, but a typescript of the story survives. Chris Cooper, a movie script-writer, meets Judy Downs while he is "riding the rails" to get material for a hobo movie. They join Velia Tolliver, who is supposed to star in Chris's film, and the three travel by train to Hollywood. During the trip, Velia's unusually large diamond is stolen. Judy is suspected of the theft, but a search proves that she doesn't have the gem. Arriving in Hollywood, Chris learns that the studio is no longer interested in his story; so he quits his job and hits the road with Judy. Then he discovers that Judy did take the diamond because it was rightfully hers—it had belonged to her wealthy father. The story ends with the promise of a happy future.[4]

No Fitzgerald letter remains with word that "Travel Together" was sent for the first time, and no Ober letter acknowledges receipt or gives his reaction. On 10 January 1935, Fitzgerald wrote to Ober saying: "So glad you liked 'Travel Together.' Don't forget to send me the carbon so we can get a version together to offer the movies." This story seems never to have been improved enough to make it salable, because the story is not mentioned again until it is included in Constance Smith's list of unsold stories on 15 June 1936.

"Travel Together" is another story with promise, but the parts seem to be at odds with one another as though Fitzgerald did not really know what he wanted the story to do and say. There is the potentially romantic plot of the director gathering material for a movie—except that he seeks the material among the very unromantic hobos of the Depression; there is the glamorous, sophisticated movie star contrasted with the beautiful and innocent young girl; there is mystery and implied theft and backgrounds of questionable repute; there is the director blithely throwing over his career in picaresque style. Yet these aspects do not work together to create a successful unity. This is one of Fitzgerald's imagined plots, which, like most things that he drew upon without real experience, became a badly contrived story.

"Lo, The Poor Peacock!"—1935

A typescript of this story survives. Jason Davis is having financial problems. His wife is in the hospital, and he must let his secretary go and take his teen-aged daughter, Josephine, out of a private school. Josephine goes to public school, but she gets expelled for something not her fault. The Davis's financial situation worsens so much that Davis has to pawn some of their silver. Then they hear from the school that Josephine's dismissal was an error. Davis gets an appointment for a large contract and works all night preparing for it. The man wanting the contract appears unexpectedly early the next morning and Josephine cannot wake her exhausted father. She entertains the client, telling him her father has the flu. The man, charmed by little Josephine, decides to give Davis the contract. A happy ending is tinged by melancholy as Davis and Josephine visit the peacocks in the park and she compares themselves to the peacocks.

There is no reference to this story in the correspondence. Attached to the typescript is a note in Ober's hand, which reads: "file in retired box Poor Story HO".[5]

This story appears to be one in a series known as the "Gwen stories" in which Fitzgerald tried to write about Scottie and himself. With the material gone that he had drawn upon during the 1920's, he searched for new material among his experiences. He found some in his associations with doctors and hospitals. During the middle years of the 1930's, when Scottie became a teenager, Fitzgerald began using their father-daughter relationship as a basis for stories. The idea (the father-daugher relationship) was a good one, and Fitzgerald was utilizing experiences close to himself once again. "Lo, The Poor Peacock!" is potentially a good Fitzgerald story, but events happen without reason, the plot becomes increasingly contrived, and the denouement is too pat. Perhaps worst of all, the coda ending borders on the maudlin. This story may have been revised or altered in some way, though, and sold after all (see footnote 5) but it is extremely doubtful.

Stop-press note: "Lo, The Poor Peacock!" has been published in Esquire (September, 1971).

"I'd Die For You" ("The Legend of Lake Lure")—1935-36

The surviving file card on this story contains a synopsis by Constance Smith, which reads: "No. Carolina background. Motion picture star on location falls in love with man for whom several women have committed suicide. Man is hiding from process servers. Nurse, also in love with him comes up. Threatens throw herself off nearby mountain peak. Instead she betrays his whereabouts to process servers. He commits suicide. Star marries director with whom she has also been in love. C.S."

Considerable correspondence remains about the story "I'd Die For You," revealing literally months of work by Fitzgerald. In November 1935, Fitzgerald and Ober exchanged several letters about the story. As the correspondence will show, the story had been sent in during October and returned to Fitzgerald. On 11 November 1935, Ober asks: "How are you getting along with the short story that you are revising?" The next day, from Hendersonville, N. C., Fitzgerald wired Ober: "STORY LEAVES HERE THURSDAY . . . ." Ober immediately wrote back to Fitzgerald on the 12th saying he was pleased that the story was coming. In a letter received by Constance Smith on 14 November 1935, Fitzgerald explains about the enclosed story:

> What I am enclosing looks scrappy but is a *second* revision from what you've seen—entirely new in construction + plot at the end. I hope for this one that the *Post* might like it + am sending it this way with the hope that if it reaches you Thurs. you could get a quick typing + get it to them Fri for a wk. end decision.

The next day, 15 November 1935, Ober wrote Fitzgerald saying that he had given the story to Graeme Lorimer of *The Saturday Evening Post* and adding some remarks of praise (though qualified praise) about the story:

> As you know, I hadn't read the first version. It seems to me an extremely good story. There is of course a feeling that at any moment almost any one of your characters may commit suicide but you have handled the climax in a very clever way and the story ends happily. I think the Saturday Evening Post will make a mistake if they decline this story and if they do I think we can sell it well and quickly somewhere else.

On or about 18 November, Fitzgerald wrote to Ober, commenting on the two versions of "I'd Die For You" he had written that fall. Meanwhile, Ober was trying to sell the story, and on 20 November, he reported to Fitzgerald:

I'D DIE FOR YOU is now at the American. Graeme Lorimer hadn't read the story and wanted to see it but couldn't get their editors to buy it. He let me have it back right away and I hope the American will buy it. . . .

I'm sure I can sell I'D DIE FOR YOU fairly quickly and things will look better when I get the money for that.

By 14 December, Ober's polite enthusiasm was beginning to wane, because most of the magazines which had used Fitzgerald stories in the past had turned this one down. Ober again expressed the reservations about the story he had offered on 15 November:

I liked I'D DIE FOR YOU but I am afraid it is going to be difficult to sell. The Post, American, McCall's, Cosmopolitan and Red Book have declined it. Littauer[6] of Collier's liked it but Chenery[7] didn't. Littauer, who also reads stories for the Woman's Home Companion, has turned it over to the Companion and he thinks they might possibly be able to use it. One difficulty with the story seems to be the threat of suicide all the way through the story. Cosmopolitan thought the man who was hiding from the process servers was altogether too mysterious and didn't really come to life. If the Companion doesn't buy the story I think there is a chance I can sell it to Liberty and there are of course other possibilities for it.

Fitzgerald began to give up on the story when he wrote Ober on 21 January 1936, suggesting Ober return the story to him. "I'm not going to touch it myself again but I know a boy here who might straighten it out for a share of the profits, if any." On the file card for this story there is a note by someone in Ober's office which reads: "Fitzgerald gave to Bill Warren[8] —said he'd go 50-50 on a sale. Says it's dead as far as he is concerned 4/7/36". Meanwhile, Ober continued trying to sell the story on 27 January 1936, he wrote Fitzgerald saying: "I thought of offering I'D DIE FOR YOU next to Pictorial. Let me know if you want me to do this or send it back first for revision." In response to Ober's letter, Fitzgerald wrote on 29 January again asking him to send the story back, and Ober did so on 1 February. The same day, Ober wrote again about the story; this time he included criticism from an unidentified magazine editor:

One editor commented on the fact that the man in the story was too mysterious and this editor thought he ought to be explained. The main difficulty with the story, however, has always been that there is so much about suicide in it.

The final reference to this story comes from Ober on 30 March 1936. He reminds Fitzgerald of their January correspondence concerning the story, and then, if Fitzgerald has "discarded further plans for rewriting," he offers to "remove the story from the active list."

Neither Ober nor Fitzgerald mentions it again, and "I'd Die For You" is not included in Constance Smith's 15 June 1936 list of unsold stories. However, a copy of a typescript of the story survives.

Ober's criticism of this story remains valid upon a reading of the typescript today. Trying to sustain suspense, Fitzgerald overdoes the threat of suicide on all sides; it seems that any character is liable to leap into the lake at any time. The character of the protagonist has been purposely kept mysterious and shadowed to achieve the full impact of the revelation of truth about him at the end; nevertheless, there is a forced and contrived aspect to the plot and some of the characterizations are sketchy and seem extraneous when they are not and should not be.

"Make Yourself at Home"—1935-36

No manuscript or typescript of this story survives, and though it was sold, it is a lost story.

The historical thread of this story runs concurrently with that of "I'd Die For You" during the end of 1935 and beginning of 1936. Fitzgerald submitted "Too Cute for Words" as the first of the Gwen series to *The Saturday Evening Post,* and it had been accepted. He then planned a story to precede "Too Cute for Words," and on 29 December 1935, he wired Ober to ask the *Post* to hold the story until the one he was working on was completed in early January. This second story in chronology of actual writing, which Fitzgerald intended to be the first Gwen story, was "Make Yourself at Home." Fitzgerald promised the new story by 9 January 1936, but Ober wrote to him on 14 January saying: "I have your telegram saying that the second Gwen story won't be here until the 25th. I am sure you are right in waiting until the story is just as you want it before you send it on." Explaining that the delay was due to a hospital stay, Fitzgerald asked Ober on 21 January to tell the *Post* "not to schedule 'Too Cute for Words' until they get the new one." On 1 February, Ober reported that the editors of the *Post* were wondering when the story would be coming because they were holding the first story out of schedule until they got the new story. By 6 February, Fitzgerald had finished the story, sent the original to the *Post* and a carbon copy to Ober. That day Ober wrote to Fitzgerald, telling him that Graeme Lorimer had been in and he had urged Lorimer "to give me a quick decision on it . . . . " Ober also comments on the copy he received—comments which set the tone for the future troubles this story ran into: "My carbon copy is evidently an uncorrected one as there are several places in it that are not clear." Because Fitzgerald had sent the original directly to them, the *Post* informed him directly of their decision. Fitzgerald in turn wired Ober on 7 February: POST REFUSED STORY CAN YOU WIRE ME TODAY YOUR REACTION TO IT SHALL I REWRITE OR MERELY CHANGE NAMES AND TRY TO SELL IT TO ANOTHER MAGAZINE REWRITING WOULD TAKE FOUR DAYS NAMES CHANGED CAN BE DONE IMMEDIATELY. (The rejection wire from A. W. Neall of *The Saturday Evening Post* and a copy of the letter Fitzgerald wrote in response to her wire are published in *As Ever, Scott Fitz—*.) Ober wired back immediately: THINK STORY NEEDS REWRITING MAILING SPECIAL DELIVERY LETTER. His letter reads:

> As I have just wired you, I think MAKE YOURSELF AT HOME needs rewriting. The question is, however, whether you feel like rewriting it and whether you have any idea that might make the story salable to the Post. If you haven't, I suppose the only thing to do is to change the names and let me try it on some other magazine. I do not, however, feel very confident of placing it. The story seems to me to get too melodramatic. The two crooks in the story seem too violent for this kind of story. I am not going to send you any detailed suggestions, in the first place because I have not studied the story from that point of view, and in the second place I am not sure that you want them.
>
> I am very sorry you sent the story direct to the Post but there is no use talking about that now. Did the editors of the Post send you any suggestions? If they did, I suppose it would be wise to try to rewrite the story according to these suggestions if you can.
>
> I am afraid I am not being very helpful but I do not see how you can make this the first story in the Gwen series without a good deal of rewriting. Is there any reason now why we shouldn't let the Post publish the first the one they have? I am going to take this story home with me tonight and study it carefully and if I have any ideas about it and if you want them I'll be glad to send them on to you.

When Ober saw Fitzgerald's correspondence with *The Saturday Evening Post,* he wrote Fitzgerald saying: "I judge by this that you are going to write a new story in the Gwen series for the Post and that you will rewrite MAKE YOURSELF AT HOME for another magazine . . . ." Receipt of the revised version "with the names changed" was acknowledged by Ober on 19 February. The next reference to the story is 8 April 1936, when Ober wrote Fitzgerald announcing: ". . . we have sold MAKE YOURSELF AT HOME to the Pictorial and they are paying $2500 for it." Ober reported receiving payment from the *Pictorial Review* on 17 April. Several months later, apparently in response to Fitzgerald's query, Ober wrote on 19 November telling him about the status of several stories which had been sold but had not been published. On 27 November, Ober added another note, particularly about "Make Yourself at Home" and "The Pearl and the Fur"—"I don't know why I forgot about the two girl stories when I wrote you about unpublished stories. These were sold to the Pictorial Review and the editor tells me they will probably be published in the Spring not before March or April." But the *Pictorial Review* closed down publication early in 1937 before either story was published. No manuscript or typescript remains in the Ober archive.[9]

As a side-note, this story—"Make Yourself at Home"—and the next one, "The Pearl and the Fur," are the only ones in this entire group of stories that Fitzgerald listed in his ledger. They were, of course, the only unpublished stories for which he was paid.

"The Pearl and the Fur"—1936

No manuscript or typescript survives, and though it was sold, the story is lost.

The first reference in the correspondence shows that some communication about the story had already taken place, and that Fitzgerald had submitted it to Ober. In a wire on 6 April 1936, Ober expresses concern about the story: "BEGINNING AND END DELIGHTFUL MIDDLE NEEDS REWRITING RETURNING STORY WITH SUGGESTIONS FOR REVISION IMPORTANT THIS STORY BE JUST RIGHT." Ober returned the manuscript with one of his more detailed statements of criticism and suggestion:

> I think the beginning and the ending of the new Gwen story are delightful. The middle part of the story, however, seems to me very complicated and improbable and I think this part of the story should be rewritten before it is sent to the Post. It is most important to have the story just right because it will make a great deal of difference about the Post going on with the series. I understand that there was some division of opinion about the last story and I am sure this story will have to be better than the last to get by.
>
> A good deal of the taxicab material seems to me improbable and two other readers independently reached the same conclusion. It doesn't seem possible that an expensive coat would be left in a taxicab from one evening to noon of the next day. If the taxi driver went back to his company's garage reporting that something had been found, the company would take charge of the lost property.
>
> I have checked up on the subway station at Kingsbridge and 230th Street and it is as closely settled as any part of New York City. The subways leave every four or five minutes. If anyone were in a hurry to get

from 230th Street to 59th Street one would never think of taking a taxi-cab and there are no subway terminals that are in unpopulated districts as you describe.

Wouldn't it be simpler if Gwen found some small article like a pocket-book with the richwoman's card in it and perhaps with the tickets for the trip. She might have driven downtown and taken the cab that the rich woman had left in going to the boat. I think this middle section of the story ought to be simplified and shortened and more of it written in the style of the beginning and the end.

I hate to suggest all this just as you are leaving for Asheville but as I have said before it is much better to have a story right and have it bought than to hurry it and have it declined.

By 21 April 1936, Fitzgerald had revised the story and sent it to Ober, for Ober wires that the story is "much improved" and they are having it typed to send the *Post.* But the next day, 22 April, Ober had second thoughts about the revision and wrote another detailed letter to Fitzgerald expressing his reservations:

It is true that the story is improved but when I gave the new typed copy a careful reading it seemed to me to contain a great many improbabilities. I have since had other readings on the story and every reading seems to disclose further improbabilities. In your letter accompanying the new version you said you didn't feel able to do any more work on the story so we have tried to fix up the most glaring inconsistencies.

After thinking the matter over very carefully I think that it would be a great mistake to offer this story to the Post. Mr. Lorimer made it very clear to me that he could not buy another Gwen story unless it were very much better than the last one he bought. In my opinion this story is far below the first two. The story starts very well indeed but it is terribly full of holes and when you try to patch up one hole, another one appears somewhere else. I feel it is very important for your future relations with the Post that the next story they see of yours shall be an extremely good one. This is what I'd like to do: We would like to work on the story for a few days and see if we can't fix up the inconsistencies in it, then I'd like to have the story retyped changing Gwen's name to the name used in the story I just sold the Pictorial. I feel sure that you do not want to work any more on the story just now and any changes I make in the story will be merely changes of timing and correction of inaccuracies. None of your dialogue will have to be changed. Let me know how you feel about this. In the meantime I hope you will be able to start work on a new story. I think you have excellent material for these Gwen stories.

If on the other hand you want to do further work on this story let me know and I'll send you a list of the improbabilities we have found in the story. The Post is a very difficult magazine to get by with improbabilities. They ferret them out with a fine-tooth comb.

Ober felt so strongly about wanting this to be a marketable story (and if at all possible a *Post* story) that on 25 March, at Ober's instructions because he was out of the office, Constance Smith sent to Fitzgerald (1) a list of cuts and changes, (2) a list of inconsistencies, and (3) a carbon of the story with the suggested changes and cuts made in it. The list of cuts, changes, and inconsistencies follows to show the degree to which Ober went in changing a Fitzgerald story.

THE PEARL AND THE FUR

F. SCOTT FITZGERALD

All numberings refer to original copy.

Page 4. -Direction changed because of Pier number change (Pier 97 is at foot of West 75th St. and most boats for West Indies sail from there)

Timing changed to fit further incidents.

Page 5. -Timing changed to make it logical for Mrs. TenBrook to come aboard so early. "Central Park Zoo specified—also for timing. Explains cut on page 7.

"In a new uniform" cut. N.Y. taxi drivers don't wear uniforms.

Deadhead stuff cut because seemed irrelevant and all this part had to be speeded up. (See page 6 for similar cuts)

Part about his looking up zoo cut, because of change to Central Park Zoo whose location should be known to any New Yorker.

Page 6. -Age cut because N.Y. law requires hack drivers to be 21.

Page 8. "in front of the church" cut, because they are in Park.

Page 9. -Directions changed for obvious reasons. "Chateau" changed to mansion because existence of chateaus in N.Y. doubtful.

Page 10. Cuts and changes made for timing purposes.

Page 14. Insert to explain how other taxi-driver knew about the cape.

Page 18. "windowless" changed to "dark" because doubted any room would be *without* windows.

Further changes: Eliminate "mention" on Page 18 of chauffeur so as not to raise question in reader's mind *why* Mrs. TenBrook went in a taxi.

1. No girls school (from out of town) would let girls of 13 wander around New York alone.
2. Why would anyone take a chinchilla coat to West Indies in Spring?
3. The four boys wouldn't let girl go off in taxi with the chinchilla coat. One of them at least would go with her, or they would all go to the boat together.
4. Gwen goes down to boat for the romance of travel (presented earlier) why doesn't she stay as long as possible to see people on board, etc. Instead she gets off very early to go to the zoo—why? It isn't time for lunch.
5. Gwen gets on board the boat—no passengers, not even a guard at gangplank—unlikely—why go so early? (page 5)
6. Why does a rich woman board a boat several hours before it sails?
7. Why do all four boys go back to house for coat? Why do any of them go if rich woman telephones and finds it isn't there?
8. Exchange of drivers not plausible. I think a driver would always finish his fare and get his tip.
9. Women do not have their names in their coats.—or addresses?
10. Gwen after protecting coat so carefully wouldn't let driver carry it when he gets to boat.
11. Nobody could be locked in bird house at noon?
12. Why does rich woman go down in taxi—while the boys seems to have come back in a limousine?
13. Taxi drivers have to be 21 in N.Y. City.
14. No taxi driver in N.Y. would start out with a passenger the first time he ever drives a cab. (Page 6)
15. Its long after 12—boat sails at 1—boys haven't much time to dance. (Page 10)
16. Tough taxi driver—his arriving comes as a surprise—still seems improbable—also the maids telephoning. Perhaps the rich woman should have telephoned—if she remembered taxi Co. Better say—"Rich woman telephoned to say she had left a coat in the

taxi she took to the pier 97—and then word came in coat had been found in taxi? (Page 15)

17. Boat is being cleared—Rich woman says she could arrange by long distance for Gwen to sail—Pretty quick work. (Page 18).

Ober followed up on 27 April 1936 with another detailed letter to Fitzgerald about the cuts, changes and inconsistencies.

I am delighted that you have decided to do a little more work on THE PEARL AND THE FUR. I am sure you can make it a story that the Post will be delighted to have.

The list of comments I sent you needs a little explanation. These were the combined comments of three readers. Some of them are trivial and some of them apply only to the changes that we made in the version we had typed.

While all of these inconsistencies might not occur to any one reader, some of them would I think be noticed by any reader of the story, so I hope you can get rid of as many of them as possible.

It seems to me that the most necessary thing to do in the story is to arrange Gwen's adventure so that it will take place in a very short space of time. A rich woman used to travelling would not board a boat very long before its time of sailing. It seems to me therefore that the finding of the coat, etc. ought to be arranged in such a way that everything could happen within the space of three-quarters of an hour or an hour.

Couldn't you have the young taxi driver lose his job for not reporting the loss of the coat? This would do away with the second taxi driver who I think is very difficult to introduce in a plausible manner.

I hope you know that no one reads your stories with more pleasure and with more partiality than I do and that I wouldn't suggest your making changes in a story unless it seemed to me important that you should do so. Of course much the easiest thing for me to do would be to have had your copy typed and send it as it was to Philadelphia but I am sure you want me to use my best judgment and so far I think we have agreed very well on the changes that are advisable to make in your stories.

Fitzgerald reworked the story, and by 4 May Ober had the new version. He wrote to Fitzgerald commenting on how the story had been improved: " . . . although I have gone over it a number of times I really enjoyed it this time and I think you have done a very good job on it. It is already on the way to the Post." But the story was not destined for the *Post*, and on 8 May, Ober wrote saying he had word from Miss Neall that the *Post* had already informed Fitzgerald of their rejection and their decision to drop the Gwen series. His alternative suggestion is: "to sell this story to the Pictorial after you have changed the names." The day before, he had sent Fitzgerald the names of the characters in "Make Yourself at Home." On 11 May, Ober expressed his disappointment over the *Post* rejection and referred to the new version he now had (presumably the revision for submission to *Pictorial Review*), saying: "THE PEARL AND THE FUR is very much better than any other version and I am sorry the Post could not have seen it first in this version. However, I think you are probably right that it would be a mistake to ask them to read the story again. We are having it typed and I'll show it to the Pictorial." By 28 May, Ober was able to offer Fitzgerald some hope that *Pictorial Review* would buy the story; he hoped to have a decision "by Monday," which was 1 June. On 5 June, Ober gave Fitzgerald an answer, but it was an answer with qualifications:

> I have been talking to the editor of the Pictorial and the best I have been able to get him to do is to say that he will pay $1000 for THE PEARL AND THE FUR and this on condition that they can make some changes in the story where it doesn't seem to them plausible. The editor says he doesn't want you to feel that he is trying to take advantage of you but he doesn't feel that this story is anywhere near as good as the first one they bought. He says he likes the character Dolly and if you have ideas for other stories about this character, he might like to have another one or two and I think he would pay the same price as he paid for the first story but he would want first a paragraph or two telling him what the story would be about. You might let me know what you want me to do about this. I am afraid we are rather at the mercy of the Pictorial as I think it would be very difficult to change Gwen's name again and try to sell it to a third magazine.

Although there is no further correspondence about these changes, Fitzgerald must have met the request of *Pictorial Review*. The last reference to the story is Ober's 27 November 1936 letter about "the two girl stories," which has already been quoted. The two stories were to be published "in the Spring not before March or April," but the *Pictorial Review* died.

"Cyclone in Silent Land"—1936

No Ober synopsis remains, but a typescript of the story survives. Fitzgerald entertained the idea of a series of stories about a nurse, and he published one, titled "Trouble" (*The Saturday Evening Post,* 6 March 1937). This story—"Cyclone in Silent Land"—is an earlier story about a nurse named Benjamina Rosalyn, nicknamed Trouble. Dr. Bill Craig, who has become irritated because of difficulties he's having with a cantankerous, wealthy patient, Mr. Polk Johnston, goes to teach a class of student nurses. He finds Trouble (a pretty young girl who has charmed him) crying over the rabbit which is to be dissected, loses his temper, and swears at the girls. When the superintendent of nurses reports the incident, Dr. Craig loses his job, and Trouble is dismissed from school. In a moment of frustration, Trouble decides to tell the patient, Mr. Johnston, that she'll marry him, but arriving at his room, she discovers Mr. Johnston has "escaped" from the hospital. She follows him. Dr. Craig pursues them both. Just after Dr. Craig finds them together, Mr. Johnston has a heart attack. Dr. Craig saves him and calls for an ambulance. On the way to the hospital, the ambulance is hit by a school bus. Endangering his own life, Dr. Craig breaks into the burning bus to save one of the children, and then he and Trouble give first aid to the others. Finally able to look after Mr. Johnston again, Craig learns that Mr. Johnston has been hiding the fact that he has six toes on one foot. He promises to perform an operation to remove the embarrassing appendage from Mr. Johnston's foot. Johnston is so pleased, that he promises to build a new pediatric wing for the hospital, if the hospital will take Dr. Craig and Trouble back.

No letter or wire remains to pinpoint when Fitzgerald submitted the story to Ober. The only evidence about it is a reference in Ober's letter of 5 June 1936, and all he says is: "Graeme Lorimer was in yesterday and said that you had talked on the telephone to Miss Neall about CYCLONE IN SILENT LAND, but he didn't know what had been decided about it. He said there were some things about the story he liked very much indeed. I presume from your telegram that Miss Neall gave you some suggestions and that you are rewriting the story." The story is not mentioned again, and there is no record of it being offered to any other magazine than *The Saturday Evening Post.*

"Cyclone in Silent Land," as can be seen from the synopsis, has far too complicated a plot for a typical Fitzgerald story. So much happens by accident (literally) and without reason, that the story takes on aspects of a farcical movie—a Mack Sennett comedy, only this story is not meant to be funny. Though no evidence remains as proof, Fitzgerald seems to have abandoned this story and completely reworked one about the character of Trouble, one which proved salable in 1937.

"Thank You For The Light"—1936

A typescript of this vignette survives, and on a file card there appears a synopsis by Constance Smith, which reads: "Weird little piece about tired corset saleswoman, dying for a cigarette, who goes into cathedral. Falls asleep and Virgin comes down and lights her cigarette. C.S."

Very little mention of the piece occurs in the surviving correspondence. There is no record of when Fitzgerald submitted it, but on 25 June 1936, Ober informed him that *The New Yorker* had it. A week later on 2 July, Ober quoted to Fitzgerald *The New Yorker* comments in rejecting the story:

> "We're afraid that this Fitzgerald story is altogether out of the question. It seems to us so curious and so unlike the kind of thing we associate with him and really too fantastic. We would give a lot, of course, to have a Scott Fitzgerald story and we hope that you will send us something that seems more suitable. Thank you, anyhow, for letting us see this."

According to the file card, "Thank You For The Light" was also offered to and rejected by *College Humor, Harper's Bazaar, Vanity Fair,* and *Vogue.*

To call this vignette a "story" would be to misclassify it, for its brevity and slenderness of plot as well as its caricature, rather than characterization, do not qualify it as a story. The action of a miracle occurring over such an inconsequential need borders on the ludicrous and absurd rather than clever and humorous. Fitzgerald must have thought it would earn him a quick fifty dollars from *The New Yorker.*

"They Never Grow Older"—1937

This is also a lost story. On the surviving file card, there appears a synopsis by Ober, which reads: "Story about a cartoonist. He and boyhood friend both love same girl. The friend finally becomes owner of the syndicate which owns the cartoonist's comic strip. The girl carries on the strip when cartoonist is shot for no reason by a crazy man who thinks he is originator of strip. When they are about 50 the cartoonist and girl decide to get married. Very poor story— improbable and has none of author's best writing in it. H.O."

The first mention in the correspondence is Fitzgerald's letter of 2 January 1937, when he writes Ober hoping that the new story, which is at the typist's, "will sell quick." But it was another month before he sent the story to Ober. In a letter received by Ober on 2 February, Fitzgerald explains: "This will reach you with the story I imagine + I have no illusions about it—it was written, delayed, re-written, finished twice re-written. If you think it is *too* bad don't show it to the *Post,* but unless you have some extraordinarily good suggestions you might show it to some one + get a reaction." After reading the story, Ober wrote to Fitzgerald on 4 February that he would try to sell it, but did not think it should be offered to the *Post.* He explains: "The next story I show them I want to be a really good Scott Fitzgerald story. If you will wait about a week and read the story over I think you will agree with me that it hasn't the quality your stories ought to have." Another month passed before any reference was made to it, and in a letter Ober received on 2 March 1937, Fitzgerald dejectedly comments: "About the cartoonist story I don't care." Yet the next month in a letter received by Ober on 6 April, Fitzgerald suggests: "You might send me the cartoon story to look over." On the same day, Ober returned the story with a very discouraging letter saying: "I don't feel very hopeful of this story and it doesn't seem to me wise for you to spend much time on it. The few people who have seen it haven't had a good word to say for it. The idea of the story has been used several times and it is not a very good one anyway."

According to the file card, two magazines saw and rejected the story—*Cosmopolitan* and *Redbook.* Ober's last remarks about the story may have been predicated on the following readers' reports he received from one of the magazines (probably *Cosmopolitan*).

READERS' REPORTS ON "THEY NEVER GROW OLDER"
by F. Scott Fitzgerald

This story of the comic strip—in life and in the papers—seems to me rather a clumsy parallel. The author apparently thinks he has a unique and clever idea but he doesn't pull it off. There never seems to be any good reason for keeping the characters apart just to draw the parallel. I don't think we'd miss this if we rejected it.

* * *

The pity is that they do, both Fitzgerald and his characters. This is a dreary badly written unbelievable story about a comic strip artist and his love and his rival, and by the time they've lived their comic strip till they're all fortyish I for one don't care for them or the comic.

* * *

One of the most cockeyed nightmarish stories I have ever read.

*   *   *

It is a confused, muddled story about a famous cartoonist, the girl he has loved since college days, and a rival who has also loved her all his life. For some reason which the author may know but I couldn't discover the cartoonist never proposes and the girl waits around until she is forty before they finally decide to get married. Just by way of pretending that it is a story, a madman breaks into the cartoonist's studio and shoots him in the middle of the story. This particular scene reminds us that Fitzgerald can write but it has very little connection with what should be the thread of the story.

"The Vanished Girl"—1937

This is another lost story. The record includes a synopsis by Constance Smith, which reads: "Girl leaves N.J. town to go to college in N.Y. and isn't found for 10 years. Man who doesn't know her has interested himself in case and traced her. Forced to marry a man to save father she has deliberately forgotten earlier life. Carried on several careers under different names including demonstrating inflated suits for window jumping. Not credible and I fear a very dull and silly story. C.S."

Ober received word that the story was sent from Fitzgerald on 11 March 1937, in a letter in which Fitzgerald comments: "it is, I think, a pretty good story—at least it reads and isn't muffed, even if the conception isn't very full-bodied." According to the file card, Ober submitted the story to *Redbook* on 17 March 1937. He informed Fitzgerald on 22 March that *Redbook* had not decided anything yet, but on 24 March he wrote Fitzgerald that *Redbook* had declined it. In that letter he offered a criticism of the story: "I like the first few pages of this very much indeed but when the girl floated out the window, it began to be improbable and all the latter part of the story seemed to me weak." Also in this letter, and in a telegram the same day, Ober said he would return the story special delivery and suggested that Fitzgerald try to sell it to *Esquire*. The story was never published.

"Offside Play" ("Athletic Interview" and "Athletic Interval")—1937

In the file there survives a card on this story containing an Ober synopsis, which reads: "Interesting. Girl at football game. Man she is in love with throws her over—she meets hero of game and finds he has no money. She gets a rich man to give him money so he can continue to play. In the end she goes back to man she loves. H.O."

On 13 April 1937, Ober received the story (entitled "Athletic Interview") and a letter from Fitzgerald in which he says: "At least I have taken my time on this story as I should have started doing two years ago." Ober answered the same day, saying: "I think it is a good piece of work." After offering the story to *The Saturday Evening Post*, Ober wrote to Fitzgerald on 20 April to say that the *Post* had rejected it. Ober also proposed suggestions for making the story more salable and showed a rare irritation with the magazine editors.

> The Post has declined ATHLETIC INTERVAL. They say it is much too long for their present requirements—but this is a minor point. It is over 9000 words and ought to be cut before I show it to anyone else. (It's at the Cosmopolitan now and they can use long stories). I'm sending you a carbon and if Cosmopolitan declines I'll wire you to try and cut it to 6000 or 7000 words.
>
> To go back to the Post. They say it lacks the warmth of your best work and that it hasn't the "incandescent" quality your readers expect. This gives me a pain. This story may not be your very best—no author can be his very best all the time; but it is so much better than 9/10 of the stories they buy that their criticism is absurd.
>
> If Cosmopolitan declines the story I think you ought to cut it and while you are doing it perhaps you can do something to Kiki or Considine that will make them more likable. Considine is rather a shadowy character. I think the story would sell to the more popular magazines if you could make Considine an undergraduate who is not an athlete—but who has qualities that Rip lacks. And couldn't you motivate Kiki's rather hard headed business plans for Rip? All this, of course, in case Cosmopolitan doesn't buy the story.

The next day Fitzgerald wired that he wanted a carbon of the story so he could make changes; particularly, he thought he "HAD BETTER SUPPRESS THE ACTUAL NAMES OF THE COLLEGES . . . ." Apparently Fitzgerald got right to work on the story, because on 23 April he wired Ober that he was sending a cut version. On 26 April Ober received a letter from Fitzgerald in which he expressed some optimism about the shortened version: "I've cut it without difficulty to about 7300 instead of 9100 + it's vastly improved. This is the way it should have been at first—inevitable result of pressure + hurry. I think the Post might have taken it as it is now." That same day Ober answered that he thought Fitzgerald "did a good job of cutting" the story, and he was sending the shorter version to *Cosmopolitan*, who had not made a decision yet on the longer one. Nothing had happened by 2 May, for Fitzgerald, in his habitual need for money, wired Ober to "TAKE ANY PRICE FOR INTERLUDE . . . ." On 5 May Ober wired that *Cosmopolitan* still had the story and that if they refused it, he would try *American Magazine*. The next day Ober sent Fitzgerald the bad news: "I have just received ATHLETIC INTERVAL from Cosmopolitan. They told me that it had been touch and go whether they accepted it or not. The final verdict . . . has been against it . . . ." The readers' reports from *Cosmopolitan* follow.

May 24, 1937

ATHLETIC INTERVAL by F. Scott Fitzgerald
REPORTS

It is shorter and therefore somewhat better than formerly. . . . But it still is strangely complicated in motivation. . . . The emotional parts are strangely UNemotional and static. . . . The plot concerning the orphanage brother is frankly dragged in.

* * *

Strangely unemotional this story is, but it holds you to the end and the football element gives it an added value.

* * *

I kept feeling that it was good, then bad, then that it was going to be good—then it didn't. Actually, there's a sense of frustration and dullness and anticlimax in the girl's romances—she is pretty much deadened to emotion, and her final compromise is so routine and valueless. Worse, however, is the unfinished and unsatisfactory story of the two collegians, the football star and his orphanage "brother"—you have a feeling that the brother is still a crook, and that the girl has prostituted the football star to commercialism and has given him nothing in return—except a security income wangled out of a nitwit alumnus, for which the hero has sold all the glory which the public and his own deeds have given him. Altogether, it's unsatisfactory—although the color and background are just what we'd like.

* * *

Mr. Fitzgerald seems pretty far away from his characters in this. The idea of the plot is perfectly satisfactory but Kiki's switch from one man to the other and back again never seems very convincing and what should be a fairly emotional story is pretty cold.

Ober next offered it to *American Magazine*. On 10 May he informed Fitzgerald that the story was at *American,* and on 18 May he apologetically told Fitzgerald "the American doesn't like ATHLETIC IN-TERVAL and I have given it to Balmer of the Red Book."

Undaunted by three rejections, Fitzgerald completely rewrote the story and on 16 June wired Ober: "FOOTBALL REVISE CAN YOU ORDER RETYPEING AND SEND POST." The cycle began again on 17 June when Ober reported that he had had the story retyped and given it to Graeme Lorimer. On 21 June, Fitzgerald sent Ober a postcard on which he remarked that he was "Glad you liked football." But the story was not good enough yet. On 23 June, Ober wrote Fitzgerald about the *Post's* decision with their remarks: "'The new version of Scott Fitzgerald's story is a vast improvement over the first one. The writing has all the old Fitzgerald quality, but the plot values are a bit hazy. For that reason, we must regretfully return the story.'"

In July 1937, Fitzgerald signed a six-month contract with MGM and went to Hollywood as a script-writer. Nevertheless, Ober continued to try to sell the story. On 26 July, he wrote to Fitzgerald saying that Kenneth Littauer of *Collier's* "is going to read over the football story and see if he can write a letter making suggestions that he thinks will make the story all right." Ober followed up on 4 August with a letter to Fitzgerald containing Littauer's comments on "Offside Play":

> There is a great deal of good stuff in this story but the action is altogether too complicated. Unless we are mistaken the whole thing needs to be simplified and very sharply focused. For instance, the introduction of a co-ed wife for Van Kamp is a piece of strong-arm work that ought to make a master of subtleties like Fitzgerald blush for shame. There is too much about Kiki and the Old Grads. There is too much about all sorts of major and minor irrelevancies. If this story ran a true course it would end in the neighborhood of page twenty. The only thing that carries it all the way to page thirty-one is a conglomeration of ellipses and detours that do nothing but confuse the issue and bewilder the reader. Therefore, won't you ask Mr. Fitzgerald to make this the story of Alex and Rip and the girl. Tell us what they do to each other. Throw the spotlight on them in the center of the stage and shove everything else into the background or out in the wings as much as possible. Emphasize particularly the importance and poignancy of the romance of Alex and Kiki.

On 29 September Ober encouraged Fitzgerald to do some work on the two stories for *Collier's* and make them salable. The final word on this story comes from Fitzgerald in October 1937, by which time he was thoroughly engrossed in his script work on the movie *Three Comrades* (his only screen credit). He wrote to Ober on 8 October regarding "Offside Play" and "Dentist Appointment" ("End of Hate," published in *Collier's,* 22 June 1940)—two stories for *Collier's:*

> . . . I am going to do something about them but have definitely postponed it until after THREE COMRADES is in the bag—as I told you which is a matter of three weeks more. Then I will either take a week off or simply find time some way in early morning. So tell Colliers not to fret about it. The longer I wait the more I am liable to get a fresh point of view. I think maybe you are dead on them and so is Collier, and I will have them both read here by someone who can put their finger on the trouble. Both of them come so near being right that I am sure the actual writing won't be any trouble. To get the right point of view is the question—which seems to be all [off] right now.

Apparently nothing satisfactory was ever done with the story, for it was never published.

"Temperature" ("Women in the House")—1939

This is a lost story.

Throughout 1938, Fitzgerald's time and energies were largely devoted to his script work. The only short story reference during that year is about his revising of "End of Hate" for *Collier's.* His revision on that story took over a year and a half. At the end of 1938, MGM did not renew Fitzgerald's contract, and he turned to free lance script-writing to support himself. Not until 20 June 1939, did he submit a new short story to Ober. That day he wired that he was sending a 14,000 word story; it was "The Women in the House." Ober reacted as soon as he had the story, wiring Fitzgerald on 29 June 1939: "STORY JUST RECEIVED AND READ. MUCH TOO LONG FOR SUBJECT. ADVISE CUTTING TO SIX THOUSAND WORDS WILL OFFER AS IS IF YOU INSIST BUT THINK VERY UNWISE. WRITING." The next day he did send Fitzgerald his criticism and suggestions:

> I'm returning THE WOMEN IN THE HOUSE by airmail so that you can cut it as much as possible. As I tried to tell you over the telephone last night, this is in my opinion, a story that would be very difficult to divide into two parts. It is a light, amusing story and hasn't enough suspense. It is also too long for any magazine that I know of to use as a short story and it is not long enough for a novelette.
>
> I know from experience that it is the length of story that the Post finds it very difficult to use. And since it is some time since you have shown the Post a story, I think it is important to show them a story that there is a chance of their buying.

I hope you will cut it just as much as you can. It is a light, farcical story and such stories do not stand a lot of words. I think the closet scene and a lot about the nurses could be cut. Also the part of the story where Monsen is intoxicated. The first part is really good, but after that it seemed to me to get rather exaggerated.

Fitzgerald responded on 3 July:

I made a first cut from the original 14,500 words (58 pages) that I sent you, to 10,850 words and now at the last moment I have made an additional cut to 9,350 words which is the last that can be pried out of the story. (by this old hand)

I don't see how the incident of Emmet getting the brandy bottle can *possibly* be eliminated, and I know it's a difficult length, but unfortunately that's the way the story was.

On 5 and 6 July, they exchanged a wire and letter as Fitzgerald asked Ober to hold the new version and Ober agreed. On 7 July Fitzgerald sent Ober a letter saying:

This is about right, I think. I took one more whack at it. My God, what a waste of energies. What I cut out is long enough for another short story, only it might not fit together. Littauer gave me to understand that they had nothing at all against the two-parter. I know there was no trouble with the *Red Book* with the "Rich Boy" or the *Post* with the "Popular Girl."

He wired on 8 July that the third version was mailed. He also wrote a letter the same day, sending Ober further corrections to the latest version. Ober wrote on 10 July, that he had received the third version—titled "Temperature"—and would show it to the *Post*. Fitzgerald, obviously concerned about the story and not having heard from Ober wired on 11 July—"HOW DO YOU LIKE IT NOW." Ober answered him the next day, giving a mixed appraisal of the story:

The story is a lot better now that you have shortened it but I do not think and I do not believe you think that it is anywhere one of your best stories. A slight story like this one cannot stand the length that a more important story would. That is why I was sure you ought to cut it down before we showed it to anyone. It is true that magazines sometimes use a two-part story but here again it is necessary that the story be one that will divide and has suspense enough to hold over for a week or a month as the case may be.

At this same time, the Fitzgerald-Ober break over financial matters occurred, and on 14 July, Fitzgerald wired requesting that "Temperature" be returned to him and saying it shouldn't be offered. But the story had already been offered to the *Post,* and on 18 July Ober wrote to tell Fitzgerald of the *Post's* rejection:

> I have the following letter from The Post regarding your last short story, TEMPERATURE:
>
> "There is, it seems to us, a real story idea in Scott Fitzgerald's TEMPERATURE, but the thing has been so garbled in the telling that you can't see the story for the words. You, I know, realized this yourself when you gave the manuscript to me.
>
> I wish you'd tell Scott that we are anxious to see more stories of his and suggest to him to put this away for awhile and have another try at it later."
>
> I also have your telegram suggesting that I do not offer the story further. The story, even now, is about 8,200 words in length which is worse for other magazines that it is for the Post. I think you have enough material for a very light, very short, amusing story, but it isn't a good story now and I don't think it would help you to offer it. . . .
>
> I haven't lost faith in your being able to write. I do know though that without exception every author I have ever known who has worked in Hollywood has had a transitional period of several months in which it has been difficult for him to get away from the motion picture technique of writing.

In the postscript, Ober said he was returning the story. Apparently Fitzgerald had not received Ober's letter when on 22 July, he sent the following petulant letter to Ober's office:

> Dear Sirs:-
>
> From lack of communication in regard to my story "Temperature," I am assuming that Mr. Ober is on his vacation. I wired about a week ago directly to the *Post.* They answered suggesting some specific changes whereupon I wired you to return the manuscript to me and have expected it by airmail daily.
>
> As I said in the wire, I want to do a revision before showing it to any other magazine.

On 24 July, Ober patiently explained that the story had been sent "on the day you asked me for it." He also told Fitzgerald that he "didn't send it airmail because you said you might look it over later on." The last word on the story is from Fitzgerald in his 2 August 1939 letter to Ober, when he adds a postscript saying the story finally arrived. It had gone to the wrong post office.

"The Couple"—n.d.

No mention of this story by this title occurs in the correspondence. Attached to the surviving typescript is a synopsis, unsigned, which reads: "Story about a couple who are on the verge of getting a divorce; have just arranged to separate, but husband agrees to let the wife stay in the house for another two weeks. An English couple she has engaged as servants arrive the next morning, but they are so terrible and the experience of having them in the house is so hideous that the dissident pair is reunited and they fire the Englishman, Reynolds, and his wife, Katie. The pet poodle who had hated the English servants too and fled returns to find the servants gone and his master and mistress happy in their home." A note added in Ober's hand reads: "no record we have ms." There is no way of knowing when it was submitted to Ober or to which magazines he offered it. The story was never published.

The absence of any record of this story suggests that Ober did not try to sell it. The story, weakly plotted and with thinly drawn characterizations, is one of Fitzgerald's lesser attempts. The idea of the contrasting couples could have been turned into a charmingly ironic story, but Fitzgerald does not seem to have decided exactly what he wanted the story to do, and the result is a vague and uncertain story.

This record—a record of the struggles of both author and agent—tells clearly the professional suffering Fitzgerald experienced during the disastrous years of the 30's. He was unable to do consistently the one thing he had long been capable of doing well—writing good, marketable, popular short stories. Writing, whether stories or novels, was his profession, and these rejections, sometimes after two or three complete revisions of a story, represent lapses or failures in Fitzgerald's practice of his profession. No matter how much help Harold Ober tried to be, and the evidence shows that he strived with Fitzgerald to keep that great talent flowing, these were times when Fitzgerald's literary well-spring ran low.

This is not to say that the 1930's were a complete waste for Fitzgerald. After all, between 1931 and 1939, he wrote and published 48 stories—including such stories as "Babylon Revisited" and "Crazy Sunday"—plus the "Crack-up" articles for *Esquire*. Fitzgerald never ceased being a professional writer; he never stopped being a regularly published author. Even the slim years were not bone dry.

Nor is this to suggest that Harold Ober ever stepped in and took over the writing of Fitzgerald's stories. His first "letter of advice" was sent to Fitzgerald in August 1933. Before that time he had not offered criticism in any detail, or presumed to direct Fitzgerald in the writing of a story—and in the 1920's Fitzgerald was so in command of his writing abilities that it would have been an insult on Ober's part. But when times were hard, Ober patiently encouraged Fitzgerald to work, revise, and improve his stories. He made general suggestions to Fitzgerald—suggestions designed to make a story more appropriate for a particular market or magazine. For example, he would suggest taking out an inconsistency, or making an incident more realistic, or simply cutting the length of a story. Sometimes Fitzgerald listened to his advice; sometimes he did not.

There were various reasons for Fitzgerald's failures with these stories—reasons which include his own emotional and physical instability as a result of his dissipation and the pressures on him of Zelda's illness during this time. However, the most significant reason may be because his material was gone—his life with Zelda from which source he drew so much for his stories and novels. The efforts on Ober's part are designed to aid Fitzgerald in problems of plot and structure; he does not offer suggestions on style revision. Fitzgerald was having difficulty with matter more than manner, and the record of this failure is meant to show both Ober's concern for and energies in behalf of his client and Fitzgerald's troubles. For a writer of Fitzgerald's stature, it is important that the record of his professional output be as complete as possible.

University of South Carolina

---

[1] Matthew J. Bruccoli, ed., and Jennifer McCabe Atkinson, *As Ever, Scott Fitz—, The F. Scott Fitzgerald/Harold Ober Letters* (New York: J.B. Lippincott, 1971).

[2] Henry Blackman Sell.

[3] *The Saturday Evening Post.*

[4] Though not based on Fitzgerald's story, the film *Sullivan's Travels* (1941), original screenplay by Preston Sturges, is an interesting parallel to the story.

[5] Henry Dan Piper claims that *Pictorial Review* bought this story, though they never published it *(F. Scott Fitzgerald,* p. 232). He cites an Ober letter of 2 June 1939 as his source. However, the Ober letter does not name the story; it simply tells of *Pictorial Review* suspending publication. No other evidence has turned up to show where the story was offered, and the note attached to the typescript implies that it was never sold.

[6] Kenneth Littauer.

[7] William Ludlow Chenery.

[8] Charles Marquis Warren.

[9] *Pictorial Review* was bought by the Hearst Corporation. *Cosmopolitan* and *Woman's Home Companion,* both Hearst publications, have been asked to check their files for copies of these two stories. They have found nothing.

Fitzgerald's Marked Copy of
This Side of Paradise

Matthew J. Bruccoli

Fitzgerald's marked copy of *This Side of Paradise* is inscribed: "Personal Property of the W. K. F Scott Fitzgerald". As in his copy of *Gatsby*, he indicated passages that had been mentioned in reviews and noted the publication in which the review appeared.[1] These notes have not been included in the list that follows. The queried passages are puzzling: In some cases they seem to be passages Fitzgerald had come to regard as weak; but in other cases they appear to be passages mentioned in unidentified reviews.

The references to Compton MacKenzie indicate Fitzgerald's awareness of—and perhaps chagrin at—the impression *Sinister Street* made on him.

---

[1] See Jennifer E. Atkinson, "Fitzgerald's Marked Copy of *The Great Gatsby*," *Fitzgerald/Hemingway Annual 1970*, pp. 28-33; and my "A Collation of F. Scott Fitzgerald's *This Side of Paradise*," *Studies in Bibliography*, IX (1957), 263-265.

Published with the permission of Frances Fitzgerald Smith and the Harold Ober Associates. All rights to this material are the property of Mrs. Smith.

while, why he had determined to use to the utmost himself and his heritage from the personalities he had passed. . . .

He stretched out his arms to the crystalline, radiant sky.

"I know myself," he cried, "but that is all."

? New Reprint,

Phila Ledger
Phila ?

I like this book for the enormous emotion, mostly immature and bogus, that gives every incident a sort of silly "life".

457 1925.

But the faked references and intellectual reactions + cribs from MacKenzie, Johnston, Wells Wilde, Tarkington give me the pip.

Fitzgerald's Marked Copy of *This Side of Paradise*

title	Fitzgerald queried Brooke epigraph
dedication	Sigorney [Sigourney
4.1	Margaritta [Margherita
4.34	"Frank on the Mississippi," ["Frank on the Lower Mississippi,"
5.25	fed [*Fitzgerald put X in margin*
6.2	-struck [-stricken?
6.7	raconteur [*Fitzgerald wrote "Fem." in margin*
6.25	amendments, memories [amendments, and her memories *Fitzgerald wrote "notice" in margin*
7.28	Ashville [*Fitzgerald wrote "Sp" in margin*
7.33	Ashville [Asheville
10.2	Collar and Daniel's "First-Year Latin," [*Fitzgerald queried hyphen and wrote "Sp" in margin*
14.25	Mysterieuse [*Fitzgerald underlined*
17.3	'Casey ["Casey
18.14	Three-fingered [Three-finger
18.15-16	Christie Mathewson [*Fitzgerald wrote "Sp" in margin*
18.17-23	*Fitzgerald bracketed and wrote "Ainslees" in margin*
18.22	Ghunga [*Fitzgerald deleted h and wrote "Sp" in margin*
18.26	Rhinehart [Rinehart
22.8-15	Fitzgerald wrote in margin: "Touch of McKenzie here"
27.9-16	Fitzgerald wrote in margin: "Strange to say this really happened tho I *had* read McKenzie"
30.6-10	Illegible marginal note.
36.2	Mont Martre [*Fitzgerald wrote "Sp" in margin*
36.6	moonlight [*Fitzgerald queried in margin*
41.	Fitzgerald wrote in top margin: "Here begins COMTOM M^{c}KENZIE"
41.26	Allenby [*Fitzgerald wrote "Hobey Baker" in margin*
49.15	flambuoyant [*Fitzgerald wrote "Sp" in margin*
49.24	tetotalling [*Fitzgerald wrote "Sp" in margin*
50.20	swathe [*Fitzgerald wrote "Sp" in margin*
50.27-29	Fitzgerald queried in margin
51.9	Litt. [*Fitzgerald underlined*
51.29	Cumizza [*Fitzgerald circled the m*
52.4-8	Fitzgerald queried in margin

52.18-24	Fitzgerald queried in margin
53.18-22	Fitzgerald wrote in margin: "This vulgarity is my own"
55.11-22	"Come into the Garden, Maude," [*Fitzgerald wrote "Sp" in margin*
56.2	*Litt.* [*Fitzgerald underlined*
56.15-21	Fitzgerald queried in margin
59.4	Ballades [*Fitzgerald deleted e and wrote "Sp" in margin*
61.5	Fitzgerald queried in margin
63.32-33	Fitzgerald queried in margin
64.	Next to "PETTING" subtitle Fitzgerald wrote: "And this is *all* mine"
67	Next to ISABELLE subtitle Fitzgerald wrote: "This too!"
73	Next to BABES IN THE WOODS subtitle Fitzgerald wrote: "This too!"
78	Next to CARNIVAL subtitle Fitzgerald wrote: "Return to Mac"
79.7-12	Fitzgerald wrote in margin: "Oh Yeah! 1933"
80.7	Cambell [Campbell
89.27-29	Fitzgerald queried in margin
94	Next to UNDER THE ARC-LIGHT subtitle Fitzgerald wrote: "MINE"
98.29	high point [*Fitzgerald underlined and put in margin F. P. A.*
99	Next to THE EGOTIST CONSIDERS chapter title Fitzgerald wrote: "MINE"
104	Next to THE SUPERMAN GROWS CARELESS subtitle Fitzgerald wrote: "Here it becomes quite mixed—half his"
105.6	master [muster
116.6	flare [flair
117.30	*Litt.* [*Fitzgerald circled second t*
119.14	Esquadrille [*Fitzgerald wrote "Sp" in margin*
119	Next to THE DEVIL subtitle Fitzgerald wrote: "Enter Robert Hugh Benson"
120.13	Dachari [Daiquiori
131	At head of page Fitzgerald wrote: "Always remember this is all true—or I thought it was sincerely"

131.13-20	Fitzgerald bracketted and underlined, and wrote "Quoted" in margin
132.20-21	Fitzgerald queried in margin
134.35	Tolstoi [*Fitzgerald wrote "Sp" in margin*
135	Fitzgerald wrote at head of page: "Enter Wells of 1919"
154.20	Cecelia [Cecilia
169	Fitzgerald queried INTERLUDE section title
176.16-17, 23-24	Fitzgerald queried in margin
176.36	Johnston. [*Fitzgerald deleted t and wrote "Sp" below*
179	Fitzgerald wrote "MY OWN" at head of page.
180.24	tickle-toe on the soft carpet [*Fitzgerald underlined*
184.1	impeachable [unimpeachable
199.30	juvenalia [juvenilia
200	Fitzgerald wrote in top left margin: "McKenzie touch"
200.12	her [hers
202.13, 15	his [*Fitzgerald underlined*
212.12	rather grosteque [*illegible marginal note*
224.18	Fitzgerald wrote in margin opposite this paragraph: 'Here I reject my prophet. "For each man kills" ect.'
224.24	Jenny [*Fitzgerald circled y and wrote "Sp" in margin*
224.25	McKenzie [MacKenzie
224.25	Bennet [Fitzgerald underlined and wrote "Sp" in margin
226.11-18	Fitzgerald wrote in margin: "Rather patheticly naive —what?"
227.9	tres [*Fitzgerald wrote grave and accute accents over both appearances of this word*
227.34	surnamed [nick-named
228.23	I [I'm
229.9-13	Fitzgerald wrote in margin: "Rotten Prophecy"
229.17	Gunmeyer [Guynemer
230.4-7	Fitzgerald queried in margin
232.22	Gouveneer [Gouveneur
232.22	Fanny [*Fitzgerald underlined and put "Sp" in margin*
232.20-33; 233.1-7	Fitzgerald queried in margin

233.14	Bennet [Bennett
234.8	Juvenalia [Juvenilia
234.13-35	Fitzgerald wrote in margin: "1925 My God!"
235	Fitzgerald wrote after section break: "Thank God
235.15	that Junk is over"
235.24	sight, [sight
235.25	*life* [*Fitzgerald underlined*
238	*One* [*Fitzgerald underlined*
	Fitzgerald wrote in top margin: "This is so funny I can't even bear to read it"
240.28	*langeur* [*langueur*
242.26	Celleni [Cellini
249.6	*foreborne* [*Fitzgerald wrote "Sp" in margin*
251.9	Stretch [Scratch
252.34	tens [teens
259.22	Our [One
260.	At bottom of page Fitzgerald wrote: "Bunny says he could see the sawdust leaking out of her all through. But what I can see leaking out is not named in books F. S. F. 1925"
264.6	moisture, [moisture;
264.12, 14	Fitzgerald circled the repetition of "became"
267.13	kill [take a paste at you
273.17	portcullis [*Fitzgerald wrote "cochere" above*
285.4-6	Fitzgerald queried in margin
286.3	O'Neill [*Fitzgerald circled and wrote "Cardinal?" in margin*
296.28	Fitzgerald underlined "deep profundity"
297.22	moralist, reformer, doctor [physician, inventor
299.14-15	I was. . .decent education [*Fitzgerald underlined*
300.27	born [borne
303.1-9	Fitzgerald queried in margin
304.28-33;	
305.1-6	Fitzgerald queried in margin
305	Fitzgerald wrote at bottom of page: 'I like this book for the enormous emotion, mostly immature and bogus, that gives every incident a sort of silly "life". F. S. F. 1925. But the faked references and intellectual reactions & cribs from MacKenzie, Johnston, Wells, Wilde, Tarkington give me the pip'

University of South Carolina

RUGGIERO AUTO AND CYCLE CO.

Donate this space to the Girl Scouts this week

I am glad of the chance to march along with the Girl Scouts.—**James Hay, Jr.**

I know the work the Girl Scouts are doing and it has my enthusiastic approval. It will certainly make them all better voters, wives and mothers.——**Arthur Train.**

Gertrude Atherton writes from Culver City, California, where she is working on the production of a movie from one of her books: "I heartily endorse the Girl Scout idea and you are welcome to use my name."

Don't you think that after being hymned in the press as the creator of a particularly villainous type of flapper that it would be somewhat ironic for me to come out for the Girl Scouts?

Nevertheless as I passed two very beautiful Girl Scouts on Fifth Avenue today I am inclined to feel rather friendly toward the organization.

Very sincerely,

(Signed)   **F. Scott Fitzgerald."**

Daily

Unlocated clipping in Fitzgerald's scrapbook

Hollywood Canteen

A memoir of Scott Fitzgerald in 1937*

Anthony Powell

In May, 1937, having survived six months of script writing of a humble kind with a film company at Teddington, termination of contract and a local recession in the industry caused me to consider an attempt to gain a livelihood by similar means in America.

It was said that, if you stayed in Hollywood only a year, some winnings might be retained. Longer sojourn, entailing an ever-increasing standard of existence, was better avoided; could even result in a life sentence on the weariest of treadmills. My agent, thinking the ambition not too hopelessly irrational, opened up negotiations on the other side. Plans were known to be on foot for making a picture to be called *A Yank at Oxford*. The services of an experienced script writer, who had also spent three years at that university, might well be acceptable.

Deciding to arrive in the first instance "on the Coast," we sailed by Panama. It was a voyage of four weeks. The *Canada* (a Danish vessel subsequently torpedoed by a German submarine in World War II) put into port three or four times on the way. In the Virgins, reached the morning after celebrating King George VI's coronation, the green downs of St. Thomas seen through a porthole shimmered and heaved no less than the waves of the Atlantic. Tom Collinses in the shade of Morgan's Castle to some extent restored the equilibrium. Our ship sailed on through Panama, past the luxuriant marine foliage and forlorn remnants of the canal Lesseps had planned; out into the Pacific, until we docked at Los Angeles.

Of efforts to become a Hollywood script writer there is little more to say than that they were unsuccessful. My American agent

*First published in *The Times Saturday Review* of *The London Times* (3 October 1970), 1. Reprinted here with the permission of Anthony Powell and Harold Ober Associates. All rights to this article are the property of Mr. Powell.

had died during our weeks on the high seas. The replacement was antipathetic. This was getting off to a bad start. I did a round of the studios, told my life story to a series of executives often agreeable enough, but it was pursuing the mirage. One became familiar not so much with the bum's rush, to use an old fashioned expression, as that stagnation of movement, total inanition where any action is concerned, to some extent characteristic of all theatrical administration, more especially when the art of the film is in question.

After a couple of months I gave it up. We flew from coast to coast, spent a week or more in New York, where they were having a heat wave, and sailed homeward on the old *De Grasse,* a leisurely barque dating from the days of the boom. Wine flowed, *vin d'honeurs* the order of the day, and a taste expressed for *bouilla-baisse* resulted in a whole string of individual dishes cooked as reward for appreciation of *la cuisine provençale.* We landed at Plymouth in the middle of August. The security officer glanced at my passport.

"Author? Where's your pipe?"

As a money-making venture the trip could not be called a success, but, as sometimes happens, the side issues were more rewarding than the main intent. To illustrate that, a word must be said of how we lived during this exile, since certain aspects were unexpected.

The accommodation itself was to some extent defined by a male songster in one of the night spots:

> I'd like a little shack
> The other side of the track,
> And a man who doesn't limp
> To be my p . . .

The final word was lost in the moaning of saxophones. The physically active entrepreneur apart, that was much our case. We were among the Untouchables on the "wrong side of the track," one of four self-contained furnished flats of a two-storeyed house, No. 347 North Palm Drive, Beverly Hills. It cost what now seems a low figure, rather less than a hundred and fifty pounds a year, including one day a week's cleaning. With a secondhand car at sixty pounds, living could therefore be called reasonably cheap. Such an existence would not, of course, have been tolerated had one landed a job. It is interesting to speculate what nemesis might be visited on a highly paid script writer who drew his salary, and firmly insisted on an equally modest way of life.

72

The car deserves a word. It was of a kind only briefly produced, then withdrawn from the market. At first, when asked by the parking attendant: "What make?," I would reply: "An Oakland." Later, even when row upon row of shining automobiles stretched away to the horizon and beyond: "The Oakland." That was enough. When we left, the Oakland was returned to the "lot" of its original salesman, who in due course forwarded a very reasonable proportion of what had been paid in the first instance.

While trying out this famous car for the first time in some secluded avenue, I nearly ran into a vehicle driven by Ronald Colman, beside his then wife, Benita Hume. This recollection provokes the question of film stars, who always bulk large in any inquiry as to what life in Hollywood was "Like." To see stars in the flesh was simple enough if you were prepared to pay the prices, naturally expensive, of the bar currently fashionable. At the time it was called, I think, The Cock—possibly The Cock and Bull—and on our sole visit Marlene Dietrich was there, with others no less famous as far as the eye could reach.

We met a few stars personally at different times: Douglas Fairbanks Sr., Lupe Velez, Freddie Bartholomew. The last of these, whose laurels as Little Lord Fauntleroy had recently been conspicuously renewed as the small boy hero of *Captains Courageous*, revealed to me with charming candour the cat's cradle of delicate wires and filaments that remodelled his back teeth.

Most of the time we led a sequestered life in North Palm, where, after an unavailing offer of my services during the day, I read *War and Peace* in the evening. There was a glimpse of Ernest Hemingway one night, when he spoke a personal commentary in a hall at Los Angeles for the showing of the film—rather an indifferent one—*Spanish Earth*. Sometimes, an unheard of thing locally, we would take a picnic basket and bottle of wine for an alfresco lunch outside the town.

The countryside of California is varied. Some of it presents a wilderness, exotically tinted during the rainy season with bursts of wild flowers. In other regions, tiers of oil derricks resemble plantations of a sinister space-fiction shrub. Round about the accumulation of townships loosely known to the world as "Hollywood", the eucalyptus tree flourishes among outcrops of rock and dusty palms. Bougainvillea grows, a few cacti, while red and white cistus, among the tall yuccas, wafts a faintly Corsican perfume. Here large artificial humps in the ground suggested prehistoric burial mounds, or remains of medieval motte-and-bailey castles. They marked the place where yet more film star-villas had been begun, then abandoned owing to the slump.

So odd was this habit of picnicking regarded that, when from time to time a patrolling police car shot swiftly down the highway, the driver would slow up, its crew of Keystone cops give a long appraising stare. I believe there was indeed some danger from snakes.

A bottle of wine has been mentioned. It would hardly be going too far to say that the fact of being resident in wine-producing country was the chief, almost the only element, to make Hollywood life tolerable. Without wine the place would have been a wilderness indeed, and one without wild flowers. It cost about a dollar, roughly four shillings a bottle. Gin could also be bought for a dollar, but a British proprietary brand was a shade more than in England, say, 14s. Obviously, if people were prepared to pay 14s. for what could be purchased for four, some advantage was offered.

More than once that fact was vigorously emphasized. I do not think one's own acquaintances spent so little as a dollar on the gin they provided. On the other hand, they did not perhaps always get the best on the market. There was at least one occasion when I doubted whether I should be able to drive the car home after a single drink: the hangover the following day, of formidable dimensions.

This was, of course, only a few years after the repeal of Prohibition, when, at least in theory, vineyards had been ploughed up, or converted to produce raisins. Nevertheless, the Cabernet of California, Sonoma Valley Chablis, wine "of the German colony," or "of the Swiss colony," carried one through. The two last vintages named, with others similarly planted as "national" grapes, usually by missionaries, were promulgated by a Beverly Hills vintner with a keen interest in the vinicultural history of the state.

The natives of California were by no means universally aware of their good fortune in living in a wine-producing land. In the eyes of those who restricted their potations to spirits, the wine drinkers were almost a race apart; esoteric to the point of intellectual pretension. We were fortunate enough to enjoy the hospitality of one of these wine drinking families, the Morgans, introduced to them by Rex Evans, whose songs to the piano in London of the Twenties had been to the Café Anglais much what the Café de Paris had enjoyed during the same era from Douglas Byng.

Elliott Morgan, son of the house, was employed in the research department of Metro-Goldwyn-Mayer; indeed occupied in "researching" *A Yank at Oxford*, the film on which I had once pinned hopes of attaching myself to the movie business. It turned out that these activities had quite recently brought him in touch with Scott Fitzgerald, just arrived in Hollywood to work on that very script.

It is hard these days to remember that in 1937 the name F. Scott Fitzgerald, as a novelist, was scarcely at all known in the United Kingdom. *The Great Gatsby* had appeared in England in 1926, making no stir at all. Indeed, when *Tender is the Night* followed in 1934, the London publisher did not even bother to list *Gatsby* opposite the title-page. Fitzgerald's reputation, such as it was, rested on the individual efforts of one or two of the younger critics.

In America, though in quite a different manner—an essentially American manner—his position was almost equally unsatisfactory. This famous figure, once the golden boy prototype of the "Jazz Age"—which thought itself every bit as momentous as those who see a fresh renaissance in the pop life of today—was all but forgotten.

There were several reasons for this. Fitzgerald—that rare phenomenon, a "bad" writer who became a "good" writer—had lost much of his former wide public simply because he began to produce immeasurably better books. When the going was good, he had lived recklessly, drunk too much, involved himself in financial embarrassments. In addition, his personal life had suffered unforeseeable and tragic blows. At the same time, he had always managed to keep himself afloat by writing short stories, some accomplished, some less accomplished. All this was outlined by himself in his collection of autobiographical pieces, *The Crack Up,* which I had not then read. However, one could not fail to notice the way people in Hollywood spoke of Fitzgerald. It was almost as if he were already dead; at best risen from the dead, and of somewhat doubtful survival value.

"Meet him? Of course. Scott will be crazy to find an Englishman who knows his work. He says he's never gone over in England, and never will."

So it was all arranged. Elliott Morgan was to bring Scott Fitzgerald to luncheon with us. For convenience sake that was to be at the M.G.M. "commissary." I noted it in my engagement book for Tuesday, July 20; a date, as it turned out, of a certain significance.

After undergoing the accustomed formalities demanded for entering the premises of a film studio—security precautions that might be deemed excessive for gaining access to a nation's most secret atomic plant—we met Elliott standing outside the commissary. This turned out to be a hangar-like restaurant, of no great charm. We found a table by the wall.

The luncheon break for the lower echelons of the film world, such as writers, was not yet due, but a sprinkling of loiterers of one kind or another had begun to congregate in the neighbourhood of the commissary, most of them in ordinary clothes. Through these was suddenly led a girl in a blue Louis XV dress, her makeup bright yellow, powdered and curled hair contained under a cellophane bag. Her sunburnt hands suggested the beach at Santa Monica, rather than the *parterres* of Versailles. Meanwhile, at the central table of the dining room the senior executives were beginning to gather.

These Big Shots appeared just as they might be imagined. Like most people in Hollywood, they seemed to be passionately acting the part life had assigned them; looking almost too much like movie magnates in one of their own films. It should be added that the legend representing every Hollywood waitress or usherette as a failed film star of unimaginable beauty was soon found to be without foundation. One would even hesitate to affirm with any certainty that the Hollywood standard of looks, female or male—the top executives did little to augment the latter—sustained a good working average.

Now, all at once, a vast throng emerged from their offices at the same moment, surging towards the commissary. It may be of interest to record that I immediately recognized which figure was Fitzgerald's. In an inexplicable way he was quite different from anyone else. Then for some minutes he was lost to sight, reemerging near our table from somewhere in the background. Elliott jumped up.

"This is Mr. Fitzgerald."

He was smallish, neat, solidly built, wearing a light grey suit and lightish tie, all his tones essentially light. Photographs—seen for the most part years later—do not do justice to him. Possibly he was a person who at once became self-conscious when before a camera. Even snapshots tend to give him an air of swagger, a kind of cockiness, he did not at all possess. On the contrary, one was immediately aware of an odd sort of unassuming dignity. There was no hint at all of the cantankerousness that undoubtedly lay beneath the surface. His air could be thought a trifle sad, but not in the least broken down, as he has sometimes been described at this period. In a railway carriage or bar, one would have wondered who this man could be.

Food and drink were ordered. Talk began to flow at once. That is certain. Scarcely a moment was required for conversation to warm up. Adjustment was all but instantaneous. Fitzgerald, who was off alcohol, drank milk, ate "cold cuts"; the rest of us had beer, and—my wife's unbigoted belief—pork chops with spaghetti. Naturally *A Yank at Oxford* cropped up almost at once. The question of dialogue. Would an undergraduate say a "shiner" for a black-eye? Could the American public be made to understand that "the Prog," and his "bullers," meant the Proctor and bowler-hatted "bulldogs," the university police?

This opened up a delicate theme, obviously a favourite with Fitzgerald, the differences between the American and British way of life. It was something about which he had speculated a lot, one felt, and loved discussing. I said—what I have so often thought—that Americans allow other Americans such small powers of comprehension. Surely, if American policemen are sometimes called "bulls," only a minimum of imagination would be required to guess the meaning of "buller" in the context. After all, the British public had been expected to essay far greater feats in mastering alien language and behaviour in days when all films were American. Fitzgerald seemed delighted to find someone with whom to argue about that sort of thing. In a moment he was well away on what Americans were like.

"At a party some time I used the term *cinquecento.* Donegall—do you know who I mean—was present. He said how unexpected to hear that word on the lips of an American."

For some reason I had the idea the party in question had been a year or two before. Perhaps it had; perhaps, on the other hand, as things turned out, it had been the previous Wednesday. The dating is not without interest. Fitzgerald explained how this assumption—that Americans would not use the word *cinquecento*—had brought him up with a start. In the past, in his grandfather's day, even in his father's, Americans had been noted for being well educated, well informed, culturally aware; possibly even too much of these things. He did not deny the imputation that had been made at the present day; at the same time it saddened him.

He took a pen from his pocket and piece of paper. On this he drew a rough map of America. Then he added three pointing arrows. The arrows showed the directions from which culture had flowed into the United States. I am ashamed to say I cannot now remember precisely which these channels were—possibly the New England seaboard; the South; up through Latin America; yet I retain some memory of an arrow lancing in from the Pacific, whence we ourselves had come. However, the point is the manner in which Fitzgerald revealed what was certainly a characteristic side of him. He loved instructing. There was a schoolmasterish streak, if at the same time an attractive one; an enthusiasm, simplicity of exposition, that might have offered a career as a teacher or university don.

77

We talked of his own books. He dismissed any idea that they would ever be read in England. It certainly seemed unlikely then—a good example of the vicissitudes of authorship—that within 10 years and a world war everything Fitzgerald had written would be in print in a London edition. He said that the American diplomat in *Tender is the Night*, wearing a nocturnal moustache bandage, was drawn from life; also that a rather rackety lady rescuing a British compatriot from arrest in Switzerland had suggested a somewhat similar incident in the novel.

This led to the subject of what Fitzgerald called "Dukes." In short, the nettle of snobbishness must be firmly grasped in the interests of our story. Fitzgerald himself was not at all averse from a little "smart" life. That is clear from his Collected Letters. He also possessed a writer's characteristic desire to categorize people. At the same time, his own experience of English life was not extensive. Consequently some of his judgments in this field were less than wholly reliable.

The particular instance was that, after praising the aristocratic picturesqueness of Napier Alington, a figure with undeniable claims to be thought aristocratically picturesque, he spoke of a lady (whose name, rightly or wrongly, had been coupled with that of a royal duke) as the wrong sort of "English aristocrat." There was some demur at this. Fitzgerald was disinclined to accept that, whatever other qualities the lady might possess, she could not, for practical purposes, be thus defined. This trivial—to some even unpalatable— matter is mentioned only on account of its repercussion.

In any case the subject was at that moment changed owing to an interruption in the shape of two film stars, Spencer Tracey and James Stewart, table-hopping round the commissary. James Stewart had come to rest not far away. Fitzgerald indicated him.

"A Princeton man, I believe."

That, at least, was to move into a more serious realm of conjecture. He went on to say that "Ernest" was in Hollywood. I was interested to know that he was on first-name terms with Hemingway, but then by no means aware of the love-hate obsession that professionally raged between the two of them. It has to be admitted that all this time Fitzgerald and I had been hogging the conversation, hardly allowing a word to my wife or Elliott Morgan. Fitzgerald must have become aware of this. In a good mannered effort to make conversation less monopolized, he brought back the subject of American and British degrees of difference. The Morgan family, as it happened, were first generation in the States. Fitzgerald posed a question:

"Now what about Elliott? British or American?"

Eliot? I made a great mental effort. At that time I had never met T. S. Eliot, was familiar with no more than the obvious poems. I had given little or no thought to the matter of nationality. Of course Eliot had been born an American, though now himself such an essential feature of the British intellectual landscape. This was certainly an occasion for a brilliant exemplification. It failed to materialize.

"You mean his poems?"

"Does Elliot write poems. I wasn't aware of that."

Fitzgerald obviously found the revelation amusing.

"*The Waste Land* and all that . . ."

There was laughter when this confusion of identities was put right. It sounded loud in the silence that had fallen on the commissary. In fact, our laughter was embarrassingly loud, a change had come about in the room. It was all but empty. Time had passed so quickly, talk been so lively, I was unaware a metamorphosis had taken place. It had, however, been noted in its various stages by my wife.

First of all the less important executives had hurried back to their desks. Then some of the writers, uncertain about renewal of contract, had made some pretence at being industrious. Executives of a superior sort had drifted away. Finally even the most undisciplined slaves of the celluloid had returned to work. In short, except for the table of Big Shots, only our own table remained occupied. Worse than that, not only was the luncheon break being grossly extended, but we were talking and laughing, as if nothing mattered less than making commercial films. A gloomy silence had fallen on the table of top executives as they smoked their cigars. Like the patrolling policemen glaring at picnickers, they gave us the same fishlike stare. They looked puzzled; not exactly angry, but hurt. Perhaps some of them had heard of Fitzgerald, even spelled out one of his early books. It was unlikely any would know him by sight, but you couldn't tell. It was certainly time to move.

When we said goodbye, I asked if I might send Fitzgerald a novel of mine called *From a View to a Death,* a copy of which I had with me. This was done. He replied a couple of days later. The reference is, of course, to those British social distinctions which had been adumbrated in the commissary.

Metro-Goldwyn-Mayer
Corporation Studios
Culver City
California
July 22, 1937
Dear Powell:

Book came. Thousand thanks. Will write when I have read it.

When I cracked wise about Dukes didn't know Mrs. Powell was a Duke. I love Dukes—Duke of Dorset, the Marquis Steyne, Freddie Bartholomew's grandfather the old Earl of Treacle.

When you come back, I will be in a position to have you made an assistant to some producer or Vice-President, which is the equivalent of a Barony.

Regards,

F. Scott Fitzgerald.

Two or three days later we drove down to Mexico for a short visit, although in the other direction, a stage on our journey home.

It is a mark of Fitzgerald's good manners, his niceness, that he had found time to acknowledge the book at all, especially in so characteristic a style. At that particular moment a lot was happening in his own life. Some of this is recorded in Sheilah Graham's autobiography *Beloved Infidel.*

On Wednesday, July 14 (the night after the Hemingway film, when we ourselves had been watching a W.P.A. performance of *Macbeth* staged by a Negro cast), a party had been given in Hollywood to celebrate the engagement of Miss Graham and Lord Donegall. There she met Fitzgerald for the first time. They had liked each other. Two or three days later, after another meeting, he asked her to dinner on Tuesday, July 20, the day of the M.G.M. lunch.

That afternoon a telegram from Fitzgerald's daughter announced her arrival in Hollywood that evening. Fitzgerald called up Miss Graham to excuse himself from keeping the date. She describes in her book how she held him to it, suggesting he should bring his daughter with him. The dinner took place. Two young men were also present. The evening, so it appears, lacked sparkle. At the end of it, Fitzgerald drove Miss Graham home. That night was the beginning of their love affair. It lasted through the years that remained to him.

Fitzgerald died on December 21 (my birthday, as it happened), 1940, at the age of 44. I did not hear about it until nearly two months later. By that time I was in the army, doing a course at Cambridge. Fitzgerald, Hollywood, writing, all seemed a long way away. Nevertheless, the luncheon at the Culver City studios remained—and remains—very clear in my mind.

Fitzgerald's Film Scripts of "Babylon Revisited" [1]

Lawrence D. Stewart

When Scott Fitzgerald came to the Pacific coast in 1937 he did not come with that sense of fulfillment which characterized earlier and more ambitious American migrations. "All gold rushes are essentially negative," he reaffirmed to Gerald Murphy near the end of his Hollywood life. Fitzgerald's third and final Hollywood sojourn is the best documented, and yet the most puzzling, phase in his career: he created the promissory brilliance of *The Last Tycoon* and the discountable cheapness of Pat Hobby. And in a final effort to keep himself going financially, he turned to "Babylon Revisited." "Cosmopolitan"—the second film script he made of it—was his last completed work. To explain what went wrong with the film scripts of "Babylon Revisited"—and I believe they did indeed go wrong—we need to re-examine the understandable, but romantic, assumption that the man who suffers and endures is also the one who will prevail; and that, if he is a writer, his last completed work must somehow be an ultimate illumination of experience.

It has long been insisted that Fitzgerald's final Hollywood trip was superficially colored with optimism. But did he really ever repudiate his attitude toward the place, an attitude expressed over a decade earlier? "If . . . [my next novel] will support me with no more intervals of trash I'll go on as a novelist. If not, I'm going to quit, come home, go to Hollywood and learn the movie business . . . there's no point in trying to be an artist if you can't do your best."[2] He dismissed film writing as the collaboration of hacks; and in the thirties he wrote some lines which must be taken into any account of the Hollywood years:

I saw that the novel, which at my maturity was the strongest and supplest medium for conveying thought and emotion from one human being to another, was becoming subordinated to a mechanical and communal art that, whether in the hands of Hollywood merchants or Russian idealists, was capable of reflecting only the tritest thought, the most obvious emotion. It was an art in which words were subordinate to images, where personality was worn down to the inevitable low gear of collaboration. As long past as 1930, I had a hunch that the talkies would make even the best selling novelist as archaic as silent pictures.[3]

So in 1937 he tried to cross over, to change his natural allegiance. And in the land which gave off dreams to the millions, the last of his own dreams gave out.

Fitzgerald's Hollywood plans had rested on no notion of converting his own stories and novels into scripts. But by the beginning of 1940, there was no alternative open—the big studios made him no offers, and only the independent producer, Lester Cowan, thought him still capable of a script. On 21 February Fitzgerald thanked Maxwell Perkins "for sending the release on 'Babylon' " and said he had sold the story to Cowan. That brought him $800—not much by Hollywood standards; but there was a chance to do the script for as much as $5,000. And what Fitzgerald did to that memorable story in that final year of his life reveals far more about what had happened to him in Hollywood than do our anecdotal records of the days and nights at the Garden of Allah, in the Horton cottage in Encino, and on Laurel Avenue around the corner from Schwab's.

Fitzgerald's 1936 prediction that his future lay along less intensely felt and creative ways was not entirely wrong. The old capacity to feel deeply and simultaneously in opposite directions—that power which so distinguished his earlier works—seemed by the late thirties to have been exhausted. His notes from the Hollywood years show indisputably he worked as intensely as ever. But, as he himself had predicted, the performance was measured by a different standard, here in the city of "the ceaseless compromise." In *The Last Tycoon* he noted, "It was everyone's secret that sustained effort was difficult here"; everyone agreed "the climate wears you down." And even when he was adapting "Babylon Revisited" and insisting "It is fun to be working on something I like," he would still grumble about the "monotonous climate and already I am tired of the flat, scentless tone of the summer." If the movie scripts of "Babylon Revisited" reveal Fitzgerald's picture world as two-dimensional black and white, rather than his once-beheld luminous universe of shimmer and the gleam, we must never forget his own explanation: "I have now at last become a writer only."

The earliest of the extant movie scripts is a carbon, titled: "HONORIA: A Screenplay by F. Scott Fitzgerald—based on his Saturday Evening Post story—'Babylon Revisited.' First draft May 29, 1940." Fitzgerald had begun work on 12 April; his letters for April and May complain of the low pay but generally express pleasure with what he was doing. Although on 4 May he groused to Zelda that he was overworking "on the goddamn movie," three days later he was writing his daughter that "My movie progresses and I think it's going to be damn good." On 11 May, in his most optimistic moment, he wrote Zelda again: "I think I've written a really brilliant continuity. It had better be for it seems to be a last life line that Hollywood has thrown me. It is a strong life line—to write as I please upon a piece of my own." And on 20 May he told Perkins he was "in the last week of an eight week movie job. . . . I just couldn't make the grade as a hack—that, like everything else, requires a certain practiced excellence."

Fitzgerald divided his 146-typed-page manuscript into five sequences; and by late July he had entered slight revisions. He also altered the title page: "BABYLON REVISITED: A Screenplay by F. Scott Fitzgerald—based on his Saturday Evening Post story of the same name. Revised, July 30th 1940." In the two months between "First draft" and "Revised," much had happened to change the intention of the script. "First draft" had begun with:

> A note on casting:
> Honoria has been drawn from the memory of a child of eight and nine years old. This age was chosen because it is a period of *complete* childhood, unmarred by adolescence. The effects have been attained by contrasting the innocence of a child's world with a series of adult situations. Casting a child over the age of ten for the part would be a fatal mistake—it would give the effect of precocity and throw every situation out of balance. A nine year old child and a twelve year old child have reactions as entirely different as a girl of sixteen and one of twenty-five.
> It is unfortunate that there is no current star of eight or nine and that there are several aged twelve or thirteen but any of these latter playing the part would strike a completely false note from the beginning. This is a Child—*not* Daddy's little helper who knows all the answers—but a living child.

By mid-June Lester Cowan decided that the picture's best chance would be with Shirley Temple. So Fitzgerald modified his "Note on casting" to state that "Honoria has been drawn from the memory of a child of eleven"—but then he canceled it all. Perhaps if Honoria were eleven, the objections to a child over ten playing the part would not be so clear. This seemingly trivial page, however, with its assured statement of immediately contradicted aesthetic principles emphasizes the compromise Fitzgerald accepted in Hollywood. Even writing alone, with no one writing behind him, and working on his own carefully constructed story he could not master circumstances. By 26 June he was eagerly agreeing with Cowan that the script could be redone for Shirley Temple. But on 12 July he wrote Zelda, "I spent a silly day yesterday with Shirley Temple and her family. They want to do the picture and they don't want to do the picture." He liked Shirley Temple herself, however: "She reminds me so much of Scottie in the last days at La Paix, just before she entered Bryn Mawr." And he told Cowan that he wanted to move her into the film exactly as she was: she wouldn't play a part but would *be* Shirley Temple. All through that fall he kept hoping the film would be produced and give him, as he wrote Zelda on 21 September, "some real status out here as a movie man and not a novelist." But one week later he was fearing that "Shirley Temple will be grown before Mrs. Temple decides to meet the producer's terms. . . . It wouldn't even be interesting if she's thirteen." To the end of his life, Fitzgerald kept hoping for positive word on the picture; but, like the dreams of his earlier heroes, that dream too eluded him forever.

"Babylon Revisited" had always been an odd choice for a film script. In 1939, probably before Lester Cowan had even suggested the cinematic possibilities of the story to him, Fitzgerald had written Kenneth Littauer that "I not only announced the birth of my young illusions in *This Side of Paradise* but pretty much the death of them in some of my last *Post* stories like 'Babylon Revisited.' " In his Hollywood years Fitzgerald culled his discarded stories for "primarily passages of sentimental romance"; these he would type into his notebooks.[4] And now he was writing a script of a story which he insisted to Cowan was to be "felt in the stomach first, felt out of great conviction about the tragedy of father and child—and *not* felt in the throat." So, working at cross purposes with his past—even with the immediate re-creation of it—Fitzgerald produced a movie script that has little in common with its excellent source. Only the character of Charlie Wales has come from the story, and his journey has worn him down.

The movie was to open with a long shot of Paris in November 1929 and pull down to a view of the Petrie home (the Lincoln Peterses have become a French family) where Richard and his cousin, Honoria, both eleven, are getting ready for school. Soon we see

Honoria breaking her piggy bank and stuffing her belongings into her school sack; she is preparing to run away. Eventually she arrives at Altgelt, Switzerland. As she approaches the cold and deserted Chalet Gilmont, she suddenly calls "Daddy, Daddy!"

> A man, whom we will later know as Charles Wales, is standing in front of the open door of the chalet, apparently alone. We see his eyes straining down toward the sleigh which is perhaps one hundred feet below. An expression of absolute horror comes into his eyes. He raises his hands and makes the motion "Get away!" Then he puts his hands to his mouth. . . . "Get away! Go back! Turn around, I tell you! Obey me!" . . . Honoria [is] still standing up. Her face changes from joy to amazement, then to bewilderment. . . . "But Daddy-"

And the scene dissolves slowly with the end of Sequence A.

From this enigmatic beginning we flash back; and:

> there is a short but definite pause on the sound tract. Then we hear Honoria's voice speaking, not in the startled tone which has just said "But Daddy," but calmly and quietly. We don't know who she is talking to nor do we ever know, any more than we ever knew who Joan Fontaine in "Rebecca" was telling her story to. We assume that Honoria is telling the story to someone several months after the events shown in our picture.

The scene is New York, late June 1929; Honoria and Charles Wales, who had just retired from the stock market, were meeting Helen on board ship. Charlie, "a vital, confident, immediately likeable man of thirty-five," is being plied by his chauffeur for stock market tips, while Charlie hurries aboard ship with his daughter to reenact the introduction scene from the short story: "I'm Charles T. Wales, 16½ Wall Street." "I'm Honoria Wales. 193 Park Avenue."

To the ship to see them off comes Wales' partner, Lloyd Garside:

> an old college friend of Wales. He has a certain talent as a customers' man in the bull market but is actually the type of reckless spender. In spite of his large earnings, he's probably always a little in debt; keeps a small yacht he can't afford and possibly has a couple of mistresses hidden away somewhere. He wouldn't tell all this to Wales because Wales is essentially a serious character and though they have been drifting apart for some years, they've managed to get along amicably. during this long prosperous time.

Garside is annoyed at Charlie's retirement and failure to fulfill his "duty to his partners"—"the moral side," as Garside phrases it. But Charlie is adamant, and his "gift of the—divine guess" will no longer be available, for his sick wife attributes all of her afflictions to Charlie's business. She hears "the ticker in her sleep all night" and sees the tape issuing from Charlie's mouth.

During the voyage, Charlie takes Honoria to the broker's office on board ship; he is explaining the notations when suddenly he discovers a possibility in the market. Almost unconsciously he has acquired a stock boy and a page. Twenty-four hours pass, while his wife tries to get him to come to her; but he delays, preoccupied with his trading. Several shifted scenes disclose Charlie triumphing in the broker's office, and Honoria playing or wandering aimlessly about the ship. Soon everyone is searching for Helen; and while "the ship's dance orchestra is playing tunes of 1929 in a nervous rhythm," Charlie keeps hearing voices: "Not here, Mr. Wales," "Not there, Mr. Wales," "Not in her room," "Not in the bar, Mr. Wales," "Not in there, Mr. Wales." The sequence closes with a shot of a dark sky filled with sea gulls:

> The sudden sound of a wild shriek, which breaks down after a moment, into the cry of the gulls as they swoop in a great flock down toward the water. Through their shriek we hear the ship's bell signalling for the engines to stop.
> Ship receding from the Camera as the awful sounds gradually die out.

Sequence C opens with a long shot of Le Havre on 4 July 1929. There wait Helen Wales' sister and brother-in-law, Marion and Pierre Petrie. Lawrence Peters, the short story's bank executive, has been reduced to:

> a Frenchman with a family tradition of past nobility which makes him very pompous and ceremonious in his personality. However, nature has equipped him only to be a minor clerk. His wife, Marion (Helen Wales' sister), is an American woman of thirty-four who must have hoped for a better match.
> Marion is in a state of desperate grief. Though she controls it outwardly, she is agitated almost to the breaking point by the news of her sister's suicide which reached her last night in Paris.
> Petrie's grief is mingled with awe. There has always been something so magnificent about his brother-in-law, Charles Wales, so that even Helen Wales' suicide seems on a great magnificent scale.

When Charlie sees Marion, his "immediate instinct is to share his grief with hers." But Marion is having none of it. "She is the impersonation of outrage and hatred, which she hides under a thin insincere mantle of pity and of accepting something inevitable which she had always foreseen." Charlie immediately senses her attitude but asks the Petries to take Honoria for awhile.

A montage of newspapers covers over two weeks. 20 July in the Petrie home finds Honoria asking her aunt if Charlie is better. Marion is annoyed. "She is a decent woman and not yet prepared to admit that she would like to separate father and daughter, but that's exactly what she would like." Pierre returns with the news that Charlie's partner, Garside, has just arrived from the States and is coming to see Honoria. When Garside enters, he comes:

> in a different mood from when we last met him on the dock in New York. Then he was furious at Charles Wales' desertion. Now there is almost a sparkle in his eye. In the bull market stocks have continued to rise and money has been easy to make even without Wales' help. Moreover, he has been to see Wales at the Ritz and, though we only gradually disclose to the audience what he is thinking, it is apparent from his manner that he is full of some purpose deeper than his actual words.

Garside speaks of his visit to Charlie and describes him as a drunkard who never had known trouble before and therefore cannot face it now. Garside quickly perceives that "Marion is the more intelligent of the two and, also, that Marion hates Charles Wales with deadly hatred." She wants Charlie committed to a sanitarium, but Garside has other plans: he replaces Charlie's doctor and nurse with an unscrupulous physician who will prolong Charlie's convalescence.

Garside and Honoria visit Charlie's hotel suite; there they meet Mary Waldron, the new nurse. Having been suspended from the Registry of the American Hospital in Paris because she had been caught sneaking in by a fire escape, she has been without work for some time; Dr. Franciscus, the new doctor, has hired her because he feels she will do exactly what she is told.

> Mary Waldron is about 24. She is not dressed expensively but very attractively. It is not a beautiful face but distinctly a pretty one. . . . (NOTE: It is important that the audience doesn't say at this point "Here comes the love interest." Therefore, this girl's prettiness should not be the first thing that we notice about her, and this must be remembered in the casting.
>
> At present, she is *just a nurse,* perhaps cast by some such actress whom one no longer visualizes in a straight romantic role. Kay Francis at this writing, 1940, is the type of casting I mean, though I don't believe Miss Francis is at all suitable to this part. She must not awaken a romantic pull in the audience, but rather she will justify or damn herself by her actions.)

Honoria's presence upsets Charlie who insists she not be brought back. The doctor tries to calm his patient: "We're going to get your mind off yourself and your immediate family. What are your hobbies, Mr. Wales, besides business, I mean? What interests you?" Char-

lie waits a moment and then answers, "Well—since you ask—death."
Honoria comes back into the room to say goodbye: "Daddy! I just
want to tell you I'll do everything you said. Everything you had time
to tell me on the boat. Everything, I'll do, Daddy. Don't ever
worry." The camera shifts to Mary Waldron's face: "She is terribly
moved and disturbed by what the child has said." The next day in
Charlie's Ritz bedroom a lawyer reads a deed by which Charlie relin-
quishes the guardianship of Honoria to Pierre and Marion until the
child reaches her majority; at the same time he establishes a trust
fund for her and places it in their control. The Petries, Garside,
Dr. Franciscus, and Mary surround the heavily drugged Charlie as he
signs. In that silence only the nurse tries to warn him.

A second time-montage spans the months from 21 June to
24 October 1929. Then we cut to Pierre, Richard, and Honoria out
for a walk in Paris. As they pass an American-French Brokerage
House, Pierre idly tells the children "This is where they make their
millions, those Americans." Immediately the three pool their money
for a try at the market. A brief interior shot reveals the frenzy from
the falling stocks; and the three leave, their money gone. They meet
Marion at the Moto-France Travel Agency where Pierre is an assistant
manager. After Marion and Richard have left, Pierre prepares to take
Honoria on a visit to Charlie; but suddenly Garside appears. He has
"only just heard about the crash. His face is serious, frightened. He is
on business long planned, but now it must be done immediately."
Garside spreads some papers before Pierre. "You merely authorize
our investment trust to re-invest the child's money as the market
changes. Everything happens so fast that it's our duty to the child to
increase her profits. Sign here." Pierre is reluctant and says that the
market had just fallen. Garside pretends that what was only a temporary flurry has since quieted. But Pierre holds out, so Garside
invites him and Honoria to have an ice-cream soda next door. "As
the three start out, we notice that Honoria is unimpressed by the
offer of the soda."

Pierre finally signs, but only after Garside has loaned him a hundred francs to cover his own impetuous entry into the market. Garside explains that he himself prefers to tell Charlie about their trans-
action. The scene shifts to the Ritz where Charlie prepares for
Honoria's arrival. Honoria spends the afternoon with her father who,
now recovered, dismisses the doctor and then takes her to a toy shop
and then to Rumplemayer's Tea Shop where they replay substan-
tially the restaurant conversation of the short story. No Duncan or

Lorraine appear, but the scene concludes with the realization reached in the short story: Charlie wants Honoria as much as she wants him. They then return to the Petrie apartment where, much condensed, the short story scene between Marion and Charlie is restaged. When the question of regaining control of Honoria arises, Marion says her duty is to her sister and she's presently too upset to consider the matter. Charlie leaves, and Honoria discovers that her aunt doesn't want her to see her father ever at all.

On Tuesday, five days later, Honoria goes unannounced to her father's Ritz suite and finds him deep in the market again. A private phone is being connected; there is also a hotel trunk line to New York set aside for him. Meanwhile, messengers bring and carry away a series of cables. Honoria sits knitting as she visits with her father. Suddenly Garside bursts in. Terribly upset, his clothes in disarray, he vividly describes the loss of fortunes and the universal panic. But "It cannot be too much emphasized that Wales is as calm as a store-keeper measuring out a pound of sugar." Anticipating the bear market, he had sold out the previous May and put his money in conservative investments! But now Garside reveals that Charlie's money—or, rather, Honoria's—was in the market too. Charlie immediately assumes that Garside and *Marion* had changed the investments. Garside complains, "Well, you asked for it. You quit us. You left me alone there. . . . You've always been so smart about the market,—solve this one. Try and get it back."

Despite the news being "a terrific blow," Charlie has within seconds "put the past behind him and turned to the question of what is to be done." Selling by phone, he saves some money for Honoria. Meanwhile Garside lies on the couch, trying to devise a plan to save himself. Dinner arrives for Honoria and Charlie; when Charlie takes a pill with his drink, he collapses half asleep. Garside then brings Marion and Pierre to the room where the debris from the day's transactions makes them believe that Charlie is in a drunken stupor. Marion indignantly takes Honoria home, leaving Pierre and Garside to argue over the responsibility for the lost trust fund. Garside threatens Pierre with ten years at Devil's Island; at the same time he emphasizes that if Pierre will do one trivial—but unspecified—favor for him, the money can be recovered. Pierre agrees reluctantly. Sequence D ends with Garside watching the sleeping Charlie who says out of a dream, "I'm going to get my daughter."

The E—and final—Sequence begins in the cabin of a Swiss bound plane; in it a seated Charlie is speaking to his fellow passenger.

89

Wales, in ordinary clothes, seems tired but not in bad condition. His manner is serious without being either somber or anxious. At the moment we have, of course, *no indication as to how much time has passed* since we last saw him asleep at the Ritz. Also we don't know *any of the reasons for this* journey.

They land at Lausanne, and Charlie and his plane companion share a taxi to Montreux. We soon learn that this is the day following Charlie's stock market transactions. He has come to Switzerland, believing himself to be in pursuit of Honoria. (He had "forced" Garside to admit where she was being kept.) When the two men arrive at the hotel, they find it boarded up; and when they enter, Charlie recognizes a trap. His companion—now revealed as Henri Le Basquette, champion de boxe of Western Europe—holds a gun on the puzzled financier. Had not Pierre phoned that Marion was taking Honoria to this hotel? But suddenly Charlie understands Garside's plan: Charlie is to have an "accident," mountain climbing. Since he has no will, his money will revert to Honoria. But with the signed paper Garside has from Pierre, Garside himself can get the estate.

At seven o'clock that evening, Le Basquette prepares to take Charlie on their fatal expedition. Charlie steps to the door. It is at this moment we see almost an exact replay of the scene which closed Sequence A: Charlie warning the approaching Honoria to leave. Honoria senses danger, but Le Basquette presents himself only as Charlie's trainer. With Honoria's arrival the two men decide to postpone their ascent until the following morning before Honoria awakens. But she is the first one up, and she looks at the mountain through the hotel telescope.

The two men have started their climb when, suddenly, Charlie leaps down a slope, rolling against trees and shrubs. Le Basquette follows, rolling, sliding, and firing—and so they descend for a quarter of a mile. On an open snow-covered meadow, Charlie is close to death when, unexpectedly, a sleigh approaches and a voice calls out. It is Mary Waldron who, having received a note from Honoria that she was going to her father, has followed her. Mary realizes instantly that Le Basquette is not Charlie's trainer; her coachman also senses that Le Basquette is lying. Le Basquette aims his pistol at Mary, but now the coachman's rifle is pointed at Le Basquette himself. Charlie "turns suddenly and with his last strength smashes him [Le Basquette] in the face. Basquette staggers back. Wales himself, completely used up by the blow, sits down on the side of the sleigh."

The film's final scene reunites Mary, Charlie and Honoria in the lodge which Honoria has cleaned. Soon there is a fire "with three or four logs burning jovially." They set the table for dinner, comparing their "groaning board" with the scant table usually provided by Marion. Then the camera

TRUCKS in front of Honoria, as she walks away and over to a window where the blind is not drawn. She looks out and up. Then she speaks aloud to herself—her words are not quite audible to the others.

HONORIA

Star light,
Star bright,
First star I've seen tonight.
I wish—
WALES' VOICE (off scene)
What did you say, dear?
HONORIA
(Turning and smiling to herself)
You'd be the last two people I'd tell.

FADE OUT

II

To the end, Fitzgerald still occasionally had notions of turning the technique of screenwriting into an art; and on 14 September 1940 he was to write excitedly to Zelda that writers might soon be directing their own scripts. "If I had that chance, I would attain my real goal in coming here in the first place." But this melodramatic scenario gives little assurance of a new artistic perceptiveness or unsuspected talent. Frances and Albert Hackett, who were seated at the MGM writers' table that first time that Fitzgerald walked into the commissary, remember a man with a haunted look, a man with a briefcase clasped tightly to his chest. He was suffering from that disease which had killed off most of his created beings: alienation from a chosen environment. But whereas the earlier Fitzgerald had striven desperately to make his environment accord with his own desires in order to bring about a necessary unity, the man who came to Hollywood tried harder than ever before to adjust to the environment that existed. As late as 21 September 1940 he would write Zelda that "the Shirley Temple script is looking up again and is my great hope for attaining some real status out here as a movie man and not a novelist." Perhaps the greatest psychological damage done to him in Hollywood came from his nagging fear that he could succeed again only if his natural métier were repudiated.

Fitzgerald's awareness of the cheapness implicit in Hollywood did not blind him to the potentialities of the movies. His last novel reveals his excitement over the process of inspired movie-making, and his scripts to "Babylon Revisited" have long been unexamined legends of a superior talent at scenario writing.[5] But the scripts re-emphasize that the qualities which distinguished his novels failed to make the transition to the screen. A notebook entry concerned

> Six original stories written for the Screen. They will not be offered to magazines. This is not because, in any sense, they are inferior products but because the magazines expect from this author descriptive and "mental" values rather than dramatic values. Also the lengths.

Despite Fitzgerald's assertion that he could write in one form as well as the other, most would agree that his strength lay not in dramatic speech but in his imagery—those perceptive descriptions which endow his dialogue with a richness of implication. His extensive stage directions in this movie script suggest his yearning to give his conversations their customary ambiance. His characters often speak in that authentic tone which ever testifies to Fitzgerald's acute ear. But if it is true that remarks are not literature, so is it also true that these are not the reverberations from persons who are both complex and yet comprehensible in their complexity.

Dialogue weakness need not imply weakness of plot, but who can deny the tiresome conventionality of this whodunit where again bows smiling before us that capitalist hero, the wise man who sold out in 1929 *before* the crash? If Fitzgerald's attempt to conceal the film's outcome comes out well, it is despite the planning of tricks that are embarrassing melodramatic cliches: the unscrupulous doctor planted by the unscrupulous partner, an insufferably noble Charlie-as-hero who stoically receives the news that his trusted partner is a thief. When Fitzgerald disguised Mary as the "love interest," he was only trying to suspend temporarily the Hollywood-conditioned response—we all know that the pretty-nurse-as-victim-of-circumstances must end in the widower's arms.

A problem greater than the script's stereotypes, however, was its divided intention. In the beginning, Fitzgerald concerned himself only with Honoria: she is the central character, and the camera focuses on her and chops off the heads of the adults. This point-of-view gradually changed; and it is Charlie who is the central figure—Honoria is only a means of revealing her father's character and value.

Fitzgerald, as his own most perceptive reader, instantly saw these defects. He began to write a critique of the work: eighteen pages of typed notes which analyze the faults, outline the desired effects, and suggest possible remedies. The briefest of these cryptic self-conversations indicates the intensive and sceptical reading he gave his own script:

> New character of Garside. Must introduce him so that audience absolutely believes in him, not one line or hint otherwise but rather confirmation that he is a good man, even stronger confirmation than I had previously intended. If the audience senses anything wrong with him Wales trust will both give away the plot and make Wales out a fool. They are like brothers. Can't shake off mob. Million dollar insurance. . . .
>
> General note: Did he cause his wife's death. Lester [Cowan, the producer] feels it must be answered directly. . . .
>
> Marion rewritten as if to be played by Mary Astor.

Besides these random comments, these pages detailed discussions of scenes and continuity; each emphasizes how carefully Fitzgerald blocked out an action before he executed it with dialogue and condensed stage directions. There was also a five-page outline of a new conclusion for the movie; then followed a one page "Re-Examination," in which all the contemplated changes were reviewed. Fitzgerald also recast his characters:

> Lloyd Garside
> —is a combination of Richard Whitney and the sanctimonious Dartmouth football captain. Eliminate all the "moustached-and-horse-whip characteristics." Begin with him as being one to be approved if not liked and continue him as a person above reproach or even suspicion until the guardianship scene when a sharp dislike should be established. From then on break him down rapidly and sanctimoniously a la tartuffe.

One of the revisions was to have Garside (now called "Schuyler") see off his thug-and/or-gunman on the same train which carries Honoria to Switzerland. Fitzgerald said about his hoodlum:

> Think of something here along the line of Mr. Jones [of Conrad's *Victory*?] or my character in A SHORT TRIP HOME. Perhaps type him as the character in A SHORT TRIP HOME. If possible, there might be a hint here as to where Schuyler found him or how he happened to do this for Schuyler. . . . The figure of Schuyler is perhaps the last thing in our sight as the train pulls out. As he is about to turn we cut to train. He must have no identifying mark—perhaps it would be better to have some stand-in for Schuyler play the shot so that no especially keen member of the audience will spot who it is later.

Fitzgerald's second attempt to make a movie of "Babylon Revisited" was titled: " 'Cosmopolitan' A Screenplay by F. Scott Fitzgerald—based on his Saturday Evening Post story 'Babylon Revisited' 2nd Draft Revised August 12, 1940." The Princeton copy of this script consists of the carbons of 130 typed pages, plus the title page. That faded blue-green folder is labeled merely "A Screenplay by F. Scott Fitzgerald—based on his story 'Babylon Revisited.' " The title, "Cosmopolitan," was probably an afterthought: it appears on no page in the script and, when added to the folder, came as an original title page, rather than as a carbon. Princeton also owns a grey bound mimeograph of this typescript, dated 13 August 1940 and entitled *Cosmopolitan.*" The only appreciable change in it from the typescript is the young girl's name: Honoria has become "Victoria," presumably in honor of Budd Schulberg's new daughter. (Earlier that spring Fitzgerald had written Gerald and Sara Murphy that in adapting the story for the screen he was keeping the name, Honoria, which had been a tribute to the Murphys' daughter).

The first fifteen pages of the typescript carbon are a clean copy of Sequence A. Beginning with page sixteen, Fitzgerald made penciled corrections, and these continued to the manuscript's end. In accordance with the revisions on the "Characters" page of the original version, Garside's name has been changed to Dwight Schuyler. But Mary Waldron, who was to have become Julia Bell, has now been rechristened Julia Burns. Henri Le Basquette has disappeared, but there is a new character: Mr. Van Greff, who had first emerged only as an anonymous observer of the action in one scene of the original.

As in the first script, Honoria runs away, encountering the same adventures up to the moment she boards the train. Looking out the window she suddenly "starts, dismayed by what she sees, and shrinks back against the seat." The exterior scene, added to this version, shows two men talking:

> The one who is *facing* the train and whom Honoria recognizes, we cannot see—but we see the face of the one whose back is toward the train. He is a youth of nineteen, blond, weak and cruel. He wears a CLOSE-FITTING TOP-COAT.

These are, of course, Garside (Schuyler) and his henchman—the scene Fitzgerald introduced to prefigure the sinister events to follow. Honoria converses with those in her car, and then another shot reveals the youth in the close-fitting top-coat boarding the car behind Honoria's. He strolls down the aisle, looks in Honoria's compartment with "no sparkle of interest in his white, dull eyes." The sequence ends much earlier than formerly, stopping with Honoria's soliloquy on the train. The scene where Charlie Wales warned away his daughter, and gave a false impression of not wanting her, is removed. The same ominous overtones are retained, but no longer is the spectator quite so deliberately misled.

With Sequence B and the departure from New York, the new Dwight Schuyler (Garside) enters.

> *He is a respectable Wall Street banker, a pillar of the financial establishment. One of his contributions to the speculative firm of Charles T. Wales is his impeccable reputation. Wales served in the same artillery regiment with Schuyler in France and went into Wall Street in 1920. Contrastingly,* Schuyler's father and grandfather were in Wall Street before him. He is smooth-shaven, steady-going, firm of countenance and of excellent habits as is shown by his fine physical trim. He is impeccably dressed—dark suit and tie and derby, with a white carnation as the only spot of color. He carries a silver-headed cane. [I have italicized the portion that Fitzgerald deleted in his script].

The discussion between Charlie and Schuyler reveals that Charlie had decided to leave the market even before Helen developed nervousness; her condition merely reinforced that decision. "If Helen was in the pink I'd still be getting out, Dwight. I want a new job, exploring the poles, climbing mountains." This change in Charlie's motivation makes it clear that his act of entering the ship's brokerage office is not responsible for Helen's suicide.

Where Schuyler formerly had said to Charlie, "It's your talents we'll miss, old man. That gift of the—divine guess," the revision carefully inserted: "That's why we insured your life for a cool million." The new script introduces two significant, though minor, characters at this moment: Bill Bonniman, a small town banker and old friend of Charlie's who has come to see him off, and old Mr. Van Greff, "reputed one of the richest men in the world." Later, when Charlie and Honoria are feeding the gulls, Van Greff greets Charlie warmly and reminds him there is always a position for Charlie with the financier. But Charlie merely smiles and asks Van Greff about his health:

VAN GREFF

Well, every year I go to Switzerland—to die. And it never happens. It's very monotonous.

(he starts to hobble into the dining room, then turns)

It's up on a mountain, convenient for the angels.

Maitre d'Hotel and valet follow him. When Van Greff is out of hearing Honoria whispers to her father.

HONORIA

Supposing he had to go down.

(she points down)

WALES

(smiling)

Oh, that's a cinch.

This new scene prepares for that moment when Charlie does turn logically to Van Greff for aid; the conversation about death also is counterpoint for Helen's imminent suicide. In this version when Charlie looks at the ship's stock ticker he sees that Radio and Bill Bonniman are getting a pounding. His plunge back into the market comes, therefore, only from an altruistic desire to help an old friend.

While the Le Havre dock scene is unchanged, the background and psychology of Pierre and Marion are modified:

> Pierre and Marion Petrie waiting in the crowd. He is a Frenchman with a military tradition which makes him pompous and ceremonious in his personality—but when he had taken off his uniform back in 1919, it was apparent that nature had equipped him to be only a minor clerk.
>
> His wife, Marion (Helen Wales' sister), is an extremely pretty American woman of thirty-two who must have hoped for a better match. She is now in a state of great emotion—barely controlled. She is agitated almost to the breaking point by the news of her sister's suicide—which reached her last night in Paris. Always before this she has felt a certain secret jealousy of her sister who has had great wealth and luxury. Now suddenly, this has changed into a wild hatred of Charles Wales, whom she makes the scapegoat of the catastrophe. In a few hours she has fully convinced herself that her sister was the dearest thing in life to her.
>
> Petrie's grief is mingled with awe. There has always been something so magnificent about his brother-in-law, Charles Wales, that even Helen Wales' suicide seems on a magnificent scale.

Fitzgerald determined to minimize Charlie's responsibility for the disaster; when Charlie disembarks and speaks of his wife's death he no longer says "Yes, I could have stopped it" but "Yes, I *might* have stopped it." (The italics are Fitzgerald's.)

Sequence C bridges the days to 20 July 1929 with a montage. Then comes the arrival of Schuyler and the three-sided discussion with Marion and Pierre. Fitzgerald now inserted Schuyler's suggestion that a guardianship for Honoria could be arranged. Marion, for whom "the legal word means little," says, "Helen would have wanted me to bring up Honoria—I know that." The action continues as first outlined: Honoria accompanies Schuyler to the hospital, and Dr. Franciscus and Julia Burns, the new nurse, come on the case. The conversation between doctor and nurse—now more enigmatic than earlier—still emphasizes that Franciscus intends making money from Charlie by prolonging his convalescence. Schuyler, in his talk with the doctor, introduces the subject of Honoria's guardianship— preparation for the final scene in the sequence. Fitzgerald's stage directions, which had emphasized the sinister quality in Schuyler's act, disappear; but suspicion lingers in the reader's mind.

Another montage begins Sequence D—this time "showing the passage of Honoria's summer in a seaside town." Once again, Pierre and the children enter the stock market and lose. In the meeting of the Petries at the Moto-France Travel Agency, however, Marion's initial distrust of Charlie is magnified. In the first script she had said of Honoria's planned visit with her father:

> Of course I don't like this at all, but I don't suppose he'll do her any harm—or try to kidnap her. . . . (in a voice of protest) Why couldn't we have just gone on—like the last three months? Honoria's been perfectly happy—she hardly mentions her father at all. (she frowns) If things are not—quite—as they should be, don't leave her. And, in any case, you must bring her home by seven.

In revision, she announces:

> I have just talked to—to Miss *Burns* on the telephone. I told her the child is not to be left alone in the room with her father. (in a voice of protest) Why couldn't we have just gone on—like the last three months? Honoria's been happy—she hardly mentions her father to me. (almost angrily) I don't trust that nurse! If Charles is ranting and raving don't stay one minute!

The sequence continues until after the cafe scene where there is inserted a shot of Schuyler phoning Dr. Franciscus and saying deliberately that he "was surprised to learn that Mr. Wales is well enough to see his daughter." Franciscus—also surprised by the news—joins Honoria and Pierre; all see Charlie, who is attended by Julia. Franciscus, resentful of Julia's betrayal, now thinks only of getting his money, since he presumes the market crash has ruined his patient. This version de-emphasizes the quackery of Franciscus and Charlie's realization that his illness has been "prolonged"; it also underscores the friendship between Honoria and Julia: all the time the child was not seeing her father she had been writing the nurse.

Charlie and Honoria leave the hotel and have their famous conversation in the restaurant. When they return to the Petrie home, Marion's reaction to Charlie and his recovery now reveals itself as "indignant surprise." The new Charlie is more determined than the old; whereas he had once said to Marion "(with stubbornness coming into his voice) I understand how you feel, Marion, but of course I don't want to lose Honoria's childhood—you can understand that," he now insists "(stubbornly) I'm not going to lose Honoria's childhood, Marion—you can understand that."

The original script blanketed the period from Thursday evening to Tuesday afternoon with a time dissolve. The revision shows Charlie returning to the hotel and entering the men's bar where he bumps into some old friends who tell him they are there to meet Schuyler. Surprised that Schuyler is in Paris, Charlie instantly senses that the firm has been ruined. Schuyler starts to enter the bar when, catching sight of Charlie and still being unnoticed himself, he leaves quickly. In the background a voice sings, "Last night was the end of the wor—l—l—ld!" The scene closes as "CAMERA PANS OFF TO SINGER, a fair haired man of thirty with tears flowing down his cheeks."

Charlie returns to his room, attempts to locate Schuyler, and begins opening cables. He also arranges for a radio phone to New York. Honoria appears and the New York call goes through; Charlie orders the short sale of shares, using as capital $350,000 which he had entrusted to Schuyler. But then Schuyler himself enters and admits that both Honoria's trust fund and Charlie's money have been lost. Pierre phones for Honoria, but Charlie—speaking firmly to his brother-in-law—insists that she stay with him for dinner. The two partners then have their recrimination scene, Schuyler defending himself simply:

> "I rode with the times, Charles. You weren't there to help and you were all we had. That's why we insured your life for a million dollars—your brain! And then you quit." (he is breathing hard) "There's nothing I can do. There isn't any million dollar policy on my life."

Charlie replies contemptuously, "Don't worry, I'll jump out the window in a minute. I wouldn't want to have you not get your million, Dwight." Schuyler leaves the room unharmed—but not before Charlie "breaks his cane dispassionately over his knee and hands the fragments to Schuyler: 'Your sword, Monsieur.' " Shortly afterwards we pull into the Ritz bar at 4:30 that afternoon. Schuyler sits alone;

nearby is Dorini, a New York bootleg chief, with three friends. Paul at the bar complains that Dorini's gang are killers, and Schuyler suddenly takes interest.

Later in the hotel room, Julia, Charlie and Honoria are finishing dinner and Charlie's birthday cake when Marion enters with the French lawyer who drew up the guardianship papers. "Do you realize that bringing Honoria here is kidnapping under French law?" she demands. Marion exclaims, "her voice low and full of hatred,"

> "You've got to understand that this is the end. You've spoiled one life and you can't spoil another. I don't care about your dirty gambling, whether you make money or lose it. I don't want it for the child. Stick to your women who will have you." (her eyes flicker momentarily toward Julia, then to the bottle on the table)—"And your drink and your luxury."

Despite Charlie's deliberate "Oh, bananas!" he knows that only an expensive court battle can restore Honoria to him. His remark to Julia that he can't abandon Honoria—"they'd take her like they're taking my good name"—forces a new decision: he will fly that night to Switzerland to see Van Greff "who believes in me."

At the Grand Hotel in Hautemont, Van Greff's secretary asks Charlie to dine with the financier that evening; Charlie sits on the hotel terrace, watching the view of the funicular. The camera shifts to Honoria, rising to the hotel; in the rear seat is the Youth in the Close-Fitting Top-Coat. At the hotel the youth overhears Honoria ask for her father, and he follows her to the porch where she surprises Charlie. Honoria tells Charlie about her pursuer, but when she turns to point him out he is gone.

That evening Charlie goes to his dinner appointment while Honoria sits at another table, eating alone and pantomiming to Charlie across the room as he waits for Van Greff. Suddenly the secretary appears with the news that the financier has just died. Charlie then crosses the room to eat with Honoria, determined to conceal their new bad fortune. But he sends a note with some money to the orchestra to play Honoria's favorite song, "I'm Dancing with Tears in My Eyes." As they are about to dance together, two old tight acquaintances come up (the Duncan and Lorraine of the story, transformed here into Cornelia and Tom), but Charlie breaks away and dances off with his daughter. Honoria asks who the couple were, and Charlie replies, "Parasites." He explains they are found everywhere and always want something you yourself have—sometimes, even your happiness. When Honoria asks how they got that way, Charlie answers, "Oh, they begin by not doing their lessons."

(with a sigh)

I knew there'd be a moral in it. (pause) I wish there was some person who could talk to you without always ending up with a moral.

Charlie promises, "word of honor, that'll be me." The scene fades with Honoria's hope that the parasites have found someone to annoy so they can be as happy as she: "the happiest that you can ever get."

Back in their room, Honoria tells her father that Schuyler is her parasite; she describes the day he got Pierre to sign the trust fund paper. Charlie immediately realizes the conspiracy, and he starts to phone Paris, overjoyed that Schuyler and Marion (through Pierre) are now in his control: it means he can regain Honoria. But hidden in the hotel room is the youth who confronts Wales with a gun and forces him to an open window. Charlie is about to be pushed out when the telephone rings. The distraction gives Wales his chance, and he knocks out the boy. The voice on the wire, we gather, is Julia's. Honoria has fallen asleep nearby, and the movie ends with Charlie's *sotto voce* "Ah, there's a lot to live for."

Twenty-nine of this revised script's mimeographed pages were redone by 17 August 1940 and—marked "CHANGES"—were inserted in this second version. There was also appended a page of commentary which defined Fitzgerald's intention, as he conceived of having it after he thought it fulfilled:

AUTHOR'S NOTE:

This is an attempt to tell a story from a child's point of view *without* sentimentality. Any attempt to heighten the sentiment of the early scenes by putting mawkish speeches into the mouths of characters—in short by doing what is locally known as "milking it," will damage the *force* of the piece. Had the present author intended, he could have broken down the sentimental section of the audience at many points, but the price would have been *the release of the audience too quickly from tension*—and one would wonder at the end where the idea had vanished—or indeed what idea had been purchased. So whoever deals with this script is implored to remember that it is *a dramatic piece*—not a homey family story. Above all things, Victoria is a *child*—not Daddy's little helper who knows all the answers.

Another point: in the ordinary sense, this picture has no more moral than "Rebecca" or "The Shop around the Corner"—though one can draw from it any moral one wishes about the life of the Wall Street rich of a decade ago. It had better follow the example of "Hamlet," which has had a hundred morals read into it, all of them different—let it stand on its own bottom.

Finally—the author wishes to acknowledge the valuable help of Lester Cowan in keeping the line straight and giving many valuable suggestions.

Fitzgerald's insistence that he knew precisely what he was doing and that he had fulfilled his intentions is understandable. But do these synopses suggest that the film script of "Babylon Revisited" is a literary achievement? Or that it could make an effective film? All Fitzgerald had succeeded in doing was drawing stock characters into the standard situation of the Class B mystery. And there is no mystery why the script has never been filmed.[6]

When Fitzgerald warned that his script had no—or innumerable—morals, he was arguing against any interpretation which would reduce the film to a homily. Where morals are principles of action, however, the story has many. And on a fundamental one does the story—and do the scripts themselves—turn. A considerable portion of the dramatic interest in "Babylon Revisited" derives from conflicts more significant, and less apparent, than those between Charlie and Marion. There are conflicts, in the story itself, between the Charlie of the pre-crash (that ineluctable ghost which haunts his descendent in every Parisian shadow) and the successful businessman from Prague. There are also contrasts between the Charlie who returns to Paris and the man who leaves it a few days later. The new Charlie has overcome obvious faults: most notably, he is no longer a drunk. But Charlie is unaware that a portion of his tragedy may be attributed to imperfect notions about responsibility; and these shortcomings have not been corrected in his penitential exile.

The more basic fault in Charlie is his belief that money is omnipotent: having it, one can afford the greatest of luxuries—irresponsibility. The villains of *The Great Gatsby* have become the hero of the short story, for here even the new Charlie keeps trying to buy his way into and out of emotional involvements. He repeatedly tries to buy an Honoria he already owns; and when he encounters a prostitute at night, he gives her money "to elude her encouraging stare." The knowledge that money is only money—a knowledge that Tom and Daisy never received—comes to Charlie only at the conclusion of the story. He never had it before. In the perception of this truth he becomes tragically admirable. The weakness of the film scripts is their failure to work with the number of parallel balances which enrich the story where the conflict between having money and having Honoria is a consistent theme.

The change of the film's title to "Cosmopolitan" was perhaps necessary; the Babylon of the scripts seems not to have been revisited. The original title held a wealth of connotation, however, which the revision lost; and Fitzgerald himself appears ever to have thought of his script as "Babylon Revisited." There was reason to do so: for though Charlie does not come from and return to Babylon, are not we—the audience—making the return across so many years when we see this experience at the end of an era? The detached point of view came only with time for the rest of us. It was Fitzgerald's good fortune that in the years before his crack-up he had so much of it simultaneously with the initial experience. Yet even then, it was only through his assiduity that he was able to crystalize it and make it impervious to the unimaginable touch of time.

Admirers of Fitzgerald, especially those who regard the Pat Hobby stories and *The Last Tycoon* as aesthetic accomplishments, reject the suggestion that the post-crack-up author failed to equal the achievement of the earlier writer. The theory of rehabilitation has won over so many that few remember that restoration brings one to, at best, a functioning adequacy. Fitzgerald himself, however, recognized that the cracked plate which he had become, however so well mended, could never be trusted with anything more valuable than left-overs. His self-analytical essays are the mature, honest, and reasoned expression of a man who knew that through the fissure in his emotions had drained away that distinctive talent he once had possessed.

After his deterioration, he never could see simultaneously both sides of an issue or the antipodes of emotion. And, alas, it is true that "the test of a first-rate intelligence is the ability to hold two opposed ideas in the mind at the same time, and still retain the ability to function." All his life he had made lists, planning the future, preserving the immediately fading past. The lists were enumerative and they were analytical. Students of Erik Erikson could probably use them as evidence of an unending identity crisis. Among the documents from the Hollywood years is a yellow work sheet labeled "Since the Depression (10 yrs.)." It lists all the stories written from 1929 to 1939 and classifies each by quality and theme and possibility for republication. Fitzgerald was trying to find out what had once worked and what might work again. He concluded that "Babylon Revisited" was a first-class story, essentially unhappy, based on himself and Scottie, and should be republished. On the verso of this same sheet, Fitzgerald listed it with five "A" stories ("Family in the Wind," "Crazy Sunday," "First Blood," and "The Intimate Strangers") and said of it, "glamorous, sad, love." We sense his Hollywood apprehension that the best that he could do would be to imitate his once successful self.

If the older Fitzgerald lacked the ability to see dualistically, there is little wonder that the film script of his famous short story should reveal all the myopia which characterized his later work. Occasionally he tried some of his old tricks, and in his script revisions he inserted symbols where they did not arise naturally from the context. He made much of Honoria's camera as a double symbol—sentimental as a preserver of the past, realistic as the objective eye of reality—and had it appropriately crushed at the moment she leaves the past to go forward into the future as Charlie's support. But it served inadequately. When Fitzgerald sold his story to the films, he complained to his daughter that the money received "wasn't worthy of the magnificent story—neither of you nor of me." Nor was the script worthy of its origin. We have met all these flat and conventional characters many times before. The tragedy is that we met them not in Fitzgerald's short story but in the lesser works of those whom he had once contemned.

San Fernando Valley State College

---

[1] This article is based upon a study of the "Babylon Revisited" film scripts (and notes for scripts) that are in the F. Scott Fitzgerald Collection at Princeton. All quotations from those unpublished documents are made with the permission of Lester Cowan and Frances Fitzgerald Smith, the copyright holders. I am also indebted to Mr. and Mrs. Albert Hackett for their conversations with me about Fitzgerald's life in Hollywood.

[2] Letter to Maxwell Perkins, 24 April 1925 in *The Letters of F. Scott Fitzgerald,* ed. Andrew Turnbull (New York: Scribner's, 1963), pp. 180-181.

[3] "Pasting It Together" [mistitled "Handle with Care"] in F. Scott Fitzgerald, *The Crack-Up,* ed. Edmund Wilson (New York: New Directions, 1945), p. 78.

[4] Robert Sklar, *F. Scott Fitzgerald: The Last Laocoön* (New York: Oxford, 1967), p. 324.

[5] cf. Arthur Mizener, *The Far Side of Paradise* (Boston: Houghton Mifflin, 1965; revised edition), pp. 326-327 for the anecdote about the scriptwriter who said this was "the most perfect motion-picture scenario I ever read." Kenneth Eble, *F. Scott Fitzgerald* (New York: Twayne, 1963), pp. 147-148 believes the script, which he calls "The Cosmopolitan," is "a very interesting revision of the original story." Henry Dan Piper, *F. Scott Fitzgerald: A Critical Portrait* (New York: Holt, Rinehart & Winston, 1965), p. 258, thinks the screen adaptation was "not especially good." I agree with his judgment but do not find his plot summary accurate. A more recent study of Fitzgerald in Hollywood insists upon the script's excellence and relates it to *The Last Tycoon;* cf. Aaron Latham, *Crazy Sundays* (New York: Viking, 1971). But cf. Alan Margolies, "F. Scott Fitzgerald's Work in the Film Studios," *Princeton University Library Chronicle,* XXXII (Winter 1971), 82, 102-106, for a less favorable evaluation of the "Babylon Revisited" scripts. Incidentally, Messrs. Latham and Margolies and I

appear to have worked without awareness that we were on each other's trail; neither of their studies alludes to the findings of the other, and both of their works appeared while this essay was in press.

[6]Sheilah Graham, *The Garden of Allah* (New York: Crown, 1970), p. 172 says that Lester Cowan "brought in the Epstein brothers to do another script after Scott died. He sold that one to MGM for one hundred thousand dollars, and it came out *The Last Time I Saw Paris*. . . . He still has Scott's original scenario, and one of these days he will sell it and make another fortune." Mr. Cowan says that within the next year he hopes to publish Fitzgerald's "Cosmo-politan" as Fitzgerald's "last finished work." He will also publish an essay on his recollections of Fitzgerald as writer-at-work—particularly at work upon *The Last Tycoon*. Many of Mr. Cowan's film experiences, and especially his dealings with Thalberg and Mayer, were recounted to Fitzgerald for his novel. A few years ago Mr. Cowan himself prepared a film script of *The Last Tycoon*, and the ending used in the film is *not* the ending as outlined by Edmund Wilson; nor are the details as remembered by Sheilah Graham. Mr. Cowan says that Fitzgerald outlined the novel's plan very clearly to him, and he believes that only his script is true to Fitzgerald's announced intention. It is expected that the film will go into production within the next year or two. Meanwhile, Mr. Cowan has promised to write up some of his Fitzgerald recollections for a forthcoming *FHA*.

A Note on F. Scott Fitzgerald's Monsignor Sigourney Fay and his Early Career as an Episcopalian

The Rev. R. C. Nevius

One of the important influences on the life of F. Scott Fitzgerald was Monsignor Sigourney Webster Fay, the Headmaster of the Newman school, and a convert to Roman Catholicism. The purpose of this paper is to present some facets of Monsignor Fay's life prior to his conversion to the Roman Church. Fay was one of a group of Anglo-Catholic clergy of the Episcopal Church who seceded to Rome following the General Convention of 1907, and at the time of his conversion he was the Professor of Dogmatic Theology at the Nashotah House, an Episcopal seminary on Lake Nashotah just outside of Milwaukee, Wisconsin.

Nashotah House had been founded in 1842 as the result of a missionary appeal by Bishop Jackson Kemper. From the beginning there had been some conflict as to the ideals of such a seminary, and the influence of the English Oxford Movement was strong. Some of the earliest students, who had come from the General Seminary in New York, felt that the new seminary should be modeled after the Roman Tridentine pattern; others wanted it to be a monastic community as well as a training school for priests. One of the young deacons, Breck, was a strong advocate of a religious house run on semi-monastic lines, while Bishop Kemper, the first missionary bishop of the Episcopal Church, saw it as a theological seminary, not unlike the General Seminary, which would serve as a source of clergy supply for his missionary work in the West. Nashotah's early history is closely bound up with the history of Episcopal missionary work in Wisconsin and Minnesota as well as further West.[1]

When the ideals of the Oxford Movement, led by John Henry Newman, John Keble, and Edward Pusey, crossed the Atlantic, they first found favor at the General Seminary, but its official position made it impossible for the General to become the kind of "Catholic" stronghold that many of the students wanted. Numerous investigations were run by bishops and other representatives of the General Convention to ensure that the ideas of the Tractarians did not take root in the Episcopal Church's oldest and only official seminary. But Nashotah House was under no such constraint and from its earliest days began to put into practice the outward manifestations of the Anglo-Catholic revival.[2] By 1895, Nashotah had lost some of its earlier role as a supply for missionaries, and had a more monastic appearance than any other Episcopal seminary. Nashotah had a daily Mass for the community, a daily private Mass for each priest, eucharistic vestments, choral services, incense, and was busy turning out parish priests for the (largely) Anglo-Catholic dioceses being formed in the Mid West.

It was to one of these Anglo-Catholic dioceses, the diocese of Fond du Lac in Wisconsin, that Sigourney Fay came seeking ordination to the Episcopal ministry. J. G. H. Barry, later to become the Dean of Nashotah House at the time of the secession, was then a Canon of Fond du Lac, and in his autobiography he describes the arrival of Sigourney Fay. Fay "was a Philadelphian, with apparently an ample income, who had chosen to be a candidate from Fond du Lac because of its Catholic reputation. He had all the notes of an Easterner. One day he asked a friend where he was born and on receiving the answer 'In Omaha, Nebraska' he could only ejaculate 'Fancy!' "[3]

Canon Barry and the young clergyman (who soon became the Archdeacon of Fond du Lac) became close friends. Barry describes him as "a most fascinating person; a brilliant talker, and notwithstanding the drawback of imperfect sight, very widely read. He had a prodigious memory which, it seemed, retained all that he had ever read or heard."[4]

But there were drawbacks too. "He was life and joy whenever he appeared—the only trouble was to make him disappear: Bed meant nothing to him, and some of us, I in particular, liked a few hours sleep."[5]

Fay had been characterized by Canon George DeMille, an historian of the 20th century Episcopal church, as brilliant and unstable. Barry certainly found this to be the case. "Fay seemed to have, apart from the fundamentals of the Christian religion, no opinion that he could not change over night. When I first got to know him well he had just returned from a visit to Russia with Bishop Grafton. . . . He came back an enthusiatic devotee of the Eastern Church, as was also Bishop Grafton. The difference was that the Bishop remained so, and Fay did not. But for the time the Orthodox were everything and the Anglican Church should do everything it could to achieve union with them. The West? Rome? Not to be thought of! Anglican orders? Indisputably valid. It was, so he would go on, Roman orders that were invalid; he could write a book proving it. I am sorry that he did not. . . ."[6] Barry characterized Fay as the "most perfect example that I have ever known of the 'will to believe' ".[7]

Shortly afterwards, William Walter Webb, who was the president of Nashotah House, was elected as bishop of the diocese of Milwaukee. Webb had strengthened the scholarly side of Nashotah and there was much speculation about his successor. At that time very few of the seminaries of the church had much contact with the rapidly changing world of the universities. The academic reforms begun by such men as Charles Eliot at Harvard, had not yet penetrated the theological schools. Eliot and others had taken the lead in establishing new patterns of education, abandoning the old method of 'recitation by rote' and molding the American universities on a German rather than the English pattern. The German degree of Doctor of Philosphy was imported, and genuine graduate programs in the arts and sciences were established.[8] The reforms begun at Harvard and Johns Hopkins were to spread to other colleges and universities, not without some opposition, as Woodrow Wilson, then president of the college of Princeton, learned when he attempted to turn that pre-revolutionary Presbyterian college into a model university. Few of the students in a theological college were college men, and those that were graduates of the modern universities were often dismayed by the antiquated teaching methods then in use. Nashotah had found itself running a preparatory department, almost a miniature college, to bridge the gap between high school training and the demands of a theological education. Nashotah was fortunate that one of their graduates, Hughell E. W. Fosbroke, a native of England and son of a missionary priest in Wisconsin, had taken two years at Harvard and had been exposed to the new teaching methods in Cambridge. Few of the men applying to Nashotah had a college education and most of the faculty at the turn of the century were men who had been trained at Nashotah. The question of the new Dean was important in determining the direction of the seminary's future.

Dr. Webb approached J. G. H. Barry to determine whether he would be interested in accepting the presidency of Nashotah House. "I said not at all. As time went on, no name was suggested that appealed to Webb. I talked the situation over with Fay and he of-

107

fered, if I would accept the presidency, to go with me and take a professorship. In the end . . . I consented. . . ."[9]

One thing which Dr. Barry insisted on was that the title be changed from president to Dean, and this was arranged. In due course he arrived at Nashotah as Dean and brought Sigourney Fay with him as Professor of Dogmatic Theology. One result was that "Fr. Fay obtained from his family very generous gifts which enable me to set out an extended improvement of the property."[10]

Walter Gardner, who had been an associate of Bishop Grafton of Fond du Lac, had been the Dean before Bishop Webb. Monsignor Hawks (one of those who defected with Fay to Rome) left a picture of the 'Catholic' life at Nashotah House during Gardner's reign. "The life was centered in the daily 'sacrifice of the mass,' which was celebrated in almost exact accordance with the Roman rite. Every student began his day by assisting at one of the celebrations which took place in the chapel, or in one of the numerous oratories which were scattered through the different buildings. There was a daily meditation directed by the professors in turn. The divine office was recited at the canonical hours, the deficiencies of the Book of Common Prayer being supplied by the Roman breviary. Vespers was sung before supper with incense and cope on the eves of the greater feasts. The Gregorian chant was followed faithfully; in later days the Solemnes method was the norm, the teacher having taken a course of study at the Benedictine monastery in the Isle of Wight. Compline ended the day. . . . Liturgical vestments were worn, the altars were adorned with lights and flowers, and incense was used on Sundays and holidays. Before I left, the "Sacrament" was reserved for the purpose of adoration."[11]

Thus the seminary that Dr. Barry consented to run with Fr. Fay becoming the professor of dogmatic theology was, far and away, the most High Church or 'extreme' of the Episcopal Church's theological seminaries.

At the same time, it was beginning to gather a small group of scholars who were to make this period what Canon DeMille has called 'the golden age of Nashotah House.' Hughell Edgar Woodall Fosbroke had graduated from Nashotah in 1900, and was immediately hired as a teacher of Hebrew and principal of the preparatory department. With Fosbroke, Biblical criticism entered Nashotah House. Fosbroke at this time was struggling through the problems of inspiration and Biblical authority, steadily moving in what must have seemed to some as a liberal direction. (In fact, he became a radical source critic.) The earlier leaders of the Oxford Movement, John Henry Newman, John Keble, and Edward B. Pusey, had been distinctly opposed to liberalism, theological or political. Pusey who had studied in Germany later recanted his earlier opinions on becoming canon of Christ Church and Regius Professor of Hebrew in the University of Oxford. Very little of the critical study of the Bible which had been going on for almost a century in Germany had penetrated the American theological schools. At the same time that young Fosbroke began teaching the mysteries of J,E,D, and P at Nashotah, a Presbyterian professor by the name of Briggs was being tried for heresy by the presbytery of New York for teaching the students the same Graf-Wellhausen hypothesis.

There had been some shift in the High Church wing of the Church of England between the publication of *Essays and Reviews* in 1860, which presented a conservative view of the latest German scholarship, and the publication of *Lux Mundi* in 1889 in which Charles Gore and other contributors gave an Anglo-Catholic imprimatur to the documentary hypothesis for the Old Testament and the Marcan priority for the New. But to America, these ideas were still new, and to many people, particularly in the Mid-West, dangerous. And it was ideas such as these that Fosbroke was teaching in the Old Testament department and an impish young man, Burton Scott Easton, taught in the New Testament department at Nashotah.

At this point, Professor Sigourney Fay, their colleague, was also teaching a *Lux Mundi*, liberal catholic line. Barry suggests that Fay was impressed by the mild modernism being taught in some Roman continental schools, but shortly after this, the Pope in his encyclical *Pascendi* condemned this kind of thinking, and the propapal Anglo-Catholics recoiled in horror from it. Pius X's word had become law for some extreme members of the Episcopal Church. And the very tendencies the Pope discouraged, they found being taught by the Biblical professors at Nashotah.

So closely identified with each other as these Anglo-Catholics tended to be, it is not difficult to understand that some unsympathetic to the ideals of the group saw in it a conspiracy designed to win the whole Anglican Communion over to Rome. Yet the defections when they came were small as the group of extremists had been small. The group was close knit in spirit though separated geographically, and their focal point was in a priest in Philadelphia, the Rev. William McGarvey.

McGarvey, William Walter Webb, and several others had been

associated with an eccentric High Church rector, the Rev. Henry R. Percival. McGarvey became rector of the parish of St. Elizabeth, a daughter parish of Percival's parish. Webb went to be president of Nashotah and then Bishop of Milwaukee. McGarvey began in 1891 a religious organization known as the Companions of the Holy Saviour. One of the companions was the Rev. Sigourney Fay. Though McGarvey became the leader of this group, and literally led them to Rome, he was not a theologian. Burton Scott Easton, then professor of New Testament at Nashotah, and later at General, wrote: "McGarvey's great difficulty was his ignorance. He was a street boy whom Percival picked up and educated in his own image, without sending him to college; he knew nothing at all except the Percivalian theology. And we used to say in Philadelphia that Percival never accepted the Copernican theory; I knew him and I am sure it did not interest him. He had no sense of humor whatever, but was convinced that he had; something that made conversation with him trying. He was a valetudinarian and celebrated in an oratory surrounded by plate glass. *And* he used to declare that true Christianity demanded an absolute monarchy."[12]

The Anglo-Catholic movement was highly unpopular in many quarters. For almost fifty years every ritual or ceremonial advance had been bitterly fought out on the floor of the General Convention, but attempts to bar the outward signs of the Anglo-Catholic revival proved unavailing. Many of the older High Churchmen and almost all of the Evangelical and Low Church party regarded the Tractarians and their followers as part of a conspiracy to bring the Episcopal Church into the Roman fold. An historian of the period deplored the fact that the church was forced to spend its time arguing about matters that properly belonged, as he put it, to *modistes* and dressmakers instead of the urgent tasks facing the Church and nation following the Civil War.[13]

The group of clergy who were associates of McGarvey were distinctly pro-Roman. Their ideals of theology and ceremonial were modeled on post-Tridentine models. The Papal encyclical condemning modernism created a problem because they saw Anglican scholars, even those associated with an Anglo-Catholic institution like Nashotah House, teaching a method and conclusions in a spirit distinctly contrary to the views of the Pope. A second problem was to arise as a result of the General Convention of the Episcopal Church in 1907.

Fr. Fay apparently had been teaching in the Lux Mundi, or liberal catholic, vein. Politically, too, he had some unconservative thoughts. Dr. Barry had devoted much of his outside reading to a study of social problems. In time he was drawn to socialism, and two of his companions, Delay and Fay, were also interested.

"Though in the case of Fay there was nothing serious about it, he simply came along to keep us company. He did take to preaching mildly socialistic sermons. After a time he got nervous and one day asked me if we did not think that when the confiscation of property by the proletariat took place they would draw the line at about two hundred thousand of private ownership; that, I gathered, was what he expected to have."[14]

Fr. Fay was as naive about geography as about politics. Barry related how on one occasion "Fr. Fay was going to spend some time in Los Angeles and wrote a friend in San Francisco that he would run up and preach for him on Sunday morning. Apparently, he thought Los Angeles was just a trolley ride from San Francisco."[15]

At the General Convention of the Episcopal Church in 1907, a slight revision was offered to the existing Canon 19. This addition would permit "the preaching of sermons or the delivery of addresses by Christian ministers, or men, who may be invited thereto by any priest in charge of any Congregation, or in his absence by the Bishop, who may license them for the purpose." In the ensuing debate the word 'sermon' was deleted, the bishop's permission made mandatory, and it was specified that this was to be for 'special occasions only'. With these changes the canon passed the House of Deputies and the House of Bishops. (Several High Church or Anglo-Catholic dioceses voted against it in the House of Deputies; only one clerical deputy from the Diocese of Milwaukee—in which diocese Nashotah House was—voted for the amendment. I suspect that this lone clerical affirmative was cast by Fay's colleague, H.E.W. Fosbroke, who was one of the clerical deputies from Milwaukee to that convention.)

At first the canon caused little stir. The majority of Bishops, clergy, and laity in the High Church dioceses were not upset by it. But it came as a shock to the McGarvey group.

From the very beginning of the Oxford Movement, unsympathetic observers (such as *Punch* and Sir William S. Gilbert) expected to see the entire group move in a body to the Roman Church. But when John Henry Newman made his submission, it was only a handful of Tractarians who went with him. Again, in 1907 when the McGarvey group began agitating and declared that the Episcopal Church had forfeited any claim to catholicity, some observers (including Dr. Barry) saw the prospect of a large defection. Barry had been convinced by Fr. Fay that there was, in fact, a conspiracy. But, as Burton Scott Easton observed, the conspiracy was largely in Fay's own mind.

In February, 1908, two of the priests who were teachers in the preparatory department of Nashotah under Dr. Fosbroke resigned and immediately joined the Roman Church. Their defection was followed by several members of the student body. The Dean gave Fr. Fay an indefinite leave of absence. Barry wrote: "Fay's unstable temperament called for a new thrill. He had by this time given up writing a book to prove the invalidity of Roman orders; he was tired of socialism and the mild form of modernism he had adopted. He was looking Romeward and the papal condemnation of modernism led him to declare publicly: 'We must obey the Holy Father.' "[16] Sigourney Fay shortly afterwards made his submission to Rome. Dean Barry left Nashotah to become the rector of New York's famous Anglo-Catholic parish, St. Mary the Virgin. H.E.W. Fosbroke moved to the more liberal atmosphere of the Episcopal Theological School in Cambridge, Massachusetts, and Burton Scott Easton moved to Seabury. The Golden Age of Nashotah House was over.

Heathwood Hall Episcopal School

---

[1] A fascinating picture of Nashotah in its earliest days is found in Sinclair Lewis' novel, *The Godseeker* (N.Y.: Random House, 1949).

[2] A faithful picture of early Anglo-Catholic practices in England is found in Compton MacKenzie's *Sinister Street.* The kind of incense laden parishes young Michael Fane frequented during his religious period were models for other High Church parishes, particularly in the United States.

[3] J.R.H. Barry, *Impressions and Opinions*, (N.Y.: Gorham, 1931), p. 219.

[4] *Ibid.*

[5] *Ibid.*

[6] *Ibid.*, p. 220.

[7] *Ibid.*

[8] Herbert J. Mueller, *Freedom in the Modern World*, (N.Y.: Harper & Row, 1964), pp. 300-301.

[9] J.R.H. Barry, *Impressions and Opinions*, p. 227.

[10] *Ibid.*, p. 233.

[11] E. Hawks, *William McGarvey and the Open Pulpit*, (Philadelphia: Dolphin, 1935), pp. 85-86.

[12] Quoted in G. DeMille, *The Catholic Movement in the American Episcopal Church*, (Philadelphia: The Church Historical Society, 1949), p. 164.

[13] S.D. McConnell, *A History of the American Episcopal Church from the planting in the colonies to the end of the Civil War,* (N.Y.: Whitaker, 1890), p. 318.

[14] J.R.H. Barry, *Impressions and Opinions*, p. 238.

[15] *Ibid.*, p. 143.

[16] *Ibid.*, p. 245.

"Oh, Sister,

Verse: I may be a What-ho, a No-can-do
Even a banker, but I can love you
As well as a better man
a letter-man of fame
As well as any Mr. Whosis you can name

———————————

The little break in my voice
—or Rolls-Royce
take your choice
I may lose
You must choose
So choose

———————————

A hundred thousand in gold
and you're sold
to the old
and I'm broke
when our days a
are gold
I'm begging
begging
Oh, Sister, can you spare your heart?

****

Can You Spare Your Heart," [1]

A Fitzgerald Lyric

Those wealthy goats
In racoon coats
　　can wolf you away from me
But draw your latch
For an honest patch
　　the skin of necessity

(we'll make it a tent, dear)

****

The funny patch in my pants
　　take a chance
　　ask your aunts
　　　What's a loss
　　　You must toss
　　　　So toss!
A gap inside that's for good.
　　　You'll be good
　　　As you should
　　　　Touch *wood!*
　　　I'm begging
　　　　begging
Oh, Sister, can you spare your heart?

---

[1] Attachèd to a Fitzgerald letter to Harold Ober, 12 June 1933. *Published with the permission of Frances Fitzgerald Smith. All rights to this material are the property of Mrs. Smith.*

Dear Sinclair Lewis; Joe just sent for Arrowsmith. My hope is that this the Great Gatsby will be the second best American book of the spring.

F Scott Fitzgerald

Slip pasted in *The Great Gatsby* (1925). Collection of R. L. Samsell

"A Sort of Moral Attention":
The Narrator of *The Great Gatsby*

Oliver H. Evans

Arthur Mizener, in *The Far Side of Paradise,* suggests that F. Scott Fitzgerald, by using Nick Carraway as narrator of *The Great Gatsby,* was able "to keep clearly separated for the first time in his career the two sides of his nature, the Middle-Western Trimalchio and the spoiled priest who disapproved of but grudgingly admired him."[1] As Mizener goes on to say, "a great deal of the book's colour and subtlety comes from the constant play of Nick's judgment and feelings over the events."[2] It is with the question of the adequacy of Nick's "judgment and feelings," the adequacy of his understanding of what he tells us about the other characters and about himself, that this paper will deal.

While Mizener's description of Nick as one side of Fitzgerald's nature is useful up to a point, it is too limited a view of both Nick and Fitzgerald. To understand Nick Carraway it is necessary to understand something of the sensibility of Fitzgerald, and to understand that sensibility it is necessary to recognize distinctions that exist within both the poetic, or Trimalchian, and the priestly side of Fitzgerald's nature. An examination of Fitzgerald's works, particularly *Gatsby* and the novels preceding it, reveals a sensibility which, for purposes of analysis, may be broken into the following four categories:

1) The vision of the "romantic" poet. It is this vision that permeates, or tries to permeate, *This Side of Paradise.* The young, in this vision, are beautiful, wise beyond their years and alive to the possibilities of life. To the romantic poet, the young are capable of fulfilling their dreams by creating the lives they imagine.

2) The vision of the "satiric" priest. This vision undercuts the vision of the romantic poet. The satiric priest recognizes the hollowness of the dreams and the shallowness of the people trying to fulfill them. But the satiric priest and the romantic poet both react to people and events in a somewhat superficial way, and the satiric priest is himself undercut by the romantic poet. If the romantics ultimately have little real possibility for life, so too does the satiric priest, who has shut himself off from whatever possibilities of life may exist. Furthermore, the moral judgments of the satiric priest display about as deep an understanding of the human condition as do the dreams of the romantics. While absent, for the most part, from *This Side of Paradise,* it is the voice of the satiric priest we hear at the opening of *The Beautiful and Damned.*

3) The vision of the "historically conscious" poet. It is this poet who sees the events of the present as recapitulations of "mythic" events. In order to create the beautiful new life they imagine, the romantics must create for themselves a new past. This is done most often by the romantic's rejection of the natural father, the true past, and the adoption of a new father. Amory Blaine ignores his natural father and chooses the Monsignor for his father. The natural father is often an ineffectual man and is sometimes seen as a kind of animal. Gatsby's father reports that Gatsby once told him he " 'et like a hog,' "[3] and it is the natural, sexual, father who corrupts the possibilities of life as Nicole's father has done in *Tender is the Night.*

4) The vision of the "historically conscious" priest. Like the historically conscious poet, the historically conscious priest sees the present as a recapitulation of past events, but the past of the historically conscious priest is represented, not by the adopted father, but by the natural father. The historically conscious priest knows that one cannot deny one's natural father, and, in Fitzgerald's novels, the natural father appears at significant times in the hero's career. The natural father is a kind of original sinner, who, like the grandfather, significantly named Adam, in *The Beautiful and Damned,* destroys the poet's vision, or what in that novel is meant to be the poet's vision, and forces the hero to contaminate himself. Like his forefather Adam, Anthony Patch must fight for money and soil himself in the process. He creates, as did his grandfather, "much fuss, fume, applause, and ill will."[4] One does indeed relive the past in the present, but the historically conscious priest finds a very different past and present from those of his poet counterpart.

This discrimination of the various aspects of Fitzgerald's sensibility is important in understanding Nick's role as narrator because, as narrator, Nick speaks in all these voices. I think it an error to hold that Fitzgerald, sometimes too close to his material, achieved the necessary distance by splitting the poet-priest between two characters and having Nick narrate the book. There are, actually, two poets and two priests in Fitzgerald, each with his own voice and vision, and Nick Carraway presents all four of these. He speaks not only with the naivete of the romantic poet and the smug superiority of the satiric priest, but also with the voices of historically conscious poet and priest. Fitzgerald has created a highly perceptive and intelligent narrator who, caught in a complex world, tries to understand that world by looking through many windows. He tries to be an honest man in both his actions with, and judgments of, other men.

That Nick is not up to his task is the position taken by R. W. Stallman in "Gatsby and the Hole in Time." Stallman is correct in suggesting that there is some inadequacy in Nick, but his most fundamental error in reading *Gatsby* is his failure to realize that the priest in Nick goes beyond the simple moralizing of the satiric priest one finds at times in him. Stallman, in seeing Nick as an "archprig all dressed up in a morally hard-boiled starched shirt of provincial squeamishness and boasted tolerance,"[5] goes too far in the direction opposite those who see Nick as the moral center of the novel.

Nick is inadequate, finally, not because he "cannot bring himself to keep any commitments to life,"[6] but because his final judgment of Gatsby, which he makes on the basis of Gatsby's refusal to betray Daisy after the accident, represents an inadequate understanding of Gatsby and his motives. As I shall show, Nick fails to understand why Gatsby refuses to betray Daisy and, on the basis of that misunderstanding, proceeds to turn Gatsby into an ideal. Gatsby becomes for Nick what Daisy was for Gatsby, an embodiment of an ideal, and Gatsby is as far removed in reality from the ideal Nick imagines him to be as Daisy was far removed from what Gatsby imagined her to be.

II

The opening pages of *Gatsby* are masterful in their presentation of the several facets of Nick's sensibility. Points of view and perspective shift unobtrusively in this opening section and if these shifts are missed, an entire aspect of Nick is missed. The first point of view presented is that of the moralist, the view associated with the satiric priest. Nick tells us that, following the good advice of his father, he is "inclined to reserve all judgments" when dealing with people, and he goes on to tell us that this "habit . . . has opened up many curious natures to me and also made me the victim of not a few veteran bores."[7] The attitude Nick takes toward the confessions he has heard is condescending. The "wild, unknown men" were not, for Nick, that "wild" or that "unknown."[7] As a good satiric priest, Nick knows that the people he has met were not as glamorous or exciting as they were thought to be. Rather, they are bores whose confessions are usually plagiarized and "marred by obvious suppressions."[8]

Yet quietly Nick changes his perspective. There is more to his attitude than that of simple moralizing. He is, as was noted, "inclined to reserve all judgments," and reserving judgments, he tells us, "is a matter of infinite hope."[8] Nick Carraway is also a romantic, as

119

Gatsby is. He, like Gatsby, has a "gift for hope," and he is "afraid of missing something" if he forgets his father's advice and criticizes people too quickly.[8]

Nick goes on to modify this position by telling us that his reserving judgments "has a limit."[8] After a time, Nick says, he does not care whether conduct is "founded on the hard rock or the wet marshes;" he prefers instead to put the world "in uniform and at a sort of moral attention forever. . . ."[8] There is more here than at first may be suspected. Nick says he does not care whether conduct is founded on a rock or a marsh, but to want the world in uniform is, in effect, to want conduct founded on a rock. Secondly, the either-or position, that conduct is founded on a rock or a marsh, suggests a dualism that leaves no room for conduct founded, as Gatsby's is, "on a fairy's wing."[9] Yet Nick will later approve of Gatsby. He will appear able to transcend this either-or position and to exempt Gatsby in spite of the fact that he tells us Gatsby "represented everything for which I have an unaffected scorn."[8]

The scorn Nick feels for Gatsby is contradicted before the paragraph is over, for "Gatsby turned out all right at the end."[10] It was the "foul dust" that destroyed Gatsby, but it could not destroy what Gatsby represents for Nick.[10] The "foul dust" is the people and events associated with the ashen wasteland. It is Wilson, a figure of ashes, who crawls through the trees toward Gatsby's pool and who finally kills Gatsby. At the beginning of the novel, Nick, writing after Gatsby's death, suggests that what Gatsby represents for him is not dead. His interest in character was only "temporarily closed," and it was closed not by Gatsby, but by the "foul dust."[10] Nick's own capacity for hope is not destroyed by Gatsby's death.

Fitzgerald never lets go of this complex sensibility, but continues to develop the romantic and satiric aspects of Nick. His family is Middle Western, indicative that Nick's sensibility is neither that of the West nor of the East, but a mixture of both. His family is in the hardware business, and he, Nick, is supposed to resemble a "hard-boiled" great-uncle.[10] Nick has left what he calls "the ragged edge of the universe" to come East in search of the "warm center of the world."[10] Once in the East, however, he chooses to live where there are lawns rather than to do "the practical thing" and "find rooms in the city."[11] There are overtones of initiation suggested by the references to prep school, and there are more things to suggest that Nick is a parallel to Gatsby. Nick comes East in the spring and, like Gatsby, begins life over. He wants to pull "so much fine health . . . out of the young breath-giving air,"[12] and part of what he wants to pull out of the air is not unlike what Gatsby wants: money. It is money that Daisy's voice suggests to Gatsby, and it is money, "the shining secrets that only Midas and Morgan and Maecenas knew,"[12] that Nick hopes for. There is for Nick, as there is for Gatsby, a mythic past congenial to the historically conscious poet.

There is also for both Nick and Gatsby a dream of culture, undercut to be sure, but present nevertheless. There are Gatsby's books and Nick's dream of becoming a "'well rounded man'" in spite of the fact that "life is much more successfully looked at from a single window, after all."[12] Nick is a new man, "a guide, a pathfinder, an original settler,"[11] in a new world, but, true to the priestly side of his sensibility, Nick recognizes that his new world is not perfect "like the eggs in the Columbus story."[13]

Before five pages of the novel are done, Fitzgerald has sketched the four parts of Nick's sensibility. Nick is the romantic poet who, at base, is hollow, the satiric priest and the poet who finds in the past mythic prototypes for the dreams of the present. The historically conscious priest, whose voice is heard most strongly on the last page of the novel, is present at the beginning in the mention of the "foul dust," the corruption that destroys Gatsby.

Early in the novel, we see Nick exercise the various aspects of his sensibility as he moves through the social world of the East. In the first scene of the novel, the dinner at Daisy and Tom's, two aspects of Nick's sensibility are at work. Nick is attracted by the glamour of the place while at the same time he makes accurate judgments of the quality of the people and of their lives. Nick recognizes that underneath his "swank" exterior, Tom Buchanan is rough, powerful and cruel. He recognizes that Tom's theory of culture, Tom's attempt to create a past for himself, is "pathetic . . . as if his complacency, more acute than of old, was not enough for him any more,"[14] and he recognizes the "basic insincerity" of Daisy's statement that she is "sophisticated."[15]

It is the Buchanan house, the style of their lives, that most amazes Nick. When he first enters the house, it is not a room, but "a bright rosy-colored space" that he finds.[16] This description of the room illustrates a motif recurrent throughout the novel. Whenever a scene takes on romantic qualities, whenever the romantic poet in Nick is aroused, it is accompanied by some change in natural objects. Thus the room is described figuratively. The grass grows into it; the ceiling is a "frosted wedding-cake"; the rug is "wine-colored"; and the wind makes a shadow on the rug "as wind does on the sea."[16,17] Only the women and the couch on which they sit are

121

immovable, but even the women are not real. They look as though "they had just been blown back in after a short flight around the house."[17] The room retains its romantic overtones until Tom slams the windows, an action suggestive of his character, and the illusion is destroyed.

Similarly, when Nick and Daisy return from their talk outside the house, the room again takes on romantic overtones. We are told that "the crimson room bloomed with light" and that words read by Jordan Baker from *The Saturday Evening Post* ran "together in a soothing tune."[18] If Nick is acute in his judgment of these people, he is also highly attracted to what they represent.

The second chapter acts as an ironic comment on the first. The structure of both chapters is circular. In the first chapter, we begin in West Egg, move into the romantic heaven of Tom and Daisy's house, move back to West Egg where Nick catches his first glimpse of Gatsby and then stands alone "in the unquiet darkness."[19] The second chapter also begins in West Egg, moves us through the wasteland to the hell represented by the New York apartment and ends with Nick alone in the train station.

Characters in one scene act as foils to those in the other. Tom and Nick in the second chapter act as foils to the Tom and Nick of the first chapter. Myrtle becomes a foil to Daisy, and Catherine a foil to Jordan since both she and Jordan act as sources of information for Nick.

While it is true that Nick exercises both aspects of his sensibility in the second chapter that he exercised in the first, in the second chapter his enchantment and repulsion are directed at the "inexhaustible variety of life," not at the glamour of it.[20] The party in the apartment has no glamour associated with it, and the final vision of the party is a vision of hell and not of heaven. "The little dog was sitting on the table looking with blind eyes through the smoke, and from time to time groaning faintly. People disappeared, reappeared, made plans to go somewhere, and then lost each other, searched for each other, found each other a few feet away."[21] At the height of the confusion, Tom Buchanan breaks Myrtle's nose, an action that parallels his destruction of the romantic illusion in the earlier chapter.

What is most suggestive in these two chapters is the concluding scene of the second chapter in which Nick stands beside the photographer's bed and its structural relationship with the concluding scene of the first chapter when Nick first sees Gatsby. In the first chapter,

Nick feels that Gatsby has "come out to determine what share was his of our local heavens."[19] The photographer, who earlier in the second chapter said he had " 'done some nice things out on Long Island,' "[22] also owns space by capturing it in photographs, but there is no romance associated with either the photographer or his pictures.

Both chapters end with Nick alone. In the first, he is alone on the beach with the "unquiet darkness," while in the second, after a series of images of descent, he is alone on the lower level of the train station face to face with the kind of reality represented by the newspaper.

Thus by the third chapter, where we meet Gatsby for what is really the first time, we have been prepared to understand the complex sensibility with which Nick views him. When Nick first meets Gatsby, Gatsby is, for him, a character of remarkable qualities. Nick meets Gatsby after having drunk champagne, and, the romantic side of his nature once again aroused, the scene changes "before [Nick's] eyes into something significant, elemental, and profound."[23] But almost immediately Nick's perspective alters; his sensibility shifts. Gatsby now becomes, as we have been prepared to expect, "an elegant young roughneck" whose way of speaking "just missed being absurd."[24]

But even though we have been prepared for Nick's shifting sensibility, we still have in Nick a character we only partially understand. One moment he sees a scene as something fine and romantic; the next he sees it as something essentially hollow. He gives the impression that he is viewing the world through a number of windows in trying to have us understand the several things Gatsby represents.

What Gatsby represents begins to be developed almost immediately after Nick meets him, and this development takes the form usual in Fitzgerald. Nick sets out to search for Gatsby's past. He wants to know who Gatsby is, and who Gatsby is, is for Nick a matter of "where is he from. . . . And what does he do."[24] Such things are important to Nick largely because his own past will not allow him to accept Gatsby as something spontaneously generated. All people, for Nick, have ancestors of one kind or another whose portraits are hung on walls and whom one resembles in some way. "I would have accepted without question the information that Gatsby sprang from the swamps of Louisiana or from the lower East Side of New York. That was comprehensible. But young men didn't—at least in my provincial inexperience I believed they didn't—drift coolly out of nowhere and buy a palace on Long Island Sound."[25] Gatsby has no concreteness, and it is "with an urban distaste for the concrete" that Jordan Baker changes the subject of Gatsby's past.[25]

All of the possible pasts mentioned for Gatsby early in the novel are pasts congenial to the historically conscious priest. Gatsby may be a murderer, a bootlegger, or a spy. All these pasts suggest some corruption, some mortality, that is destined to prove fatal to Gatsby's dream. But there is also a past, beside the imaginary ones suggested by Gatsby himself, congenial to the historically conscious poet. Gatsby denied his natural father and adopted Cody, a much more attractive figure, as his new father.

The final vision of Gatsby includes both these pasts. Gatsby's natural parentage has been noted; he is also involved in some kind of criminal activity. But he did live with Cody and is an incarnation of what Stallman calls "the power of dream and illusion by which new worlds have been conquered since the beginning of civilization. . . ."[26] Nick adequately understands Gatsby as a modern exponent of the American Dream, and he also recognizes that this dream is corrupt and futile.

But to understand Gatsby and his dream is to understand Gatsby in terms of the American past and present. This does not explain Nick's attitude toward Gatsby "at the end," despite the attempts of several critics to explain Nick's attitude in just this way. Stallman says that "Gatsby exemplifies an ideal and remains faithful to it, and that is why Nick in admiration exempts him from his general condemnation."[27] Mizener says that the slightly ironic tone of the last page of the novel "does not seriously qualify Nick's—and Fitzgerald's— commitment to Gatsby, to the romantic 'capacity for wonder' and its belief 'in the green light, the orgiastic future,' which justifies by its innocent faith Gatsby's corruption."[28] Similarly, Thomas Hanzo finds that Nick admires Gatsby because of his "capacities of will: a tremendous energy to accomplish certain purposes, and a self-imposed delusion which makes those purposes meaningful," and, Hanzo continues, it is Gatsby's defense of Daisy, his "last heroism in protection of the mistress of his dreams," that "confirms Nick's judgment."[29]

There are two problems with these explanations. First, as will be made clear in a moment, Nick, toward the end of the novel, believes Gatsby recognizes the futility of his dream and gives it up. But even were this not the case, these critics are faced with the problem of having Nick admire a man who, as Nick knows, wilfully deludes himself into believing in a corrupt and futile dream that could have been fulfilled at no time in American history.

Nick says that Gatsby "turned out all right at the end," which implies he was not all right at the beginning. Nick knows Gatsby was corrupt, and, while "there was something gorgeous" in Gatsby's "sensitivity to the promises of life,"[8] Nick believes that not only can one not "'repeat the past,'"[30] but that there never was a time when the American Dream in either its original form or in the form Gatsby conceives it, was viable. At the end of the novel Nick thinks the whisperers of the first dream were panderers.[31] The eyes of the Dutch sailor and the eyes of Dr. Eckleburg are the same eyes; the land they brood over, the same land.

Gatsby is "'worth the whole damn bunch'" because Nick sees in him, "at the end," a way of acting in a world that has lost, if it ever had them, its possibilities of life and the values that went with them. By the end of the novel, Nick has had to modify his early dreams to a great extent. What he had hoped was "the warm center of the world" has become "haunted" and "distorted."[32] He has learned from Gatsby's mistake that dreams of a New World are illusory, and so he returns home convinced that "life is much more successfully looked at from a single window, after all."

But while he returns home having learned the possibilities of life are very limited, Nick does not return devoid of hope. He has one last hope—that in a world that has lost everything else, it is still possible and best to act from what he calls "a sense of the fundamental decencies."[8] Nick returns home convinced of the rightness of his father's morality.

It is the fundamental indecency of the East, the fact that people do not know or care about one another, that causes Nick to reject it. He breaks off his relationship with Jordan because it is the fundamentally decent thing to do, and he thinks Tom a child because, like Daisy, Tom lacks "a sense of the fundamental decencies." "They were careless people, Tom and Daisy—they smashed up things and creatures and then retreated back into their money or their vast carelessness, or whatever it was that kept them together, and let other people clean up the mess they had made. . . ."[33]

Following Myrtle Wilson's death, the other characters in the novel, as they do after Gatsby's death, become concerned with their own interests and with retreating from the "mess" with as little trouble as possible. It is only Nick who shows concern for anyone other than himself. As has been suggested, Gatsby remains faithful to his dream. Even after Daisy has told him she did love Tom, he refuses to believe she did, or, if she did, " 'it was just personal.' "[34] Gatsby is also, then, concerned with his own interests, attaining Daisy, and, by his refusal to betray Daisy, attempts to prove himself worthy once more.

But Stallman points out, and I think fails to draw the proper conclusion from the fact, that Nick believes Gatsby, like himself, has been disillusioned by the East.[35] Nick, who understands why Gatsby dreamed, thinks Gatsby may have realized he has "lost the old warm world."[36] Since this is the case, Nick cannot admire Gatsby for remaining faithful to his dream as even Stallman suggests. Nick believes Gatsby has awakened from his dream and, therefore, must think Gatsby's refusal to betray Daisy has nothing to do with that dream. His refusal to betray Daisy is, rather, an act of fundamental decency. Nick thinks he and Gatsby are the only two who do not retreat, who have a capacity for going beyond their own interests and caring about someone other than themselves.

What Nick appears to have done, then, is something no other character in Fitzgerald is able to do. As I pointed out earlier, characters such as Amory Blaine and Gatsby attempt to discard the natural father and to adopt a new father. Usually the natural father and the adopted father are opposed. The natural father is unimaginative and ineffectual; the adopted father is glamorous.

Nick also has two fathers: his natural father and Gatsby. Unlike the fathers of the other characters, however, both Nick's fathers ultimately agree on how to live one's life. Nick embraces the morality of his natural father and believes he has seen confirmation of that morality in the actions of the adopted father. Nick, "afraid of missing something," has reserved judgment long enough to discover that Gatsby, who both repels and attracts him, turns out to be as fundamentally decent as himself.

But since Gatsby has, in fact, remained faithful to his dream, it is impossible not to see Nick's understanding of Gatsby's final act as inadequate. As Hanzo says, Nick "assumes that evil may be clearly enough determined."[37] Because of this, it seems to me, Nick never escapes from the either-or position established at the beginning of the novel and so fails to realize that, like his other acts, Gatsby's apparent decency toward Daisy takes place in that realm which, according to "Absolution," "has nothing to do with God,"[38] nothing to do with the "fundamental decencies." Nick's understanding of what Gatsby represents is, in this one instance, inadequate.

126

The conclusion of the novel must be seen, therefore, as ironic. On one level, Nick's final statements are an accurate and moving account of what he has learned in the East. Nick has matured while in the East, and Hanzo, in opposition to Stallman, is correct in saying that Nick's discoveries about himself and others do not lead him to wish to regiment the world on the basis of his "private convictions."[37] The morality Nick affirms is, so far as one can tell, a morality for him alone. Nick's "private convictions" are a way for him to function in the world, and "his hopes are modest because he regards the good only as a private, incommunicable possession."[37]

Nick's final statements are, furthermore, a sympathetic explanation of Gatsby and, perhaps, all mankind. All men are caught in dreams that cannot be fulfilled; all believe, as Gatsby did, in some kind of "green light," and, in trying to capture that light, all are "borne back ceaselessly into the past."[39]

But since, according to Nick, one cannot repeat the past, the implication is that he wants us to exempt him from the judgment of the final page of the novel. Nick becomes aware of what the New World was for the Dutch sailor and for Gatsby; he understands what they felt and why they failed. Supposedly, from what he has learned in the East, Nick has freed himself from the futile pursuit of the "green light."

But even though Nick has wisely modified his initial hopes, and perceptive as his final insights are, the last sentence of the novel does not allow us to exempt him entirely. Not only has Nick returned home with his hope that it is possible and best to act from "a sense of the fundamental decencies," which is perhaps true, he returns thinking Gatsby exemplified that hope, which is certainly false. Nick, for all his experience, remains something of an innocent. For all his fine perception and intelligence, he, like Gatsby, never fully understands the reality before him, and the novel is a moving account both of what Nick learns and of what he fails to learn.

Ironically, Nick is himself "borne back . . . into the past" and, whether he believes it possible or not, repeats the past—reenacts it—by writing about it. At Gatsby's funeral, Nick tries to "think about Gatsby, but he was already too far away. . . ."[40] Gatsby—Nick's past—recedes before Nick as Daisy—Gatsby's past—had receded before him. Yet Gatsby, the past as Nick imagines him, is not "too far away," because Nick, in search of his own version of the "green light," has been forced to repeat, and to remake, that past.

The novel is, among many other things, Nick's attempt to justify

127

his conception of Gatsby. In justifying that conception, Nick provides himself with one uncorrupted possibility of life, one value, in a world in which the other possibilities of life, the other values, are hopelessly corrupt and futile. Stallman to the contrary, Nick, finally, is able to commit himself to life. He revives his "interest in the abortive sorrows and short-winded elations of men,"[10] "temporarily closed" to him, because he now has what Hanzo called an "incommunicable possession" with which to deal with the "foul dust" that had closed his interest. Gatsby, standing "at a sort of moral attention," is for Nick an embodiment of this last remaining possibility of life just as Daisy had been an embodiment of an ideal possibility for Gatsby. Nick knew the real Daisy was far removed from what Gatsby imagined her to be. That Nick does not know Gatsby is just as far removed in reality from what he imagines him to be "at the end" is the final irony of the novel.

Purdue University

---

[1] Arthur Mizener, *The Far Side of Paradise* (Boston: Houghton Mifflin, 1951), p. 171.

[2] Ibid., p. 172.

[3] F. Scott Fitzgerald, *The Great Gatsby* (New York: Scribners, 1925), p. 209.

[4] F. Scott Fitzgerald, *The Beautiful and Damned* (New York: Scribners, 1922), p. 4.

[5] R. W. Stallman, *The Houses That James Built* (East Lansing: Michigan State University Press, 1961), p. 137.

[6] Ibid., p. 139.

[7] Fitzgerald, *Gatsby*, p. 1.

[8] Ibid., p. 2.

[9] Ibid., p. 119.

[10] Ibid., p. 3.

[11] Ibid., p. 4

[12] Ibid., p. 5.

[13] Ibid., p. 6.

[14] Ibid., p. 17.

[15] Ibid., p. 21.

[16] Ibid., p. 9.

[17] Ibid., p. 10.

[18] Ibid., p. 22.

[19] Ibid., p. 26.

[20] Ibid., p. 43.

[21] Ibid., p. 44.

[22] Ibid., p. 38.

[23] Ibid., p. 57.

[24] Ibid., p. 59.

[25] Ibid., p. 60.

[26] Stallman, Op. cit., p. 147.

[27] Ibid., p. 150.

[28] Mizener, op. cit., p. 178.

[29] Thomas Hanzo, "The Theme and Narrator of *The Great Gatsby*," *Modern Fiction Studies*, II (Winter, 1956-1957), p. 188.

[30] Fitzgerald, *Gatsby*, p. 133.

[31] Edwin Fussell, "Fitzgerald's Brave New World," *ELH*, XIX (December, 1952), p. 298.

[32] Fitzgerald, *Gatsby*, p. 213.

[33] Ibid., p. 216.

[34] Ibid., p. 182.

[35] Stallman, op. cit., p. 149. Stallman writes in opposition to Norman Friedman's "Versions of Form in Fiction: *Great Expectations* and *The Great Gatsby*," *Accent*, XIV (Autumn, 1954), pp. 246-264. Friedman believes Gatsby was disillusioned by the East; Stallman points out that Nick *thinks* Gatsby was. There is, then, a discrepancy between what Nick thinks is going on in front of him and what the actions he describes tell the reader.

[36] Fitzgerald, *Gatsby*, p. 194.

[37] Hanzo, op. cit., p. 189.

[38] M. Cowley, ed., *The Stories of F. Scott Fitzgerald* (New York: Scribners, 1951), p. 159.

[39] Fitzgerald, *Gatsby*, p. 218.

[40] Ibid., p. 210.

Nick Carraway's Self-Introduction

A. E. Elmore

> Nick Carraway, Fitzgerald's narrator, is, for the book's structure, the most important character.
>
> —Arthur Mizener[1]

The first character one meets in *The Great Gatsby* and the only character one comes to know directly is Nick Carraway, the narrator. It is necessary, of course, that Nick introduce himself, since no other character can introduce him without violating the first-person point of view. That Fitzgerald recognizes and abides by this necessity marks an advance in his technique, for in the earlier novels his handling of point of view is never entirely consistent. To fail to come to terms with Nick's self-introduction in the opening paragraphs is to fail to understand not only the structure of the novel but perhaps its meaning as well. Nick Carraway, in short, is the most important character both for the book's structure, as Mizener says, and, in some ways, for the book's meaning.

The story is basically a story of initiation, with a difference. As Jerome Thale says, "The formula is the coming to knowledge of the self through seeing the self in another. . . ."[2] Thus, though it is Gatsby who suffers through the obvious rituals of initiation—rejection, pain, dream-building, disillusionment, and so on—it is Nick Carraway who learns, if in part only through vicarious suffering, the lessons which these rituals can teach. That is not to say Gatsby learns nothing or that Nick learns only the usual lesson of what it means to grow up. It is simply to say that whatever is learned is presented to the reader through the medium of Nick's consciousness and that that consciousness reflects, in the course of the novel, a growing understanding of the nature of the human experience it observes.

Thus, when Nick introduces himself in the opening four paragraphs, which form a sort of prologue to Chapter I and to the novel as a whole, as well as in the paragraphs immediately following the prologue, we must not assume that his education is already complete and his understanding already entirely clear. In one sense, it is true, the ritual of initiation is over, having ended with Gatsby's death or, more exactly, with Nick's return to the West; both events occurred the year before Nick begins to tell the story. "When I came back from the East last autumn I felt that I wanted the world to be in uniform and at a sort of moral attention forever; I wanted no more riotous excursions with privileged glimpses into the human heart."[3] When the ritual had first ended, Nick's response had been one of revulsion and withdrawal; he wanted to avoid the implications of the experience, the pain of looking again into the unguarded human heart. But now, as the novel begins, the pain of the ritual has subsided, and Nick is able to begin sorting out its meaning. The ritual "temporarily closed out my interest in the abortive sorrows and short-winded elations of men," Nick recalls, but the fact that he is beginning, despite the danger of recurring pain and revulsion, to recount the sorrows and elations of the ritual is evidence that his interest has now returned. It bears repeating, however, that his understanding is *not* entirely complete as he sits down to recount the story. The recounting, the sorting out of the story, will itself be the final stage of the initiation ceremony. Therefore Nick's final reactions at the end of the novel will not necessarily be the same as those he displays at the beginning.

It is necessary to distinguish between two kinds of time at work even in the very opening pages of the novel. Using one kind of time, we can say that the prologue (paragraphs one through four) postdates any of the action which follows it in the novel. The remainder of the novel is devoted to the events of 1922 up to the time of Nick's return to the West, while the prologue, written sometime in 1923, is devoted in large part to explaining Nick's reactions *after* his return to the West, right on up to the moment he begins to tell the story. But using the other kind of time, we can say that the prologue antedates everything which follows because it is the first thing Nick tells or writes down. Thus some of the things which come clear to Nick as he actually tells the story are not necessarily reflected in the prologue. For example, it is hard to believe, after one has read the entire story, that Nick's statement, "Gatsby . . . represented everything for which I have an unaffected scorn," must stand as his final understanding of Gatsby's life and personality. Yet the statement employs the present tense, "everything for which I *have* an unaffected scorn." At the end of the novel (two years after the events of autumn, 1922, as we learn from the first sentence of the final chapter) it is evident that, if anyone represents everything for which the initiated Nick has an unaffected scorn, it is Tom and Daisy Buchanan, certainly not Gatsby.

The point is not only that Nick learns from recounting the story but also that he makes every effort to be faithful, when recounting the past, to the attitudes he held *at the time.* When Nick returned from the East after the events of the summer of 1922, only Gatsby was "exempt" from Nick's mood of revulsion and withdrawal. Yet as he writes the prologue in 1923, Nick is careful to add that, despite the exemption, Gatsby still represents certain qualities for which Nick can feel only scorn. This scorn, or most of it, evaporates as Nick writes the story. For the story portrays an almost constant movement on Nick's part away from "his own people" (represented by his cousin, Daisy Buchanan, her alter ego, Jordan Baker, and her husband Tom) and toward Gatsby, a movement which culminates in Nick's climactic declaration to Gatsby, " 'They're a rotten crowd. . . . You're worth the whole damn bunch put together,' " and, at the very end of the novel, in his symbolic act of erasing an "obscene word" from Gatsby's "white steps." The use of the present tense in "I have an unaffected scorn" thus serves to indicate that the story is not a pat account of initiation (what I learned from my summer experience) at the same time it serves as an early instance of the basic honesty of Nick's historical sense. To put it crudely, we may say that Nick did not allow himself to return to the prologue after finishing the story but that instead he left the prologue to reflect what he felt at the time he began the story. This at least is the fiction which, it appears, the novel as a whole would have us accept.

Not everything Nick says in the prologue is finally to be discounted, of course. Undeniably Nick retains, after the fact, a distaste for *some* of the things Gatsby represented, for some of the bad taste of the *nouveau riche*, for some of the excesses of the romantic. Nick's vision of the world is dramatically modified by his contact with Gatsby, but not totally reconstructed. Furthermore Nick's initial understanding of the *nature* of Gatsby's experience does not appear to change in the recounting of the story. That "Gatsby turned out all right at the end" remains essentially true even after the reader has viewed Gatsby's end and come to the end of Nick's account. For *The Great Gatsby* proves to be neither at the beginning nor at the end essentially a tragedy.

We have seen some of the things which can be learned from Nick's introduction of himself and of his story—in particular, the sense in which the story is one of initiation. But let us begin at the beginning.

> In my younger and more vulnerable years my father gave me some advice that I've been turning over in my mind ever since.

From Shakespeare's sonnets to Eliot's *Prufrock* and beyond, it has been characteristic of modern young writers to identify their voice with that of an older, an aging man. "I grow old, I grow old," laments Eliot's *persona*. And perhaps he does. But Fitzgerald's narrator, as we are soon to learn, has only turned thirty late in the year before he begins his story. Yet he too sounds at the very beginning the note of encroaching age by contrasting his present years with his "younger and more vulnerable" ones. Throughout the novel Nick's growing awareness that the past is that which takes him ever nearer a time when he can no longer live merely on the promise of precocity or youth or education, ever nearer old age, ever nearer death is contrasted with Gatsby's abiding faith that the past is a great security which the future will soon redeem. Nick is modern man in much the sense that Prufrock is. Spiritually Gatsby belongs to a more optimistic and older generation, an older century which produced the romantic poets and the robber barons and, perhaps of no less importance for Gatsby's career, the latter-day evangelists and reformers. Thus it is Gatsby who comes to represent the vitality and the promise of youth, even though Gatsby's spiritual antecedents are older and even though the two men are, in point of chronological fact, almost exact contemporaries.

The advice of Nick's father is a Midwestern and thus somewhat democratized version of the old principle of *noblesse oblige*.

> "Whenever you feel like criticising any one," he told me, "just remember that all the people in this world haven't had the advantages that you've had."

Nick's family is not quite *noblesse*, though they are "prominent, well-to-do people," and thus Nick's obligation to the lower orders is simply to "reserve all judgments," a mode of social operation he applies to all sorts and conditions, even to "wild, unknown men" who take advantage of his toleration to burden him with their "secret griefs"—so it had happened in college and so it is shortly to happen again in Nick's relationship with Gatsby.

Nick's reserve in applying social and moral judgments contrasts in interesting ways with the calculated abandonment of reserve in much of his speech. His diction is frequently hyperbolic—"the secret griefs of wild, unknown men" is an early example. When Nick's temperamental reserve is juxtaposed with his hyperbole of statement, the result accounts in large measure for the distinctiveness of his style: "*Reserving* judgments is a matter of *infinite* hope." (My italics here as elsewhere, unless otherwise noted.) Nick himself associates the reserve with his Midwestern background. The hyperbole is more nearly characteristic of the East, a thousand novels and movies having assured us that understatement is the way of the West. More specifically the hyperbole is characteristic of the upper classes of any region who draw on the East for their education and manners. That Nick does not say "utterly ridiculous" or "perfectly charming" is only because his education serves him as more than an ornament. He says the same sort of things, only with more wit and with the slight mockery inherent in the detached and divided (because partly Midwestern) mind. Nick's speech combines with his clothes (he wears characteristically Buchanan white, for example, to Gatsby's first party), his family ties, and his education to ally him with other members of his social rank, with the Buchanans in particular, even though Nick's family is evidently less wealthy and "aristocratic" than Tom's.

Nick's distinctive way of talking (or writing) by constantly juxtaposing the reserved and the hyperbolic, the limited and the expansive, the finite and the infinite, the small and the large takes many forms in the novel and creates a dominant motif throughout. Without leaving the prologue, one finds a good example of the extended use of this motif.

> If personality is an unbroken series of successful gestures, then there was something gorgeous about him, some heightened sensitivity to the promises of life, as if he were related to one of those intricate machines that register earthquakes ten thousand miles away. This responsiveness had nothing to do with that flabby impressionability which is dignified under the name of the "creative temperament"—it was an extraordinary gift for hope, a romantic readiness such as I have never found in any other person and which it is not likely I shall ever find again. No—Gatsby turned out all right at the end; it is what preyed on Gatsby, what foul dust floated in the wake of his dreams that temporarily closed out my interest in the abortive sorrows and short-winded elations of men.

It is clear from this passage that the use of elevated, absolutist, or hyperbolic speech does not function merely (as it often functions among upper-class conversationalists like the Buchanans) to insulate against the more disconcerting emotions and to frame the witticisms of the clever. Here there is a crucial tension between Nick's native reserve and his recognition of the magnitude of Gatsby's capacities. Thus, at least in this passage, it is not the usual hyperbole which restrains the emotion, but the reserve itself. "*If* personality is an unbroken series . . . *then* there was something gorgeous. . . ." And after all the words and phrases suggesting great size or degree— "unbroken," "successful," "something gorgeous," "heightened," "intricate," "ten thousand miles away," "nothing to do with" (at least in the present context), "extraordinary," "such as I have never found in any other person and which it is not likely I shall ever find again"—come the words and phrases suggesting finiteness, smallness, shortness, incompleteness—"temporarily closed out," "abortive," "short-winded." The clause in the middle of this description, "This responsiveness had nothing to do with that flabby impressionability which is dignified under the name of the 'creative temperament',," cuts both ways. It is another way of indicating the magnitude and legitimacy of Gatsby's capacities, but its negative syntax is perhaps another expression of Nick's reserve and his vision of a finite world, a mortal existence, and a limited hope. If so, some form of that reserve and the vision which produces it run throughout the description, framing the description at beginning and end and anchoring it in the middle.

Because Nick, following the conventions of his class, characteristically overstates when he is being whimsical, his elevated language for a serious purpose (as when he is describing Gatsby's capacities) almost never seems excessive or out of character, as by all rights it should seem once we have granted that he is basically a man of great restraint. Nick persuades us to take him seriously partly by refusing to insist on the necessity for doing so. He has two saving graces— humor and candor. He makes little jokes about his tolerance (feigning sleep to avoid hearing confessions) and then brings us up short by saying flatly that it has a limit. He overstates in jest and then what would otherwise appear to be overstatement in a subsequent and serious context seems intense in an almost muted way. The reason, or part of the reason, is that Nick avoids the comedian's tired transition, "seriously, though, folks." The "secret griefs of wild, unknown men" merge with the secret griefs of Gatsby, separated only by the transitional qualification that Nick's tolerance has a limit which was somehow reached during the time Nick knew Gatsby, though Gatsby himself was "exempt" from the reaction. We have already noted another part of the reason—that the elevated language is anchored by phrases suggesting reserve and restraint. Still another part is the use of an image in a light-hearted, even jocular form which is repeated in the subsequent and serious context in a more somber and resonant form. An example in the prologue is martial imagery. When Nick is almost whimsically describing his tolerance as an undergraduate, he says, ". . . I'm inclined to reserve all judgments, a habit that has opened up many curious natures to me and also made me *the victim of not a few veteran bores.*" But when he turns to describing the limits of his tolerance, preparatory to extolling Gatsby's "heightened sensitivity," he uses the martial imagery in a way that demands it be taken with utter seriousness: "When I came back from the East last autumn I felt that I wanted the world to be in uniform and at a sort of moral attention forever. . . ." However, to take Nick seriously is not to assume, say some critics, that his judgments are morally reliable.

No one has questioned Mizener's view of Nick as an extension of one side of Fitzgerald's personality: "His use of a narrator allowed Fitzgerald to keep clearly separated for the first time in his career the two sides of his nature, the middle-western Trimalchio and the spoiled priest who disapproved of but grudgingly admired him."[4] And nearly every critic agrees with Mizener that artistically this separation works well, that indeed the use of a narrator-participant who judges not only the other characters but himself as well accounts in large measure for at least the technical superiority of *Gatsby* to Fitzgerald's other novels. What is not universally agreed upon is the extent to which, if at all, Nick is, to use R. W. Stallman's phrase, the "moral center of the book."[5] To regard Nick as the moral center is possible, says Stallman, only for the "duped reader."[6] In an article which appeared the same year as Stallman's, W. M. Frohock said much the same thing, declaring that Nick is "short on moral perspective."[7] These views perhaps stem in part from Mizener's description of Nick as a "spoiled priest," though the phrase is Fitzgerald's own, employed in the short story, "Absolution," which Fitzgerald planned at one time to incorporate in *The Great Gatsby* as an account of Gatsby's boyhood. In any case the argument of Frohock and especially of the more insistent Stallman is, to say the least, near-sighted.

Undeniably Nick Carraway is, like most of us, something less than a saint. But his moral limitations are not lost on himself. He is a highly self-conscious and consistently candid person ("as my father snobbishly suggested, and I snobbishly repeat"). His mind is receptive, active to the point of restlessness, and relentlessly analytical.

In my younger and more vulnerable years my father gave me some advice that *I've been turning over in my mind ever since.*

136

He didn't say any more, but we've always been *unusually commun-
icative in a reserved way*, and I understood that he meant a great deal more
than that.

I am still a little *afraid of missing something....*

Throughout the novel Nick analyzes the social and moral implications of the experience he is describing and does not spare himself.
Stallman discounts Nick's candor as the mask of the hypocrite, but
Stallman's "evidence" is that Nick is symbolically betrayed by his
"ragged lawn" lying next to Gatsby's "well-kept expanse" of yard, as
if morality consisted, Franklin-like, in orderly appearances. Jordan
Baker is said to "call his bluff," so that Nick is "identified" in his
immorality with her,[8] but what is obvious beyond words (though
not to Stallman) is that Nick has no bluff to call at that point, is
fully conscious of participating in a common guilt with Jordan and
others well before Jordan condemns his behavior it is clearly Jordan
Baker and the Buchanans who can never admit sin, never learn from
experience, not the Nick Carraway who after all is our only source of
knowledge about *anyone's* morality in the book. No—Carraway turns
out all right at the end, as does Gatsby. Insofar as he is part of the
foul dust in the wake of Gatsby's dreams, he knows it all too well.
    The crucial fact about Carraway, in terms of the story, is that, as
Thomas A. Hanzo has argued,[9] he serves both as a foil to Gatsby
(thus intensifying and "justifying" the reader's sympathetic involvement with Gatsby from the beginning precisely because Nick at first
does not share it) and as a participant,, through his relationship with
Jordan Baker, in the common guilt which he alone of all the guilty
characters recognizes. This recognition allows him first to return to
the West, as Hanzo says, and then to sort out the meaning inherent in
Gatsby's story, as none of the other characters can do.
    Actually Nick's most conspicuous moral flaw, to which he is
chronically subject and against which he struggles throughout the
story, is precisely his tendency to reserve judgment, to retreat from
human involvement, to allow his interest in the abortive sorrows and
short-winded elations of men to shrivel up every time those sorrows
and elations encroach upon the almost narcist complacency to which
his class and generation are so susceptible. Shortly after Nick comes
East, he begins to extricate himself from an unsuccessful love affair,
and one of the last things he does before returning to the West is to
extricate himself from another unsuccessful love affair. Like Prufrock and Hemingway's Jake Barnes, he seems somehow incapable of
establishing a fulfilling love relationship (although, unlike them, he is

able to exercise some imaginative sympathy with the women in his life).

Nick's failure in love is associated, as is Jake's, with his experience in the War. The association is made more explicit later in the novel, but even in the prologue, as we have seen, Nick begins to employ the imagery of war which he maintains throughout the story. The imagery begins as apparent whimsy—"the victim of not a few veteran bores"—but grows into more substantial stuff when Nick recalls his desire for "the world to be in uniform and at a sort of moral attention forever." Nick's characteristic movement from light or humorous forms of an image to quite serious forms of the same image fits in nicely with those hyperbolic tendencies we have observed in his speech. What begins as merely clever and socially characteristic often becomes structurally and morally significant. Thus his progressively more serious references to war prepare us for his first direct reference (in the first paragraph following the prologue) to the real war in which he had recently participated: "I graduated from New Haven in 1915, just a quarter of a century after my father, and a little later I participated in that delayed Teutonic migration known as the Great War. I enjoyed the counter-raid so thoroughly that I came back restless." The martial images and even the very phrasing tie this reference to the martial references in the prologue; "I came back restless" echoes "When I came back from the East last autumn. . . ." Thus the great shock of Nick's experience with Gatsby is allied with the great shock for most young men of his generation— the experience of world war. As the shock of the war created in young men a heightened sense of inadequacy in various forms, so the shock of Gatsby's experience created in Nick the sense of an inability to share in the experiences of any other human being—"I wanted no more riotous excursions with privileged glimpses into the human heart." If Nick's first love affair is perhaps soured partly by the war, certainly his second is turned to gall by Gatsby's death. Yet, like other returning veterans, he searches for a way to regain his losses by rebuilding his life, except that it is Gatsby's life he reconstructs as a way of regaining his own emotional and moral equilibrium.

We have noted that Nick is fond of pairing the small and large. We can expand the point by saying that he is fond of pairing in general and especially fond of pairing all sorts of opposites.

The *abnormal* mind is quick to detect and attach itself to this quality when it appears in a *normal* person. . . .

And, after *boasting* this way of my tolerance, I come to the *admission*

138

that it has a limit. Conduct may be founded on the *hard rock* or the *wet marshes*, but after a certain point I don't care what it's founded on.

Such pairings are merely stylistically interesting at first, especially when they involve simple rhetorical repetition without antithesis: "as my father *snobblishly* suggested, and I *snobbishly* repeat." But the repetition of Gatsby's name slightly later in the prologue seems almost incantatory.

> Only Gatsby, the man who gives his name to this book, was exempt from my reaction—Gatsby, who represented everything for which I have an unaffected scorn.

> No—Gatsby turned out all right at the end; it is what preyed on Gatsby, what foul dust floated in the wake of his dreams that temporarily closed out my interest in the abortive sorrows and short-winded elations of men.

The incantatory, ritualistic elements in Nick's style combine with the hyperbolic and antithetical elements and with references to the mysterious and supernatural—"abnormal," "unusual," "strangest," "shining secrets," and "curiosities"—to suggest the presence of something larger than life and more significant than mere biography or history, the presence, in short, of myth. Certainly the self-introduction is far too weighty if all that follows is simply, to use Richard Chase's description, a novel of manners.[10]

After the prologue Nick proceeds to introduce himself in more direct ways. He comes from a good family with three generations invested in an unspecified "Middle Western city." The family is evidently Scottish, with a tradition that "we're descended from the Dukes of Buccleuch"—maybe *noblesse* after all, since Buccleuch is almost as good and venerable a name in Scotland as Buchan, the root of Buchanan—but Nick, the cool realist, makes nothing of it, turning instead to "the actual founder of my line. . . , who came here in fifty-one, sent a substitute to the Civil War, and started the wholesale hardware business that my father carries on today." Nick's rather light-hearted candor about his family background can hardly represent dishonesty or hypocrisy, even to Stallman. Nick is said to resemble this founder of his line—"with special reference to the rather hard-boiled painting that hangs in father's office." This is one of the very few hints in the entire novel about Nick Carraway's physical appearance. After all that has been written about Gatsby as a shadowy figure, one can still probably "see" his physical outlines and features more clearly at the end than Nick's.

Immediately after the "hard-boiled" description occurs the description, partially quoted above, of Nick's war experience and its immediate consequences.

> ... I participated in that delayed Teutonic migration known as the Great War. I enjoyed the counter-raid so thoroughly that I came back restless. Instead of being the warm center of the world, the Middle West now seemed like the ragged edge of the universe. ...

The term "hard-boiled" derives from a manner of preparing eggs, and the phrase, "the warm center of the world," also suggests an egg with a warm center or yolk where the unborn is protected and nourished. Thus begins an important image-pattern which takes its most conspicuous form in two of the major settings of the novel, West Egg and East Egg. Not surprisingly, this pattern is often associated with another image-pattern, involving birds and winged flight, as in the subtle image, "migration," above. Fitzgerald's pencil-written holograph of *Gatsby* in the Princeton Library reveals the conscious artistry which formed these image-patterns. The "hard-boiled painting" of Nick's grandfather, for example, was originally the "stern, pig-headed painting."

Another important description of Nick in the above passage is "restless." Like "hard-boiled," it seems to denote both a physical and temperamental characteristic. "Restless" was one of Fitzgerald's favorite words. In *This Side of Paradise* his protagonist, Amory Blaine, describes restlessness as a state beyond boredom. Like Nick, Amory associates the mood with the effects of World War I. Amory is talking with Thomas Parke D'Invilliers (the same D'Invilliers who is credited with the poem prefacing *Gatsby*).

> This particular day on which he announced his ennui to Tom had been quite typical. He had risen at noon, lunched with Mrs. Lawrence, and then ridden abstractedly homeward atop one of his beloved buses.
> "Why shouldn't you be bored," yawned Tom. "Isn't that the conventional frame of mind for the young man of your age and condition?"
> "Yes," said Amory speculatively, "but I'm more than bored, I['m] restless."
> "Love and war did for you."
> "Well," Amory considered, "I'm not sure that the war itself had any great effect on either you or me—but it certainly ruined the old backgrounds, sort of killed individualism out of our generation."[11]

If, at the time of *This Side of Paradise*, the conventional frame of mind for the young men of Amory's age and condition was boredom, by the time of *The Great Gatsby* Amory's restlessness has itself become conventional; at one time or another Nick describes the following characters, in addition to himself, as restless: Tom Buchanan, Jordan Baker, and Gatsby. Jordan is said to be restless on only one occasion—after she has been sitting on a sofa reading to Tom. Gatsby, too, is associated with restlessness only once, and there the context points to an almost purely physical application, "a tapping foot somewhere or the impatient opening and closing of a hand." Nick describes himself as restless only on the occasion we have been remarking unless one counts the generic reference in Chapter III: "I began to like New York, the racy, adventurous feel of it at night, and the satisfaction that the constant flicker of men and women and machines gives to the restless eye." The supremely restless character is Tom Buchanan. With the exceptions already noted, the word "restless" and its variant forms such as "unrestfully" are always applied to Tom. Tom is the dominant member of that class of which Nick and Jordan are somewhat borderline members and to which Gatsby is a tireless if ill-fated aspirant. Note, too, that "restless" is nearly always applied to men whose common experience has been the war; the single exception is the application to Jordan Baker (a rather masculine type herself) and that, to repeat, occurs when she is mostly closely identified with Tom. Perhaps "restless" would have served as well as "lost" to describe Nick's generation of the twenties, or at least that part of it which set the standards.

Restlessness, of course, implies a more or less purposeless motion. Gale H. Carrithers, Jr., sees images of drift and purposeless action as one of the four or five major patterns of imagery in *Gatsby*, contrasting with a "pattern of imagery [which] helps to define purposeful and orderly action: winged flight; sailing toward a goal."[12] Guy Owen observes that the images of drift in *Gatsby* "show the artificiality, the insincerity and the emptiness of Daisy and Tom Buchanan's world."[13] But we must keep in mind that Nick is bound by blood, class, and background to the Buchanans and that what is true of them tends also to be true of Nick—true, that is, of the uninitiated Nick.

So, restless like the cousin and her husband whom he is shortly to visit, Nick decides to go East, unable to endure any longer the region of his birth, that "ragged edge of the universe" which no longer seems like the "warm center of the world." Once again Nick pairs opposite or at least strikingly dissimilar things, this time in a manner which suggests and perhaps even echoes Matthew Arnold's famous stanza in "Dover Beach":

The Sea of Faith
Was once, too, at the full, and round earth's shore

Lay like the folds of a bright girdle furl'd.
But now I only hear
Its melancholy, long, withdrawing roar,
Retreating, to the breath
Of the night-wind, down the vast edges drear
And naked shingles of the world.[14]

"The Sea of Faith" and "the warm center of the world" both imply the presence of life and health (fullness, warmth), while "the vast edges drear / And naked shingles of the world" inevitably suggest, as does "the ragged edge of the universe," the utter absence of animation and warmth. Arnold employs imagery drawn from clothing ("bright girdle") and houses ("shingles"), and it is hard to say whether "edges" refers to clothing, houses, or both, or something else. Nick's "ragged edge" seems more clearly to be an image of clothing, though it too could be architectural. In any case the vision of a complete world is contrasted with the vision of a fragmented world in both citations.

Nick decides to go into the bond business in the East--hardly a surprising choice for a business career in the 1920's, when everybody seemed to be in the market. Actually he decides to "learn the bond business," so that in a sense he must remain a student for a time, supported by his father, who "agreed to finance me for a year." Although approaching thirty, Nick is still not entirely independent. But when he comes East "in the spring of twenty-two" his mood reflects the "warm season"–"And so with the sunshine and the great bursts of leaves growing on the trees, just as things grow in fast movies, I had that familiar conviction that life was beginning over again with the summer." He has come East to cure his restlessness, to make a career and settle down: "I came East, permanently, I thought, in the spring of twenty-two."

Yet we already know from the prologue that Nick returned to the West in the autumn. "The frame that Nick creates," observes Robert Sklar, "is a circle, a circle that begins as it ends, in the West."[15] Sklar is correct but not comprehensive. Just as there is more than one time-scheme in the novel, there is more than one frame or structural principle. Nick's movement from West to East to West does describe a circle (in precisely the sense of a round trip), a circle Nick had made even earlier as an undergraduate and then as a soldier. But the events of 1922, falling *between*, on the one hand, his coming to the East in the spring and, on the other, his returning to the West in the fall, form a smaller frame which, in the words of

Thomas F. Staley "follows the pattern of the arc of summer."[16] Thus, instead of a single, simple structural pattern in the novel, we see patterns within patterns, commonly in the form of circles or partial circles (arcs) within still larger circles. A major theme of *Gatsby* is renewal, return, restoration—beginning over again, to use Nick's own words—and it is not hard to see how the very structure of the novel reflects this theme.

Nick's account of his first days in the East gives us some information about him which is of interest chiefly because it balances with similar information we get later about other characters. We learn that Nick has a dog, an old Dodge, and a Finnish maid. Nick later has to search for the maid in order for her to make her next ineffectual appearance in the novel, the dog runs away, and the Dodge seems to disappear until Nick sells it to the grocer near the very end: all about as lost to us as Thoreau's hound, bay horse, and turtledove. But these details have their structural and even thematic importance. References to animals (Wolfsheim's very name, for example, or the dog Myrtle Wilson buys in Manhattan), to servants (Daisy's silver-polisher or Gatsby's butler), and especially to automobiles form significant motifs which even become symbolic in some cases later in the novel. For example, the gap between Daisy's and Gatsby's worlds can be measured by the difference between the clean white or conservative blue cars she drives and the yellow "circus wagon" Gatsby favors. Once again the narrator unobtrusively begins crucial patterns of imagery and symbolism while appearing merely to toss off casual details about himself.

Perhaps the most important fact about Nick's settling in is his renting (alone, as it turns out) a bungalow in a "commuting town" outside the city. For by this fortuitous move he places himself next door to the title character, a man who is already in love with Nick's cousin. How very convenient for Gatsby and for the narrator! Fortunately Fitzgerald presents the contrivance so gradually and skillfully that it is noticed, if at all, only well after the fact. Nick does not even see his neighbor until the very end of the first chapter, does not meet him at all until the third, and knows nothing of Gatsby's love for Daisy until Jordan tells him near the end of the fourth. By that time we are willing to accept Nick's choice of a house which he had after all moved into four chapters and several weeks before. Furthermore, once we accept the premise that Nick is describing events of the past year, we can accept the improbable on the same grounds we accept it after it has occurred in real life—namely, that things simply happened that way.

143

The commuting town is West Egg, and Nick begins to feel at home after he directs a stranger to West Egg village. "And as I walked on I was lonely no longer. I was a guide, a pathfinder, an original settler." These images of the discoverer, the explorer, despite the relative inconsequence of the context in which they first appear, are repeated in the crucial, concluding section of the work, Nick's final vision of the Dutch sailors who once viewed the "fresh, green breast of the new world." Again we see Nick's fondness for pairing—in this case, the pairing of the small and the large, the private and the public, the autobiographical and the historical, the anecdotal and the mythic.

In the very next paragraph there is another pairing of opposites: "And so with the sunshine and the great bursts of leaves growing on the trees, just as things grow in fast movies, I had that familiar conviction that life was beginning over again with the summer." The leaves of course are an emblem of pastoral nature; Nick has chosen to stay as close as he can to the sort of countryside he left behind in the Midwest, "a country of wide lawns and friendly trees." But there is nothing pastoral about movies: movies are nature at third or fourth hand, artificiality itself, a product of the machine age and urbanization. Again and again Nick invokes similar antitheses, usually associating pastoral qualities with the Midwest and urban qualities with the East, so often in fact that Arthur Mizener has called *The Great Gatsby* "a kind of tragic pastoral, with the East exemplifying urban sophistication and culture and corruption, and the Middle West, . . . the simple virtues."[17] Of course, in the quotation above, the antithesis is not strictly West *vs.* East (most movies, then as now, were produced in the Far West, though the East contributed a greater share then than now) and the context is typically, for the introduction of an image-pattern, slight and even humorous. But the interested reader will easily discover many more substantial instances of nature contrasted with what J. S. Westbrook has called "a disparity of elements" which "all represent an assault upon nature."[18]

The succeeding paragraph concludes Nick's self-introduction as such. Afterward we continue to learn about him, but only indirectly as he introduces other characters and the major settings of the novel. The concluding paragraph has two main functions: (1) to induce the reader to accept the convention that a literary non-professional can write so well and (2) to reveal that the final part of Nick's initiation is the sorting out and shaping of the story. As for the first, we learn that Nick "was rather literary in college," having written "a series of very solemn and obvious editiorials for the Yale News." Again Nick's self-deprecating humor and candor persuade the reader to give him the benefit of the doubt— the editorials must not have been *all* that solemn and obvious; this man can *write*. After all, anyone who would choose Midas and Morgan and Maecenas as representatives of wealth-making must have been literary all along. All three figures in their own ways were patrons or connoisseurs of the arts—Midas, who preferred Pan's pipe to Apollo's lyre; Maecenas, who patronized Horace and Virgil; Morgan, who collected more paintings than railroads. As for the second function, Nick sees that he must give up being "that most limited of all specialists, the 'well-rounded man,' " if he is to sort out and shape Gatsby's story into a meaningful whole. The "single window" through which Nick (like Fitzgerald himself) has learned to view life sucessfully (that is, by the time he begins to write the story) is precisely the window of art. [19]

In summary, as Nick introduces himself, he makes us aware of his habits of thought and begins to unfold those patterns of thought which condition and shape our response to the story. The self-introduction (including the prologue and the seven subsequent paragraphs) undergirds the reader's confidence in Nick's intelligence and honesty and induces the reader to accept Nick as a credible narrator and stylist. Nick is an ideal narrator for a novel of this sort (that is, for a novel which is, at least in its technique, impressionistic). For in addition to any strictly literary skills and talents we may presume from his background, he has a certain detachment of temperament which allows him to observe the actions of others and of himself with a clear eye, at the same time he is developing a firm and credible moral groundwork which allows (indeed causes) him finally to make the necessary judgments he withholds earlier. It is not, of course, that Nick becomes more conventionally moral; he is no more likely at the end than at the beginning of his experience to sit in judgment on dishonest women ("Dishonesty in a woman is a thing you never blame deeply") or unfaithful husbands and wives (remember that Nick not only accompanies Tom on a liaison but actually arranges one between Daisy and Gatsby). It is essentially that he comes to see that the moral carelessness typified by the Buchanans, who "smashed up things and creatures and then retreated back into their money or their vast carelessness," is the great spirit-breaking, death-dealing sin of the age.

If Nick Carraway is then, as I have argued, the ideal kind of narrator for this kind of novel, may we conclude that he is finally the central character, not only structurally but thematically as well? I think not. For all his importance, he remains essentially a screen on which Gatsby's story is enacted. Fitzgerald's master stroke in this novel was to separate himself somewhat from the romantic idealism which his earlier novels had celebrated—not, as Henry Dan Piper has argued,[20] in order to criticize romantic idealism (or egotism, as Piper calls it) but in order to present it more truthfully and therefore more effectively. *The Great Gatsby* celebrates romantic idealism as surely as *This Side of Paradise* celebrates it, only more maturely and poignantly. Gatsby does indeed turn out all right at the end, this "son of God" living out the principles of his "religion" and even dying for them. He is, of course, not literally resurrected, but he lives again through the words of his convert and high priest, Nick Carraway. It is true that Nick is more of a St. Paul than a St. Mark, for he begins in opposition and even after conversion goes on to interpret and elaborate. But he does not subvert the lessons or the life of his subject. He is faithful to fact from the start and finally faithful to truth itself as he has come to see it—"faithful," like Gatsby, "to the end."

Hampden-Sydney College

[1] Arthur Mizener, *The Far Side of Paradise* (Boston: Houghton Mifflin, 1951), p. 172.

[2] Jerome Thale, "The Narrator as Hero," *Twentieth Century Literature*, III (July 1957), p. 72.

[3] F. Scott Fitzgerald, *The Great Gatsby* (New York: Scribners, 1925), p. 2. All subsequent quotations from the novel refer to the first printing.

[4] Arthur Mizener, *The Far Side of Paradise*, p. 171.

[5] R. W. Stallman, "Gatsby and the Hole in Time," *Modern Fiction Studies*, I (1955), p. 7.

[6] *Ibid.*

[7] W. M. Frohock, "Morals, Manners, and F. Scott Fitzgerald," *Southwest Review*, XL (Summer 1955), p. 227.

[8] R. W. Stallman, "Gatsby and the Hole in Time," p. 8.

[9] Thomas A. Hanzo, "The Theme and the Narrator of *The Great Gatsby*," *Modern Fiction Studies*, II (Winter 1956-57), pp. 183-190.

[10] Richard Chase, *The American Novel and Its Tradition* (New York: Doubleday, 1957), Chapter VIII, esp. pp. 157-167.

[11] F. Scott Fitzgerald, *This Side of Paradise* (New York: Scribners, 1920) p. 228.

[12] Gale H. Carrithers, Jr., "Fitzgerald's Triumph," in *The Great Gatsby: A Study*, ed. Frederick J. Hoffman (New York: Scribners, 1962), p. 316.

[13] Guy Owen, "Imagery and Meaning in *The Great Gatsby*," in *Essays in Modern American Literature*, ed. Richard E. Langford (Deland, Florida: Stetson University Press, 1963), p. 50.

[14] Matthew Arnold, *Poetry and Criticism of Matthew Arnold*, ed. A. Dwight Culler (Boston: Houghton Mifflin, 1961), p. 162.

[15] Robert Sklar, *F. Scott Fitzgerald: The Last Laocoön* (New York: Oxford University Press, 1967), pp. 175-176.

[16] Thomas F. Staley, "F. Scott Fitzgerald: A Study of His Development as a Novelist," (unpublished Ph.D. dissertation, University of Pittsburgh, 1962), p. 75.

[17] Arthur Mizener, *The Far Side of Paradise*, pp. 175-176.

[18] J. S. Westbrook, "Nature and Optics in *The Great Gatsby*," *American Literature*, XXXII (March 1960), p. 80.

[19] In this concluding paragraph of his self-introduction, Nick describes his financial volumes as "red and gold." Once again he introduces an important type of imagery and symbolism in a slight and relatively insignificant way. For a detailed study of the color imagery and symbolism in the novel, see my article, "Color and Cosmos in *The Great Gatsby*," *Sewanee Review*, LXXVIII (Summer 1970), pp. 427-443.

[20] Henry Dan Piper, *F. Scott Fitzgerald: A Critical Portrait* (New York: Holt, Rinehart and Winston, 1965), p. 111.

The Great Gatsby:
Troilus and Criseyde Revisited?

Nancy Y. Hoffman

Fitzgerald's *The Great Gatsby* and Chaucer's *Troilus and Criseyde,* apparently so disparate in form and tradition, actually are hauntingly similar. In fact, their resemblances and their differences lend a larger reading to Gatsby than the chauvinistically American one of the failure of that euphemism, "The American Dream"; they also apply a peculiarly modern "relevance" to Chaucer's rendering of the legend of Troilus. The attempt here, then, is to see the medieval and the modern worlds with one view, to overcome the customary bifurcation between modern American literature and its predecessors, while not denying the external environmental pressures of time and place, nor denying Chaucer's and Fitzgerald's responses to these pressures.

It may behoove the reader at this juncture—or later—to mutter, "So what?" So this: The great body of Fitzgerald criticism links author and works to the loss of the "American Dream." Fitzgerald as *persona* is wedded indissolubly to the Jazz Age he so gratuitously named. His novels and his short stories seem locked in an American frame, to which the key has been thrown away. His—or Gatsby's—or Dexter Green's—dream of innocence usually is connected with a pre-Civil War, pastoral, possibly Jeffersonian tradition. And while this approach to Fitzgerald as *genus Americanus* is valid, it is astigmatic; thus, the "universality" of Gatsby is limited by the American socio-historical view.

While Fitzgerald, with Pound and Eliot, is aware of standing on the threshold of the new art and the new sensibility of the twentieth century, he firmly fixes his novel of the "new" to the rhythms of the past with Nick's famous last line: "So we beat on, boats against the current, borne back ceaselessly into the past."[1] The stories of Gatsby and Troilus are then essentially anachronistic. Chaucer presents the tale of the Trojan and Greek camps in medieval Christian terms, an anachronism itself, as a story of the old days. Gatsby retreats from the new and clings to his dream of recapturing the past, unchanged, untarnished, undiminished. Both are "tragic pastorals,"[2] presented in a pagan, yet Christian, framework. Both straddle epochs. If Chaucer can be said to mark the beginnings of the Renaissance in England, perhaps Fitzgerald can be seen as marking the end of the Renaissance ideal in twentieth century American fiction. The linkage of the two juxtaposes the birth and perhaps the death of an attitude of mind.

And despite the multiplication of speculation on Fitzgerald's literary heritage, we know for sure that Fitzgerald *did* study Chaucer in depth, in that fall term of 1916, when he returned to Princeton apparently determined to really study.[3] Fitzgerald's nostalgia for the past, his elegiac sense of what was and can never be again, probably was reinforced by his course on Chaucer and His Contemporaries that fall, although Chaucer himself is a far greater realist than is the Fitzgerald of *Gatsby*. For the elegiac movement of *Gatsby* is the movement backward of a young land without ancestors to a time of tradition and legend, a time in which the implied legend of the knight's chivalric ideal mutely contrasts with present reality. This movement backwards transcends even "the old island here that flowered once for Dutch sailors' eyes,"[4] to a past before this past, when Fitzgerald warns young writers to "remember also, young man, you are not the first person who has ever been alone and alone."[5]

II

The structures of the two tragedies (if one accepts *Gatsby* as a tragedy), or of the two novels (if one accepts *Troilus and Criseyde* as the first psychological novel) are strikingly similar. In each work are three main characters: the boy, the girl and the seemingly well-intentioned friend. In each, themes of pursuit, flight and geographical displacement predominate. The vision of society and its corruption is central to these non-sociological works. Perhaps the view of society as a destructive force is more evident in *Gatsby* than in *Troilus*, but only superficially so. The course is backward into time past and forward from innocence lost to experience, and beyond experience to disillusionment—propelled by the ritualistic initiation of love.

In some ways, the customs and artificial values of East and West Egg reflect the medieval courtly love code, and the seeds of corruption that it spawned within itself. Although Chaucer's interpretation of the artificiality of courtly love conventions is debated, certainly Fitzgerald's theme is the falsity of standards in Gatsby's El-Greco-like world. Throughout *Troilus,* people constantly posture, try on

149

masks, much as they play roles in the society of East and West Egg, and in the world of the Wilsons.

Fear of what their peers will say dominates the medieval and the modern. While Gatsby does not seem to care what society will say about the way he makes his money, he does care deeply what Daisy will think. Nick's grass must be cut, because Daisy might notice its ragged edge; Gatsby's "career as Trimalchio" ends because Daisy disapproves; and so the lights go out in his mansion. Troilus is impotent in preventing Criseyde's departure, because—despite his protestations—he fears what people will say about their romance. Both couples are united in the rain. Pandarus exploits the elements to bring Troilus and Criseyde together at his home while a storm rages outside (the "Baby, It's Cold Outside" principle is eternally efficacious). Daisy and Jay are reunited, again at the home of an intermediary, in the midst of a rainstorm which symbolically destroys Gatsby's plans for remaking Nick's unkempt grounds. East Egg and West Egg are like the two armed camps of Greece and Troy. Self-enclosed, trapping and yet trapped by their own walls, ancient and modern stand as synecdoches for the people within.

The essence and the failure of Troilus and of Gatsby focuses about Chaucer's use of *gentilesse,* a use simultaneously "straight" and ironic, in *Troilus.* The narrator *wistfully* comments, ". . .for every wyght, I gesse, /That loveth wel, meneth but gentilesse."[6] And Troilus reassures Pandarus:

> But he that gooth, for gold or for ricchesse,
> On swich message, calle hym what the list;
> And this that thow doost, calle it gentilesse,
> Compassioun, and felawship, and trist.[7]

The crux of the problem for us is to define *gentilesse*; for Troilus and Gatsby, it is to translate true *gentilesse* into action. Alan Gaylord's definition of *gentilesse* is helpful here:

> . . .at one pole the word may be associated with manners of court and castle as an aspect of curteisie entailing genteel social conduct and gentle private relations, and at the opposite pole be more philosophically defined as *verray gentilesse,* true nobility, identified as moral virtue deriving from the Divine Idea. Between these two poles flow the alternating currents of the theme of *gentilesse* in *Troilus and Criseyde.*[8]

Between these two poles of "alternating currents" also flow the theme and the movement of *Gatsby*—both individual and social. In fact, Mr. Gaylord's description of Troilus sounds like a medieval Gatsby:

Troilus' fall and the destruction of his love dramatize the same kind of superficiality and even self-deception in the use of courtly language and morals which Chaucer recognized in the nobility of his own day. Troilus' characterization in its entire development is the depiction of a potential for one kind of *gentilesse* which is never realized because another is held in its place. The tragedy of Troilus is then the tragedy of his *gentilesse*.[9]

How closely this resembles Nick's perceptive accounting:

The truth was that Jay Gatsby of West Egg, Long Island, sprang from his Platonic conception of himself. He was a son of God—a phrase which, if it means anything, means just that—and he must be about His Father's business, the service of a vast, vulgar, and meretricious beauty. So he invented just the sort of Jay Gatsby that a seventeen year-old boy would be likely to invent, and to this conception he was faithful to the end.[10]

Both Troilus and Gatsby, then, substitute a false concept of *gentilesse,* a concept of the self conceived in their youth, a concept to which they devote a pure fidelity unworthy of their vision. Yet it is this very fideltiy that elevates them, while the clay feet of the object destroys them as they enact their dream.

Both Troilus and Gatsby present as protagonists in "the archetypal theme of the young man from the provinces." It may seem strange to so view Troilus, mighty Priam's son, whose valor and societal position act as a cynosure for Criseyde. But Troilus has experience on the battlefield only, just as Gatsby is knowledgeable with big-time gamblers and lost in the worldly jungles of Tom Buchanan and Daisy Fay. Troilus and Gatsby thus demonstrate the theme of a man thrown back on his own character, cut off from society. Troilus already is cut off by the exigencies of the way between the Greeks and the Trojans. He further removes himself by his dream of love, by his loss of or distortion of *gentilesse,* by his abdication of responsibility as the king's son. Gatsby, as James Gatz from North Dakota, is cut off by his birth as a Westerner in an Eastern culture, by his circumstances initially as a poor boy among the rich and later as a nouveau riche among the decadent Old Guard, by his lack of hereditary *gentilesse.*

Chaucer's and Fitzgerald's internal theme is of the man from the outer moral provinces moving into society, from innocence to experience within the self, as well as moving toward the common experience of all men. For the ideal of love, although unworthy in both instances, returns them to a greater society—that of all men. In Chaucer's terms, they learn *caritas.* The Troilus, who mocked the

151

lovers in the first scene, finds he is no better than they. The Gatsby, who first kisses Daisy, consciously before the kiss (in contrast to Troilus) realizes its implications, the sacrifice of personal ambition for its own sake.

But love, as expressive of the will of the self, is destructive of society, as well as being destroyed by that society's code. If Fitzgerald's elephant crushes the fox, at least the fox bites back. Love makes Troilus an even more ferocious killer; and perhaps this accounts for Gatsby's Army success, his collection of medals from every Allied government, even "little Montenegro down on the Adriatic Sea!"[11] Modern civilian life, however, frowns upon open killing as a means of attracting feminine attention. Gatsby must substitute wealth and its accoutrements for medals. This is less a transformation of Troilus' standard, than a replacing of older values with an updated price-cost ratio.

An acute sense of society's transiency, of human mutability, permeates the two stories. Troilus visits Criseyde's empty house, while Gatsby spends the last of his Army pay to walk the streets of Louisville. Both erect false shrines to their false goddesses in the romanticization of "The Street Where You Live." And there is another visit to an abandoned house of dreams, perhaps even another romanticization of an empty house of possibility: Nick's final homage to Gatsby's empty mansion, when he erases the obscene commentary on the front stairs. None of these "homes" are real, any more than is Troilus' room where he mourns and moans of his love for Criseyde, the Buchanan's mansion, or Tom and Myrtle's apartment. Significantly, the confrontation between Gatsby and Tom takes place in that home away from home, a rented New York hotel room. The sense of displacement is acute in both works. Both protagonists are displaced emotionally, sexually and psychologically. The implicit question arises whether it is possible for any man to find a home in a society bifurcated by war into armed camps, or by financial and social barriers into insiders and outsiders, *alazons* and *eirons*.

But if Troilus and Gatsby are innocents, then Criseyde and Daisy represent experience. Neither girl is a virgin. Criseyde is a widow, Daisy a married woman. Color is absent in their dress. Criseyde appears in widow's black, just as Daisy reclines on the couch in her invertedly symbolic white. Described as exemplars of womanly perfection—externally, each has an aura of something heavenly, not quite human. For the modern, the discrepancy between appearance and reality in Daisy reveals that even heaven has gone sour, is not possible in a universe where "Whirl is king, having driven out Zeus."[12] For the medieval, heaven never is possible in human terms, only in the extra-human, the Christian concept of the universe. Both women are idealized objects for their lovers. The dream must be greater than reality at all times. Nick limns the impossibility of Gatsby's illusion of love in words that suggest Troilus as well:

> There must have been moments even that afternoon when Daisy tumbled short of his dreams—not through her own fault, but because of the colossal vitality of his illusion. It had gone beyond her, beyond everything. He had thrown himself into it with a creative passion, adding to it all the time, decking it out with every bright feather that drifted his way. No amount of fire or freshness can challenge what man will store up in his ghostly heart.[13]

At the risk of sounding cynical, perhaps the insurmountable differences between men and women, the lack of communication between the sexes thematic throughout literature, are symbolized by the difference between Criseyde and Daisy, on the one hand, and Troilus and Gatsby, on the other. Troilus and Gatsby are romanticists. Criseyde and Daisy are pragmatists, self-interested realists, who are romantically idealized by their lovers' distorted ideal of *gentilesse*. Criseyde and Daisy opt for life with all its defects—and they are well aware of its defects. Criseyde swoons, Troilus contemplates suicide, but Criseyde revives and shudders to think that she might have followed him in death. At the nexus of the story, she chooses life and briskly offers her own solution:

> But hoo, for we han right ynough of this,
> And lat us rise and streight to bedde go,
> And there lat us speken of oure wo.[14]

With the same concern for her own life at any cost, Daisy apparently never thinks of offering the information that she was driving the death car. The Buchanan-Fay law of self-preservation modernizes the medieval "lawe of kynde."

Lest Daisy and Criseyde sound too much like the "bitch-goddesses" of the twenties, there is a malleability about them, a need for direction and a responsiveness to male captaincy that is eternally feminine (Women's Lib to the contrary). They need a man to take charge of them. The problem is that one man is almost as good as another. When Gatsby goes off to war, Daisy. . .

...was feeling the pressure of the world outside, and she wanted to see him and feel his presence beside her and be reassured that she was doing the right thing after all. . . . And all the time something within her was crying for a decision. She wanted her life shaped now, immediately—and the decision must be made by some force—of love, of money, of unquestionable practicality—that was close at hand.[15]

Criseyde responds to Diomede, as she has responded to Pandarus' offer to join "the dance of life," much as Daisy does hundreds of years later:

> Retornyng in hire soule ay up and down
> The wordes of this sodeyn Diomede,
> His grete estat, the peril of the town,
> And that she was allone and hadde nede
> Of frendes help. And thus bygan to brede
> The cause whi, the sothe for to telle
> That she took fully purpose for to dwelle.[16]

An attempted defense for Criseyde and Daisy should be offered, for they have been excoriated by their critics. Criseyde's name is, as she predicts, a synecdoche in literature for the tramp, particularly in the versions of her tale by Henryson and Shakespeare. Daisy represents the corruption of the American dream. In some ways it is easier to defend Criseyde, alone in an alien land, than to defend Daisy, who responds to Gatsby's idolatry with a myth of her own, who approves Gatsby's ends but not his means—and never really believes in his ends either. And Daisy has Tom, no matter how dubious his morality—or hers. Criseyde has no one, for certainly Calchas is no ally. Gatsby dies, ever the romantic, in protecting Daisy's name, in shielding her from the consequences of her crime. He assumes a responsibility for her that Troilus does not assume for Criseyde, when the suggestion is made that she be bartered for Antenor. With Criseyde, only the nobly-detached Hector, like Gatsby a defender of lost causes, will speak out against the trade. But Hector's nobility also is deluded. He says his society will not traffic in women; and yet, of course, it does—for this traffic is the basis of the Greco-Trojan conflict.

Tom inherits something of both Calchas and Diomede. Calchas, the uncaring father who runs off to the Greek camp, claims Criseyde in an outburst of belated fatherly emotion just when she needs or wants him the least. Tom can play around with women whenever and wherever he wishes, but he is upset at the thought of Daisy's meeting Gatsby when he did not know about it. His sense of husbandly responsibility is as ill-timed and hypocritical as is Calchas's paternalism. Diomede's direct approach to Criseyde is translated into Tom's cynical relationship with Myrtle Wilson. In Calchas' and Diomede's attitudes toward Criseyde, in Tom's responses to Daisy and Myrtle, there is a sense of the supreme male ego striving for domination. And this male sense of "look what you have missed" crops up in Pandarus' campaign for Criseyde, in contrast to Nick's initial rôle of disinterested intermediary.

Nick plays a dual rôle, however. He is both Pandarus and Chaucer, the narrator as *naïf.* In "Winter Dreams," the short story that is father to *Gatsby,* Fitzgerald is narrator and advisor to the reader, much as Chaucer comments on the action of *Troilus.* But in "Winter Dreams" there is no intermediary between Dexter Green and Judy Jones. Time, instead of disloyalty, renders the dream worthless. In *Il Filostrato,* Pandarus is of the same generation as Troilus, but Chaucer transforms him into the older, meddling but well-meaning, friend; Fitzgerald, on the other hand, creates his agent, Nick, as the same generation as his protagonist. The difference in generations between Pandarus and Nick may account for the difference in their motivations to action. Pandarus, older, devoting himself to an unreturned love—a devotion which he warns Troilus against when Criseyde is found wanting—is motivated by the desire for vicarious life and love that is the hallmark of the generation that "has been there before." Nick is animated by the unfolding mystery of Gatsby's life; he is caught in the tension of the romance of Gatsby as *persona,* as holder of the dream inviolate.

Despite their difference in age, both Pandarus and Nick recapitulate experience through their relationships with Troilus and Gatsby. When Criseyde fails, Pandarus wishes her dead, just as Nick offers his one tribute to Gatsby's concept of *gentilesse* that pronounces the world of Daisy and Tom as dead:

"They're a rotten crowd," I shouted across the lawn. "You're worth the whole damn bunch put together." [17]

At this moment in each story, the go-betweens assume the responsibility of a moral judgment on the action. They reveal that they have become involved, whether willingly or unwillingly. Just as Troilus and Criseyde must be drawn into the "dance of life," so, too, must Nick and Pandarus enter the action. They have reached the point of no return with the spectatorial attitude. And yet, although involved, finally they withdraw. Pandarus walks off; he can offer Troilus no more, and he is seen no more. Nick returns to the stability of the Mid-West; he wants "no more riotous excursions with privileged glimpses into the human heart."[18] The fascination for a Nick and a Pandarus of the Gatsbys and the Troiluses may be rooted, however, in the envy of the "unillusioned" of those who still hold fast to illusion, no matter how mistakenly based.

The question of the honesty of Nick and Pandarus has been raised, and their very ambivalence links them. Both carefully and pointedly protest their honesty, although R. W. Stallman and D. W. Robertson feel they "protesteth too much."[19,20] To view Nick as a dishonest narrator would be to deny the validity of the story he tells; yet no one can be as straightforward as he claims, so that the question of his honesty may be another form of self-delusion in Fitzgerald's novel. In contrast, Pandarus sees the problem as it is and says his actions will be viewed as "pandering" by the outside world. Troilus overcomes Pandarus' objections with a little pandering of his own: he offers his sisters to Pandarus in an action that anticipates Gatsby's offering Nick an interest in one of his "deals." Both Pandarus and Nick reject their offers. And significantly, after lunching with Gatsby and Meyer Wolfsheim, Nick "insisted on paying the check."[21]

III

Gatsby and Troilus are then in hot pursuit of the grail. The irony of both their stories is that, while the quest may be holy, the grail has been desecrated; and it is this that destroys them. And Gatsby's grail quest is influenced directly or indirectly by the tradition of Troilus. It is Gatsby's fate to be pursued by the Furies in Chaucer's Proems, to have to "find a way to live as man once had lived with a purpose and a meaning which transcended personal fate."[22] Yet while transcending the personal, as in his memorable remark that Daisy's love for Tom was "just personal," while depersonalizing the ideal, he still remains circumscribed by the boundaries of the self. Gatsby's and Troilus' romance is that of seeing themselves in the center of something that doesn't have any meaning. The tragedy of their *gentilesse* is that they believe so fervently in their own words and in the life that they believe these words describe. Thus, Nick judges Gatsby's tragedy as the loss of Eden, the loss of the ability to believe in Eden, judges that "he must have felt that he had lost the old warm world, paid a high price for living too long with a single dream."[23]

Classical and Romantic tragedy by definition emphasize the hero's choice as dictated by his *hamartia,* his fatal flaw. It is Troilus' and Gatsby's single-mindedness, their looking at a pluralist society through a "single window," their "heightened sensitivity to the promises of life,"[18] that destroys them. Yet it is just their individualistic tenacity to the promises of a "meretricious" ideal that lends them a tragic dimension impossible in contemporary literature, where the protagonist operates "not with a bang but a whimper."

The epigram for both Gatsby and Troilus is inscribed by Robert Frost, the modern poet who resembles Chaucer:

> Possessing what we still were unpossessed by,
> Possessed by what we now no more possessed.
> Something we were witholding made us weak
> Until we found out that it was ourselves
> We were withholding from our land of the living.[24]

We not only are possessed by our possessions, we are possessed even more by that which we would possess, for appearance and reality bear no relation to each other. Paul MacKendrick reflects that "The Gatzes of this world can never long possess the Daisy Fays."[25] Troilus' lesson for Gatsby is that the pursuit is pointless, for even the Troiluses of this world (if there are any) can never long possess the Criseydes. This is the meaning of Troilus' epilogue—that all human endeavor comes to nothing when potential for greatness, when *gentilesse,* is wasted on that which is unworthy of it. This is possibly the meaning too of *Gatsby* as envisioned by Fitzgerald—Catholic, Puritan, moralist and "mediocre caretaker" of his own "talent."[26]

St. John Fisher College

---

[1] F. Scott Fitzgerald, *The Great Gatsby* (New York: Scribners, 1925), p. 218.

[2] Sergio Perosa, *The Art of F. Scott Fitzgerald* (Ann Arbor: University of Michigan Press, 1965), p. 52.

[3] Janet Miller, Department of English, Princeton University, personal communication, 1970. "F. Scott Fitzgerald took English 303 in the fall term of 1916. The catalog describes the course: '303—Chaucer and His Contemporaries. Reading will include the greater part of Chaucer's poetry, with selections from Langland, Gower, Wyclif and the author of Sir Gawain and the Green Knight.' " Unfortunately, the Fitzgerald collection of the Firestone Library at Princeton does not contain the required thesis for this course, "a thesis of considerable length, embodying the results of independent investigation."

[4] Fitzgerald, op. cit., p. 217.

[5] F. Scott Fitzgerald, "Introduction to the Modern Library Edition" of *The Great Gatsby* (New York: Modern Library, 1934).

⁶ Geoffrey Chaucer, *Troilus and Criseyde* in *The Poetical Works of Chaucer*, 2nd. ed., ed. F. N. Robinson (Boston: Houghton Mifflin, 1937), p. 433, III, Ll. 1147-1148.

⁷ Ibid., p. 425, III, Ll. 400-403.

⁸ Alan T. Gaylord, *"Gentilesse* in Chaucer's *Troilus,"* *SP*, LXI (Jan. 1964), p. 21.

⁹ Ibid.

¹⁰ Fitzgerald, *Gatsby*, p. 118.

¹¹ Ibid., p. 79.

¹² Walter Lippmann, *A Preface to Morals* (1929) (New York: MacMillan, 1947), p. 1, citing Aristophanes.

¹³ Fitzgerald, *Gatsby*, p. 116.

¹⁴ Chaucer, op. cit., p. 454, IV, Ll. 1242-1244.

¹⁵ Fitzgerald, *Gatsby*, p. 181.

¹⁶ Chaucer, op. cit., p. 470, V, Ll. 1023-1029.

¹⁷ Fitzgerald, *Gatsby*, p. 185.

¹⁸ Ibid., p. 2.

¹⁹ R. W. Stallman, "F. Scott Fitzgerald," *The Houses that James Built* (East Lansing: Michigan State Univ. Press, 1961), pp. 131-157.

²⁰ D. W. Robertson, Jr., *A Preface to Chaucer* (Princeton: Princeton Univ. Press, 1962), *passim,* especially pp. 472-502.

²¹ Fitzgerald, *Gatsby*, p. 89.

²² Thomas Hanzo, "The Theme and the Narrator of *The Great Gatsby,"* *MFS,* II (Winter, 1956-1957), p. 187.

²³ Fitzgerald, *Gatsby*, p. 194.

²⁴ Robert Frost, "The Gift Outright," *In the Clearing* (New York: Holt, Rinehart and Winston, 1962).

²⁵ Paul MacKendrick, *"The Great Gatsby* and Trimalchio," *Classical J.,* XLV (April, 1950), p. 309.

²⁶ Lionel Trilling, "F. Scott Fitzgerald," *The Liberal Imagination* (New York: Viking, 1950), p. 235, citing Fitzgerald.

The Dramatic Novel, *The Great Gatsby*, and *The Last Tycoon*

Alan Margolies

Despite his well-known defense of *Tender is the Night*—"*Gatsby* was shooting at something like *Henry Esmond* while this was shooting at something like *Vanity Fair*. The dramatic novel has canons quite different from the philosophical, now called psychological, novel. One is a kind of *tour de force* and the other a confession of faith. It sould be like comparing a sonnet sequence with an epic"[1] — F. Scott Fitzgerald was never completely satisfied with his philosophical novel. Thus, when he began to plan *The Last Tycoon*, he was determined to return to the more successful format of *The Great Gatsby*. The new work would be "between 50 and 60,000 words long" (the length of *The Great Gatsby*), he wrote Maxwell Perkins in January 1939, and "one of those novels that can only be written at the moment and when one is full of the idea—as *Tender* should have been written in its original conception, all laid on the Riviera."[2] Later that year, in a letter to Kenneth Littauer of *Collier's*, he further stressed the relationship among these works. "Unlike *Tender Is the Night*," he wrote, "[*The Last Tycoon*] is not the story of deterioration—it is not depressing and not morbid in spite of the tragic ending. If one book could ever be 'like' another, I should say it is more 'like' *The Great Gatsby* than any other of my books. But I hope it will be entirely different—I hope it will be something new, arouse new emotions, perhaps even a new way of looking at certain phenomena."[3]

Inasmuch as Fitzgerald never completed his Hollywood novel, one can never be entirely certain whether he would have achieved these effects. On the other hand, from the author's papers as well as from other material, it *is* possible to demonstrate how heavily he relied on his knowledge of the drama, and specifically, on *The Great Gatsby*, his previous dramatic novel.[4]

I

The young Fitzgerald had become aware of dramatic form while writing plays in St. Paul and later as a participant in the Triangle Club productions at Princeton University. In a number of early stories, to obtain stage-like effects, he had used theatrical metaphors; in some, he had used play dialogue and stage directions, at times employing these devices to avoid a too-intrusive narrator; and in others—for example, the ending of *The Beautiful and Damned*—he had successfully used the dramatic scene. During the summer of 1922, he seemed to be moving even closer to the form of the dramatic novel when he proposed that his next major work, about the Middle West and New York in the 1880s, would "be centered on a smaller period of time"[5] than *This Side of Paradise* or *The Beautiful and Damned* and would be "something extraordinary and beautiful and simple and intricately patterned."[6] Undoubtedly, he also was becoming aware of other writers at that time who were experimenting with these methods. "A single subject, embodied in a dramatic situation, developed logically, without interruption and without interference, to its inevitable conclusion—this," said Joseph Warren Beach some years later, "was their idea of a novel."[7] Finally, in 1925, after having devoted the major portion of two years to his unsuccessful play, *The Vegetable*, and having absorbed even more about the theatre, Fitzgerald completed *The Great Gatsby*, a work that fell squarely within the tradition of the dramatic novel.

In his method of narration, Fitzgerald eliminated himself entirely from the work, and, instead, focusing upon Nick Carraway, re-created in fictional terms the aesthetic distance between the audience in the theatre and the actors on stage. At one point, while in Myrtle Wilson's apartment, Nick suggests his dual role as observer and participant. "High over the city," he states, "our line of yellow windows must have contributed their share of human secrecy to the casual watcher in the darkening streets, and I [was] him too, looking up and wondering. I was within and without, simultaneously enchanted and repelled by the inexhaustible variety of life."[8] Maxwell Perkins understood and approved of this effect. "You adopted exactly the right method of telling it," he wrote Fitzgerald, "that of employing a narrator who is more of a spectator than an actor: this puts the reader upon a point of observation on a higher level than that on which the characters stand and at a distance that gives perspective. In no other way could your irony have been so immensely effective, nor the reader have been enabled so strongly to feel at times the strangeness of human circumstance in a vast heedless universe."[9]

Fitzgerald also placed great emphasis upon the scene, and Perkins recognized this when he wrote, "If one enjoyed a rapid railroad journey I would compare the number and vividness of pictures your living words suggest, to the living scenes disclosed in that way."[10] In the novel, Fitzgerald assisted his readers in visualizing these scenes by introducing a number of them with a precise and terse account of time and place. He bathed his characters in all kinds of light and frequently delineated them by placing them in front of the light source. Conversely, a type of romantic darkness ends five of the nine chapters. Nick's first view of Gatsby at the end of chapter one, for example, is of a figure stretching his arms out to the green light at the end of Daisy Buchanan's dock. Nick looks away for a second; then he turns back, but the figure is gone. "When I looked once more for Gatsby he had vanished," says Nick, "and I was alone again in the unquiet darkness."[11] It is as if the theatre curtain has suddenly dropped—or a motion picture scene has faded out—before the eyes of the audience.

The following year, while reviewing a number of Ernest Hemingway's short stories, Fitzgerald alluded to this type of effect:

> The next two stories ["The End of Something" and "The Three Day Blow"] describe an experience at the edge of adolescence. You are constantly aware of the continual snapping of ties that is going on around Nick [Adams]. In the half-stewed, immature conversation before the fire you watch the awakening of that vast unrest that descends upon the emotional type at about eighteen. Again there is not a single recourse to exposition. As in "Big Two-Hearted River," a picture—sharp, nostalgic tense—develops before your eyes. When the picture is complete a light seems to snap out, the story is over.[12]

The tradition of the dramatic novel also necessitated the suggestion that time move relentlessly towards a conclusion, and the limited time span in *The Great Gatsby*, from late spring to early fall, intensifies even further this feeling of destiny. At the very beginning of the work, Nick optimistically compares the movement of time in the novel to a speeded-up movie. "And so with the sunshine and the great bursts of leaves growing on the trees, just as things grow in fast movies," he says, "I had that familiar conviction that life was beginning over again with the summer."[13] Later, in the middle of a hot summer day, Jordan Baker, also hopeful, says, "Life starts all over again when it gets crisp in the fall."[14] But Nick and Jordan are unable to foresee what is to come. Myrtle Wilson is closer to the reader's understanding of what will happen when she describes how she felt when she first was attracted to Tom Buchanan: "All I kept thinking

161

about, over and over, was 'You can't live forever; you can't live forever.' "[15] "In the dramatic novel," said Edwin Muir, "fate is visible; we see it unfolding in the world, on which beats for the time being a more intense light than that of ordinary day; and because we see it manifested we understand it and acquiese in it."[16]

But this swift movement from introduction to conclusion also occurs in *The Great Gatsby* because of the novel's structural similarity to that of a play. The work contains an exposition; a crisis in the exact center of the book where Gatsby regains Daisy Buchanan, and, for the moment, succeeds in recapturing the past; a climax ending with the death of Myrtle Wilson; and a conclusion, Gatsby's death.

More specifically, chapter one is equivalent to a first act; chapters two through five, ending with Gatsby and Daisy once more together, make up a second act; chapters six and seven, ending with the conspiracy of the Buchanans, are equivalent to a third act; chapter eight, ending with Gatsby's death, is the fourth act; and chapter nine, Gatsby's funeral, is the concluding act.

Did Fitzgerald consciously structure the work into these five acts? No plans are available to prove or disprove this. However, during the next fifteen years, the novelist increasingly indicated his awareness of the relationship between the drama and his fiction. In 1930, for example, while inquiring about the possibility of selling the short story "Majesty" to Hollywood, he suggested its adaptability to the screen. "It's constructed dramatically like a play," he wrote, "and has some damn good dramatic scenes in it."[17] Five years later, in 1935, he told Laura Guthrie that his usual story had a three-part quality similar to that of a stage work.[18] Finally, while working in Hollywood during the last three years of his life, he fashioned a number of film outlines divided into episodes, acts, and, in at least one case, chapters of a novel.[19] At about this same time, while planning *The Last Tycoon*, he drew up a number of diagrams divided into five acts as well as episodes and chapters. The last of these contains sufficient parallels to *The Great Gatsby* to affirm that, if not earlier, by the time of *The Last Tycoon*, Fitzgerald recognized that *The Great Gatsby*, too, was constructed on a five-act dramatic curve.

II

Fitzgerald constructed the earliest extant diagram for the Hollywood novel probably during the late spring of 1939. In this schema, labeled "version Y," he divided the work into ten chapters, one more than *The Great Gatsby*, broke down the chapters into major episodes, estimated the number of words per sequence, and, further, determined a total number of words about equal to that of the earlier novel:

CHAPTERS   (version Y)[20]

I.	The airplane trip; and Cecelia decides to tell her story	7500
	A. Introduction	
	B. In some stop—Schwartz and Rogers	
	C. With Stahr in Front	
II.	A. Stahr meeting Thalia	2500
	B. Stahr meeting Rogers—Rogers conversation with Stahr	2500
III.	Thalia's response to Stahr	2500
IV.	Thalia and part of her story	2500
V.	How Stahr worked out a picture	5000
	A. Story conference	
	B. Railroad episode and idealism about making non-profit picture	
	C. Stahr's Visit to Sets	
VI.	A. Cecelia's seduction and her love for Stahr)	
	B. A good part of Stahr's story)	7500
	C. Cecelia takes her father off guard)	
VII.	Stahr and Thalia alone—Stahr's house	5000
VIII.	A. Robinson, the Cutter & Dartmouth	2500
	B. Stahr sick in East hears.	
	C. On Coast. The meeting of writers, etc.	2500
	D. Firing of secretaries, technicians, etc.	2500
IX.	A. Stahr's return and anger	
	B. Bradogue Plot	
	C. Stahr's departure to include big scene for Thalia	2500
X.	A. The Fall of the Plane	5000
	B. Epilogue in Hollywood	2500
		52,500

In addition, the novelist planned to use the ending of *The Great Gatsby* as a pattern for the second half of the tenth chapter. He wrote:

> The epilogue can model itself quite fairly on the last part of Gatsby. We go back to Cecelia as a narrator and have her tell it with the emphasis on herself so that what she reveals about what happened to her father, to the company, to Thalia [Kathleen in later versions] seems to be revealed as if she was now a little weary of the story, and told all she knew about it and was returning to her own affairs. In it she might discuss whom she married and try to find an equivalent of that nice point in Gatsby where the narrator erases the dirty word that the boy has scrawled in chalk against the door step. . . . I think that I'll leave Thalia's life in the air, her character unimpaired, deepened without quite the pettiness in the end of Gatsby. . . .[21]

Then, later that year, he drew up four diagrams within what seems to be a very brief period and used the last as a guide for his manuscript. The first of these plans was far more detailed than the "version Y" schema. On the left side of the page Fitzgerald divided the novel into eight chapters, one less than *The Great Gatsby*, and thirty-two, then thirty-one episodes. In the center he structured the novel as if it were a play, dividing it into five acts and also subtitling each act as had been the custom in the theatre at one time. He wrote: "Act I (The Plane) . . . Act II (The Circus) . . . Act III (The Underworld) . . . Act IV (The Murderers)." For "Act V," at first he wrote in parentheses, "Fade Out," possibly an allusion to the slow "dying fall" ending of *Tender is the Night* or, more likely, an allusion to a film technique. But then he crossed out these words and in their place wrote "End" in parentheses. Finally, on the right side of the page he included a few notes for the first four chapters.[22]

The novel was to have a dramatic curve similar to that in *The Great Gatsby*. Producer Stahr's seduction of Thalia, his girlfriend, extremely crucial to the plot (Fitzgerald had written earlier, "This love affair is the meat of the book")[23], was to occur in the "DEAD MIDDLE" exactly where, in *The Great Gatsby*, Gatsby meets Daisy Buchanan again after five years. An episode titled "Last fling with Thalia. Old Stars in heat wave at Encino" was intended to evoke the same mood as the scene on the hot summer day in the New York hotel in the earlier novel. Each of these episodes was intended to lead directly to the climactic section—in *The Great Gatsby* to Myrtle Wilson's death and in *The Last Tycoon* to Thalia's husband's awareness of her affair with Stahr. To underscore this dramatic movement, Fitzgerald wrote in the diagram, "Baird [an early name for Brady,

Stahr's partner] gets to Smith [Thalia's husband]." In a separate note he wrote, "Climax is the discovery of Smith."[24]

The novelist even tried to repeat the effect of the parties at Gatsby's house. For the chapter illustrating Stahr's day at the studio he wrote, "Chapter C is equal to guest list & Gatsby's party. Throw everything into this."

In his second diagram, he added a time scheme appropriate to the dramatic novel, the spring to fall pattern of *The Great Gatsby*. Act I, chapter A, the plane ride bringing Stahr and a number of others from the East to Los Angeles—the exposition—was to take place in June. The next three chapters (B through D), which comprised the second act and introduced Thalia, portrayed Stahr's average day at the studio, and ended with the crisis, the seduction scene, were to occur during July and early August. The remainder of August and September was to be the time period for act III (chapters E and F), and this act would end with the climax, Smith's discovery of Thalia's affair with Stahr. The producer's departure on the doomed airplane would take place at the end of September and bring act IV (chapter G) to its conclusion. And act V, the plane crash and the funeral, would occur from September 30 through October.

At another place in this diagram Fitzgerald alluded to the Waste Land symbolism previously used in *The Great Gatsby*. Next to chapter D, which was to end in episode 15 with Stahr's seduction of Thalia, he wrote, "Three episodes. Atmosphere in 15 most important. Hint of Waste Land of the house too late."

Finally, in this second diagram, Fitzgerald added additional titles or directions next to each act. Near "Act I (The Plane)" he wrote "Stahr"; "Act II (The Circus)" was now also labeled "The Movement toward Thalia"; "Act III (The Underworld)" was now also "The Struggle"; "Act IV (The Murderers)" was also "Defeat"; and "Act V (End)" was also labeled "Silence."

These directions were revised slightly in the third diagram. Instead of "The Movement toward Thalia" (in act II), Fitzgerald substituted "Stahr and Kathleen" (Thalia's new name). Act V was also changed. Now it read "The End" and "Epilogue." In addition, Fitzgerald reordered his chapters in this third schema, splitting the third chapter into two parts. Apparently this too was a purposeful effort to achieve a closer relationship to the form of *The Great Gatsby*, for the chapter with the seduction scene marked "DEAD MIDDLE" was now the fifth chapter, the same number as the equivalent chapter in the middle of the earlier novel. And now both novels had nine chapters.

III

While writing *The Last Tycoon*, Fitzgerald alluded a number of times to the effect he was trying to achieve. "I am deep in the novel, living in it, and it makes me happy," he wrote ecstatically to his wife. "It is a *constructed* novel like *Gatsby*, with passages of poetic prose when it fits the action, but no ruminations or side-shows like *Tender*. Everything must contribute to the dramatic movement."[25] His concern with form also can be seen in a note pertaining to Vardis Fisher's *Children of God*, published the previous year, as well as pertaining to a projected scene later in *The Last Tycoon* in which Stahr wants to produce an artistic but unprofitable film about the Mormons. "In Fisher's Mormon Book," Fitzgerald wrote, "there are interesting questions of tempo *contrary* to the dramatic assumptions or at least uneasy to answer in dramatic terms. For example: at the end we get the brave men yeilding—how does Fisher show the background of that to unbelievers. I *know* it is true—but there is lack of art. On the other hand, in dramatic inevitability such as a [George S.] Kauffman scenario or an expert picture there is too much inevitability."[26]

Again, the basic unit was to be the scene. "I want to write scenes that are frightening and inimitable." he wrote in another note. "I don't want to be as intelligible to my contemporaries as Ernest who as Gertrude Stein said, is bound for the Museums. I am sure I am far enough ahead to have some immortality if I can keep well."[27]

"ACTION IS CHARACTER,"[28] he asserted in yet another note, a statement recalling not only Henry James's 1884 rejoinder to Walter Besant ("What is character but the determination of incident? What is incident but the illustration of character?")[29] as well as Edwin Muir's 1928 comment that in the dramatic novel, characters and plot are "inseparably knit together," that "the given qualities of the characters determine the action, and the action in turn progressively changes the characters, and thus everything is borne forward to an end,"[30] but, in addition, the arguments of the many dramatic critics of the late nineteenth and twentieth centuries who took issue with Aristotle's dictum giving precedence to action over character.[31] And this effect of characterization was no simple matter to achieve. "The novel is hard as pulling teeth," he wrote his wife in another letter, "but that is because it is in its early character-planting phase. I feel people so less intently than I did once that this is harder. It means welding together hundreds of stray impressions and incidents to form the fabric of entire personalities. But later it should go faster."[32]

The published version of *The Last Tycoon* shows the effect of these influences of the drama. Each act increases in intensity as it moves towards its conclusion. Act I (chapter one), the plane trip from New York to Los Angeles, ends with heightened prose as well as a lighting effect. As the plane lands, Cecelia Brady, Fitzgerald's narrator, compares Stahr favorably with Daedalus. Stahr, she says, "had flown up very high to see, on strong wings, when he was young. And while he was up there he had looked on all the kingdoms, with the kinds of eyes that can stare straight into the sun. Beating his wings tenaciously—finally frantically—and keeping on beating them, he had stayed up there longer than most of us, and then, remembering all he had seen from his great height of how things were, he had settled gradually to earth." Cecelia then describes the descent of the plane "into the warm darkness,"[33] a conclusion reminiscent of the ending of so many of the chapters in *The Great Gatsby*. In addition, the completion of the journey also lends a feeling of finality to the chapter.

In act II (chapters two through five), chapter two ends with moderate suspense, chapter three leads directly to chapter four, and chapter four again ends with a moderate amount of suspense. Everything in this second act, including the events in Stahr's day in chapters three and four, was to revolve around the relationship between Stahr and Kathleen. Despite the fact that the "DEAD MIDDLE" of the novel was to be the seduction scene, the act continues for two more episodes, and again, similar to an act in a play, ends at its most heightened pitch, the point where Stahr receives the unexpected telegram from Kathleen telling of her marriage that noon.

The influence of the drama also can be observed in the foreshadowing and contrasting of events in *The Last Tycoon*. The first plane flight, for example, contrasts with the planned plane crash in the final chapter. An ominous note at the beginning of the novel to Schwartz, the has-been film producer, foreshadows a number of deaths including Stahr's. Cecelia and Wylie White's inability in chapter one to enter the Hermitage and to grasp the meaning of its tradition was to be echoed later with Stahr's visit to Washington, where, ill with fever, he would be unable to visit the Capitol. The series of conferences at the studio in chapters three and four were to be contrasted with a later series of conferences in chapter seven.

Even so minor a character as the old-time movie actor Johnnie Swanson, who appears for a split second at the beginning of chapter two as one of the very first characters Cecelia sees when the plane lands in Hollywood, was to return at the end of the story to be a pallbearer at Stahr's funeral and eventually achieve stardom again. Here as well as elsewhere, Fitzgerald took pains to make certain that all loose ends would be tied up at the conclusion of the story.

Another aspect of the use of contrast is the manner in which Fitzgerald introduced a theme and then played variations on it. One example, related to Stahr's loss of vitality and its corollary, a need for a type of rebirth, appears a number of times. When the earthquake in chapter two shakes the set, Cecelia perceives its symbolic meaning. "For a full moment," she says, "our bowels were one with the bowels of the earth—like some nightmare attempt to attach our navel cords again and jerk us back to the womb of creation."[34] At first, Stahr is "grey with fatigue." But as reports of the ensuing floods on the sets come "his eyes . . . pick up shine."[35] Soon after, he becomes aware of Kathleen, who resembles his late wife, riding in the flooded area on a huge floating studio model of Siva, a phallic deity representing both destruction and restoration of life. Later, at a charity ball, Kathleen and Stahr "smil[e] at each other as if this was the beginning of the world." As Stahr approaches Kathleen, "vitality well[s] up in him."[36]

Sometimes this theme of the search for vitality and rebirth is handled humorously. After Kathleen and Stahr consummate their love in the roofless house on the beach, they walk outside and watch a parallel action, the grunion coming ashore at full moon to spawn.

The theme is apparent also in Stahr's ability to transmit life to others. At one point, Rodriguez, the impotent actor who has sought help widely but in vain, comes to Stahr for assistance. "I even—one day in desperation I went down to—to Claris," he confesses to Stahr. "But it was hopeless. I'm washed up."[37] Claros had been the location at Iona of one of the oracles to Apollo. Stahr, who has been described as an oracle as well as a type of Daedalus (the builder of a temple at Cumae), is able to succeed where others have failed. Within minutes, the actor leaves the producer's office apparently cured.

Stahr also give a form of new life to Pete Zavras, the Greek cameraman who has attempted suicide because rumors of his impending blindness have blackballed him throughout the film industry. The producer sends Zavras to an oculist, discovers the cameraman's eyesight to be perfect, and has the report circulated. In the published version of the novel, Zavras tells Stahr: "Before the Delphic oracle . . . . The Oedipus who solved the riddle. I wish I had my hands on the son-of-a-bitch who started the story."[38] But his statement in what seems to be the final unpublished manuscript is even more germane. " 'Before the oracle,' said Garcia [Zavras' previous name],

'The solver of Elusianian mysteries. I wish I had my hands on the son-of-a-bitch who started the story.' "[39] Here Fitzgerald united the themes of the oracle, vitality, and rebirth in a humorous reference to the Eleusinian Mysteries, a series of purification fasts, rites, and dramas portraying the legend of Demeter, Persephone, and Dionysus, supposedly forecasting resurrection and immortality, and insuring the happiness of the initiated in the future world.

Although Stahr can give vitality and permanent rebirth to others, his own rebirth is only temporary. An omniscient narrator suggests that Stahr's relationship with Kathleen can mean "new life," but the producer rejects the opportunity to abandon his work for a weekend to be with Kathleen. "It is your chance, Stahr," the narrator pleads. "Better take it now. This is your girl. She can save you, she can worry you back to life." But Stahr has hesitated, ironic for one who must make quick decisions involving millions of dollars, and the moment is lost: "He knew he could not let her go now; but something else said to sleep on it as an adult, no romantic. And not to tell her till tomorrow."[40]

Here, another theme in the novel intervenes. Kathleen's boyfriend, "the American," has changed his plans and soon will arrive to marry her. Fate does not work in one's favor all the time, as Wylie White, without grasping the irony in his statement, indicates to Schwartz at the beginning of the novel. "You'll get it all back," he says. "Another turn of the wheel and you'll be where Cecelia's papa is."[41] But White can not know that at that moment Schwartz is probably considering suicide and that within five months both Stahr and Cecelia's father, Pat Brady, also will be in the grave.

IV

Thus the tragedy would have ended. But all that Fitzgerald managed to complete were some six and a half chapters, a large amount of notes, and a reminder at the top of the last draft of chapter one, "Rewrite from mood. Has become stilted with rewriting. Don't look [at previous draft.] Rewrite from mood,"[42] suggesting that had he lived, his final version would have differed in a number of ways. After all, despite the original conception, he had already written more words than planned and the novel was only two-thirds finished. But it does seem likely that the final version still would have retained the many structural similarities to *The Great Gatsby*.

John Jay College Of
Criminal Justice, CUNY.

169

---

[1] Fitzgerald to Bishop, 7 April 1934, *The Letters of F. Scott Fitzgerald,* ed. Andrew Turnbull (New York: Scribners, 1963), p. 363. Hereafter cited as *Letters*.

[2] Fitzgerald to Perkins, 4 January 1939, *Letters*, p. 283.

[3] Fitzgerald to Littauer, 29 September 1939, in F. Scott Fitzgerald, *The Last Tycoon: An Unfinished Novel,* ed. Edmund Wilson (New York: Scribners, 1941), p. 141. All quotations from the novel are from this edition and hereafter are cited in the text. All references to the notes in this edition, however are cited in the footnotes.

[4] Others who have written about the influence of the drama and *The Great Gatsby,* to whom I am indebted for a number of ideas in this article, include Robert E. Maurer ("F. Scott Fitzgerald's Unfinished Novel, *The Last Tycoon,*" *Bucknell University Studies,* III [May 1952], pp. 139-156); Sergio Perosa (*The Art of F. Scott Fitzgerald* [Ann Arbor: Univ. of Mich. Press. 1965], pp. 163-178); and Henry Dan Piper (*F. Scott Fitzgerald: A Critical Portrait* [New York: Holt, 1965], pp. 277-286).

[5] Fitzgerald to Perkins, 20 June 1922, in Arthur Mizener, *The Far Side of Paradise: A Biography of F. Scott Fitzgerald,* 2nd ed. rev. (Boston: Houghton Mifflin Sentry, 1965), p. 162.

[6] Fitzgerald to Perkins, July 1922, in Ibid., p. 184.

[7] *The Twentieth Century Novel: Studies in Technique* (New York: Appleton, 1932), p. 307.

[8] F. Scott Fitzgerald, *The Great Gatsby* (New York: Scribners, 1925), p. 43. I have emended the quotation to conform with Fitzgerald's emendation in his copy of the novel. See Jennifer E. Atkinson, "Fitzgerald's Marked Copy of *The Great Gatsby,*" *Fitzgerald/Hemingway Annual: 1970* (Washington: Microcard Editions, 1970), p. 32.

[9] Perkins to Fitzgerald, 20 November 1924, *Editor to Author: The Letters of Maxwell Perkins,* ed. John Hall Wheelock (New York: Scribners, 1950), p. 38.

[10] Ibid., p. 40.

[11] Fitzgerald, *Gatsby*, p. 26.

[12] F. Scott Fitzgerald, "How to Waste Material: A Note on My Generation," *Bookman,* 63 (May 1926), pp. 264-265. The image appears again at the end of the last scene on the Riviera in *Tender is the Night* ([New York: Scribners, 1934], p. 406).

[13] Fitzgerald, *Gatsby*, p. 5.

[14] Ibid., p. 142.

[15] Ibid., p. 43.

[16] *The Structure of the Novel* (1928; rpt. London: Hogarth Press, 1963), pp. 110-111.

[17] Fitzgerald to Ober, [Received 13 May 1930], *Letters*, p. 396.

[18] The statement, made on 12 September 1935, is on p. 136 of Laura Guthrie Hearne's diary on file in the F. Scott Fitzgerald Papers, Princeton University Library, Princeton, New Jersey. Hereafter cited as Fitzgerald papers.

[19] See e.g., Fitzgerald's outline for a movie based on the Basil Duke Lee stories, Fitzgerald Papers.

[20] Fitzgerald Papers.

[21] Ibid.

[22] Fitzgerald's method for the formulation of these later diagrams was to enter changes in longhand onto the typed diagram, have it retyped, and then make further changes on the newly typed plan. It is possible to order chronologically the diagrams from these changes. In all cases, I have considered the hand corrections as part of the diagram on which they have been entered. All diagrams are in the Fitzgerald papers; the fourth plan, the retyped version of diagram three, is reproduced in *The Last Tycoon*, pp. 142-143. For a discussion of the titling of acts of a drama see, e.g., William Archer, *Play-making: A Manual of Craftsmanship* (Boston: Small, Maynard and Company, 1912), p. 143.

[23] Fitzgerald to Littauer, 29 September 1939, in *The Last Tycoon*, p. 139.

[24] Fitzgerald Papers.

[25] Fitzgerald to Zelda Fitzgerald, 23 October 1940, *Letters*, p. 128.

[26] Fitzgerald Papers. After this, Fitzgerald wrote and then, in red, lined out, possibly because he wished to use it elsewhere, "In life too much luck, in drama too much destiny."

[27] Fitzgerald Papers.

[28] Fitzgerald, *The Last Tycoon*, p. 163.

[29] Henry James, "The Art of Fiction," in *The Art of Fiction and Other Essays*, introd. Morris Roberts (New York: Oxford Univ. Press, 1948), p. 13.

[30] *The Structure of the Novel*, p. 41.

[31] See, e.g., Archer, pp. 22-24.

[32] Fitzgerald to Zelda Fitzgerald, 2 November 1940, *Letters, p. 129.*

[33] Fitzgerald, *The Last Tycoon*, p. 20.

[34] Ibid., p. 23.

[35] Ibid., p. 24.

[36] Ibid., p. 73.

[37] Ibid., p. 35.

[38] Ibid., p. 61.

[39] Fitzgerald Papers.

[40] Fitzgerald, *The Last Tycoon*, p. 115.

[41] Ibid., p. 9.

[42] Ibid., p. [134].

"The Falsest of the Arts"

R. L. Samsell

I suppose any biography will have its share of errors. By nature, the dramatization of facts becomes an onorous task. Then, too, it may be part of the biographer's role to assume the kind of breezily authoritative tone which does not admit to narrative difficulties. This rationale is the kindest apology for the professorial tenor of most biographical pap. In a word, scholars seem so coolly cocksure of themselves. Witness: In the *Harper's* excerpt of John Aaron Latham's *Crazy Sundays*—"Fitzgerald died in Hollywood shortly after two o'clock on a winter afternoon in December 1940." The words "shortly after two" have a knowledgeable ring about them. Not at two, two-thirty, etc., but "shortly after." Henry Dan Piper belongs to the two o'clock school: "On the twenty-second, he had a second attack while escorting Miss Graham to the opening of a new film, and died two days later in her living room from another attack, a few minutes after two o'clock in the afternoon." Here, we have the knowledgeable "a few minutes after." Assuming, without deciding, that Latham and Piper have an authoritative basis for their agreement as to time, it is painful to report that Prof. Piper is three days wrong as to Fitzgerald's date of death. His "a few minutes after" seems to come from his footnoted source, *Beloved Infidel* (p. 330). But witness pp. 329, 330: "It was a little after two o'clock."

"I prepared sandwiches and coffee for lunch while Scott glanced through the newspapers." Subsequent, then, to "a little after two," there is at least lunch, candy bar(s), Fitzgerald's doodling of football plays on the *Princeton Alumni Weekly*. By Miss Graham's depiction, we are closer to two-thirty, perhaps later. In her recent *Garden of Allah*, she corrects those who apparently relied on her earlier depiction, setting the time "at three in the afternoon." On safer ground, Prof. Arthur Mizener states, simply—"after lunch." Then *Beloved Infidel's* movie version sees the fatal ambulance pull away from Miss Graham's apartment in harsh sunlight. However, without further hair-splitting, perhaps we can agree, for the moment, that the time can be securely placed in mid-afternoon. But then along comes Prof. Jay Martin in his Nathanael West biography. Witness: "—preoccupied with the news of the death of his friend, F. Scott Fitzgerald, who had died on December 21 at 5:30 of a heart attack. . . ." This, at least, was intriguing. So I turned to the redoubtable R. Wooster Stallman. His introduction to "Bowery Tales" in the Stephen Crane *Omnibus*—but, no, witnesseth: "He [Crane] died at the same sinister hour as Fitzgerald, three in the morning." Undaunted, I reached for Andrew Turnbull. He testifies: "Sitting in an armchair after lunch, he was eating a chocolate bar and making notes on next year's football team in a *Princeton Alumni Weekly*, when suddenly he stood up as if jerked by a wire, clutched the mantelpiece, and fell down with his eyes closed, gasping for breath. It was over in a moment." Six scholars, one infidel, one movie. All, wrong?

But at least we know where Scott Fitzgerald died. Scholars occasionally visit the shrine at 1403 North Laurel. Or, was it 1403? That is, certain authorities have Fitzgerald dying in Miss Graham's first floor apartment, and, rightly, or wrongly, it has been assumed her apartment was on North Laurel. No scholar tells us, however, in which of the first floor apartments Miss Graham resided. But how do we know she lived on North Laurel? The process of literary folklore hazards much conjecture. Perhaps the North Laurel address achieved prominence because of its presence in Fitzgerald's *Letters*. Prior to the publication of the *Letters*, Edmund Wilson's *New Yorker* review of *Beloved Infidel* may have entrenched in many minds that Fitzgerald and Miss Graham domiciled in the same apartment building. "They rented two apartments in the same building, one above the other. He knew now that he had a bad heart, so lived on the bottom floor." More recently, in *Zelda*, Nancy Milford seems to make the same error. "In order to avoid the strain of climbing stairs he moved into Sheilah Graham's apartment on the first floor; his had been on the third." A close reading of *Beloved Infidel* is inconclusive as to where. At page 310, a brief sentence blurs by: "I found him an apartment in Hollywood on the street next to mine." This one sentence quakes Mr. Wilson's "same building"; the North Laurel folklore becomes tottery. But *Beloved Infidel* says more. At page 323, the impression of togetherness exudes, and at an episodic time when the reader's attention is intensified to the climactic finish—"Yet Scott must take care of himself. His apartment was on the third floor, mine on the first. 'All right,' I said. 'You move in with me right away.' Frances and I would look for a suitable ground-floor apartment nearby." Now, Arthur Mizener: "In April they gave up the house at Encino and Fitzgerald moved into an apartment in town near Sheilah's." Mizener is wrong, then right. "They" did not give up the house at Encino, because "they" never lived in the house in Encino. But, significantly, they did not live in the same North Laurel apartment building. Andrew Turnbull's clear statement should have partially clarified the record. "At $110 a month he rented an apartment a block from hers, and they shared the same maid and dined at each other's places on alternate nights." Although Turnbull vividly portrayed Fitzgerald's *when*, he is content to place the *where* a block away. But, be it a block, or a mile, Fitzgerald's last days were not passed at the celebrated North Laurel address. Ironically, Fitzgerald's *Letters*, although a primary research source, have apparently confused the less earnest scholars into a North Laurel fixation.

Because I frankly did not know what to make of the scholars—they were either contradictory or cavalierly assertive—I simply resorted to public records, requesting the County Recorder send me a copy of Fitzgerald's death certificate. F. Scott Fitzgerald died December 21, 1940. December 21 was the shortest day of the year. The certificate says the time was 5:15 P.M. It was quite dark at that hour. Further, the address was 1443 North Hayworth. This address is one block due east of North Laurel. Fitzgerald's secretary, Frances Kroll Ring, has graciously verified the facts she had provided authorities some thirty years before.

The difficulty with Miss Graham's *Beloved Infidel* is that the unceasing shower of detail lulls us into forgetting that she was recalling events which transpired some seventeen to twenty-one years before. In *College of One*, Miss Graham tells us—"After Scott died, I told Frances, I had deliberately erased him from my memory, with everything that had concerned us. It was the only way to survive the shock and the dreadful loss." In spite of this candor, the earlier *Beloved Infidel*'s compelling close is vividly exact. Miss Graham speaks familiarly of a Dr. Wilson—Dr. Lawrence Wilson—yet for more than twelve months, Fitzgerald's attending physician was Dr. Clarence Nelson, an error Miss Graham corrects (subsequent to Nelson's appearance in Fitzgerald's *Letters*) in *College of One*. Her mid-afternoon statement as to time persists in *Garden of Allah*—"three o'clock." To inquire of the time-gap—three to five-fifteen—is, then, the next step in order. The certificate, after all, is only hearsay. A glance informs us of its inaccuracies. Fitzgerald was a veteran; Dr. Nelson had attended Fitzgerald since at least December 1939 (see Fitzgerald's *Letters*, p. 598). Dr. Nelson, deceased, cannot tell us the basis for his time estimate. Frances Kroll Ring, who arrived at Miss Graham's apartment prior to the ambulance's departure, states she simply doesn't know the time of Fitzgerald's passing—and provides us, thereby, with perhaps a plausible state of affairs. But Miss Graham is her own research source. Interestingly, when another source (the certificate) touches upon a few facts detailed by Miss Graham, we have contradiction. At this writing, it is too early to say more. Perhaps Fitzgerald said it all—"Biography is the falsest of the arts."

Recollections of Fitzgerald and Hemingway

Donald Ogden Stewart

These excerpts are from Donald Ogden Stewart's autobiography-in-progress. All rights to the material are the property of Mr. Stewart. We gratefully acknowledge the help of Barrows Dunham.

One unmistakable reality, however, which came crashing down on me on July first, 1919, was a terrific hangover. This was the morning on which America woke up to begin the noble experiment of Prohibition. The final night of slavery to alcohol had been celebrated at the University Club on Summit Avenue, not far from my boarding house. At least, it didn't seem far until I tried to get home that night. Although I was unaware of it, the "gay 1920's" were just around the corner, and as though to be a herald of these glad tidings there arrived shortly after a young, blond, good-looking Princeton grad named Francis Scott Key Fitzgerald. Kay Tighe had said "You'll like Scott"—and I did. He had just come up from Montgomery, Alabama where he had been unsuccessfully trying to get Zelda Sayre to marry him. I told him about Diana and we became commiserative "rejects" under the skin. He still had hoped, however, of getting somewhere with his girl.

Zelda sounded wonderful. Scott told me of one incident just after they first met. They had gone swimming in the river, and, like me, he was a bit timid about diving from even moderate heights. While he stood hesitantly rather far above the water on a rock from which he had intended to impress her with his daring, a body suddenly shot past him in a perfect dive from shudderingly high above him. It was Zelda. He made up his mind right then that she was the girl for him. What interested me particularly was that he had just finished a novel and I got him to give me a cardboard box full of *This Side of Paradise*, written in pencil. I approved of it, with Yale reservations which are happily forgotten. I didn't know enough to appre-

177

ciate his style and form, but the content excited my praise. Scott was really a godsend to me at that time, and filled the educational void left by my separation from Put and Doc. We were neither of us interested in political happenings at home or abroad. He took me to see a very intelligent Catholic priest named Father Barron and we spent exciting hours in Scott's home (also on Summit Avenue), arguing religion and literature. From Scott I first learned to love the poetry of A. E. Housman; to him I owe my delight in many novelists, Compton McKenzie's *Sinister Street* and the Catholics like the English Benson and the French Huysmans. I myself was flirting a bit with mysticism and the reality of Satan, and Scott was watching me with that green-eyed Mona Lisa smile, as though he were taking notes. Actually, it was that note-taking aloofness of his that kept me from ever feeling that he was really a friend. And I, too, kept somewhat aloof, but this was due more to my Yale conformity: When Scott got drunk he embarrassed me, although in those early days of Prohibition there was very little drinking. Scott had an outrageous way of asking the wrong (actually the right) questions about one's private and confidential feelings—questions which one just didn't ask. Or so I had been taught. He was very curious about my humor. "How did I go about making people laugh?" Part of my answer to that one lay in a technique which I had slowly been developing since Yale by imitating the "funny men" who were so popular at parties and as ushers at weddings.

I was lucky with Scott, too, because I knew him so intimately first in that comparatively calm period before he skyrocketed to the somewhat unapproachable dizzy heights. In a way he and I had one thing in common. We were both impoverished ambitious "outsiders." I think that he was almost as obsessed as I with the magic of great names, both in Finance and Society. We were both products of Eastern upper-class universities, and both insecure and unprepared for sudden success in the post-World-War-I world. My 1920's were, on a smaller scale, the Fitzgerald 1920's; my 1930's likewise. And when, just before his death, we had one final blessed month of togetherness, of a return to our 1920 relationship, I was able again to be understandingly grateful for those few months in St. Paul "at the beginning."

La Vie de Bohème was beginning to look a bit insecure—and then Scott Fitzgerald came to my rescue. *This Side of Paradise* had been published while I was in Dayton, he had married Zelda, and they had exploded brilliantly into the sky over New York. They were living in an apartment on 59th street, convenient to a drug store on Sixth

Avenue where Scott could get pure alcohol made into gin. I had not kept up with their exploits and the first time I called, expecting to have a quiet dinner, I found myself eventually swept along dinnerless with ten or fifteen others to a ball at the Savoy Plaza given by the Daughters of the Southern Confederacy. It was not the same Scott I had known in St. Paul, and I wasn't sure that I was as crazy about Zelda as everyone appeared to be. She seemed much more interested in her own conversation than in mine; so did Scott, and I felt like some embarrassed spectator caught by the unexpected rising of the curtain on the stage of a comedy in which the two stars were competing for the spotlight. Neither then, nor in the years to follow, did I ever have any sense of a relationship between Zelda and myself. I just couldn't get through to the real girl, and God knows I tried, especially on that first acquaintance. At one point that evening, however, the gin gave out, Scott took me with him to the drug store for a refill, and I had a chance to tell him what had happened in Dayton and why I had come to New York. He was immediately sympathetic and told me to go to Frank "Crowny" Crowninshield, the editor of *Vanity Fair*, who might have something for me in the advertising department.

On my first trip to the *Vanity Fair* offices I found that Scott had prepared the way for me with "Crowny" as well as with the two assistant editors Edmund "Bunny" Wilson and John Peale Bishop. "Crowny", white mustached, elegant, soft-voiced, suave, listened to my plea for "any kind of work" with benevolent courtesy and shook his head. "Unfortunately, my dear boy, there is nothing." I asked if he could suggest any possibilities; perhaps on a newspaper, as an assistant music critic, or in the *Vanity Fair* advertising department. He smiled sadly and I rose to go; I too had good manners. He offered to give me letters of introduction to other magazines, but it would be better if I could let him look at something I had written, so that he could judge what sort of position he might recommend me for. I thought of my only published work and didn't feel encouraged; "Dear Queenie" was not apt to be "Crowny's" dish of tea. Well, Scott had done his best. The Depression had obviously hit the cultural field, too. Tomorrow I would try Tommy Tompkins at the Bankers Trust. On my way out I heard Scott's laugh. He had dropped in on Wilson and Bishop who had been at Princeton with him. I poked my head in to thank him for his help, then continued on my way to the elevator. I could hear the laughter behind me. I felt very envious, and very out of it.

It wasn't long before I began to wonder if I wasn't capable of much more important work than humorous pieces and parodies of other authors. I didn't let anyone in on this secret ambition, but I began to read novels and short stories for the purpose of seeing how it was done. I had certain favorites, headed by Anatole France. Scott had introduced me enthusiastically to France's philosophy of "irony and pity," and I became equally a devotee. I couldn't share Scott's interest in Dreiser whose plodding grimness was to me just bad writing in spite of what Menken and Nathan might say about it.

It was a perfect fling. On my first night there I found myself occupying Ernest Hemingway's lodgings. John Peale Bishop had suggested, in a letter to Capri, that I do two things: (a) read a new poem by T. S. Eliot called "The Waste Land," and (b) look up an interesting young writer in Paris named Hemingway. I had got a copy of the Eliot poem and found it fascinatingly expressive of my own feelings at the time. As I have said, I have never felt at home with poetry, but this one seemed (as had *Ulysses*) to strike some deep-lying bell within me in spite of my inability to understand the difference between this and other poetry, most of which had left me comparatively unmoved. I could only say that "The Waste Land" seemed to have been written for me and I felt extremely grateful to John Bishop for having sent it my way.

I was even more grateful to him for Hemingway. On my first night in Paris he happened to be at a restaurant on the Ile St. Louis which John Dos Passos had told me about, and I liked him immediately. I didn't know anything about him as a writer, but he seemed to be my kind of a guy, which meant, among other things, that there wasn't any phoniness about him and he liked good food and liked to drink and he understood my kind of humor. He was going to take an early morning train for Switzerland where his wife and baby son were staying, but we got on so well that he insisted, with characteristic enthusiasm, that I occupy his rooms until he brought them back. I was to learn later that when Ernest was enthusiastic about something it was extremely dangerous to resist, but after six months of solitude I had no desire to resist anything, especially friendliness, and I woke up the next morning in his room, very happy, with a note from him telling me where I could get eggs and milk.

My God, it was good to be back in Paris. The Barrys went down to their villa in Cannes, but the Murphys welcomed me with their matchless open arms. Ernest and Hadley Hemingway's open arms weren't so bad, either, and Madame the proprietor of the Hotel

Venetia gave me a big kiss and my old room. My only cloud on the horizon was a financial one, since *Aunt Polly* had sold very few copies and I had got out of the habit (and the desire) of writing short humorous pieces for magazines. I rather hesitantly showed Ernest my abortive attempts at novel writing and to my delight he said that he wanted to publish some of it in a magazine called the *transatlantic* which he was publishing with Ford Madox Ford. It was a bit about an old college graduate at his fraternity house and I was delighted that Ernest approved of it, but *transatlantic* didn't pay any money to its contributors—or at least they didn't offer any to me. Ernest and Ford, however, did set me up to a gay wine-filled luncheon, after which we saw Ford off on his train for London and embarrassed him unspeakably with our boisterous American farewell at the station.

. . . the fiesta of San Firmin. Ernest and Hadley Hemingway had gone the year before, come back full of enthusiasm, and arranged for the party. This incidentally wasn't the one which Ernest wrote about in *The Sun Also Rises*; that was to come the next year. Besides Dos and myself on this first occasion there were his Paris friends William and Sally Bird, Robert McAlmon and Bill Smith. There may have been one or two more. It was a gay friendly party, every minute of which was fun. We stayed at a hotel on the square which I think was called the "Montana." Pamplona had not yet been popularized, and we were, as far as I can remember, the only foreigners in town.

Ernest was terribly concerned about bullfighting and I was equally concerned about not letting Ernest down in his opinion of me. I liked him tremendously, and after I had heard him sound off on people who didn't care for bullfighting I wouldn't have wanted to criticize the sport. Ernest was somebody you went along with, or else. A couple of years later I was to get the "or else" treatment, but fortunately here in this around-the-clock wine-drinking street-dancing gayety I discovered that I also like bullfighting almost as much as Ernest did. I didn't care for the cruelty to the horses, but when Ernest explained to me the technical necessity for this second stage in the ritual I accepted it as part of the dramatic ballet of courage and grace which engrossed and fascinated me. I also acquired two other bits of more or less useful information, one being that on entering the ring the bull instinctively seeks a "corner" which he can call his own and from which he can be tempted to his death only with great difficulty, a tactic of self-preservation which I have found exceedingly effective at literary and other cocktail parties. The other helpful morsel of tauromachy was that a *cow* cannot be used as the

victim, for the simple reason that she can only be fooled into charg-
the cape once; the next time it is waved at her, she charges at the
man.

So I went happily through the fiesta, excited, drunk, hot, hung-
over, enjoying the warm friendship, worshipping Ernest's hero Maera,
dancing enthusiastic solos in the square, drinking even more enthusiastically from the hospitable native wineskins, and being uncomfort-
able only in the early morning when Spanish ideals of courage required that the young men run through the streets ahead of the
swiftly running bulls. I am not, as I have said, possessed of much
physical courage and the animals terrified me, so that to this day I
can associate the hot smell of the Spanish wood used in the street
barriers with a feeling of panic in my stomach. Until the very last day
I avoided facing Ernest's challenge to go down into the ring in the
morning when the Pamplonian youth show off their bravery by performing as amateur toreros against three or four nonlethal small bulls
whose horns are padded so as to prevent any serious accidents. They
didn't look small or nonlethal to me and I wandered miserably
around the edge of the arena hoping that Ernest would be too triumphantly occupied with his own fearlessness to notice my abstention.
Dos had the excuse of his extreme nearsightedness, but even he
ventured into the ring and there was one tense moment when he
leaped back into what he thought was the safety of the grandstand
without being aware that the bull had also made the same leap. Two
natives rescued him just in time, but in avoiding the bull I had
jumped into the arena and was quietly tiptoeing along the sand mind-
ing my own business when two Spaniards spied me and noisily extended to me the warm hand of Pamplonian guest-friendship. To my
horror I realized that in these outstretched hospitable hands was a
large red cloak, and that they were offering it to me so that I might
feel assured that a visiting American was being permitted to give
proof of his own country's bravery. I started modestly to decline the
honor, but a crowd of happy Spaniards quickly gathered, all apparently determined to show me that they had no hard feelings against
the country which had taken Cuba and the Philippines away from
them in the 1898 war. I was hustled towards the nearest bull, and
found myself standing alone in the midst of a large audience (not to
mention the thousands in the grandstands and bleachers) with the
bull glaring at me from a distance of six feet. I gulped, grinned, and
raised the red cape in front of my body in what I thought to be the
proper gesture. The movement attracted the bull's attention, he
started towards me, and I quickly moved the cape into position

number two—outside my right leg. Unfortunately that should have been position number one. The bull did not swerve as I had expected; I was hit full force, my glasses flew in one direction, the cape in another, and I was tossed into the air, amid a great gleeful shout from the spectators. When I hit the ground, however, an amazing thing happened. I lost my fear completely. And not only that—I got mad. I grabbed the cape and started to chase my enemy. When I got to him I held the cape, once more in front of me, yelling "Come on, you stupid son-of-a-bitch!" The bull may have been a S.O.B., but he wasn't as stupid as I was; when he started toward me and I persisted in moving the cape to the right, he again tossed me triumphantly in the air and galloped away. I picked myself up, beaming with delight. I was triumphant too. I had been hit by a bull, and it was nothing. I was right back on the football field at Exeter. I had shown that I could take it. Ernest clapped me on the back, and I felt as though I had scored a winning touchdown. After we left the arena I discovered that a couple of my ribs had been fractured, but that couldn't spoil the frenzied last night of drinking and dancing. It had been a memorable week, a male festival, a glorified college reunion.

Then came the quiet and peace of the French riviera. The Murphys were at Cap d'Antibes where they had persuaded the proprietor of the Hotel du Cap that this winter resort might possibly be attractive to summer visitors. None of the other communities along the riviera had considered this revolutionary possibility, and when Dos and I arrived we found Gerald, Sara and Co. installed at the hotel in solitary grandeur. In a way, there was a reason for this tradition that the riviera was suitable only for winter vacationists. The summer climate was a treacherous one for the unsuspecting newcomer, and the first week or so was apt to be spent in getting over a disagreeable diarrhoetic complaint known as the "mal du midi." But once that had been conquered, the life was sheer paradise. There was as yet no elegant Eden Roc restaurant or swimming pool but the Murphys had discovered a small private beach in the vicinity, and I settled down to the engrossing occupation of acquiring a bronzed body and an appetite for superb meals on the wide hotel porch. This was varied with visits to Phil and Ellen Barry at their Cannes villa where my typescript of the "Haddocks" was welcomed by them with cheering laughter. Sun, blue sea and not a cloud in the sky. There were even copies of Ernest's *transatlantic review* on sale in a Nice bookshop with "Work in Progress by Donald Ogen Stewart" advertised on the cover. Other "works in progress or to appear" were by Joseph Conrad, Ford M. Hueffer and Jean Cocteau. It was very encouraging.

In Detroit I took time off to observe the aesthetic beauty of the Ford plant belt line (which I had had described to me by a French poet in Paris) and to have lunch with Ernest Hemingway's married sister whom I tried to encourage about the literary future of her brother. Ernest had sent me his *In Our Time* short stories which I had unsuccessfully urged George Doran to publish. Actually, I didn't have any idea that Ernest was a very good writer. I liked him, and I wanted to help a friend; however, when he had sent me a "funny" piece about myself to submit to *Vanity Fair*, I had decided that written humor was not his dish and had done nothing about it. On the jacket of the first edition of *In Our Time* which Boni and Liveright published later that year there are fulsome tributes to Hemingway as a short story writer by Edward J. O'Brien, Sherwood Anderson, Waldo Frank, Gilbert Seldes and Ford Madox Ford, and I am quoted as saying "After trying to make a meal out of literary lettuce sandwiches which are being fed to this country, it is rather nice to discover that one of your own countrymen has opened a shop where you can really get something to eat." I admired him tremendously as an honest unsentimental man who was trying to write the truth about life.

But also it was time to join Ernest and Hadley in Pamplona for the Feast of Saint Firmin, so with all the boyish eagerness of a college graduate I prepared for another rowdy reunion with the gang. But when I got there I found that someone had left the door open and Eve had walked into my male Garden of Eden. Eve's name was Lady Duff Twisden and she was right out of the gay brave hell of Michael Arlen. I had never known any English ladies and she was distant and rare and beautiful in a black broadbrimmed Spanish hat and I was scared as hell of her until I discovered that she had a terrible hangover which always endears people to me. With her as what I took to be her lover, was another "Green Hat" character from the overdrafts of Mayfair named Pat Guthrie whose charming worthlessness immediately won my heart. The third new member of our club was Harold Loeb, editor of *Broom*, whose presence, as I discovered later, was not entirely in the interests of literature. Somehow or other sex rivalries didn't seem to belong in the celebration of the life of Saint Firmin, and I wondered in my innocence why Ernest and Hadley had brought in these strangers. Anyway, good old Bill Smith was there and so were the bulls and the bands and the wineskins and I determinedly set about showing myself and the newcomers the glories of the fiesta as I remembered them from the last year.

But little by little the glory began to slip away. It wasn't the same, no matter how much I drank. At first I figured that maybe it was because we were no longer the exclusive foreign participants in the show. Rolls-Royces from Madrid and France stood outside the hotel. The presence of the American Ambassador, the Pittsburgh millionaire Alexander Moore who had married Lillian Russell, didn't add anything to the spirit of peasant gaiety. Pamplona seemed to be getting ready for the hand of Elsa Maxwell. But that wasn't what was spoiling things for me. Ernest had changed. Hadley wasn't the same. One night there was almost a fight between Ernest and Harold Loeb. The fun was going out of everybody. But the dancing and singing kept going on all around us and gradually it looked as though the spirit of the fiesta had swung them up out of their triangles or quadrangles or whatever the hell it was. I had got to like everybody very much and on the last night we danced and toasted each other and made plans for next year's fiesta and goodtime Donald fell into bed very happy.

But next day the hotel bills came in and my happy world of comradeship fell to pieces. It seemed that our gay brave English companions had come down without any means of paying for anything, and it also seemed that this came as a shocking surprise to Ernest who had barely enough to settle his own bills. His bitter fury was of course more or less justified as he had trustfully introduced us all to his great friend the hotel keeper, and this was a betrayal of that trust, although not entirely surprising in view of Pat and Duff's previous performances. But for me the real moment of truth came in the revelation of the tenuity of human relations when confronted with financial considerations. It was the intrusion of that same sickness which had crept into my heart at Yale when I had tried too zealously to collect dues from my fraternity brothers. Here in Pamplona a joyful if temporary comradeship between gay people was being destroyed because of an unpaid debt. Money wasn't worth that much, I decided, and as I was luckily able to transform my decision into action the spirit of fiesta, if not some of the friendship, survived the crisis. "The proper function of mankind is to laugh" had said Rabelais and I was becoming increasingly devoted to that doubtful slogan as a guide to my conduct, at the expense, I might add, of any perhaps more worthy use of my talents. On the way from Pamplona to the Murphys in Antibes it occurred to me that the events of the past week might perhaps make interesting material for a novel. I was right. Ernest started working on *The Sun Also Rises* the next week. I bought a bottle of sun-tan lotion.

In Antibes, as at Pamplona, I was destined to experience a growing sense of "things aint what they used to be." Elsa Maxwell hadn't yet discovered it, but there were ominous signs. The Hotel du Cap was now more than half full of wealthy vacationers and the small exclusive beach on which the wonderful Murphy children and Dos and I had run wild was now shared with a Mr. and Mrs. Pierrepont Morgan Hamilton and assorted guests, including a Portuguese baron named Tony D'Almeda. Unbeknownst to me, the sands of that beach were shifting beneath me and it is an ironic comment on my own rudderless course between these worlds that within two years I was to ask the Hamiltons to be god-parents for my first son. But at the moment there was no communication between me (the Dedicated Writer) and them (the Social Rich). On our side of the beach were the Benchleys and the Barrys, the Scott Fitzgeralds and the Archie MacLeishes, all of whom had by now become close friends of the Murphys.

There were other changes at Cap d'Antibes that summer besides the transformation of Gerald and Sara's quiet little group into a celebrity circus. Ernest was beginning to become a celebrity himself. His *Torrents of Spring* had been published without much success, but *The Sun Also Rises* based on the fiesta week at Pamplona the year before, was on its way to being made known to twenty-five countries. When I first read it I couldn't see what everyone was getting so excited about, and exclaimed "But this is nothing but a report on what happened. There's no creation, no imagination. This is journalism." I had a feeling that I could have turned out a much better, much truer novel.

On Bea's birthday in October I gave a party at Prunier's where I discovered to my dismay that Ernest's marriage to Hadley was breaking up. About the same time Ernest also broke up *our* friendship in a quarrel caused by his writing of a viciously unfair and unfunny poem about Dorothy Parker which he read at a party at Archie MacLeish's apartment. There was this curious bitter streak in Ernest which I had first come across to my dismay in *The Torrents of Spring*, a book which I loathed both for the above-mentioned pettiness and for its inept attempts at humorous writing. I angrily told him what I thought of his poem, and *that* honeymoon, to my sorrow, came to an end.

Next day we fled, taking Dotty with us. The descent from Hell to Earth was almost as nerve shaking an atmospheric change as had been the sudden elevation to the mountain. On the train to Paris I exploded into my one and only row with Dotty and attacked her bitterly for a profile on Ernest Hemingway which she had written for the *New Yorker*, in the course of which she had praised Ernest as one writer who would never never never be a slave to the society inhabiting the North Shore of Long Island. *Touché*—and it hurt like hell, especially, ironically enough, from Dotty for whose sake four years before I had had a quarrel with Ernest which had helped terminate our friendship. Dotty of course disclaimed that she had been specifically referring to me, and by the time we got to Paris all was love and cognac. And by a curious coincidence Ernest with his wife Pauline were on the boat which Bea, Dotty and I took for New York.

It was an interesting meeting of two former friends whose dreams had now come true. At the time of the beginning of the friendship there had been a certain similarity in Ernest's and my dreams; we had both wanted to succeed as writers who told the truth about life as we saw it. But in the seven years since then, Ernest's ambition had not been undercut as had mine by other forces. He had held true to *his* course, and had now reached the goal. *A Farewell to Arms*, published the year before, had deservedly achieved his dream of artistic fulfillment. Incidentally, it had also been a best seller; a stage version by Lawrence Stallings was playing on Broadway; Hollywood had eagerly paid their handsome tribute to his genius.

My own tribute was sincere, with an important reservation. I had said in "Rebound" what I thought about one aspect of *A Farewell to Arms*. Ernest's heroine, it seemed to me was too exclusively the male idea of the way women *should* act. She was always there when the hero wanted her, and she even obligingly died at the end when her presence was no longer a boon. Partly in reaction to this I had in my play created a heroine who refused to become a male convenience.

At any rate, here we were, two boys who had started out with our bare hands, a pencil and a few sheets of blank paper and had in a few short years and by different paths hit the American jackpot of fame and wealth. Whose jackpot seemed to be the more important was convincingly indicated, somewhat to my surprised dismay on our arrival in New York harbor when a boatload of newspaper reporters boarded the ship. Whilst I was reminiscently thumbing over in my mind the reviews of "Aunt Polly," "The Haddocks" and "Rebound" there was a rush of journalistic feet past my cabin door, all eagerly in search of Ernest Hemingway, and I somewhat sadly but wisely tucked my scrapbooks of favorable clippings back into my memories and returned with Bea to our study of the profitable use of leisure time amid the Rich.

The only worrisome thing about *The Women* was the fact that I was expected to work on it with Scott Fitzgerald. Our paths had separated widely in the eighteen years since our St. Paul friendship at the dawn of our careers. Scott's literary skyrocket had apparently burned itself out; his *Tender is the Night* had been badly received by the Depression-era critics. Worst of all, Zelda had gone insane. I hadn't seen him since the twenties when Bea and I had walked out of one of his famous Great Neck weekends, unable to enjoy the stupid drunkenness. As I entered the gates of the new Irving Memorial Building I didn't quite know what to expect, especially as I had greatly disliked his confessional "The Crack Up," probably because it was a little too close to home. My own crack-up as a writer had been, in many respects quite as reprehensible and as disappointing to those early 1920 hopes as had Scott's. But now, I felt, I was back on my feet, still capable of fulfilling my promise.

To my great surprise and delight, so was Scott. He wasn't drinking, and he was, in fact, much more understanding than before, and infinitely more human. In our month together our old friendship came back, and it was like those eager starry-eyed days in St. Paul when he was reading Masefield to me in front of the fire in his living room. "Be with me, beauty, for the fire is dying." But, the fire still wasn't dying—in either of us. He told me of *The Last Tycoon*, and I tried to explain my "conversion." He had apparently come close to the edges of Marxism when living in Baltimore, but the "artist" in him couldn't go over the fence. He sympathized with me about Bea, and we had fatherly discussions about his daughter at Vassar. He made helpful suggestions about a speech I was writing in reply to the attack by Congressman Martin Dies on the "Communistic un-American Hollywood Anti-Nazi League." He seemed to enjoy with a sort of kind grandfatherly benevolence the spectacle of me as one of the eager socially-conscious beavers.

After Scott and I finished our version of "The Women" (which wasn't shot). . . .

"La Vie est beau avec Papa"

C. E. Frazer Clark, Jr.

Gerald and Sara Murphy were an intimate part of the "dangerous summer" of 1926, when "everything," according to Hemingway, "was all shot to hell in every direction."[1] "Everything," in this case, included the prospect that Ernest and Hadley were going to break up. Early in August the Hemingways stopped to see their friends at the Murphys' Villa América, and the plans to separate were made known. Gerald Murphy invited Hemingway to make use of a studio Murphy maintained in Paris, at 69, rue Froidevaux. On their return to Paris, Hadley was registered at the Hôtel Beauvoir, and Hemingway set up shop in the studio.

By the end of August, Hemingway had finished reading proof on *The Sun Also Rises.*[2] September found Hadley prepared to agree to a divorce, provided, at the end of a separation to last a hundred days, Ernest and Pauline Pfeiffer were still in love. Hemingway stayed in Paris; Pauline went to New York; the Murphys had gone to New York, where they ran into Pauline. In October, Hemingway and Archibald MacLeish went to Zaragoza to close out the bullfight season. By mid-November, Hadley felt she had to get away and think things out by herself. She left Bumby Hemingway with his father and went to Chartres.[3]

Soon after Bumby's stay, Hemingway heard from the Murphys. Always interested in his work, they had sent a clipping of a review of *The Sun Also Rises.* Hemingway acknowledged their interest by inscribing a copy of *Today is Friday.*[4] in which he found space to add a personal note reporting events.

---

[1] Carlos Baker, *Ernest Hemingway: A Life Story* (New York: Scribners, 1969), p. 172.

[2] Corrected proof left for America on 27 August 1926. Baker, p. 173.

[3] When Hadley returned to Paris, terms were reached, a divorce agreed to, and the Pauline-Ernest separation treaty abandoned. Baker, p. 178.

[4] Ernest Hemingway, *Today is Friday* (Englewood, New Jersey: The As Stable Publications, [1926]). The Murphy copy of *Today is Friday* is in the Clark Collection. I acknowledge my appreciation to Professor Michel Fabre, who was instrumental in securing this copy.

The As Stable Pamphlets

Edith Finch : George Platt Lynes : Adlai Harbeck

I. GENESIS OF PEACE *by* Paxton Howard,
   with drawing by A. E. H.

II. DESCRIPTIONS OF LITERATURE
   by Gertrude Stein,
   with drawing by Pavel Tchelitchew.

III. 1830 *by* René Crevel,
   with drawing by H. Phelan Gibb.

IV. TODAY IS FRIDAY *by* Ernest Hemingway,
   with drawing by Jean Cocteau.

Three hundred numbered copies printed.
Two hundred and sixty for sale.
Number

The As Stable Publications
125 Engle Street, Englewood, New Jersey.

1926

Dear gents —

Thanks for the review.
Archie read me a grand letter
from Sara to ada. I will
write you a fine letter soon —
but today it is raining.

I am very comfortable at
69 (rue Froidevaux he hastens to
add) and about as happy
as the average empty
tomato can.

Archie and I went to
Zaragoza and had a fine trip.
He took away from me — with a
couple of books and his fine legal
mind — the Popes, Caesar and
Shakespeare (all Fairies) and, the
Holy grail (Just a goddam lie) and gave
me in exchange A great Yale
Football Team (They'd just beaten
Dartmouth).

Well we got home and the next
Sunday I read the paper and Holy Cross

or some place like that had beaten
Yale 33-6. So wrote archie a
[piece] and said I was sending back
his great Yale Team including their
great new quarterback and would
he return me by return post all
The Papers, Caesar, Shakespeare and
The Holy Grail.

But so far I haven't got them
back.

However I love you both
very much and like to think
about you and will be shall
we say **pleased** to see
you –

It is swell that gerald
is working so well and I will
be pretty excited to see
the stuff –

When do you come back?
My love to Patrick Booth and Honoria.
Bumby and I lived together for
10 days while Hadley was on a trip
and one day when I bought him an
harmonica and a glass and he was holding
the one and eating the other at the cafe

"So Vie est beau avec Papa"
he said.

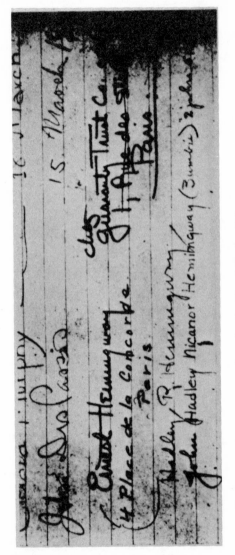

Guestbook—Hotel Taube, Schruns

Lost Hemingway Review Found

In *Fitzgerald/Hemingway 1970* we called attention to Hemingway's lost review of a Christmas play. Josef Nels (Hotel Taube, Schruns) and Günther Schulte have found it for us. This review—translated into German was published in the *Vorarlberger Landes-Zeitung* (13 January 1926).

—*M.J.B.*

Schruns (Montafon), January 12. Hans Sachs from sixteenth-century Nuremberg and Bernard Shaw, an Irishman from twentieth-century London, fought for precedence at a successful evening of theater in Schruns, brought to the stage by Mr. Norman B. Kapp, London. Mr. Kapp, who produced and directed "The Hot Iron" by Hans Sachs and "How He Deceived Her Husband" by Shaw, demonstrated in his mastery of modern stage technique that he had assimilated the discoveries of Gordon Craig and Max Reinhardt without in the process having to suppress his own fantasy and good taste. He played the lover in Shaw's comedy, as well as the deceived and deceiving husband in the 'Volksstück,' with exceptional ability and talent. Mrs. Alexa Ritter-Kapp, the well-known character actress, played the repentant wife in both the medieval and the modern comedy with superlative emotional and technical ability. A. Nels in the role of the malicious and witch-like godmother in "The Hot Iron" played the difficult role very convincingly. E. Bertle in the role of a Shavianly enraged husband was thoroughly Shavian and enraged. It will be interesting to observe him in future Kapp productions. Mr. Kapp's staging and lighting, especially in the Sachs play, were more than superlative. Both performances were attended by a large and intelligently appreciative crowd of listeners.

Ernest Hemingway

Translated by James Franklin,
University of South Carolina.

Erscheint jeden Werktag mittags.   Fernspruch-Nummer 55/4.

Vorarlberger
Landes-Zeitung.

Amtsblatt für Vorarlberg.

Wochenbeilagen: „Holunder", „Frauen-Zeitung" und Kupfertiefdruckbeilage „Zeitgeschehen im Wochenbild"

Bezugspreise:	Kalender.	Anzeigen finden Verbreitung durch das ganze Land und
Oesterreich: monatlich 2.70 Schilling, vierteljährlich 8.— Schilling, Deutschland 2.— Mark. Schweiz 3.00 Francs. — Einzelnummer: 20 Groschen.	Sonntag, 10., 1. n. Ersch. Wilh. — Montag, 11., Hyginus, Thd. — Dienstag, 12., Ernst, Be-nedkt. — Mittwoch, 13., Gottfried, Veron. — Donners-tag 14., Hilarius, Felix. — Freitag, 15., Remebius, Paul. — Samstag, 16., Priscilla, Honor. — Sonntag, 17., 2. n. Ersch. Gulpit.	werden nach Tarif berechnet; ob 3-maliger Wiederholung Ermäßigung. Für das Erscheinen von Anzeigen an be-stimmten Tagen und besonderen Plätzen kann keine Gewähr übernommen werden.

Nr. 9.	Bregenz. Mittwoch. den 13. Jänner 1926	63. Jahrgang

Schruns (Montafon), 12. Jänner. Hans Sachs aus dem Nüremberg des 16. Jahrhunderts und Bernard Shaw, ein Irländer aus dem London des 20. Jahrhunderts, stritten um den Vorrang an einem erfolgreichen Theaterabend in Schruns, von Herrn Norman B. Kapp, London, auf die Bühne gebracht. Herr Kapp, der "Das Heisse Eisen" von Hans Sachs und "Wie er ihren Gatten belog" von Shaw inszenierte und leitete, zeigte in seiner Beherrschung der modernen Bühnentechnik, dass er die Entdeckungen des Gordon Craig und des Max Reinhardt assimilert hatte, ohne dadurch seine eigene Phantasie und seinen guten Geschmack unterdrücken zu brauchen. Den Liebhaber in Shaws Lustspiel, sowie auch den betrogenen und betrügenden Ehemann im Volksstück, spielte er mit ausserordentlichem Können und Talent. Frau Alexa Ritter-Kapp, die bekannte Portrait-Künstlerin, spielte die reuige Frau sowohl im mittelalterlichen wie im modernen Lustspiel mit hervorragender gefühlsmässiger und technischer Begabung. A. Nels in der Rolle der hämischen, hexenhaften Gevatterin im "Heissen Eisen" spielte die schwierige Rolle sehr überzeugend. E. Bertle in der Rolle eines Shaw-haft empörten Ehemannes war durchwegs Shaw-haft und empört. Es wird interessant sein ihn in den nächsten Kapp-Aufführungen zu beobachten. Herrn Kapps Inszenierung und Beleuchtung besonders im Sachs-Spiel, waren mehr als hervorragend. Beiden Aufführungen wohnte eine grosse und intelligent anerkennende Zuhörerschar bei.

Ernest Hemingway

Letters of Ernest Hemingway to Soviet Writers*

Ivan Kashkeen

We are publishing letters from Ernest Hemingway to the Soviet translator and critic Ivan
Kashkeen and the author Konstantin Simonov. The
letters have been slightly abridged.

Hemingway's letters are self-explanatory. There are only two or three points that require elucidation.

At one place in his letter of 1935 Hemingway joins issue with me over my article in which, while praising his work highly, I expressed some concern about where the heavily-stressed bravado of the author's Mr. Frazer was going to lead him. Recognizing the purifying role of the revolution as a kind of catharsis, Hemingway at that time identified communism with the state, and for him then any state meant bureaucratism. In his letter Hemingway polemically stresses his attitude to the state. But to what state? His views on the state were formed in the years when he observed the birth and growth of the arbitrary fascist state in Italy; and later the heady growth of nazism in the Hitlerite state with which as early as 1934, he considered war to be inevitable. No wonder that Hemingway found the state in such forms inimical and alien and that he preferred to "look after himself" and his neighbours. But it is characteristic that a year after writing this letter Hemingway was helping not his neighbours but those who were far removed from him, dashing to the defence of a state, the Spanish Republican state, against the fascist insurgents who had risen against it. And the theory of non-intervention in politics and of the position of an observer on the side-line at once retreated into Hemingway's past. On his return in 1937 from Republican Spain to Florida Hemingway found there a copy of *La Litterature*

*Reprinted from *Soviet Literature*, No. 11 (November 1962), 158-167.

197

Internationale which had been sent him. It contained my article on his work, "La force dans le vide." And on July 24, 1937 he wrote to the editor of the magazine, S. Dinamov: "Thank you for the copy of *International Literature* with Kashkeen's article. I hope I will keep Kashkeen busy revising my ultimate biography for some time yet. . . .[1]

"Tell Kashkeen for me that war is very different when you are thirty-eight from when you were eighteen, nineteen and twenty. And what a different war. Sometime I will write him about it if there ever is time again to write letters. . . . Just now I am seeing my family before going back again."

Hemingway found time for the next letter only after his final return from Spain in spring, 1939. And then began the Second World War, in which Hemingway took direct part, a pact was concluded in Europe, there was the Finnish campaign and neither letters nor the promised galleys reached me. After the war I received from Hemingway only greetings conveyed in the letter to Konstantin Simonov or verbally through people who had visited Hemingway: V. Kuzmishchev, L. Kamynin, V. Mashkin, M. Mochnatchev.

The letter to Konstantin Simonov of June 20, 1946 is of interest not so much for the biographical details which one can now find in the literature about Hemingway as for the fact that Hemingway again gives food to revise his biography. With some reservations and apologies he writes in the letter about politics and unambiguously accuses Winston Churchill of again doing what he did in 1918-1919—trying to preserve something which could be preserved from the demands of the future only by force of arms, by war which Hemingway had come to hate more than ever.

As for the state, the practices of the anarchists who found themselves in power in Republican Spain and specially in Catalonia, had opened Hemingway's eyes to the real meaning of the "state-minimum". And Hemingway expressed himself in favour—admittedly during war—of stoutly disciplined opposition to fascism.

Another point. Hemingway's sharp words about critics. But again, one may ask, what critics? He had in mind groundless criticism that was wittingly prejudiced and malicious. Some of his critics

---

[1] A reference to the articles *Death in the Afternoon* in the magazine *Literaturny Kritik,* 1934, *The Tragedy of Craftsmanship,* 1935, and *La force dans le vide (La Litterature Internationale,* Nos. 7-8, 1936), which showed new stages in the literary development of Hemingway.

ascribed to him the products of their own imagination. The English critic Wyndham Lewis, parodying the title *Men Without Women* reckons Hemingway among his *Men Without Art* (in the article "A Dumb Ox") and the American writer and critic Max Eastman in another article referred to Hemingway himself as to a *Bull in the Afternoon*, mockingly alleging that his courage was affected and bogus. When attempts like these were made to strip Hemingway of what was dearer to him than anything else—art and courage—he delivered a sharp rebuff, all the sharper because that campaign of slander stemmed from something deeper, from a conflict of opinions about the events in Spain. But which critics did Hemingway take into consideration? Edmund Wilson and Malcolm Cowley who in 1935 struck him as being recent converts or proselytes. Then, surprising as it may seem Michael Gold, despite the fact that Gold was at that time already a veteran of the American communist movement. And, finally, with a critic in the distant Soviet Union. He took these critics into consideration in spite of the fact that all four of them, without any dissembly, addressed many bitter words to him.

Hemingway was impatient and abrupt in his dealings with critics. He rarely wrote to them. More often he scorned them. All the more noteworthy is the invariably friendly tone of his letters to Russian writers and critics. But, after all, for him they were men who spoke the language of Tolstoy, Turgenev and Checkhov, they were the compatriots of his companions-in-arms in Spain, they were the representatives of the Soviet readers who loved him so dearly.

A final point. In his mistaken conceptions of the writer being "like a Gypsy" and of the difference between a class-conscious and one for whom "all classes are his province," Hemingway treats onesidedly the concept of world-scale authors, having in mind probably the great 19th-century novelists—Leo Tolstoy, Balzac. . . . However, in his own life and literary practice Hemingway refutes his own argument. Himself a writer of world-scale he does not shun that class-consciousness to which he refers so ironically in his letter. Sometimes sharing the prejudices of his class, paying his due at a certain period to the mood which prevailed in Western Literary Bohemian circles, Hemingway nevertheless rejected the ideas expressed in his letter—not only by his acts, his personal participation in the Spanish Civil War, but his writing, the writing of an antifascist. He not only fought against Franco and Hitler with a gun in his hand; he recognized that to defeat the fascists a strict discipline was called for and he subordinated himself to it during the war.

Paradoxes and sometimes contradictions are to be found in Hemingway, both big and small. In disputing in jest with me he concludes his dithyramb to the bracing effect of liquor with the sudden reservation that in two sets of circumstances a sober head is essential. "When you write or when you fight." And fighting—struggling with refractory material at his desk and on a battle-field against the fascists —was for him the real meaning of life.

Key West, Florida
August 19, 1935

Dear Kashkeen,

Thank you for sending the book[1] and the article in *International Literature*. They came, forwarded by Saroyan today. A little while ago the article came forwarded by *Esquire* and I read it.

It is a pleasure to have somebody know what you are writing about. That is all I care about. What I seem to be myself is of no importance. Here criticism is a joke. The bourgeois critics do not know their ass from a hole in the ground and the newly converted communists are like all new converts; they are so anxious to be orthodox that all they are interested in are schisms in their own critical attitudes. None of it has anything to do with literature which is always literature, when it is, no matter who writes it nor what the writer believes. Edmund Wilson is the best critic we have but he no longer reads anything that comes out. Cowley is honest but still very much under the impression of being converted. He is also tending to stop reading. The others are all careerists. I do not know one that I would want with me, or trust with me, if we ever had to fight for anything. I've forgotten Mike Gold. He is honest too.

This is the way most criticism goes. Isidor Schneider will write a piece about me, say. I will read it because I am a professional and so do not care for compliments. Only to see what I can learn. The article will be very stupid and I learn nothing. I am not indignant; only bored. Then some friend of mine (Josephine Herbst) will write to Schneider and say why do you say such and such, what about *A Farewell To Arms*, what about what Hem says in *Death in the Afternoon*, etc. Schneider will write her in answer that he never read anything of mine after *The Sun Also Rises* which seemed to him to be antisemitic. Yet he will write a serious article on your work. And not read your three last books. It is all balls.

---

[1] A book of stories translated into Russian in 1934—*I.K.*

Your article is very interesting. The only trouble, to me, is that it ends with me as Mr. Frazer out in Billings Montana with right arm broken so badly the back of my hand hung down against the back of my shoulder. It takes five months to fix it and then is paralyzed. I try to write with my left hand and can't. Finally the musculo-spiral nerve regenerates and I can lift my wrist after five months. But in the meantime one is discouraged. I remember the study in pain and the discouragement, the people in the hospital and the rest of it and write a story *Gambler, Nun and Radio*. Then I write *Death in the Afternoon*. Then I write the other stories in the last book.[1] I go to Cuba and there is a little trouble. I go to Spain and write a damned good story about necessity which maybe you did not see called *One Trip Across*. In the meantime I write that stuff in *Esquire* to eat and support my family. They do not know what I am going to write and it gets to them the day before they go to press. Sometimes it is better than others. I write it in one day each time and I try to make it interesting and to tell the truth. It is not pretentious. We go to Africa and have the best time I have ever had. Now have finished a book[2] and will send it to you. Maybe you will think it is shit and maybe you will like it. Anyway it is the best I can write. If you like it and want any of it for the magazine to translate you can use it. It may be of no interest to you. But I think it will be, perhaps, to yourself if not to the magazine.

Everyone tries to frighten you now by saying or writing that if one does not become a communist or have a Marxian viewpoint one will have no friends and will be alone. They seem to think that to be alone is something dreadful; or that to not have friends is to be feared, I would rather have one honest enemy than most of the friends that I have known. I cannot be a communist now because I believe in only one thing: liberty. First I would look after myself and do my work. Then I would care for my family. Then I would help my neighbor. But the state I care nothing for. All the state has ever meant to me is unjust taxation. I have never asked anything from it. Maybe you have a better state but I would have to see it to believe it. And I would not know then because I do not speak Russian. I believe in the absolute minimum of government.

In whatever time I had been born I could have taken care of myself if I were not killed. A writer is like a Gypsy. He owes no al-

---

[1] *Winner Take Nothing—I.K.*
[2] *Green Hills of Africa—I.K.*

legiance to any government. If he is a good writer he will never like the government he lives under. His hand should be against it and its hand will always be against him. The minute anyone knows any bureaucracy well enough he will hate it. Because the minute it passes a certain size it must be unjust.

A writer is an outlyer like a Gypsy. He can be class conscious only if his talent is limited. If he had enough talent all classes are his province. He takes from them all and what he gives is everybody's property.

Why should a writer expect reward or the appreciation of any group of people or any state? The only reward is in doing your work well and that is enough reward for any man. There is nothing more obscene to me than a man posing himself as a candidate for the French Academy or any Academy.

Now if you think this attitude leads to sterility and the individual's becoming nothing but human waste I believe you are wrong. The measure of a man's work is not quantity. If you can get as much intensity and as much meaning in a story as some one can get in a novel that story will last as long as it is any good. A true work of art endures forever; no matter what its politics.

If you believe one thing and work at it always, as I believe in the importance of writing, you have no disillusion about that unless you are ambitious. All you have is hatred for the shortness of the time we have to live and get our work done.

A life of action is much easier to me than writing. I have greater facility for action than for writing. In action I do not worry any more. Once it is bad enough you get a sort of elation because there is nothing you can do except what you are doing and you have no responsibility. But writing is something that you can never do as well as it can be done. It is a perpetual challenge and it is more difficult than anything else that I have ever done—so I do it. And it makes me happy when I do it well.

I hope this does not bore you. I write it to you because of the care and the accuracy you have used in studying what I write so that you might know something of what I think. Even though it makes you think me a worse shit when you read it. I do not give a damn whether any U.S.A. critic knows what I think because I have no respect for them. But I respect you and I like you because you wished me well.

Yours very truly,
Ernest Hemingway

P.S. Do you ever see Malraux? I thought *La Condition Humaine* was the best book I have read in ten years. If you ever see him I wish that you would tell him so for me. I meant to write to him but I write French with so many mis-spelled words that I was ashamed to write.

I had a cable signed by him, Gide and Rolland forwarded to me by mail from London asking me to some writers congress. The cable came to me in the Bahama Islands two weeks after the Congress was over. They probably think I was rude not to answer.

This new book is out in October I'll send it to you then. I can always be reached through Key West, Florida, USA. They forward when we are away.

E.H.

P.P.S. Don't you drink? I notice you speak slightingly of the bottle. I have drunk since I was fifteen and few things have given me more pleasure. When you work hard all day with your head and know you must work again the next day what else can change your ideas and make them run on a different plane like whisky? When you are cold and wet what else can warm you? Before an attack who can say anything that gives you the momentary well being that rum does? I would as soon not eat at night as not to have red wine and water. The only time it isn't good for you is when you write or when you fight. You have to do that cold. But it always helps my shooting. Modern life, too, is often a mechanical oppression and liquor is the only mechanical relief. Let me know if my books make any money and I will come to Moscow and we will find somebody that drinks and drink my royalties up to end the mechanical oppression.

Key West
March 23, 1939

Dear Kashkeen,

Well I'm damned glad to hear from you. Not only just to hear but to know that the translation in the U.S.S.R. is being done by someone who wrote the best and most useful, to me, critique on my stuff I ever read and probably knows more about it than I do. I'm damned happy you are still doing it and I will order Scribners to send galleys of the books as you suggest. I also hereby authorize you to do the adaptation of the play.[1]

---

[1] *The Fifth Column—I.K.*

About the order of the stories in the book.[1] Scribners wanted the three new ones first and since all but those were in the order in which they appeared in books when published it seemed O.K. It would have been better, probably, to have them in the end and keep it all chronological. In future editions I think you would be wise to put them at the end and so authorize you.

There are some new stories finished. Am now writing a novel and have fifteen thousand words done.[2] Wish me luck, pal. Also a story was published in *Cosmopolitan* called *Nobody Ever Dies*. They made some cuts and before you ever publish that one I wish you would let me send you the version that I will publish when I print it in book form. Have no copy or would send it.

For your information in stories about the war I try to show *all* the different sides of it, taking it slowly and honestly and examining it from many ways. So never think one story represents my viewpoint because it is much too complicated for that.

We know war is bad. Yet sometimes it is necessary to fight. But still war is bad and any man who says it is not is a liar. But it is very complicated and difficult to write about truly. For instance to take it on a simply personal basis—in the war in Italy when I was a boy I had much fear. In Spain I had no fear after a couple of weeks and was very happy. Yet for me to not understand fear in others or deny its existence would be bad writing. It is just that now I understand the whole thing better. The only thing about a war, once it has started, is to win it—and that is: what we did not do. The hell with war for a while. I want to write.

That piece you translated about the American dead[3] was very hard for me to write because I had to find something I could honestly say about the dead. There is not much to say about the dead except that they are dead. I would like to able to write understandingly about both deserters and heroes, cowards and brave men, traitors and men who are not capable of being traitors. We learned a lot about all such people.

Well it is all over now but the people like these did nothing about defending the Spanish Republic now feel a great need to attack us who tried to do something in order to make us look foolish and justify themselves in their selfishness and cowardice. And we having

---

[1] A second book of short stories published in the Soviet Union in 1939—*I.K.*

[2] Hemingway refers to *For Whom the Bell Tolls*—*I.K.*

[3] *On the American dead in Spain*—*I.K.*

fought as well as possible, and without selfishness, and lost, they now say how stupid it was ever to have fought at all.

In Spain it was very funny because the Spaniards where they did not know you always thought we were Russians. When Teruel was taken I had been with the attacking troops all day and went into the town the first night with a company of dynamiters. When the civilians came out of their houses they asked me what they should do and I told them to stay in the houses and not go into the street that night under any circumstances and explained to them what good people we reds were and it was very funny. They all thought I was a Russian and when I told them I was a North American they didn't believe a word of it. During the retreat it was the same. The Catalans all moving steadily away from the war at all times but always very pleased to see us, the Russians, moving through the traffic in the wrong direction—that is toward the front. When the Catalans held a front up in Aragon for so many months and did nothing they had a kilometer between their trenches and the Fascists and on the road, where their front line ran, they had a sign-board that said Frente Peligro. Danger. The Front. I took a nice picture of it.

Well this is enough nonsense. I'd like to see you and I would like to come to U.S.S.R. But what I have to do now is write. As long as there is a war you always think perhaps you will be killed so you have nothing to worry about. But now I am not killed so I have to work. And as you have no doubt discovered living is much more difficult and complicated than dying and it is just as hard as ever to write.

I would be glad to write for nothing but if no one paid you you would starve. I could make much money by going to Hollywood or by writing shit. But I am going to keep on writing as well as I can and as truly as I can until I die. And I hope I never die. Have been working over in Cuba where I could get away from letters, telegrams, appeals etc., and really work. Been going good.

So long, Kashkeen, and good luck. I appreciate your care and integrity in the translations very much. Give my best regards to all the Comrades who work on the stuff. Comrade is a word I know quite a lot more about than when I wrote you first. But you know something funny? The only thing you have to do entirely by yourself and that no one alive can help you with no matter how much they want to (except by leaving you alone) is to write. Very difficult business, my boy. Try it sometimes. . . (joke).

Hemingway

Konstantin SIMONOV

A year and a half has passed since Ernest Hemingway left us.

I like many other Russian readers of Hemingway, probably, love him not only for his supremely courageous books but for his behaviour in life which was itself an example of courage. I love him for having hated fascism, all the more because he expressed his hatred not only in words but in deeds: he fought fascism wherever he found it.

I wish to acquaint readers with a letter Hemingway wrote sixteen years ago.

During our visit to the United States and Canada in the spring and summer of 1946, Ilya Ehrenburg and I were invited by Hemingway to visit him in Cuba where he was then living. To our disappointment we were unable to go. On learning this, Hemingway wrote a long letter to me in New York.

I had the impression that in this letter Hemingway felt it necessary to state his attitude to some of those problems which would probably have arisen by themselves in those days had that meeting between him and two Soviet writers taken place.

I think that today, when sixteen years have passed, the letter is interesting not only as a private letter but as a document for the public to read. Hemingway writes about his participation in the war against German fascism, about his views on the postwar situation, about the necessity of friendship and mutual understanding. His letter is full of goodwill towards the people of our country.

And here is the letter which with a few short abridgements I bring to the readers' attention.

> Finca Vigia, San Francisco
> de Paula, Cuba
> June 20, 1946

Dear Simonov,

... Your book came last night. I am reading it today and will write you to Moscow when I finish it. . . .

I should have read it when it was first translated but I was just back from the war and I could not read anything about it. No matter how good. Am sure you know what I mean. After the first war I was in I could not write about it for almost nine years. After the Spanish war I had to write immediately because I knew the next war was coming so fast and I felt there was no time. After this war I had my head very badly smashed up (three times) and bad headaches. But finally

I have gotten writing again all right but my novel, after 800 mss. pages is still a long way from the war. But if I live O.K. it will get there. Hope it can be very good.

All through this war I wanted to be with the army of the U.S.S.R. and see that wonderful fight but I did not feel justified to try to be a war correspondent there since A—I did not speak Russian and B—because I thought I could be more useful in trying to destroy the Krauts (what we call the Germans) in other work. I was at sea for about two years in a difficult job. Then went to England and flew with R.A.F. as a correspondent before the invasion, accompanied the Normandy invasion, and then spent the rest of the time with the 4th Infantry Division. The time with the R.A.F. was wonderful but useless. With the 4th Infantry Division and with the 22nd regiment of Infantry I tried to be useful through knowing French and the country and being able to work ahead with the Maquis. This was a good life and you would have enjoyed it. I remember how after we had come into Paris ahead of the army, and the Army had caught up with us André Malraux came to see me and asked how many men I had commanded. I told him never more than 200 at the most and usually between 14 and 60. He was very happy and relieved because he had commanded 2,000 men, he said. So there was no question of literary prestige involved.

That summer from Normandy into Germany was the happiest I ever had in spite of it being war. Later in Germany, in the Schnee Eifel, Hurtgen Forest and the Rundstedt offensive it was very bitter fighting also quite cold. Earlier there was much bad fighting but retaking France and especially Paris made me feel the best I had ever felt. Ever since I had been a boy I had been in retreats, holding attacks, retreats, victories with no reserves to follow them up, etc., and I had never known how winning can make you feel.

Now, since the fall of 1945, I have been writing so hard, and all the time, that the weeks and the months go by so quickly we will all be dead if we do not know it.

I hope you had a good trip in America and Canada. I wish I would have spoken Russian and gone around with you because there are really many wonderful people to meet and fine things to do. But few of those people speak Russian. I would like you to have known our Colonel of the 22nd Infantry (now General Lanham) who is my best friend and the commanders of the 1st, 2nd and 3rd battalions (those that are alive) and many Company and Platoon commanders and many wonderful American soldiers. The 4th Infantry division from D day on Utah Beach until VE Day had 21,205 casualties out of a strength of 14,037. My oldest boy was attached to the 3rd Infantry Division which had 33,547 out of their 14,037. But they were in Sicily and Italy before landing in Southern France. He dropped in ahead as a parachutist and was later wounded very badly and captured in the fall in the Voges. He is a good kid, a Captain, and you would like him. He told the Krauts (he is very blond) he was the son of a ski instructor in Austria and had gone to America after his father had been killed in an avalanche. When the Krauts finally found out who he was they sent him to a Hostage camp. But he was liberated at the end.

It is a damned shame you could not have come down here. Are your poems or the journal translated into English? I would like to read them very much. I know what you are talking about. As you say you know what I am talking about. After all the world has gotten far enough along so that writers should be able to understand one another. There is so much *govno* (probably mis-spelled) that goes on and yet people are so good, and intelligent and well intentioned and would understand each other well if we could have understanding of each other instead of the repeat performance of a Churchill; doing now what he did in 1918-1919 to preserve something that now can only be preserved by war. Excuse me if I talk politics. I know that I am always supposed to be a fool when I do. But I know that nothing stands between the friendship of our countries. . . .

There is a boy (now probably old man) in the U.S.S.R. named Kashkeen. Red headed (probably greyheaded). He is the best critic and translator I ever had. If still around please give him my best regards. Was *For Whom the Bell Tolls* ever translated? I read a review by Ehrenburg but never heard. It would be easy to publish with small changes of, elimination of, certain names. Wish you could read it. It isn't about war as we knew it the last few years. But about small hill war it is all right and there is one place where we kill the fascists you would like.

Good luck and have a good trip.

Your friend E r n e s t H e m i n g w a y

"Buying Commission Would Cut Out Waste": A Newly Discovered Contribution to the Toronto Daily Star

C. E. Frazer Clark, Jr.

Hemingway's literary apprenticeship was interrupted in the late Spring of 1918 when he left the *Kansas City Star* to go to war.[1] Twenty-one months later, a scarred war veteran, Hemingway was again back at work as a reporter in pursuit of a by-line, this time on *The Toronto Star*.[2]

Ralph Connable[3] brought Hemingway to Toronto and it was Connable who introduced Hemingway to *The Star*. Hemingway soon found an opportunity to write about Connable, with an unsigned article describing Connable's part in assisting the War Purchasing Commission investigate ". . . the haphazard, muddling, wasteful squandering of public money . . ." appearing in the Toronto *Daily Star* on 20 April 1920. A clipping of this article, initialed and dated by Hemingway, is in the Clark collection.

During his literary apprenticeship Hemingway identified a substantial portion of his unsigned work by sending home clippings. The Hemingway-Connable family association provided a further reason for Hemingway to clip this article and send it home.

Fifteen articles bearing Hemingway's by-line and eleven unsigned articles were published in the *Toronto Star Weekly* in 1920.[4] "Buying Commission Would Cut Out Waste" is the first unsigned Hemingway piece located in the *Toronto Daily Star* for 1920,[5] and raises the question of what other early unsigned Hemingway work in the *Daily Star* remains to be located.

[1] Hemingway left for France on 23 May 1918. Carlos Baker, *Ernest Hemingway: A Life Story* (New York: Scribners, 1969), p. 39.

[2] *The Toronto Star* published both a daily and a weekly edition: *The Toronto Daily Star* and the *Toronto Star Weekly*. Both published Hemingway's work. His first article appeared without a by-line in the *Toronto Star Weekly* for 14 February 1920 (Hanneman C33).

[3] Ralph Connable was at the time head of the F. W. Woolworth chain in Canada. During the summer of 1919 at Petosky, Michigan, Connable determined that Hemingway could be a useful companion for the Connable son, and invited Hemingway to Toronto to stay with the son while the rest of the Connable family went South. See Baker, p. 66. Connable introduced Hemingway to Arthur Donaldson, chief of advertising layout for both the *Daily Star* and *Star Weekly*. See Baker, p. 68.

[4] Hanneman, C33-C51, C53. See also Baker, p. 68.

[5] Tuesday, 20 April 1920, p. 3.

BUYING COMMISSION WOULD CUT OUT WASTE

Present Government System Is Faulty, According to Mr. Ralph Connable.

The present Government system of purchasing supplies is comparable to having every engineer on the C.P.R. negotiate for the coal, water and oil for his own engine, said Ralph Connable to-day.

Mr. Connable, who heads the Woolworth Company in Canada, at the request of the War Purchasing Commission, made a thorough investigation of the system of buying supplies for the twenty or more departments of the Dominion Government, with instructions to apply business methods and put the department on an efficient basis.

According to Mr. Connable, each department is now buying supplies in utter ignorance of what the others are doing. The Post-Office Department, Customs Office Department, Departments of Justice and Militia all buy their own equipment without any knowledge of what the other is purchasing. This is as wasteful of money as though each section boss of a railway negotiated for his own rails and ties and each station agent bought his own oil, soap and brooms, printed his own time tables and built the particular type of station he most admired.

Disadvantages of System.

One of the disadvantages of the present system is that the departments generally do not get the benefit of the technical knowledge and experience acquired in each department. This and a number of other faults that aid in the operation of the patronage system, but that cost the public hundreds of thousands of dollars, would be done away with by centralization of the purchasing.

For example, the quantities of goods demanded by some of the departments are not sufficient to enable them to purchase at the lowest wholesale price. Centralizing would make all the goods be bought together and combining the purchases of the departments in one would make a sufficient quantity to get the rock bottom wholesale price.

Now there is no uniform standard as to sizes and qualities for the different departments. Thus each may demand a certain size envelope or certain quality of form. Adoption of standard sizes alone would save enormously.

Departments bidding against each other for supplies have raised prices materially. Lack of standardized inspection has been another difficulty.

Handle All Buying.

Mr. Connable advocates forming a Central Purchasing Staff such as that headed by Sir Hormidas Laporte, the late W. P. Gundy and Galt, of Winnipeg, during the war. This staff would handle all the purchasing stock from budgets made up by each department the first of the year. Thus they would be able to take advantage of market conditions as all big commercial houses do.

Each department should have a requisition clerk to look after the interests of the department, to handle emergency orders, and to act as a medium of quick communication between the department and the commission. Having him an employe of the commission would be a quick red tape cutter.

Even if the men in charge of the purchasing commission were paid $10,000 to $25,000 a year salaries there would be a net gain of millions to the Government by stopping the present wasteful system of uncontrolled buying. It is necessary to pay good salaries to get men above the influence of political pull and patronage.

Give Commission Advice.

An advisory board of such men as Harry McGee, R. Y. Eaton, H. J. Daly and J. Allen Ross should be appointed to serve without pay and give the new commission the benefit of their experience during the first two or three years of its life. Management of this kind would turn the purchasing department from the haphazard, muddling, wasteful squanderer of public money that it is to-day into a compact business organization that will get the public the best value for every dollar it spends.

Toronto Daily Star, 20 April 1920. Collection of C. E. Frazer Clark, Jr.

Point of View in the Nick Adams Stories

Carl Ficken

Despite the succession of heroes from Jake Barnes to Thomas Hudson, one of Ernest Hemingway's most interesting characters remains his first creation, Nick Adams. The later heroes may seem tougher, more like the image Hemingway was building for himself; but Nick Adams has special qualities which make him stand out as one of Hemingway's most fully-revealed characters. Through a dozen short stories mentioning his name, Nick Adams grows as a person of rare sensitivity and self-perception: He is a loyal son, a wandering youth, a soldier briefly, a hospital patient, a sportsman, a father; he is capable of great friendships and he is something of a loner; he is one who has made many discoveries about life and has finally suffered a shocking wound; he is a thinker—not a sophisticated intellectual, but a man who tries to understand what has happened to him. Naturally, Hemingway must do many things well to achieve his success with Nick Adams; one of his major accomplishments is that he employs a narrative perspective which keeps the focus constantly on the hero and allows the hero to tell his own tale.

I

Early critics of Hemingway did not pay too much attention either to the Nick Adams stories as a whole or to Hemingway's handling of point of view; yet, when he published a first-person novel, he was readily identified with his protagonist. It may be that the use of the third person in the earlier stories was a sufficient fake to keep critics off the autobiographical trail: One result was that Hemingway's image began to develop more in relationship to Jake Barnes than to Nick Adams. The Baker biography and Philip Young's studies of Nick Adams have successfully demonstrated that the Nick stories grew out of Hemingway's childhood memories, his boyhood adventures and his war experiences. Baker is able to show, with almost every story, a parallel between Hemingway's life and Nick's. In some cases, it is just that Hemingway's father was a doctor and that they lived near an Indian camp in the summers; in others, it is that

Hemingway's father did commit suicide, and that Hemingway himself did experience a serious wound which he either felt to be, or made to be, traumatic.[1]

None of this is to say that Nick Adams is Ernest Hemingway or that these stories are a "Portrait of the Artist." Hemingway did bring to the stories a fertile imagination: he created Nick Adams, not *ex nihilo*, but out of both his life and his strong, imaginative powers. Nonetheless, the author's hand is deeply involved in this character: All through the stories the relationship between author-narrator-character is especially close. It was important for Hemingway to "write out" of himself the Nick stories, just as it was important for Nick to camp and fish and cook out his problems. As Professor Young has noted, Nick is, for Hemingway, a "special kind of mask."[2] Clearly, Hemingway always stands right behind his narrator no matter who that narrator might be, but in the Nick stories a side of the writer's own personality shows through, a side which he apparently at other times attempted to cover over with his inevitable bravado.[3]

At the beginning of his writing career in the 1920's, Hemingway was working at, among other things, the problem of point of view. In his first publication, *Three Stories and Ten Poems,* 1923, he told two of the stories through an omniscient third-person narrator and the other in the first person; "My Old Man," in fact, remains one of the classic examples of the unreliable, first-person narrator. Of the *in our time* sketches, one half are in the first person and one half in third person; of the *In Our Time* interchapters, six are first person and ten are in some form of third person; three of the *In Our Time* stories are in the first person, the rest in a variety of third-person forms. And, of course, the first two novels are told by their main character, although Hemingway did attempt to rewrite *The Sun Also Rises* in the third person.[4] What is most significant about all this is that, throughout the period in which most of the Nick Adams stories were written, Hemingway was working from a variety of narrative perspectives and had already begun to establish his primary point-of-view techniques.[5]

In the Nick Adams stories, written over a span of ten years, Hemingway worked out a means of relating point of view to the development of character—that is his essential achievement in the handling of narrative perspective in these stories. Besides that, of course, he demonstrates great versatility. His treatment is by no means simple or clear-cut; no two stories are exactly alike in point of view. A study of Hemingway's technique in the Nick Adams stories, limited to those stories in which Nick's name is specifically mentioned, reveals a definite correlation between Nick's own state of mind and the degree to which the narrator probes into that mind. As a general rule, subjectivity intensifies in the stories around Nick's traumatic wound. In the earlier stories, when Nick is younger and less capable of understanding what is happening to him, the point of view is more objective, so that the reader knows less of what Nick is thinking; in the stories around the wound, the narrative perspective is most complex and Hemingway departs most decisively from an easily identified point of view; then, as Nick grows past the wound, a measure of objectivity returns. It isn't quite that simple, of course, because "The Killers," in which the narrator is almost absent—the most objective story, in other words—takes place when Nick is in his teens; and, the earliest story, "Indian Camp," offers a brief, but crucial, insight into Nick's thoughts. Yet, if the stories were listed on a scale of increasing subjectivity in point of view, the wound-recovery stories would be at the subjective end of the scale. Or, the stories might be placed on a scale which moves toward and then away from subjectivity, toward and then away from the wound. On such a scale only at two places are the stories out of line chronologically, even though they were neither written nor did they appear in this order.[6] None of this is to suggest, of course, that Hemingway consciously plotted such a development or that he was aware in every story of this relationship between point of view and character development. Yet, examination of the stories reveals that Hemingway matched his narrative perspective with his hero's mental state—no small accomplishment for a writer in his late twenties, consciously done or not.

In part, it is the fact that Hemingway is working at point of view with such special skill that makes a study of the problem worth while. He is experimenting with point of view; he is working at getting into the mind of his character, just as were his contemporaries. Many of Hemingway's stories, with the distinctive point of view, were written in the years between the celebrated examples of point of view innovation: Joyce's *A Portrait of the Artist as a Young Man* and *Ulysses* in 1916 and 1919, Virginia Wolf's *To the Lighthouse* in 1927, and Faulkner's *The Sound and the Fury* in 1929. Yet, Hemingway's point-of-view technique has received little notice: In the more than forty years since the first Nick stories and the first-person novels, one general study[7] and one analysis of point of view in *The* novels, one general study[7] and one analysis of point of view in *The Sun Also Rises*[8] have appeared; a few stories raise occasional comment,[9] but for the most part Hemingway's treatment of point of view is neglected by the critics. Perhaps Hemingway's work with narrative perspective is not the most brilliant achievement of the century—one must not claim *too* much, after all—but careful study of these stories indicates that he was extremely diligent in striving for precise points of view and that he came up with something, if not new, at least significantly different from the usual literary patterns. The problem in talking about it is to say just *how* it is different.

II

One of the difficulties in discussing point of view is that of finding the precise defining terminology. It seems as though every scholar who dares to talk about the subject employs a different set of terms.[10] Clearly, the most traditional terms (first person, third person, omniscient author) do not begin to make sufficiently sharp distinctions for a great deal of modern literature; it is understandable that critics should seek new labels to capture the subtle variations of narrative perspective, but the result is additional confusion in terminology. Indeed, when one tries to apply the terms from any one general discussion of the subject to a specific author, he finds that the categories don't fit, that they don't cover the individual effects achieved by that author. Hemingway, for example, has at least three different kinds of third-person narration in the Nick Adams stories; traditional labels do not work neatly with those stories.

Still, discussion is impossible without identifying terms. Rather than invent a new set, I have chosen those terms which apply most directly to Hemingway's techniques and which can serve as fairly easy handles for this study. These stories, again, do not fit perfectly into any categories; it is more accurate to see them on a subjective-objective scale. Nonetheless, the shades of difference between the narrators need to be clarified, insofar as that is possible. Four general categories of narrator seem to work in these stories (in each category a brief quotation from one of the stories will serve as a temporary identification of the type of narration). The "Effaced Narrator" is one who merely observes the action but cannot see into the minds of the characters; this is the objective end of the scale and is represented in the Nick Adams stories only by "The Killers" ("From the other end of the counter Nick Adams watched them." [11]). The "Author-Observer" is an omniscient author in that he may know what is in the

215

mind of more than one character at any given time, but he is a mere observer in that he reports only what is immediately before him ("Majorie . . . loved to fish with Nick . . . He was afraid to look at her,[12,13])." The "Center of Consciousness" is a narrator who reflects the mind of one central intelligence (here, Nick himself), albeit with varying intensity ("Nick's hand was shaky. He reeled in slowly . . . He'd bet the trout was angry . . . That was a trout . . . By God, he was the biggest one I ever heard of"). The "Narrator-Agent" is, of course, the first-person narrator telling his own story ("That night we lay on the floor in the room and I listened to the silk-worms eating,"[14]). Of these four forms, the Effaced Narrator is farthest from the central character's mind and the Narrator-Agent is, naturally, closest.

Such variation in point of view is a way of adding dimension to the character of Nick Adams. If the reader sees Nick both from an objective narrator's position and as Nick sees himself, then the reader has a deeper, more rounded insight into the character. Such a perspective is not usually possible since one of the rules of the writing game is that point of view must be consistent; because Hemingway is writing short stories, however, and because he is willing to play with the "Center of Consciousness" narration, he gains additional development of his hero.

At the same time, through all the movement in point of view, Hemingway manages to maintain Nick's place as the central character of the stories. However far the reader or narrator stands from Nick, however little he knows of Nick's thoughts, Nick remains the key figure. Hemingway accomplishes this, not only thematically by making the meaning of the story rest with Nick, but also by keeping a spot focus on Nick, mentioning his name, identifying other characters through their relationship to him, giving brief, almost imperceptible, insights into Nick's actions. This identification of Nick as the central character, in other words, increases as the narrator comes nearer Nick's mind; but even when the narrator is barely there, when he is most effaced, the reader is still made conscious of Nick's presence. To discuss Hemingway's narrators in the order of their distance from the protagonist is to watch a camera gradually move in, closer and closer, to Nick Adams. The following study will progress from the objective toward the subjective: It will begin with the Effaced Narrator of "The Killers" and then discuss the Author-Observer, the Center of Consciousness and the Narrator-Agent.

The General Store at Horton's Bay

Effaced Narrator

"The Killers" often serves as the primary illustration of a point-of-view technique common to Hemingway and other twentieth century writers.[15] It is an especially fine example of the Effaced Narrator, since it has narration reduced to a minimum, few descriptive sentences, little stage direction, nothing added to the simple "he said," and considerable dialogue. If the story were to be made into a play, no "narrator" off-stage would be necessary to tie the action together, nor would there be any authorial direction to tell actors how to say their lines; in fact, there is less "authorial intrusion" in this story than there is in most drama (even Becket cannot resist an occasional "violently," or "indifferently"). The narrator is practically effaced.[16]

All this is true. And yet, in "The Killer," the narrator is only *practically* effaced. Hemingway allows the narrator enough power to put an occasional spotlight on Nick Adams. The story is a good example of the Effaced Narrator, but the author has made some exceptions in the technique, not so as to mar the story's effectiveness, but so as to place Nick Adams unambiguously at the center. The exceptions to the rule, then are worth noting. The story opens with a close-up of Henry's lunchroom; clearly an observer of that first scene description is necessary and that observer—or Effaced Narrator, as he should be called to avoid confusion with the next category—stands inside the lunchroom. "The door of Henry's lunch-room opened and two men *came in.* They sat down at the counter" (italics mine).[11] After an initial, conventional exchange between the waiter, George, and his customers, the Effaced Narrator again provides description, again from the inside: "Outside it was getting dark. The street-light came on outside the window." Then the focus shifts to Nick: "From the other end of the counter Nick Adams watched them. He had been talking to George when they came in." That sentence provides a focus on Nick, a still-shot showing what Nick is and has been doing, and the focus is accentuated by the use of his full name. Yet, obviously, the vantage point for the observations rests outside Nick: The Effaced Narrator stands so that he is able to see both ends of the counter. The following conversation is reported objectively, with only brief comment by the Effaced Narrator about the actions or external appearance of the characters. Even in straight dialogue lines, attention falls on Nick when the killers ask for his name, a question they do not direct to George. Even when Nick is off-stage and the external action rests with George, what is happening to Nick, tied up in the kitchen, is more important and represents a more shaking experience than what happens to George: Nick, after all, "had haver had a towel in his mouth before."[17]

Through it all, the Effaced Narrator stays with the central action of the story and never reveals anything of what could be in anyone's mind, except through dialogue. The only line suggesting Nick's feeling is the one in which the narrator said: "It sounded silly when he said it."[18] That can, of course, be taken objectively too: The Effaced Narrator is not saying that it sounded silly to Nick so much as that it sounded silly to him, or to any observer. Finally, the Effaced Narrator reveals what Nick saw, and by implication what he felt, as he left Ole: The fully dressed fighter was "lying on the bed looking at the wall."[19] Nothing in these examples breaks the rules of this kind of narration; but, within this approach, Hemingway is also able to place Nick sufficiently forward in the account so that the meaning of the story has to do with Nick's discovery of what life is like through those killers and Ole Anderson's reaction to them. This narrator is not so "effaced" then as to be nonexistent: the author's hand is clearly there directing steady, if gentle, attention to Nick Adams.

Author-Observer

The next step in the narrowing focus is to allow the narrator to look into the minds of the characters. Such a narrator, identified as an Author-Observer, handles "The Doctor and the Doctor's Wife," "The End of Something," and "Indian Camp." The former story is the only one wherein the observer has no access at all to Nick's thoughts, but does have some ability to see into the minds of the characters. The Author-Observer of this story also follows the central action from its beginning when Dick Boulton and two Indian boys come into the Adams's yard to "cut up logs for Nick's father."[20] The story continues objectively until the Author-Observer provides a small inside view of Dick Boulton: "He knew how big a man he was. He liked to get into fights. He was happy."[21] The Author-Observer stays with Dick and the boys until they leave the grounds; then he picks up the doctor inside the cottage. The Author-Observer is able to know that the doctor is "irritated"[21] about a pile of unopened medical journals, that he was "very fond"[22] of his gun, but no more than that can the reader discover apart from the objective report of action. Finally, in the last sentence of the story the doctor comes upon Nick in the woods reading and that's the first time Nick has been in the story. About Nick nothing can be known except that he prefers to go hunting with his father rather than to obey his mother's call, and that he knows how to find some black squirrels.

The difficulty with this story is that Nick is so far out of the action: He is in no sense the central character of the story; no evidence in the story suggests that Nick witnessed either one of this father's encounters that day. Some critics seem to assume that Nick did hear all this and that he was consequently initiated further into the nature of his father and mother, that he made discoveries about his parents[23]; but the text says quite plainly that the doctor went out the gate—through which Dick Boulton had entered the grounds at the beginning of the story—and followed a path into the hemlock woods where he found Nick. The boy could have witnessed both scenes, of course, and hurried back to the woods so that no one would know, but nothing in the story supports such an hypothesis. Hemingway does keep the focus on Nick by identifying the doctor at the outset as Nick's father; in fact, until Dick Boulton calls him "Doc" a full page into the story, the reader only knows of "Nick's father." It would seem then that the story is about Nick's father, and about his mother; Nick did not have to see what happened that day: The story presents for the reader the conditions under which Nick grows up. His discovery about his father and mother is no sudden thing, sprung upon him by observing these two incidents; it is a gradual awareness of what those two people are like and what they are doing to one another and that knowledge shapes him as surely as any of the initiations through which he must go. The narrative perspective of the story, through a fairly objective Author-Observer, keeps Nick in the reader's mind, simply by the use of his name and, at the same time, allows for a brief focus on Nick's parents and the role they have played in the boy's development.

Nick is the central character in "The End of Something," but the Author-Observer reveals just a little of what is in the minds of both Nick and Marjorie. He tells us that Marjorie "was intent on the rod all the time they trolled,"[12] that she "loved to fish with Nick"[12]; further, Marjorie responded "happily" to Nick's rather matter-of-fact announcement that there would be a moon. Nick's attitude throughout the early moments of the story contrasts sharply, of course, with Marjorie's, but the reader knows about that mainly through Nick's actions and the flats and sharps of his conversation. Only by slight touches does the Author-Observer let us know what Nick knows: That the moon would soon rise, that he "was afraid to look at

Marjorie,"[13] that he heard and "felt" Bill's approach. Since the story is about the break-up of Nick and Marjorie and about Nick's reaction to that break-up, it is important that the reader be able to see into the minds of both parties, even if only in such slight glimpses. It is important to know that Marjorie was happy in the relationship, that Nick was the one who took action; and the Author-Observer can do that most economically and with less strain on the dialogue, by allowing some insight into Marjorie's mind. The focus stays, finally, on Nick, inasmuch as he is the one whom the Author-Observer chooses to watch after the separation; but, the double focus at the beginning helps to enforce the sense of separation once Nick is left in the spotlight.

"Indian Camp" really belongs to this category, too, although its final sentence represents a deeper penetration into Nick's thoughts than exists in any of these first three Nick stories. It is, of course, the first story chronologically, but it belongs in this position on the objective-subjective scale because of that final look into Nick's mind. The final words of the story indicate that Nick "felt quite sure that he would never die"[24]; such a reflection by the Author-Observer parallels the language of the Center of Consciousness. While the last words qualify this story for the Center category, the rest of the story belongs to an Author-Observer; for that reason the story falls at the end of this category.

Up to that last sentence, the Author-Observer tells only what any person watching the action could assume: the facts that Nick "heard" the oarlocks,[25] that his "curiosity" about the childbirth ran out,[26] that he "felt" the warmth of the lake water,[24] that the doctor was "satisfied" with the cleanliness of his hands, that he felt and then lost "post-operative exhilaration"[27]—all these facts could be reasonable guesses by any observer. The last sentence, however, is more than a guess; it represents Nick's own thoughts, his reaction to what he had seen: "In the early morning on the lake sitting in the stern of the boat with his father rowing, he felt quite sure that he would never die."[24] That one sentence, by an Author-Observer who is able to read Nick's mind, not only attaches this story to Nick Adams, but also has thematic significance for the whole series of stories. It is the first instance of Nick Adams as a Center of Consciousness, a hint of the way Nick's thoughts were later to capture his stories. The focus of the story is kept on Nick—despite the fact that the Author-Observer allows fleeting gazes into the doctor's thoughts too—by having his name begin the third sentence of the story and by identifying the other two main characters through their relationship to Nick: "Uncle

George" and "Nick's father." In fact, Nick's father is identified as the "doctor" only four times, after the birth and while Nick is at some distance from the action.

Center of Consciousness

With "Three-Day Blow" the narrative technique of the Nick Adams stories turns sharply and with increasing depth into the personality of the protagonist. Providing almost the same effect as first-person narration, these stories offer, in varying degrees, an inside view of Nick's mind and are presented by a narrator who may best be identified as a Center of Consciousness: a narrator who sometimes stands apart from Nick and reports his actions, but who also sometimes stands within Nick and expresses Nick's mental process as though it were unmediated. It is this latter effect which muddies the point-of-view waters. Traditionally, the term "Center of Consciousness" applies to a work in which the narrator speaks of the main character in the third person, yet knows as much as that character knows. What is most significant about Hemingway's development of this narrative perspective is that he brings into the narration first- and second-person accounts in order—and this is the heart of the matter—in order to gain further penetration into the mind of the character.

"The Three-Day Blow" is a good example of a story in which the narrative focus rests clearly with Nick, moving from time to time inside his mind, behind his eyes, yet without the intense introspection of the later stories. Even though the story is mainly dialogue, Hemingway works at establishing the sensory perceptions of Nick, so that the reader is kept aware of what Nick sees, hears, feels, as well as what he thinks. When Bill leaves the room, Nick is the Center who notes: "He went out to the kitchen and came back"[28]; another observer could say that "They sat in front of the fire,"[28] but then so could Nick say, "We sat in front of the fire." Such a positioning of characters does not depend upon a neutral observer or an Effaced Narrator, as does the placement of Nick at "the other end of the counter" in "The Killers." Further, when Bill leaves the room a second time, Nick hears him walking overhead[28]; and when Nick leaves the room, we follow him and are aware of his every action.[29,30] The reader sees, as Nick sees, Bill pouring a drink: "Bill reached down the whisky bottle. His big hand went all the way around it. He poured the whisky into the glass Nick held out."[31] That is distinctly Nick's view of the scene, a view from the Center.

The total effect of the story is increased by the fact that Hemingway never really goes to Bill: The reader never knows what Bill thinks, except as Nick might guess it, as when he thinks of Bill, "He was also being consciously practical."[29] The directions for Bill's part of the conversation are consistently limited to "he said," whereas Nick "confesses" or asks "respectfully" or says "sadly."[29] This narrative perspective is strengthened in the middle of the story when Nick has had quite a bit to drink: the liquor tells on Nick, the Center, when he comes through the kitchen with a log and knocks a pan from the table. In the description of picking up his mess and then a moment later in the account of his passing the mirror, there is a sense of slowed reaction; the narrative is told not by a sober observer, but by a slightly tipsy Nick:

> He laid the log down and picked up the pan. It had contained dried apricots, soaking in water. He carefully picked up all the apricots off the floor, some of them had gone under the stove, and put them back in the pan. He dipped some more water onto them from the pail by the table. He felt quite proud of himself. He had been thoroughly practical.[29,30]

Then later, Nick

> went out into the kitchen again. He filled the pitcher with the dipper dipping cold spring water from the pail. On his way back to the living room he passed a mirror in the dining room and looked in it. His face looked strange. He smiled at the face in the mirror and it grinned back at him. He winked at it and went on. It was not his face but it didn't make any difference.[30]

Hemingway, therefore, establishes Nick as the Center of Consciousness both by revealing his thoughts and by providing an impression of his sensory responses.

"Ten Indians" follows a pattern which becomes familiar in the stories: an opening setting Nick up as the central character, a body largely in dialogue, and a conclusion focusing sharply on Nick's thoughts. Again "Nick" is the subject of the first sentence and we learn immediately that he "remembered" how many Indians he had seen on his way home with the Garners after a Fourth of July ball game. In the dialogue and the brief descriptive paragraphs, Nick *sees* the lights of Petoskey[32] (a neutral observer can reveal what a character looks at but not what he sees); he feels "hollow and happy inside" when he is teased about Prudie[32]; he hears his father moving in another room.[33] Further, the action is always with Nick: His father "brought in" the food, later "went out" of the kitchen, then "came

223

back" and the reader knows of Nick's father's movements only what Nick himself can observe. The final paragraphs of the story show Nick's reaction to the news he has received about Prudie's "infidelity"; his thought about the matter is fairly objective and subdued, but the reader is told that Nick heard and felt the cool night wind and that he finally "forgot to think about Prudence."[33] Only Nick himself could say, "he was awake a long time before he remembered that his heart was broken."[33] Even though this story was published outside the *In Our Time* sequences, its narrative technique places it properly on the objective-subjective scale for this time in Nick's life.

In "The Battler" the narrative perspective undergoes a subtle shift: The Center of Consciousness is more thoroughly revealed, is more apparent to the reader, through the use of what I shall call an indirect first person. The core of this technique, so essential to Hemingway's development of point of view, lies in sentences which stand apart from a "he thought" introduction, sentences which stand alone as thoughts of the Center, framed the way his mind would formulate them. The third paragraph of the story, for example, illustrates this variation in the usual third-person pattern:

> That lousy crut of a brakeman. He would get him some day. He would know him again. That was a fine way to act.[34]

In that paragraph, the second and third sentences are proper for a third-person narrator, the "He" referring to Nick; but the first and last sentences are Nick talking to himself, they represent what he said, even though they are not quoted and not introduced by "he said." Further, the report of what the brakeman had said to him can come only as Nick tells it. Whenever, in fact, Nick begins to talk about another man, the pronoun "he" may refer to himself or to the other man:

> "Come here, kid," he said. "I got something for you."
> He had fallen for it. What a lousy kid thing to have done.[34]

That first line comes directly from Nick and is much clearer and simpler than had an observer had to say something like, "He remembered that the brakeman had said, 'Come here, kid.' " The second "he" obviously refers to Nick and the sentence could just as easily read, "I had fallen for it. What a lousy kid thing to have done." Inasmuch as the latter sentence remains the same in either case, it represents, again, an indirect first person.

The next few descriptive paragraphs are almost objective reporting about Nick's hike along the railroad track to the fireside of Ad Francis, but Nick's sensations are constantly there (he was hungry and his eye ached[35]) and the lines could easily be done in the first person. The body of the story is, of course, largely made up of dialogue between Nick, Ad Francis and Bugs; passages of dialogue rival those in "The Killers" in objectivity, but with the difference that the reader here rarely knows anything of how Ad and Bugs say things or what they are thinking while he always knows how Nick is feeling or thinking. Almost every page keeps Nick's consciousness foremost through reminders that Nick is "embarrassed," feels "a little sick,"[36] tastes good food,[37] and finally hears and sees the fireside scene from a distance.[38] When we are told that Ad said something "seriously,"[36] or "happily,"[39] or that Bugs "soothed" Ad,[38] it is clear that these are the Center's impressions; those stage directions need not reflect insight into the characters' minds by an overseeing author: They simply represent Nick's idea of the way the voices sounded to him. In "The Battler" Nick is the Center of Consciousness, the narrator of his own story.

With "Cross-Country Snow," we interrupt the chronological order of the stories and move beyond the wound; Nick, here, is some years past the war, married, about to become a father. The story is rather objective, made up mostly of dialogue and brief descriptive paragraphs, with very little of Nick's own thoughts aside from dialogue. Only one pair of sentences really enters his mental process and there Hemingway uses the first person, without quotation marks and followed by "he thought."

> The girl came in and Nick noticed that her apron covered swellingly her pregnancy. I wonder why I didn't see that when she first came in, he thought.[40]

That unquoted first person again brings the reader a little further within Nick's mind, even though the rest of the story is so very objective. This is a more secure Nick Adams than the man of the wound stories; so it is appropriate that the narrative perspective should be as objective as it had been before the wound; still this Nick has now a store of experiences behind him, his mind is full of images and any window to them can show a great deal.

What Nick thinks, even though we know so little of it, is important for the theme of the story. A little later we are to learn that Nick's wife's pregnancy is a cause of his separation from George; our one glimpse into Nick's mind, therefore, fits the theme and causes

Nick's thoughts to stand out. Nick's mental confusion, first unaware-
ness and then marked notice, with regard to pregnancy at this point
leaves range for the reader's imagination to play with Nick's thoughts,
and it avoids what might become sentimental in direct connection
with his own wife. The only other comment in the story about the
thoughts of Nick comes in these sentences: "George and Nick were
happy. They were fond of each other. They knew they had the run
back home ahead of them."[41] That, to be sure, sounds like an omniscient narrator; but, according to the pattern already established in
the stories, it is just the sort of thing Nick could say or think: He is
confident in his relationship with George; he knows George's mind
well enough to guess that George feels as he does at this moment.

Despite some ambiguity about the narrative perspective in this
story, despite its objectivity and its heavily dramatic qualities, the
focus is no less on Nick, but it is kept there sensually rather than
mentally. In the second paragraph we are told that George had
"dipped out of sight"[42]; naturally he could not have dipped out of
the sight of an Author-Observer, but he could dip out of Nick's sight.
Then as Nick skis, "a steep undulation in the mountain side plucked
Nick's mind out and left him only the wonderful flying, dropping
sensation in his body."[42] When he falls in the snow, we are told that
he was "feeling like a shot rabbit" and that his nose and ears were
"jammed full of snow."[42] A little later, as George and Nick climb
back toward the lodge, Nick hears "George breathing and kicking in
his heels just behind him."[40] And at the end of the story, Nick feels
the cold when they go outside and sees George on the road ahead of
him. This accumulation of sensory perceptions, then, keeps Nick as
the central agent of the story so that what the reader sees and feels
come through that Center. Further, that part of the story which does
belong to the Effaced Narrator technique establishes a terse dialogue
entirely appropriate to the awkwardness and affected indifference of
this separation.

"Fathers and Sons" is also on the other side of Nick's war-time
wound; it is the final story in the Nick sequence and shows an older,
more mature Nick, reflecting on a great deal of what has gone before
and especially, since he is driving with his own son, reflecting on his
relationship to his father. These flashbacks offer a deep penetration
into Nick's mind and so represent an additional movement toward
subjectivity. Many of the flashbacks are similar to the early childhood stories, but now the action is frequently described in the
perfect or past-perfect tense rather than in the simple past. As Nick's

mind returns, however, to those childhood days, the older days get closer, so that at one point Nick's reminiscences begin to take the shape of a story, now in the past tense, about Nick and his Indian friends, Trudy and Billy.[43] And this little story, of three pages, is told from the same narrative perspective as the earlier stories, such as "Ten Indians"; that is, the story is largely dialogue, with a brief glimpse at Nick's thoughts and feelings. The effect is that of a story within a story, a narrator within a narrator; the smaller story is less subjective than the larger one; it is Nick talking about Nick talking about Nick; it is the Center becoming briefly an Author-Observer. The differences we have been noting in Hemingway's narrative perspectives are especially obvious here since two different forms appear side by side.

Most of "Fathers and Sons" is a report of Nick Adams's day-dreams as he drives along a highway in the United States: some of the thought is close to the surface, sparked by what he sees; some of the thought moves by association to his own past, even to the depth of that interior story about Trudy; a large portion of the thought is expressed in the more informal and more controlled second person ("In shooting quail you must not get between them and their habitual cover"[44]). The use of the second person is a still further step toward subjectivity; Hemingway treats the second person much the same way he treats the indirect first person, that is, in what amounts to the character talking to himself. If the work were being rewritten as a first-person narrative, all the second-person sentences could stand without change because they appear in the text just as a person might speak them. The second person as Hemingway uses it here, in other words, is a more informal, more conversational form; therefore, it moves the reader closer to the Center. Hemingway brings the second person into an easy mixture with the third, keeping the focus objectively on Nick but also adding a sense of closeness to him as the teller of the action.

> His father was as sound on those two things [fishing and shooting] as he was unsound on sex, for instance, and Nick was glad that it had been that way; for some one has to give you your first gun or the opportunity to get it and use it, and you have to live where there is game or fish if you are to learn about them, and now, at thirty-eight, he loved to fish and to shoot exactly as much as when he first had gone with his father.[45]

This story, then, has as its protagonist and as its Center of Consciousness an older Nick Adams, one who has been through a great deal, who still is troubled by his relationship to his father and by his father's suicide, yet one who is a little more in control of his life and his thought than he had been for a while after the war. It is the narrative perspective which helps to establish this kind of Center.

"Big Two-Hearted River" has only one character and so represents Nick totally as a Center of Consciousness and is perhaps the best example of the Hemingway third-person Center. This is Nick's story entirely: No other characters enter the picture except as Nick makes characters of a grasshopper or a trout, except as he remembers an old friend named Harry Hopkins. The third-person narration has those same qualities, apparent in other stories, of objective reporting and subjective identification with the protagonist. This story is too completely packed with illustrations of the technique already mentioned in connection with other stories for us to recount every one of them. Generally, however, the same principles are operating, intensified. At no point in the story does the focus come from any observer other than Nick; at every point first person would work. At the outset, Nick watches the train move "out of sight" and the reader is immediately placed so that he sees through Nick's eyes. In fact, one of the amazing things about this story is the way the author constantly surrounds the character with sensory images so that the reader feels he has stepped into Nick's skin. Many of the verbs are *look, watch, see* verbs, with the effect that the reader is always seeing what Nick sees. Furthermore, the reader feels, with Nick, a heavy pack, aching muscles, hunger and even happiness and that "old feeling" which Nick occasionally gets. It isn't just the power of clear descriptive language that causes the reader to experience all this with Nick; it is also that the perceptions come to the reader through Nick. There is nothing else to feel and see except what Nick feels and sees. And, of course, at every step of the way, the reader knows what Nick is thinking: It is as though every impression of Nick's mind makes up the continuation that is this story.

The narrative perspective of "Big Two-Hearted River" becomes most complex as the story draws to a close, as Nick comes closer to the swamp. In this story, Hemingway also uses the second person on several occasions: When Nick thinks about the proper way to handle trout, for example, the narration slowly moves into Nick's mind from the beginning of the paragraph with its objective report, "He had wet his hand before he touched the trout," to: "Nick did not like to fish with other men on the river. Unless they were of your party, they spoiled it."[46] The next to the last sentence shows Nick's mental attitude; the last sentence is Nick's own unspoken formulation of that attitude. Nick talks to himself again in the second person later on when he thinks about the difficult fishing near the bank:

> The very biggest ones would lie up close to the bank. You could always pick them up there on the Black . . . It was almost impossible to fish then, the surface of the water was blinding as a mirror in the sun. Of course, you could fish upstream, but in a stream like the Black, or this, you had to wallow against the current and in a deep place, the water piled up on you. It was no fun to fish upstream with this much current.[47]

Clearly this is a crucial moment for Nick; he is thinking everything out carefully: The narration shows all that when the Center actually talks to himself.

In this story, Hemingway takes an additional step into the mind of his hero by once slipping into a direct use of the first person. The occasion is the climactic moment after Nick loses the big trout. Here the reader is aware, within a single paragraph, of movement into Nick's mind, from an objective report of the action to Nick's thoughts to the indirect first person to first person. In quoting the paragraph here, I shall divide it and number it in order to illustrate the steps of this movement.

1) The leader had broken where the hook was tied to it. Nick took it in his hand. (An objective report)

2) He thought of the trout somewhere on the bottom, holding himself steady over the gravel, far down below the light, under the logs, with the hook in his jaw. Nick knew the trout's teeth would cut through the snell of the hook. (Third-person Center, within Nick's mind)

3) The hook would imbed itself in his jaw. (Now, third person refers to the trout; the sentence could be spoken by a narrator-Nick)

4) He'd bet the trout was angry. (Third person is back to Nick, but note easily it could be changed to "I'd bet")

5) Anything that size would be angry. That was a trout. He had been solidly hooked. Solid as a rock. He felt like a rock, too, before he started off. By God, he was a big one. (All indirect first person; could easily be placed in quotation marks)

6) By God, he was the biggest one I ever heard of.[48]

This beautiful and important story, then, makes a significant contribution to Hemingway's narrative technique because it is in this story that Hemingway achieves his deepest penetration so far into the mind, now a terribly troubled mind, of Nick Adams. Hemingway achieves this depth by complicating the Center of Consciousness role with the addition of first- and second-person sentences. Furthermore, the style of the story is fitting as a play-by-play picture of the narrator's own mind. This is the carefully controlled mind of a man meticulously searching for restoration from incoherence. The precise details, the concentration of each simple action, the tedious, logical thought of this story is exactly what Nick Adams must do for himself; since he is the Center of Consciousness, the one through whom the story is told, that very precision represents the steps he must take to regain control.[49]

The mind of Nick Adams is in a more troubled state in "A Way You'll Never Be" than it is in "Big Two-Hearted River," because that former story is closer in time to the wound Nick received. What has been true of the other Center of Consciousness stories is true of this one: The story is again told in the third person, but clearly from Nick's own point of view; it could as easily be told in the first person; much of the story still contains some of the familiar objective dialogue; sometimes, the story uses direct and indirect first person. The central episode of this story, for point of view, is that in which Nick's mind is at its most disintegrated state; when Nick tries to rest on a bunk, his mind wanders in and out of past experiences. These two pages of loosely connected thoughts come to the reader through Nick's consciousness, of course, and the movement into the first person and what we have called the indirect first person also enforces the mental disintegration. The long section begins with reference to Nick, "He was very disappointed," and moves by word and image association to:

I'd shoot one but it's too late now. They'd all be worse. Break his nose. They've put it back to five-twenty. We've only got four minutes more . . . Bail them out as you go. What a bloody balls. All right. That's right.[50]

The whole passage changes person as rapidly as it does subject and both changes work together to portray Nick's mental state: it is through his confused consciousness that the reader gets all this. The reader gets all this. The account is far different from the controlled day-dreaming of "Fathers and Sons"; a comparison of the two stories, both of which show Nick's mind moving into the past, demonstrates the greater degree of subjectivity in "A Way You'll Never Be."

Narrator—Agent

"Now I Lay Me" is the only first-person narration in the Nick Adams stories; obviously the Center of the other stories is not the Narrator-Agent. Hemingway is telling this one in the first person as, in fact, he might have told a number of the others in the first person by shifting only the pronouns. The Narrator-Agent of "Now I Lay Me" is identified concretely in one reminiscence when his father addresses him as "Nick." The basic pattern of the story is familiar since it begins and ends with that focus on the narrator and has an extended and more objective dialogue in the middle. But there are differences, even within that pattern. For one thing, the dialogue section in this first-person narrative is almost entirely dramatic:[51] the Narrator-Agent intrudes for only two short lines ("We smoked skilfully in the dark" and "We were both quiet and I listened to the silk-worms"[52]) and less than a fourth of the lines are introduced by the "I said" or "he said." Hemingway, in other words, lets the dialogue work for him and keeps his Narrator-Agent honest by not having him comment further on the conversation.

The second difference in the pattern of this story is that the opening section is longer: The Narrator-Agent gets to say more in this story than did the Center in his. And that fits too. If the author decides that he is going to write in the first person, it must have something to do with a desire to get more deeply into the mind of his narrator: it is appropriate, therefore, that the Narrator-Agent should have more time to make his case. And, in this story, Nick does probe more deeply into his own thoughts, he is more analytical, there is a greater sense of awareness in the introspection. At times, he simply reflecting—"I would think of a trout stream I had fished along when I was a boy"[53]—but at other times, he is more than a reflector —"On those nights I tried to remember everything that had ever happened to me, starting with just before I went to the war and re-membering back from one thing to another."[54] It is that very backward movement which characterizes this story in theme and in narrative technique, for Nick is trying to dig into his own mind enough to understand some things about his parents—some things which he has not heretofore been able to understand, which have been an un-absorbed part of his "education" (see "The Doctor and the Doctor's Wife"), which have contributed to his present condition.

The use of the second person in Nick's reflections in this story serves as a connection with the same practice in the other stories. In the sentence, "You can hear silk-worms eating very clearly in the night and I lay with my eyes open and listened to them,"[55] the second person does not seem at all out of place, because it is the way Nick thinks: The second person is a kind of general comment which goes well with the first person, as a personal and conversational form.

In "Now I Lay Me," then, Hemingway's narrative perspective reaches its most subjective level, goes most deeply into the mind of Nick Adams; it is his use of first person which makes it so. One of the beauties of the story is that the starkly objective dialogue section keeps the story from becoming sentimental or overladen with self-pity in the same way that Nick's conversation with the soldier pulls him out of his introspection.

IV

The Nick Adams stories, taken together, provide an overview of Ernest Hemingway's narrative technique in one segment of his literary career. Some general conclusions can now be drawn in summary of the preceding analysis.

1. The basic schema on which this paper operates—the objective-subjective scale—cannot be forced too far. Variations in the pattern clearly exist: They must, since Hemingway was not working from the pattern in the first place; they must, since too precise a pattern would call attention to itself and away from the work. The scale is useful only insofar as it serves as a tool for getting at the stylistic qualities and thematic concerns.

2. Quite obviously, then, Hemingway is working carefully and skillfully with point of view in these stories. If anything can put the lie to the charge that Hemingway's early work is mere reporting or that his writing lacked maturity, it is a realization of the precision with which he works at point of view. Even though he probably did all this subconsciously, his control of the perspective, his experimentation with the form, his ability to relate point of view to theme, all mark him (needless to say?) as a great writer.

3. Study of point of view in these stories reenforces the importance of the Nick Adams sequence for a total picture of Hemingway and his work. Nick's sensitive personality deserves a high place among Hemingway's heroes because it adds another dimension to the writing and because it reminds us of another side of Ernest Hemingway (in the sense that Nick is a special mask). The trout streams of upper Michigan are as important as (I am tempted to claim "more important than") the cafe tables of Paris.

4. Because of the relationship between the author and his mask, Hemingway needs to work these stories out mainly in the third

232

person. He is able to avoid—at least until scholars begin snooping—that easy identification in the public mind between the author and his first-person narrator.

5. A corollary of that is that Hemingway gains objectivity by presenting most of these stories in the third person. Such an observation is a commonplace of point-of-view criticism, of course; but it is appropriate here. Just because he was so close to the experiences of Nick Adams, Hemingway needed to establish some distance between himself and his hero; he needed to steer clear of any intimation of self-pity; he had to make Nick a believable narrator and character. The third person helps to do all that.

6. At the same time, Hemingway apparently wanted to get as far into the mind of Nick as he could. To put it another way, he wanted to write what he felt to be true and that meant burrowing deep into himself. He wanted to talk about initiations and traumatic wounds, and in order to do that effectively and honestly he had to show, in as many ways possible, how his hero reacted to experiences.

7. Hemingway was, therefore, unable to follow exactly the established pattern of point of view. In order to achieve the proper combination of objectivity and subjectivity, he had to work out variations of an omniscient author or a Center of Consciousness pattern. One way to do that was by allowing the Center occasional second- and first-person language.

8. Finally, most significantly, Hemingway was able to build a relationship between his point-of-view technique and his overall characterization. As Nick matures and goes through his initiations, the point of view becomes increasingly subjective. The stories immediately following the wound show a disordered state of mind and are presented through a complicated narrative perspective. In no small degree, point of view provides the means by which Hemingway develops, with such penetration, the character of Nick Adams.

University of South Carolina

---

[1] Carlos Baker, *Ernest Hemingway: A Life Story* (New York: Charles Scribner's Sons, 1969.

[2] Philip Young, *Ernest Hemingway: A Reconsideration* (University Park: Pennsylvania State Press, 1966), p. 62.

[3] See Young's chapter, "The Man and the Legend," and especially his discussion of the Nick Adams side of Hemingway: Ibid., p. 157.

[4] Baker, p. 163.

[5] The third-person narrators of the *In Our Time* interchapters are five times

233

nearly absent, three times representative of a single center of consciousness, once given limited insight into the minds of the characters, and once a narrator who sets himself apart by his use of the second person. The *In Our Time* stories have three first-person narrators, two of whom function as storytellers ("you ought to have seen"), and five non-Nick third-person narrators. Of the latter five two narrators have limited insight into the minds of the characters, while three focus on a central consciousness.

The two first-person novels are not exactly alike in narrative technique: Jake Barnes is an objective narrator, rarely revealing his own thoughts and feelings, using the more informal and personal second person in only ten passages; Frederic Henry, on the other hand, frequently probes his own consciousness, frequently uses the second person. Hemingway is doing nothing very unusual in these first-person narratives, but he does establish, partially through point-of-view technique, a distinction between the narrators.

[6] A study of the composition dates as given in Baker shows no apparent relationship between the time of writing and the type of narrative perspective.

[7] E. M. Halliday, "Hemingway's Narrative Perspective," *Sewanee Review,* LX (April-June 1952), pp. 202-218.

[8] John S. Rouch, "Jake Barnes as Narrator," *Modern Fiction Studies,* XI (Winter 1965-1966), pp. 361-370.

[9] For specific studies, see Cleanth Brooks and Robert Penn Warren, *Understanding Fiction* (New York: Appleton Century Crofts, 1943), pp. 303-312, on "The Killers"; Warren Beck, "The Shorter Happy Life of Mrs. Macomber," *Modern Fiction Studies,* I (November 1955), 28-37; Austin McGiffert Wright, *The American Short Story in the Twenties* (Chicago: University of Chicago Press, 1961), pp. 391-393, on "Cross-Country Snow" and "An Alpine Idyll."

[10] The most helpful general discussions of point of view are: Wayne Booth, *The Rhetoric of Fiction* (Chicago: University of Chicago Press, 1961), a major and essential volume; Brooks and Warren, "Focus of Narration: Point of View," in *Understanding Fiction,* pp. 659-664; Norman Friedman, "Point of View in Fiction: The Development of a Critical Concept," *PMLA,* LXX (December 1955), 1160-1184; Caroline Gordon, *How to Read a Novel* (New York: Viking Press, 1957), pp. 72-144; Wright, "The Narrator," in *The American Short Story in the Twenties,* pp. 280-288.

[11] Ernest Hemingway, *The Fifth Column and the First Forty-Nine Stories* (New York: Charles Scribner's Sons, 1938), p. 377.

[12] Ibid., p. 206.

[13] Ibid., p. 208.

[14] Ibid., p. 461

[15] Brooks and Warren, pp. 303-312; Booth, p. 151.

[16] It is interesting that of *The First Forty-nine Stories* only three can be said to have an Effaced Narrator: "The Killers," "Hills Like White Elephants," and "Today is Friday" which is in play form; the Effaced Narrator would seem, therefore, to be an atypical Hemingway technique, rather than an earmark of his style.

[17] Hemingway, op. cit., p. 384.

[18] Ibid., p. 385.

[19] Ibid., p. 386.

[20] Ibid., p. 197.

[21] Ibid., p. 199.

[22] Ibid., p. 200.

[23] See Young, pp. 32-33 and Joseph DeFalco, *The Hero in Hemingway's Short Stories* (Pittsburgh: University of Pittsburgh Press, 1963), pp. 33-39.

[24] Hemingway, op. cit., p. 193.

[25] Ibid., p. 189.

[26] Ibid., p. 191.

[27] Ibid., p. 192.

[28] Ibid., p. 214.

[29] Ibid., p. 218.

[30] Ibid., p. 219.

[31] Ibid., p. 215.

[32] Ibid., p. 430.

[33] Ibid., p. 434.

[34] Ibid., p. 227.

[35] Ibid., p. 228.

[36] Ibid., p. 229.

[37] Ibid., p. 232.

[38] Ibid., p. 236.

[39] Ibid., p. 231.

[40] Ibid., p. 283.

[41] Ibid., p. 284.

[42] Ibid., p. 281.

[43] Ibid., pp. 591-593.

[44] Ibid., p. 586.

[45] Ibid., p. 588.

[46] Ibid., p. 323.

[47] Ibid., p. 327.

[48] Ibid., pp. 324-325.

[49] I have treated this story as a unit, not considering its two parts as separate stories. The objectivity of Part I, taken by itself, would cause it to be placed on the scale about where "Three-Day Blow" is. Yet, taken with Part II, as it must be, the story belongs here. I would even argue—and the paragraph above is a part of the argument—that the objectivity of Part I is an aspect of the Center's effort to retain control of a disturbed mind. The very objectivity is the careful mind's work, so it is not the same treatment, does not have the same depth, of the earlier Center stories.

[50] Hemingway, op. cit., p. 506.

[51] An objective story by a first-person narrator is not unusual for Hemingway, of course. Sixteen of *The First Forty-nine Stories* are in the first person and they show as much variety within that narrow form as do the third-person narratives. In some stories, the Narrator-Agent gives no hint as to his own thoughts ("Che Ti Dice La Patria" and "Canary for One" are examples of extremely objective narratives); in some the Narrator-Agent gives only brief insight to his own thoughts ("Day's Wait," "Wine of Wyoming"); in others he is consciously a storyteller ("The Mother of a Queen"); in others he is very subjective ("After the Storm," "Alpine Idyll").

[52] Hemingway, op. cit., p. 466.

[53] Ibid., p. 461.

[54] Ibid., p. 463.

[55] Ibid., p. 465.

CONTENTS

Harry Crosby's pencil ranking of Hemingway's stories in *In Our Time*.

The Crosby Copy of *In Our Time*

C. E. Frazer Clark, Jr.

In the fall of 1968, I submitted a mail bid for a lot of eight Hemingway titles coming up at auction.[1] I needed one of the books described in the lot. The bid was successful. To my surprise and delight, the lot contained a magnificent "sleeper," a specially bound copy of *In Our Time*[2] from the library of Harry and Caresse Crosby. It was inscribed to Harry Crosby by Hemingway, and annotated in a number of places in pencil by a second hand.

I wrote to Caresse Crosby because I wanted to know more about the book—about how it had escaped from her library—and to ask her if she could help me decipher the pencil annotations and explain Hemingway's inscription. She provided all the information she could.

The book had been part of the Crosby library, but Caresse had not seen it after Harry's death. She explained that various books, including copies of Hemingway's work, had been specially bound for them by several binders. In the case of *In Our Time*, she had asked Luichon to do the work.

Luichon provided a full red morocco binding, with marbled end-papers, and centered in both covers is a gilt-stamped crest the Crosbys had designed before, as Caresse explained, "we adopted the simpler crossed ex libris of our names."[3] The book also bears, on the front paste-down endpaper, the Crosby bookplate she described.

The pencil annotations Caresse identified as in the hand of Harry Crosby. The notes on the Contents page indicated Harry's ranking of Hemingway's stories. Harry always did this, according to Caresse. Not all of Harry Crosby's markings in the book were clear. Harry had " a cabala all his own." Caresse could not add any interpretation to Hemingway's inscription to Harry; it was apparently something private between them.

This was the Crosbys' favorite Hemingway title: "Both Harry and I thought that *In Our Time* was the best of all."

---

[1] *The Library of Charles E. Feinberg*. Part III. Parke-Bernet, 18 June 1968.
[2] Ernest Hemingway, *In Our Time* (London: Jonathan Cape, 1926). The Clark Collection.
[3] This and other quotes from Caresse Crosby's letters to the author.

CHAPTER I

*Everybody was drunk. The whole battery
was drunk going along the road in the dark.
We were going to the Champagne. The
lieutenant kept riding his horse out into the
fields and saying to him, "I'm drunk, I tell
you, mon vieux. Oh, I am so soused." We
went along the road all night in the dark
and the adjutant kept riding up alongside
my kitchen and saying, "You must put it
out. It is dangerous. It will be observed."
We were fifty kilometers from the front, but
the adjutant worried about the fire in my
kitchen. It was funny going along that road.
That was when I was a kitchen Corporal.*

† † †

Hemingway's inscription in Harry Crosby's copy of *In Our Time*. The three plus signs are in the hand of Harry Crosby.

"The Snows of Kilimanjaro":
A New Reading

Lawrence A. Walz

Ernest Hemingway's "The Snows of Kilimanjaro" is a carefully-wrought story; it contains, as Philip Young rightly says, "a conscious and explicit use of symbolism—which is unusual with Hemingway."[1] Thus a close reading, with attention paid to minute and even seemingly unimportant details, would be appropriate—yet much past criticism has ignored or misinterpreted these details. The crucial meaning of the snows at the summit of Mount Kilimanjaro, for example, has been widely misunderstood. Alfred G. Engstrom says that there "is no need to explain the meaning of the snows of Kilimanjaro" and then says that they mean "Death."[2] This interpretation, though part of one of the more perceptive studies of the story, is inexact; also misleading is William Van O'Connor, who believes that Harry's dream signifies defeat.[3] According to E. W. Tedlock, Jr., the snow and the mountain are related to "the good life of the past"; they represent a "preservation of integrity."[4] His statements are true but not close to the precise meaning of those objects. On the right track but vague is Joseph DeFalco, who sees the mountains as "a kind of redemptive Avalon."[5] William B. Bache is quite correct in stating that "the hallucination that he is flying toward the snows of Kilimanjaro" is "Harry's victory,"[6] but he does not say what exactly the snows signify. I would propose that a way to arrive at the meaning of the snows of Kilimanjaro—and of Hemingway's short story—is to consider the many contrasts set up in the course of the story.

The contrasts fall into three main groups. The first is a series of contrasts which emphasizes the external differences between Harry's past life and his present state, and which leads to the theme of the story; the second involves a character contrast between Harry and his wife Helen, which points toward one of Hemingway's major themes; and the third shows the differences between what Harry is and what he finally becomes at the end of the tale. These patterns merge to form the total meaning of "The Snows of Kilimanjaro," which will become more evident after an analysis of the contrasts.

The external differences between Harry's past life and his present condition are revealed by a number of subtle contrasts. Harry remembers that in skiing down the glacier near Schrunz, "you dropped down like a bird";[7] at present, the only birds Harry can see are the vultures, symbols of death.[8] He tranquilly recalls riding a bicycle in Paris, and the bicycle racer whose wife lived across the hall from him[9]; now death moves "in pairs, on bicycles."[10] The policemen were only policemen in the past, but in the present they are associated with death, which "can be two bicycle policemen,"[8] as Harry tells Helen. The strong, almost violent sensuality of the episode with the "hot Armenian slut" contrasts to Harry's present sterile, sexless state. The joyous drinking of the past is contrasted to the fact that now drink is "bad" for him.[11] Hemingway's inclusion of these contrasts, "skiing like a bird—nostalgia about bicycles—policemen as policemen—violent sensuality—good drink" as opposed to "birds as death—death on bicycles—policemen as death—sexlessness—bad drink," subtly brings across to us the full force of Harry's physical predicament.

Of course not all the details in the story fit neatly into this pattern; for example, there was much violent death in Harry's past, whereas there is none on the plain in Tanganyika. There were quarrels, fistfights, "things that he could never think of."[12] The simple equating of the past with happiness and joy and the present with unhappiness and pain will not hold; Tedlock's reference to "the good life of the past" is a slight oversimplification. Rather, the past is larger than the present, more heroic, a world of triumph and disaster that a writer would wish to be part of. The present is petty, sterile, empty.

Not only are there details that do not fit into this pattern of contrasts, but, more significant (in fact crucial), there is one detail that goes against this pattern. The images of snow in the story form a reversal. In the past, snow was dirtied: there were bloody tracks in it, and a snow-covered road was "urine-yellowed." Evacuated people died in it. Snow was unreal: "smooth . . . as cake frosting and as light as powder."[7] It was "powder-snow,"[13] and "it hurt your eyes."[7] In the present, the only snow is at the summit of Mount Kilimanjaro, which is "as wide as all the world, great, high, and unbelievably white in the sun."[14]

Hemingway reveals by this reversal of the pattern of contrasts that pure snow, the snow on the mountain, represents something that Harry has never before experienced.[15] The language used to describe "the square top of Kilimanjaro" and the detail of "the House of God" in the epigraph,[16] combined with this reversal, indicate a kind of fulfillment for Harry. The snow images reveal his past, as filled with life and death as it was, to be incomplete. At the summit of Kilimanjaro is Harry's completion—his victory.

To be more precise, Harry's victory is a kind of spiritual rebirth, which, because of his stifling world-weariness, he has sorely needed. That snow in the past is connected with three Christmases[7] hints at a rebirth. We are told that Harry "had had his life and it was over," that he had come to Africa "to start again,"[17] and that he had hoped by coming to Africa to "work the fat off his soul the way a fighter *went into the mountains* to work and train" (emphasis mine).[18] The top of the mountain, "as wide as all the world," is a new world in whose purity Harry can have a new vision; his renewal is an artistic as well as a spiritual one. The terrible irony of the story is that Harry's moment of "rebirth" coincides with the moment of his death.

The victory is also limited (and irony compounded) in that Harry, as Hemingway shows in the conclusion to the story, has not really gone anywhere. Yet he dies in a kind of victory; he is not merely the corpse with the rotted leg that he appears to be to Helen. We know that Harry's final vision is only a dream, but he believes that he has died in victory, and perhaps that is all that matters.

Besides the reversal of the pattern with the snow images, there is a reversal for at least one other detail. In the past, airplanes are associated with Barker, who machine-gunned the officers' train,[7,13] and with one of Helen's children, who was killed in a plane crash.[19] In the present, it is an airplane which takes Harry on his "journey" to Kilimanjaro. The airplane, which was associated with death, is now involved in Harry's "rebirth." Whether this reversal is deliberate on Hemingway's part or is just a coincidence is, perhaps, open to debate.

The second, and more obvious, pattern of contrasts in the story is concerned with the differences between Harry and Helen. As he does in his best works, Hemingway goes beyond these two characters to contrast two fundamentally opposed ways of living.[20] The basic difference between Helen's character and Harry's is suggested in the description of the "two kinds" in Paris, the "drunkards" (i.e., Helen), who "killed their poverty that way," and the "sportifs" (Harry), who "took it out in exercise."[21] Helen has depended for much of her life on the opiates of drink and sex: when she fell in love with Harry she no longer needed the opiates, but he became a crutch for her; she turned to him instead of facing reality. On the other hand, even up to the very end of his life (as I shall point out later), Harry tries to come to grips with the world. The contrast between them in the present is vividly underscored by his constant bickering: Harry, who once knew how to live meaningfully, realizes that in living on the money of rich women, he has come to resemble Helen, who has lived only by the aid of various opiates and crutches.

The results of their different ways of living are shown in the dreams they have at the end of the story. Harry's is a magnificent vision of "the House of God," whereas Helen's is described in two abrupt sentences: "In her dream she was at the house on Long Island and it was the night before her daughter's debut. Somehow her father was there and he had been very rude."[14,22]   There is a significant contrast between these dreams. Harry's is a great experience, a triumph (at least to him); Helen's is trivial and unpleasant. In these dreams Hemingway has crystallized the differences between a person who has come to be a kind of code hero and one who definitely has not. Helen's dream is the product of her whole way of living; we may feel that she will never have a vision of the dimensions of Harry's unless she too finds some kind of code by which to live.

But Harry does not seem to be a code hero in the same way that Manuel in "The Undefeated," or Santiago in *The Old Man and the Sea*, is a code hero. A central problem in "The Snows of Kilimanjaro" is the reason why Harry has his dream of victory. Does he really deserve to have a vision of a new world? What has he done to achieve it?

In the present Harry is in a precarious balance between a limited victory and complete failure. The forces within him, pulling him in both directions, can be noted throughout the story: these forces constitute the contrast between what he has been and what he becomes. However unpleasant Harry's railing against Helen may be, it must be remembered that he sees in her an indication of his failings and thus, in a sense, is recognizing and despising his own weaknesses. On the other hand, Harry returns to "the familiar lie he made his bread and butter by": he tells Helen that he loves her.[23] Yet finally he seems to achieve a balance in his views of her and realizes that he himself brought about his failure: "She shot very well . . . this kindly caretaker and destroyer of his talent. Nonsense. He had destroyed his talent himself."[18]

Harry's attitude toward the rite of dying is equivocal. "The one experience [death] that he had never had he was not going to spoil now. He probably would. You spoiled everything. But perhaps he wouldn't."[24] Yet Harry thinks, "I'm getting as bored with dying as with everything else."[25]   Harry may deserve his victory because he dies like a man—but in a way he dies like an animal. His death is filthy: he imagines that a hyena is crouching on his chest; yet he calls it "You stinking bastard."[8] The sordidness of Harry's death is tempered by his final act of defiance: it is quite likely that his stand before death, as weak as it may seem to be, reveals a strength in him.

Finally, Harry may deserve the vision because of his attitude toward his duty as a writer. Harry's chief regret is that he failed to do his duty; yet even while admitting failure, he continues to think of writing. He says, "I watched the way they [the birds] sailed very carefully at first in case I ever wanted to use them in a story."[16] "I wanted to write," he tells Helen. Later he asks her, "You can't take dictation, can you."[24] Finally, just before his death, he tells her, "I've been writing . . . But I got tired."[8] Obviously Harry has not been writing. This bit of "writing," like the flight toward the summit of Kilimanjaro, is imaginary; but still he has not failed as badly as he thinks.

Whether it is the realization that he destroyed his talent himself, or his courage in the face of death, or the will to keep on writing, that leads Harry to his victory is uncertain; he nevertheless does become a kind of code hero, and "the House of God" is revealed to him. Harry's victory is only partial, however; like the leopard in the epigraph, he does not reach the summit.[26]

Through the first pattern of contrasts, Hemingway portrays Harry's present state, and by reversing the pattern shows that the snows indicate a victory for him. Through the Harry-Helen contrast, Hemingway presents his belief that one must face reality unaided. The third series of contrasts shows Harry rising above his shortcomings. The theme of "The Snows of Kilimanjaro" may be summarized in this way: a person who, even though virtually destroyed, tries to act as he should and does not allow himself to be defeated can find some kind of fulfillment or victory. "A man can be destroyed but not defeated,"[27] says the fisherman Santiago in a somewhat simpler case.

The theme of "The Snows of Kilimanjaro" is treated elsewhere by Hemingway, notably in "The Undefeated" and *The Old Man and the Sea.* His handling of this theme is even more bitter and ambiguous in "The Snows of Kilimanjaro," however; Harry, unlike either Manuel or Santiago, is not a "good" man, and his victory is even less marked than theirs. But then the victory of a Hemingway hero is seldom a clear one: "Winner Take Nothing," except perhaps for a feeling, like that of Harold Krebs in "Soldier's Home," of being "cool and clear inside himself . . . when he had done the one thing, the only thing for a man to do."[28]

University of Tulsa

243

[1] Philip Young, *Ernest Hemingway* (New York: Rinehart, 1952), p. 46.

[2] Alfred G. Engstrom, "Dante, Flaubert, and 'The Snows of Kilimanjaro,' " *MLN*, LXV (March 1950), 204, 205.

[3] William Van O'Connor, "Two Views of Kilimanjaro," *The History of Ideas News Letter*, II (January 1956), 76-80.

[4] E. W. Tedlock, Jr., "Hemingway's 'The Snows of Kilimanjaro,' " *The Explicator*, VIII (October 1949), item 7.

[5] Joseph DeFalco, *The Hero in Hemingway's Short Stories* (Pittsburgh: University of Pittsburgh Press, 1963), p. 208.

[6] William B. Bache, "*Nostromo* and 'The Snows of Kilimanjaro,' " *MLN*, LXXII (January 1957), 34. For other interpretations, see Carlos Baker, *Hemingway: The Writer as Artist* (Princeton: Princeton Univ. Press, 1963), pp. 191-195; Marion Montgomery, "The Leopard and the Hyena: Symbol and Meaning in 'The Snows of Kilimanjaro,' " *The University of Kansas City Review*, XXVII (Summer 1961), 277-282; J. Golden Taylor, "Hemingway on the Flesh and the Spirit," *Western Humanities Review*, XV (Summer 1961), 273-275; Donald H. Cunningham, "Hemingway's 'The Snows of Kilimanjaro,' " *The Explicator*, XXII (February 1964), item 41; Barney Childs, "Hemingway and the Leopard of Kilimanjaro," *American Notes & Queries*, II (September 1963), 3; Gloria R. Dussinger, " 'The Snows of Kilimanjaro': Harry's Second Chance," *Studies in Short Fiction*, V (Fall 1967), 54-59.

[7] Ernest Hemingway, *The Fifth Column and the First Forty-nine Stories* (New York: Scribners, 1938), p. 154.

[8] Ibid., p. 172.

[9] Ibid., pp. 167, 168.

[10] Ibid., p. 169.

[11] Ibid., p. 152.

[12] Ibid., p. 164.

[13] Ibid., p. 155.

[14] Ibid., p. 174.

[15] Oliver Evans, in his fine study " 'The Snows of Kilimanjaro': A Revaluation," *PMLA*, LXXVI (December 1961), 601-607, points out this pattern in the snow images, but does not view this contrast between kinds of snow precisely as a "reversal of the pattern." Evans considers some of the same contrasts that I do (as in my treatment of Helen, below), but his interest lies largely in the contrasts between the mountain and the plain, and "life-in-death" versus "death-in-life."

[16] Hemingway, op. cit., p. 150.

[17] Ibid., p. 157.

[18] Ibid., p. 158.

[19] Ibid., p. 159.

[20] Compare Pedro Romero and Robert Cohn in *The Sun Also Rises*.

[21] Hemingway, op. cit., p. 167.

[22] Ibid., p. 175.

[23] Ibid., p. 156.

[24] Ibid., p. 165.

[25] Ibid., p. 171.

[26]The much-debated (perhaps too often debated) problem of the relationship of the leopard to the rest of the story is not of great importance to this analysis, but some interpretation may be appropriate. The main function of the epigraph is to help show that Harry has achieved a kind of victory. Although a case can be built the other way, it seems that Hemingway intends a comparison, not a contrast, to be made between the leopard and Harry. Some other characters in Hemingway's short stories are likened to animals: Dr. Adams in "Fathers and Sons" is like an eagle (pp. 587–588, 594); the young wife in "Cat in the Rain" is like a cat (p. 267); the narrator's friends in "In Another Country" are like hunting-hawks (p. 368); and Nick Adams in "Big Two-Hearted River" resembles the black grasshoppers (pp. 309–310). Like the leopard Harry seeks the summit of Kilimanjaro. If he and the leopard are similar, then the meaning of the last sentence of the epigraph becomes clearer: in a sense, Hemingway wrote "The Snows of Kilimanjaro" to explain "what the leopard was seeking at that altitude" (p. 150). One might object that the leopard, unlike Harry, is really on the mountain; yet the leopard, like Harry, is "near" the summit, not at it. It might also be argued that the animal is "dried and frozen," whereas the man's body is in decay; yet perhaps Harry's spirit is "dried and frozen" in death. Evans, pp. 604–605, generally agrees with this viewpoint.

[27]Ernest Hemingway, *The Old Man and the Sea* (New York: Scribners, 1952), p. 114.

[28]Hemingway, *The Fifth Column*, pp. 243–244.

ADVICE TO A SON

Never trust a white man,
Never kill a Jew,
Never sign a contract,
Never rent a pew.
Don't enlist in armies;
Nor marry many wives;
Never write for magazines;
Never scratch your hives.
Always put paper on the seat,
Don't believe in wars,

Berlin, September 1931.

Keep yourself both clean and neat,
Never marry whores.
Never pay a blackmailer,
Never go to law,
Never trust a publisher,
Or you'll sleep on straw.
All your friends will leave you,
All your friends will die,
So lead a clean and wholesome life,
And join them in the sky.

Ernest Hemingway

Hemingway in Dry Tortugas Island (U.S.A.),
March 1931

Lautrec-Ausstellung in Chicago (Art Institute 1931)

Photo Cahiers d'Art

Omnibus Almanach Auf Dar Jahr 1932 (Berlin and Dusseldorf: Verlag der Galerie Flechtheim, 1932), page 80.

Emerson, Thoreau, and Hemingway: Some Suggestions About Literary Heritage

Donald J. Greiner

The suggestion that Emerson, Thoreau, and Hemingway can be yoked together in a serious study may seem, at first, absurd, but the question raised in this paper is not one of literary influence or debt but, rather, one of literary heritage. Although many readers commonly link Hemingway with Thoreau, Hemingway is usually considered a polar figure from Emerson primarily because of the extreme differences between their philosophies. No one disputes the opinion that Hemingway has little in common with the mystical ideas of transcendental thought. But it seems to me that Hemingway's ideas about literature owe as much to certain artistic principles which were first worked out in American literature by Emerson and Thoreau as they do to the literary principles which he learned in Paris.

Hemingway himself has acknowledged his connection with an American literary heritage. Although he dismisses Emerson as one of a group who possesses no bodies, only "nice, dry, clean minds,"[1] he admits a kinship with Thoreau. Commenting in 1935 on earlier nineteenth-century American literature, he wrote, "There is one at the time that is supposed to be really good, Thoreau. I cannot tell you about it because I have not yet been able to read it. But that means nothing because I cannot read other naturalists unless they are being extremely accurate and not literary."[2] What is important in the statement, and often overlooked, is that he groups Thoreau with himself as another artist who cultivates experience in nature as the best means to truth. For Hemingway both *Green Hills of Africa* and *Walden* are works of naturalists in which the authors try to be "extremely accurate and not literary." Reading the definition which he assigns to *Green Hills* in the foreword, we realize that it could fit *Walden*: "The writer has attempted to write an absolutely true book to see whether the shape of a country and the pattern of a month's action can, if truly presented, compete with a work of the imagination." Asked in 1958 to name his literary forebears, Hemingway placed Thoreau on the list.[3] He did not mean that Thoreau had a direct influence on him, but only that Thoreau experimented with life-styles and art in much the same way that he was to seventy-five years later.

Hemingway's complaint about reading Thoreau does not suggest that he never read the "other" naturalist. Returning to Cuba in 1945, for example, he told Mary Hemingway that he planned to read Thoreau in an effort to ease his loneliness.[4] It is possible that he read Emerson and Thoreau, as well as other nineteenth-century American authors, while attending Oak Park (Illinois) High School from which he graduated in 1917. Commenting on the academic excellence of the school, Charles A. Fenton notes that the curriculum was built around a liberal arts education and that Hemingway responded enthusiastically to the English Department. Hemingway could have encountered large doses of American literature in his sophomore year. Because the heart of the syllabus was the literature of the past, it seems unlikely that he could have missed significant contact with the major nineteenth-century American writers.[5]

Several critics have suggested Hemingway's link with his American literary heritage, but so far as I know, Hugh Holman was the first to devote an article to a study of Hemingway and Emerson. Noting that the idea is "almost ludicrous," he goes on to quote extensively from *Green Hills* and *Death in the Afternoon* to suggest both the similarities between Hemingway's ideas and Emerson's and the possibility of an aesthetic tradition.[6] This paper owes as much to Professor Holman as it does to my doubts about the standard approach in literary histories toward the genesis of American writing in the 1920's. It is not that the approach is wrong, but that it is limited. *The Literary History of the United States*, for example, examines the question strictly in terms of craft. Maxwell Geismar comments in *LHUS* that Hemingway and the other American writers of the 1920's who were experimenting with structure, rhythm, and diction found the germ of their style in European literature:

> This was the age of the craftsman, and the complex interior monologue, for example, with its shifting elements of time and place and its purely personal framework of association, became a staple of the new novels. . . .These authors were joined in their determination to break the short story of fabricated action and a trick end. In such writers the most advanced European technical experimentation met a rich source of native material.[7]

Morton D. Zabel summarizes the years from 1915 to 1925 when he writes that the art of that decade was devoted primarily to an attack on tradition and those interests that "represented the time lag, the forces of reaction, the 'demon of the absolute,' to the younger forces of insurgence and rebellion."[8]

This emphasis on the break from tradition which led to an acceptance and imitation of European models is the common approach in literary histories to contemporary American writing. But the standard approach is not limited to the demonstrations of the literary historian; it is also evident in specific critical interpretations. In *Axel's Castle* Edmund Wilson is primarily concerned with the French symbolists' influence on the outburst of new writing which appeared in the 1920's. Tracing the development of the Symbolist movement from nineteenth-century Romanticism and Naturalism, Wilson argues that most characteristic modern literature springs from European sources. Indeed, Wilson feels that much of the confusion which English and American critics show when dealing with the work of modern writers in the English language is a result of the European literary revolution which occurred outside English literature.

Although literary historians and critics recognize the influence of certain European artistic attitudes which are easily demonstrated, there is nevertheless a native tradition which, while touching modern American writers less directly, is important historically because it helps to identify a certain context essential to understanding the development of American literature. Hemingway's relation to specific European influences has been thoroughly explored; less emphasis has been given to his relationship with the native tradition.

No one can date exactly the beginning of an American literature separate from European writing, because through the first third of the nineteenth century, the native tradition was subordinated to the standards and dictates of England. But in his "American Scholar" lecture in 1837 and in his essay "The Poet" (1844), Emerson assumes the leadership of a movement for the development of a distinct American literature. He proclaims America's right to distinctive subject matter, literary values, and style, and he declares that native writers need only incorporate native traditions in their work.[9] It is not enough to explain the renaissance of American writing in the 1920's as simply a result of European influences. If the native tradition is also examined, we will find that some of Emerson's ideas reappear in Hemingway's discussion of art in such a way as to suggest an American aesthetic tradition. For our purposes, Emerson's theory of language may be seen as a focal point from which we can determine those attitudes in the writings of Emerson, Thoreau, and Hemingway toward such artistic principles as the use of symbol, idealism in art, experience in nature, the organic theory of art, and self-reliance of the artist, all of which are fundamental to the American literary continuity.

Emerson first announced his theory of language in the essay "Nature," and it had a profound effect upon the use of words in the development of a native literature. He outlines the theory:

1. Words are signs of natural facts.
2. Particular natural facts are symbols of particular spiritual facts.
3. Nature is the symbol of spirit.[10]

The truth of a writer's language depends upon his desire to reveal the truth of his experiences in nature. If his desire for truth is weak, his language is corrupted, and his ability to connect his thought with its proper symbol is lost. Language finds its truth in natural facts, not abstractions, so that an artistic use of language will evoke the tangible object which is the symbol of the idea.

Acutely aware of the value of symbolic language, Emerson relies on symbols to reveal the real essence of an experience or of an object. A good symbol is proof of a good thought. The depth of the creative imagination depends upon what Emerson terms "primary" and "secondary" sight, and it is this secondary sight which determines the writer's success with symbols: "The primary use of a fact is low; the secondary use, as it is a figure or illustration of my thought, is the real worth. First the fact; second its impression. . . ."[11] The common mind views the visible object as the final fact of that object, but the artistic mind possesses a second sight to peer through the visible entity to find a symbol which best expresses the true meaning of the object.

Following Emerson's teaching, Thoreau likewise finds the origin of words in nature. If the writer hopes to command his language, he must confront nature, for experience with life's fundamentals will supply him with his words. Thoreau writes in *A Week in the Concord and Merrimack Rivers:*

> Yet poetry, though the last and finest result, is a natural fruit. As naturally as the oak bears an acorn, and the vine a gourd, man bears a poem, either spoken or done. It is the chief and most memorable success, for history is but a prose narrative of poetic deeds. . . .[The writer] is as serene as nature. . . .It is as if nature spoke. . . .Nature furnishes him not only with words, but with stereotyped lines and sentences from her mint.[12]

The writer's chief difficulty is to discover the best word which will name exactly the object, thereby releasing truth.

The language problem facing Hemingway is similar to the problem which Emerson and Thoreau speak of, one of discovering a correspondence between word and thing, of finding the exact word that will truthfully convey the meaning of the experience. We readily recall the famous passage from *Death in the Afternoon* in which Hemingway writes of the difficulty he had trying to relate what really happened and what emotions he truly felt:

> In writing for a newspaper you told what happened and, with one trick and another, you communicated the emotion aided by the element of timeliness which gives a certain emotion to any account of something that has happened on that day; but the real thing, the sequence of motion and fact which made the emotion and which would be as valid in a year or in ten years or, with luck and if you stated it purely enough, always, was beyond me and I was working very hard to try to get it. [13]

This difficulty with language is often a secondary subject in Hemingway's fiction. In "Fathers and Sons" Nick asks his father for the meaning of the word "mashing," but the father is unwilling to explain. His ambiguous answer is immediately followed by Nick's reflection on the word, and Hemingway suggests that only after experience with "mashing" will Nick be able to express it correctly. [14] Like Emerson, Hemingway feels that meaningful symbols must be created from facts only, as opposed to abstractions, because abstractions fail to reveal a concrete image. We need only turn to *A Farewell to Arms* for an echo of Emerson's belief that abstractions are best represented by natural facts and objects. Rejecting words like "sacred," Lt. Henry finds meaning only in the concrete names of roads and villages. [15]

The point is that words mean less than what they represent. Hemingway's variation on Emerson's theory of language is, of course, readily apparent: Where Emerson is primarily concerned with the revelation of spiritual significance behind every word and fact, Hemingway takes pains to reveal the absolute truth of experienced reality. Emerson's religious convictions may be missing, but Hemingway is one of many American writers who discovers the origin of words in nature or experience, who denies abstractions in favor of natural facts as the best way to meaningful expression, and who argues that the writer's primary duty is to find a precise correspondence between word and fact.

Yet both Emerson and Hemingway admit that their statements

about language are ideal, that neither they nor any writer of the past has succeeded in consistently discovering the exact equivalent between word and fact. Emerson's concept of the writer is so ideal that he finds some deficiency in all of the great poets. The writer, at best, merely imitates nature, although the ultimate end of art is to create man and nature.[16]

Because Hemingway recognizes the struggle he goes through to tell us what happens in an experience, the difficulty he faces when trying to re-create the exact emotion felt, and especially the problem he must grapple with to find a significant correspondence between word and thing, he also establishes an ideal as his goal. In *Green Hills of Africa* he speculates upon the kind of prose which can someday be written: "There is a fourth and fifth dimension that can be gotten. . . . It is much more difficult than poetry. It is a prose that has never been written. But it can be written, without tricks and without cheating. With nothing that will go bad afterwards."[17] Similarly, in "The Snows of Kilimanjaro," Harry's speculations about his own literary failures suggest his awareness of an ideal which has eluded him. He is more concerned with subject matter than with style, but as he thinks of the things about which he would never write, he reflects that perhaps such writing is impossible. But Hemingway would insist that it is his duty to write of these difficult things because he has been lucky enough to experience the world's changes. His adventures are valuable not only to his art but also to those of us who do not have his luck, who lack his opportunities for meaningful experience. But as an artist Harry has stumbled because he has traded his creative drive for the ease of the moneyed life. He should at least attempt to express what is as yet unexpressable:

> There was so much to write. He had seen the world change; not just the events; although he had seen many of them and had watched the people, but he had seen the subtler change and he could remember how the people, were at different times. He had been in it and he had watched it and it was his duty to write of it; but now he never would.[18]

Since Hemingway is concerned with rendering the very essence of human experience, to live it well and to tell it truly, his realism is, in its own way, a type of idealism. His realistic portraits consistently suggest something better. When, for example, Lt. Henry returns from his war leave in the fleshpots of Milan, he regrets his choice, for it keeps him away from Abruzzi where the hunting is good and the cold is clear and dry. Similarly, in "The Big Two-Hearted River: Part I," Hemingway names the ideal "the good place":

Nick was happy as he crawled inside the tent. It had been a hard trip. He was very tired. That was done. He made his camp. He was settled. Nothing could touch him. It was a good place to camp. He was there, in the good place.[19]

The point is that Hemingway's despair or cynicism does not negate his idealism. He lacks Emerson's serene optimism, but he is part of a native tradition that celebrates an ideal both in art and in life-styles. Thoreau's trip to Walden is much the same as Nick's trek to the good place: Both make the trip alone to a location away from society in order to discover something about themselves. The problem, of course, is that this ideal can be approached only through experience which is always at odds with the ideal.

Emerson's theory of experience corresponds to his theory of primary and secondary sight, for he sees experience as the fusion of illusion and reality. The artistic mind must see beyond the illusion of an experience to the central reality of it. He describes experience in terms of sense impressions, and, as such, experience appears to be composed of illusions—things which have surface and no depth and which occur in succession with little logical sequence. But there is a reality beneath the surface which the sensitive mind must see and relate to the illusions if he is to get a sense of the whole. Emerson wrote the essay "Experience" not only for artists but for all men to illustrate a means by which illusion and reality can be reconciled. But the essay's principles are vital for the writer who must use experience as a test for truth. Life itself is a mixture of what Emerson terms "power" and "form." Form is the surface illusion, while power is the force which takes the artistic mind beneath the surface to connect the artist to reality. "Between these extremes is the equator of life, of thought, of spirit, of poetry,—a narrow belt."[20]

Thoreau is also concerned with rendering in art the very essence of experience, to live it well and to tell it truly. This concern stems from his fidelity to life's details and from his search for the truth of an experience which can be revealed in his writing. His motive for going to Walden recalls Hemingway's reasons for learning the bull-fight—both writers feel compelled to front the essential facts of life and to create an accurate account of the meeting. We remember the chapter "Where I Lived and What I Lived For" in which Thoreau writes of his desire to live deliberately, to know by experience life's essentials, and to publish his discovery for the world. The writer must find the exact word or sentence which corresponds faithfully to the fullest meaning of the action, but a "perfectly healthy sentence" is rare. Demanding not wisdom but sureness in writing, Thoreau suggests that the best sentence is that which speaks "firmly and conclusively" as if the author knows enough to have a right to his statements.[21] He names conversation and bodily labor as aids to help the writer achieve his goal:

> The necessity of labor and conversation with many men and things to the scholar is rarely well remembered; steady labor with the hands, which engrosses the attention also, is unquestionably the best method of removing palaver and sentimentality out of one's style, both in speaking and writing. If he has worked hard from morning till night, though he may have grieved that he could not be watching the train of his thoughts during that time, yet the few hasty lines which at evening record his day's experience will be more musical and true than his freest but idle fancy could have furnished.[22]

The artist will create the "tougher truth" for the action that his body shows. Calluses give firmness to a sentence, and Thoreau argues that the mind fails to make a successful effort without the corresponding effort of the body. In a statement that sounds remarkably like Hemingway, Thoreau insists that the writer transcribe the experience as it is impressed upon him and not what he wishes might have happened: "Say what you have to say, not what you ought. Any truth is better than make-believe."[23]

Similarly, Hemingway admits that the difficulties incurred by his desire to render the ideal in prose force him to develop an extra-acute awareness of experience as a test for the truth of his writing. Both Robert Penn Warren and Alfred Kazin place him in this tradition of American artists who rely on an intense awareness of the experienced world. Warren writes, "Physical nature is nowhere rendered with greater vividness than in his work, and probably his only competitors in this department of literature are William Faulkner, among the modern, and Henry David Thoreau, among the older American writers."[24] And Kazin notes, "No writer in all American literature after Thoreau has had Hemingway's sensitiveness to color, to climate, to the knowledge of physical energy under heat or cold, that knowledge of the body thinking and moving through a landscape. . . ."[25]

Perhaps one of the best examples of Hemingway's work which illustrates his ability to create for the reader a particular place in nature and to portray a profound sensitivity to climate and color is the opening page of *A Farewell to Arms*. When we place it beside a passage from *Walden*, we see how close the two writers are in their ability to put down on paper their sensitive awareness of nature. Thoreau writes in the chapter "Solitude":

> This is a delicious evening. . . .The bullfrogs trump to usher in the night, and the note of the whip-poor-will is borne on the rippling wind from over the water. Sympathy with the fluttering alder and poplar leaves almost takes away my breath; yet, like the lake, my serenity is rippled but not ruffled. These small waves raised by the evening wind are as remote from storm as the smooth reflecting surface. Though it is now dark, the wind still blows and roars in the wood, the waves still dash, and some creatures lull the rest with their notes.[26]

Both quotations illustrate the brilliance of Hemingway's and Thoreau's descriptions, for the careful notations of individual details within the scenes contribute to the more important goals of each passage—the metaphorical effect. The accurate detail—trees which are too dusty or the presence of wind—is significant, but it is not an end in itself. The vivid awareness of nature is put to an artistic use so that naturalistic details support the authors' overall designs. In these descriptions the illusions which Emerson speaks of are penetrated so that meaningful experience is realized and communicated.

Observation of the essential facts of experience and fidelity to details are fundamental characteristics which the writer must possess. Hemingway's best prose reveals this sensitivity to facts and details, and it is for this reason that Alfred Kazin sees Hemingway's affiliation with Stein and Anderson as a surface association, whereas his connection with Thoreau is deeper and more meaningful:

> Yet what he was aiming at in one sense, F. O. Matthiessen has pointed out, was the perfect yet poetic naturalness of a Thoreau. Hemingway's surface affiliations as a prose craftsman were with his first teachers, Gertrude Stein and Sherwood Anderson, who taught him the requisite simplicity and fidelity and—Gertrude Stein more than Anderson—an ear for the natural rhythms of speech. But his deeper associations went beyond them, beyond even the Flaubertian tradition of discipline and *le mot juste*. . . . But he wanted not merely to tell 'the truth about his own feelings at the moment when they exist'; he wanted to aim at that luminous and imaginative truth which a writer like Thoreau, on the strength of a muscular integrity and arousement to nature very like his own, had created out of a monumental fidelity to the details of life as he saw them.[27]

Hemingway and Thoreau avoid the surface experiences, what Emerson would term "illusions," by throwing themselves into life in such a way as to savor all of the physical and intellectual sensations. No one can accurately judge the validity of their truths unless he, too, has lived a similar experience. Commenting on the violence in the bullfight, Hemingway writes that his duty is not to defend the danger and cruelty but to tell honestly the things that he finds to be true.[28] Experience acts as the primary means to the discovery of truth, and it is for this reason that Hemingway travels to Spain while Thoreau goes to the woods. Hemingway's motive for following the bullfights echoes Thoreau's explanation of why he went to Walden:

> The only place where you could see life and death, *i.e.,* violent death now that the wars were over, was in the bull ring and I wanted very much to go to Spain where I could study it. I was trying to learn to write, commencing with the simplest things, and one of the simplest things of all and the most fundamental is violent death. . . .So I went to Spain to see bullfights and to try to write about them for myself. I thought they would be simple and barbarous and cruel and that I would not like them, but that I would see certain definite action which would give me the feeling of life and death that I was working for. I found the definite action. . . .[29]

The thoughts expressed here turn up in his fiction. In *The Sun Also Rises,* for example, Jake comments that experience is one of the ways to pay for the good things.[30]

In this cultivation of a life-style based on a true feeling for experience in nature Hemingway approaches Emerson's and Thoreau's sense of being. While not sharing the mystical ideas of their transcendental philosophy, Hemingway reveres his communion with nature—with "country" as he often calls it—as a clue to how to live his life. What is so significant about these three writers is that they are also livers—the renown of their life-styles is every bit as important to Americans as the value of their art. Jake's comment about how to enjoy living is especially relevant here, for it recalls his fishing trip as the heart of *The Sun Also Rises.* In direct contrast with Robert Cohn, Jake is well aware of how to get his money's worth and savor the experience. Cohn falls asleep during the car trip to Pamplona while Jake drinks in the country, and Cohn does not join the fishing trip to the Irati River. Lacking any idea of how to live, Cohn is forgotten as Jake reestablishes his communion with the land. Commenting ironically to suggest how misunderstood men like Jake are, Bill Gorton says, "You're an expatriate. You've lost touch with the soil. You get precious. Fake European standards have ruined you."[31] Nothing, of course, is further from the truth because Jake continues to rely on simple experiences in nature to cleanse spirit and body. We are drawn to this fishing scene not only because we appreciate Hemingway's handling of it but also because we know that it suggests an approach to experience which can help us live our lives.

In his search for truth, Hemingway turns to empiricism, and his use of the empirical method derives naturally from a theory of language and symbol that relies on fact as opposed to abstraction. His ideas reflect Emerson's theory of power and form, of being able to see the truth of real experience below the surface. Take away experience and observation of facts, and the correspondence between action and expression breaks down. Many writers may feel as Emerson, Thoreau, and Hemingway do about experience's relationship with art, but these three do more than merely assume the necessity of experience. They insist on the relationship as an essential part of their aesthetics, as the primary foundation on which meaningful expression rests.

Believing that the writer must speak to the whole man, not to the mind alone, Thoreau argues that the best writing can re-create the sight, sound, feel, or smell of an experience. Although he writes that art has its germ in the expression of an experience truly felt, he knows that this expression must be a creation of the writer and not a report or description of the action. "A book should contain pure discoveries, glimpses of terra firma, though by shipwrecked mariners, and not the art of navigation by those who have never been out of the sight of land."[32] Obviously a report or description will not pass for the kind of prose that Thoreau hopes to write. What is needed is a created expression of the experience's effect on the writer.

Hemingway also feels that the account of an experience must not be described, that it must be a creation which the writer invents from the effect of the experience. Creation gives life to the prose, whereas description eventually loses its vitality:

> But if you can make it up instead of describe it you can make it round and whole and solid and give it life. You create it, for good or bad. It is made; not described. It is just as true as the extent of your ability to make it and the knowledge you put into it.[33]

If the artist develops his ability to render the experience to the extent that the reader, too, feels the true details, good and bad, of it, then the artist approaches good writing.

Since words are symbols of natural facts, and since the means to full comprehension of natural facts is by experience with them, creative writing is a process of organic form—the theory that the action or the object contains the words, and that the artist's success depends upon his ability to discover these words. Nearly all writers subscribe to the idea of organic form, as opposed to the more mechanical method that, for example, Poe suggests in "The Philosophy of Composition." But again the point is a matter of emphasis, for Emerson, Thoreau, and Hemingway feel so strongly about it that they stress the necessity of organic form when they discuss their theories of art. We can read "Poetry and Imagination" and "The Poet" for Emerson's thoughts on organic art. He differentiates between thought and form, arguing that in great writing thought precedes form. "The difference between poetry and stock poetry is this, that in the latter the rhythm is given and the sense adapted to it; while in the former the sense dictates the rhythm. I might even say that the rhyme is there in the theme, thought and image themselves. Ask the fact for the form."[34]

Professor Holman feels that this principle is so vital to Emerson and Hemingway that it acts as the strongest link between them. Hemingway's belief that the action contains the necessary words which are able to convey honestly the truth of that action, and that the artist's chief problem is to find these words, is strikingly close to Emerson's thoughts as expressed in the two essays mentioned. In *Death in the Afternoon* Hemingway insists that a primary difficulty is to put down the words which evolve naturally from the actual things and from the effect of the action.[35] These "actual things" excite the emotion which, in turn, triggers the expression of what really happened. Hemingway continues to distinguish between constructed characters and real people, arguing that no amount of skillful construction can equal the people that the writer projects from his experience. The experience contains the people, and the artist's worth is partially determined by how well he can carry the experience over to his prose.

Belief in organic art forces the writer to rely solely on his own intuition as he determines what and how he will write. For the two nineteenth-century writers, self-reliance amounts to God-reliance, an idea with which Hemingway has little sympathy. But all three writers discuss the self-reliance of the artist in terms of the fine line between influence and imitation. The influence of past art is not totally negative; after all the writer does not create in isolation. But the danger is, of course, that influence can degenerate to imitation. Emerson warns that the artist who bows too often to his mentors will lose understanding both of his own talent and theirs.[36] Attempting to establish an American literary tradition, Emerson's primary concern is to exhort native writers to avoid foreign influence. Each writer takes what he needs from the past, but he uses established landmarks of art as stepping stones to move beyond what has been done before him. Hemingway repeats Emerson's concerns when he writes:

> The art, the method, the improvements of doing, the discoveries remain; but the individual, whose doing of them made them, who was the touchstone, the original, disappears and until another individual, as great, comes, the things, by being imitated, with the original gone, soon distort, lengthen, shorten, weaken and lose all reference to the original. All art is only done by the individual.[37]

He goes on to insist upon the artist's right to use everything that has been discovered about his art, suggesting that the true individual artist can accept and reject the past so easily that it seems the knowledge is born with him. The writer then steps beyond what has been done before to make "something of his own."

Hemingway follows his own advice when he assimilates what the past has to offer and then makes his own contribution after paying his "percentage" in experience.[38] An examination of his statements about writing suggests, when compared to those of Emerson and Thoreau, that a native literary heritage does indeed exist of which twentieth-century American writers, either directly or indirectly, are aware. Suggestions of literary continuity do not necessarily mean that demonstrable influence exists between one writer and another. But certain fundamental attitudes regarding artistic creativity are discernible in American literature, and most modern native writers are as aware of this heritage as they are of American notions about freedom and democracy. Hemingway need not have analyzed Emerson and Thoreau to have a sense of their ideas about art.

Edmund Wilson makes a similar observation in broader terms when he notes theoretical associations between certain American writers of the nineteenth century and the Symbolists, suggesting that the artistic theories of these American authors could have a bearing on contemporary literary thought. He writes: "It was in general true that, by the middle of the century, the Romantic writers in the United States—Poe, Hawthorne, Melville, Whitman and even Emerson—were, for reasons which it would be interesting to determine, developing in the direction of Symbolism. . . ." The claim for Emerson is revealed in a statement from Proust which Wilson quotes. " 'It is strange,' he writes in a letter, 'that, in the most widely different departments, from George Eliot to Hardy, from Stevenson to Emerson, there should be no other literature which exercises over me so powerful an influence as English and American.' "[39]

Neither Mr. Wilson's remarks nor mine are intended to dismiss the standard approach to the development of Hemingway's writing which, in part, is an examination of certain European attitudes toward art. But the metamorphosis of contemporary American literature can be better understood if we also investigate the native heritage. Whether or not Hemingway is *consciously* aware of this tradition is not crucial to this study. What is significant is that his comments about writing are remarkably similar to those of Emerson and Thoreau. The fundamental difference in the variations on this literary tradition is, of course, that Emerson looks primarily for the divine in nature and, hence, God's truth, while Hemingway looks for the general truths which can be revealed in a confrontation with life. Yet Hemingway's art reveals some of the moral overtones that Emerson's shows, for both posit an ideal in art and experience which enables them to search for a sense of universal meaning and order.

University of South Carolina

---

[1] Ernest Hemingway, *Green Hills of Africa* (New York: Scribners, 1935), p. 21.

[2] Ibid., p. 21.

[3] George Plimpton, "An Interview with Ernest Hemingway," *Writers at Work: The Paris Review Interviews*, second series (New York: Viking, 1966), p. 227.

[4] Carlos Baker, *Ernest Hemingway: A Life Story* (New York: Scribners, 1969), p. 447.

[5] Charles A. Fenton, *The Apprenticeship of Ernest Hemingway* (New York: Mentor, 1961), pp. 15-16.

[6] C. Hugh Holman, "Hemingway and Emerson," *Modern Fiction Studies*, I (August 1955), 12-16.

[7] Robert E. Spiller, Willard Thorp, et. al., eds., *Literary History of the United States* (New York: MacMillan, 1968), p. 1297.

[8] Ibid., pp. 1358-1359.

[9] Ralph Waldo Emerson, *Essays; Essays: Second Series* (Columbus: Charles E. Merrill Standard Editions, 1969).

[10] Ralph Waldo Emerson, "Nature," *The Complete Works of Ralph Waldo Emerson*, ed. Edward W. Emerson (New York: Houghton Mifflin, 1903), I, p. 25.

[11] Ibid., "Poetry and Imagination," VIII, p. 11.

[12] Henry David Thoreau, *A Week on the Concord and Merrimack Rivers* (New York: Houghton Mifflin, 1929), I, pp. 94-95.

[13] Ernest Hemingway, *Death in the Afternoon* (New York: Scribners, 1932), p. 2.

[14] Ernest Hemingway, "Fathers and Sons," *The Short Stories of Ernest Hemingway* (New York: Scribners, 1953), p. 491.

[15] Ernest Hemingway, *A Farewell to Arms* (New York: Scribners, 1962), pp. 184-185.

[16] Emerson, *Essays*, "Art."

[17] Hemingway, *Green Hills*, pp. 26-27.

[18] Hemingway, "The Snows of Kilimanjaro," *Short Stories*, p. 66.

[19] Hemingway, "The Big Two-Hearted River: Part I," *Short Stories*, p. 215.

[20] Emerson, *Essays II*, "Experience," p. 68.

[21] Thoreau, *A Week*, p. 106.

[22] Ibid., p. 108.

[23] Henry David Thoreau, *Walden* (Columbus: Charles E. Merrill Standard Editions, 1969), p. 350.

[24] Robert Penn Warren, Introduction to *A Farewell to Arms* (New York: Scribners, 1962), p. xvii.

[25] Alfred Kazin, "Hemingway: Synopsis of a Career," *Ernest Hemingway: The Man and His Work*, ed. John K. M. McCaffery (New York: Avon, 1950), p. 177.

[26] Thoreau, *Walden*, p. 140.

[27] Kazin, op, cit., pp. 174-175.

[28] Hemingway, *Death*, p. 1.

[29] Ibid., pp. 2-3.

[30] Ernest Hemingway, *The Sun Also Rises* (New York: Scribners, 1962), p. 148.

[31] Ibid., p. 115.

[32] Thoreau, *A Week*, p. 100.

[33] Ernest Hemingway, "Monologue to the Maestro," *Esquire*, IV (October 1935), p. 21.

[34] Emerson, "Poetry and Imagination," VIII, p. 54.

[35] Hemingway, *Death*, p. 2.

[36] Emerson, *Essays*, "Self-Reliance," p. 69.

[37] Hemingway, *Death,* pp. 99-100.

[38] Ibid., p. 192.

[39] Edmund Wilson, *Axel's Castle: A Study in the Imaginative Literature of 1870 to 1930* (New York: Scribners, 1959), pp. 12, 136. For fuller comment regarding Emerson and Melville as Symbolists, see Charles Feidelson, Jr., *Symbolism and American Literature* (Chicago: University of Chicago Press, 1953).

The Two Styles of Hemingway's
The Sun Also Rises

Harold F. Mosher, Jr.

The purpose of this study is to identify two distinct functional styles in Hemingway's *The Sun Also Rises* and to resolve a critical disagreement about the novel's meaning by applying an approach which combines methods of the New Criticism with some fresh ideas proposed by David Lodge, a stylistic critic, and by Curtis Hayes, a linguistic critic. I shall examine a facet of the novel's style, which to my knowledge has surprisingly never been thoroughly analyzed before, although some critics like Mark Schorer and Joseph Warren Beach have "felt" the existence of Hemingway's two styles.

Some of Hemingway's commentators disagree about the nature of his moral code and the characters who live, or fail to live, according to this code. Earl Rovit most succinctly locates the problem when he observes that the reader does not know whether to judge Jake Barnes ironically or sympathetically.[1] Probably because of this reason, students sometimes find it difficult to identify the protagonist, some preferring Cohn or even Brett as the main character. Used to romantic heroes instead of disappearing ones, they cannot accept the sexually wounded Jake as the protagonist. Some critics interpret the end of the novel as if it principally revealed Brett's heroic self-abnegation in giving up Romero instead of dramatizing something about Jake's reaction to the foregoing events. Others believe that Brett's renouncement of Romero is an act tainted with self-delusion and that she really has acted the selfish bitch, which she claims to have avoided.[2] A few readers feel compelled to defend Robert Cohn against the admittedly biased opinion of Jake, the jealousy of Mike Campbell, and the impatience of Brett. To Arthur Scott, Cohn is the only normal person in the confused, drunken, and immoral world of the novel;[3] but to Earl Rovit, Cohn is the "anti-tutor" in Hemingway's moral system and, though unconscious of it, leads an empty life. In contrast, Count Mippipopolous's adventurous and full life represents the ideal or code of the novel. Mark Spilka, on the other hand, considers Romero to be the touchstone for the code; he is a sort of *bildungsroman* hero emerging with integrity from his initiation into manhood.[4]

But as Rovit has suggested, the problem of determining the code originates with Jake, the narrator through whose limited perspective the reader experiences the action. Although there are certain biographical similarities between Jake and Hemingway—they both were journalists; they both lived in Paris and Spain; they both were wounded in the war—it would be wrong to think of Jake as Hemingway's *alter ego*, spokesman, and only code hero, and although one might agree with John Rouch that Jake is "the most sensitive and complicated person in the book,"[5] it would be dangerous to assert that he is "well aware of . . . the significance of all the details, conversations, and scenes that he is transcribing."[6] One important monologue demonstrates that Jake does not speak with the authority of later protagonists like Frederic Henry and Robert Jordan. Drunk and afraid of the dark, Jake hesitatingly and contradictorily reflects about a life philosophy: "Enjoying living was learning to get your money's worth and knowing when you had it. . . . It seemed like a fine philosophy. In five years, I thought, it will seem just as silly as all the other fine philosophies I've had."[7] If Jake Barnes speaks for Hemingway, then the author is just as uncertain as his narrator. What is more likely, as E. M. Halliday has shown, is that Hemingway is manipulating the first-person point of view to dramatize with a sense of immediacy and credibility his own ideas, which are not as unformed as Jake makes them appear to be.[8]

In retrospect, *The Sun Also Rises*, considered by many critics to be Hemingway's best novel, seems to have been written with more concern for art than with the exposition of the Hemingway philosophy, the didactic quality which sometimes obtrudes awkwardly in such later fiction as *To Have and Have Not* or *Across the River and Into the Trees*. In 1926 Hemingway would probably have agreed with Saul Bellow's observation that the novel "becomes art when the views most opposite to the author's own are allowed to exist in full strength."[9] Thus the objective presentation and resulting ambiguity characteristic of the realistic school of James and Conrad —two of Hemingway's early masters—force the critic to verify statements with actions, compare characters, analyze symbols, and, in general, examine all parts of the book including style for clues of the author's intentions. In *The Sun Also Rises* and in *A Farewell to Arms*, the style is used organically to reveal the theme before style becomes, as seen later in Hemingway's career, simply an automatic trademark of the author's own voice. Mark Schorer, referring to these early novels, writes: "The style was the immediate representation of the moral attitude of the author toward his material, it objectified the author's values and thus in itself was comment in writing otherwise unhampered by comment."[10] Character, action, symbols, and style all function to reveal dramatically, not to obscure, the code in *The Sun Also Rises*. It is misleading to say, as Earl Rovit does, that "Hemingway has artfully (or accidentally) failed to provide the reader with obvious hints or standards of measurement. . . ."[11] Indeed, Rovit's own analysis shows that the code is clear enough in *The Sun Also Rises* although not necessarily always clear in Jake's mind or through Jake's actions alone. Rather, it is to a certain extent the life of Count Mippipopolous and, to a fuller extent, that of Romero which set the standards of restraint, endurance, self-sufficiency, order, sensuous enjoyment, comradeship, and fatalistic acceptance of life that form the Hemingway code.[12] By their actions may be measured the relative success and failure of the other more human but less idealized characters. Thus, Jake follows to a certain extent the code of sensuous enjoyment during the fishing expedition in Burguete (although not as fully as Bill Gorton) but betrays the code of the *aficionado* (as Montoya's reaction indicates) in arranging the affair between Brett and Romero.

As we shall see, an examination of some aspects of style—of rhythm, sentence structure, repetition, and vocabulary—will support these conclusions about the themes, will guide us in our judgment of Jake, and incidentally will help us to resolve a controversy about the ending of the novel. Critics like Earl Rovit or Dewey Ganzel believe that in the end Jake realizes his illusions about Brett and recognizes the necessity to accept a new, limited life.[13] To them the novel's structure is spiral-shaped. Other critics like W. M. Frohock feel that the novel ends in the same mood of emptiness with which it began. There is no recognition of progress; the generation of the 1920's is still lost. The structure is circular.[14] In both interpretations, though, Jake is a somewhat unreliable narrator at least until the end of the book. To understand Hemingway's code, to "go behind" Jake in order to find a system of value which this narrator either does not completely understand or does not always follow, we shall analyze the style of certain passages which reveal this deeper meaning. I do not claim that this approach will always uncover hidden meanings or that in this case it can be applied consistently to every passage in the novel; but it does in many cases reveal intentions which other techniques may fail to discover.

The approach that I have chosen for this stylistic analysis is derived from two sources. For a theory of choosing the texts to be studied, I have relied on David Lodge's *Language of Fiction*. According to Lodge, the critic of the novel "is compelled to select more drastically than the critic of poetry, and the alternative procedures open to him are (1) to isolate, deliberately or at random, one or more passages, and submit them to close and exhaustive analysis, or (2) to trace significant threads through the language of an entire novel. One might label these approaches 'textural' and 'structural' respectively."[15] I have tried to combine these two methods by choosing five passages to study individually (the "textural" method) and by showing this choice to be representative of the whole work's style (the "structural" method).

For my method of analysis I shall adapt, in part, some techniques of transformational grammar and statistics proposed in an article by Curtis Hayes.[16] Using Noam Chomsky's generative/transformational grammar, Hayes compares statistically the styles of Gibbon and Hemingway, describing them in more precise terms than "simple" or "complex"—words used by most critics. Hayes finds, for instance, after examination of one hundred sentences by each author that the percentage of generalized transformation is 98 percent in Gibbon and only 60 percent in Hemingway.[17] In Gibbon, Hayes finds an average of 4.3 transformations per sentence; in Hemingway only 1.3.[18] Although I shall not rely so heavily on transformational grammar nor on percentages, my approach will borrow some of Hayes's principles.

General critical comments on Hemingway's style are plentiful and usually accurate as far as they go.[19] Unfortunately, many of these studies do not take into account the increasing mannerism of Hemingway's style after *A Farewell to Arms*, a fact which makes generalizations misleading unless titles are specified. In addition, few critics have isolated passages for study in order to demonstrate how style functions in a particular novel or in what way it is typical of that novel or of a phase in the evolution of Hemingway's style.[20] Richard Bridgman in *The Colloquial Style in America* analyzes colloquialisms and repetition and concludes that "Hemingway's style was eclectic" and that "he polished his stylistic surfaces to reflect his meaning."[21] But Bridgman says nothing about how style reflects meaning nor anything in detail about other stylistic features like construction of sentences or rhythm. Joseph Warren Beach is more helpful in this general description of Hemingway's style:

Most of his sentences are short and simple, a single statement, subject, predicate and object. And most of the rest are strings of simple statements held together with *ands*. The rarest thing with him is the statement modified by subordinate clauses indicating reasons, causes, conditions, concessions. . . . Stimulus and response-gesture, speech, action. Let them speak for themselves.[22]

Here Beach has put his finger on a significant dichotomy in Hemingway's style—one type consisting of short, simple sentences and the other of longer, compound sentences. This very distinction may be found in the style of *The Sun Also Rises*. Furthermore, we shall see that the rarer complex sentences tend to appear in passages dominated by the short, simple sentences. As for sentence function, other than for the purpose of objective presentation, Beach points out that Hemingway's linear style reflects the simplicity and chronology of life[23] or "the behavior of people not precisely simple-minded, but who have not learned, or who have deliberately unlearned, the language of intellectual sophistication."[24] Such statements serve only as a general guide in the understanding of any individual novel where the style may play an important role in clarifying the author's intentions.

Carlos Baker's remarks apply specifically to *The Sun Also Rises:*

> Long before the middle of the book, a reader who is reasonably sensitive to changes in tone may discover that he has been silently forced into a choice between two sets of moral and emotional atmospheres. . . . [A] world of mean and snarled disorder is set off against a world clear of entangling alliances. The whole mood of the novel brightens, for example, when the men-without-women, Jake Barnes and Bill Gorton, climb to the roof of the bus which will take them to Burguete in the Pyrenees.[25]

Still, other than the references to "tone" and "mood" Baker says nothing more specific about devices forcing the reader into this choice between two moral atmospheres, and Baker's analysis of these two tones and moralities is incomplete. I hope to demonstrate more thoroughly the function of Hemingway's double style to indicate his attitude toward the two systems of value in *The Sun*.

Using Lodge's "textural" approach, I shall examine several passages from the novel to illustrate the two different styles. The following paragraph describes the fight between Jake and Cohn at the end of a particularly drunken night at the fiesta in Pamplona:

> I swung at him and he ducked. I saw his face duck sideways in the light. He hit me and I sat down on the pavement. As I started to get on my feet he hit me twice. I went down backward under a table. I tried to get up and felt I did not have any legs. I felt I must get on my feet and try and hit him. Mike had an arm around me, and I found I was sitting on a chair. Mike was pulling at my ears.[26]

This quotation is a good example of what I shall call Hemingway's "staccato" style. Immediately we can describe some obvious

266

aspects. The sentences are for the most part relatively short. The longest one has fifteen words; the shortest, four. Five range between ten and thirteen words and four range between six and nine words. The average length is about nine and one-half words to the sentence: Eight of the eleven sentences have a pronoun subject, and the three exceptions all have the same noun subject, "Mike." In every sentence the subject is immediately followed by the verb, and in every sentence except one ("As I started. . . .") the first word is the subject. There are no verbal transformations of the participle or gerund type, and there are only two compound verbs and no compound subjects or objects. This repetition of pronoun subject and subject-verb order in the sentence structure is continued by word repetitions: "I" is repeated eleven times; "he" is repeated three times; "Mike" three times; forms of the verbs "duck," "sit," and "try" each twice; "hit" three times; "felt" twice; and "feet" twice. Although this amount of repetition is exceptional even for Hemingway, it does serve as an example of this remarkable feature in the "staccato" style. It is often used in *The Sun* to suggest restrictions, boredom, or monotony. Finally, of the eleven sentences in the paragraph, five are simple; three are complex, a high ratio compared to the 20 percent which are compound. With the relatively short sentences creating frequent pauses, no long, rhythmical phrases have a chance to be developed. The result is "staccato" style. Its most frequent characteristics are repetition, the prevalence of simple or complex sentences, and short sentences.[27]

Let us now apply Lodge's structural approach. Having once described characteristics of this staccato style, we should be able to recognize it elsewhere in the novel. Indeed, it occurs frequently, and I have noted some of its significant appearances, selected mainly on the basis of the length of the passage. I have not considered dialogue, which is usually written in the staccato style. Hemingway uses this style with such consistency to describe action, character, or setting which in some way is concerned with the violation of his code of values that we can conclude that the style is a device to signal to the reader this violation whether Jake Barnes is aware of it or not. For instance, how are we to interpret the two dance episodes, one at the *bal musette* in Paris and the other with the *riau-riau* dancers in Pamplona? Is the first symbolic of the desolation of the Paris scenes and the second of the vitality of the Pamplona episodes, as Frohock describes the novel?[28] Or, rather, is the drunkenness of the dancers and spectators in both episodes to be interpreted as a mark of disorder and escape, as Carlos Baker would probably judge it when he asserts that Hemingway intends to criticize those members of his generation who drown themselves in alcohol instead of living life fully?[29] If we can trust the stylistic guide, we shall have to agree with Baker that both passages describe violations of Hemingway's values since both are written in the staccato style:

> The dancing-club was a *bal musette* in the Rue de la Montagne Sainte-Geneviève. Five nights a week the working people of the Pantheon quarter danced there. One night a week it was the dancing-club. On Monday nights it was closed. When we arrived it was quite empty, except for a policeman sitting near the door, the wife of the proprietor back of the zinc bar, and the proprietor himself. The daughter of the house came downstairs as we went in. There were long benches, and tables ran across the room, and at the far end a dancing-floor.[29]

> Some dancers formed a circle around Brett and started to dance. They wore big wreaths of white garlics around their necks. They took Bill and me by the arms and put us in the circle. Bill started to dance, too. They were all chanting. Brett wanted to dance but they did not want her to. They wanted her as an image to dance around. When the song ended with the sharp *riau-riau!* they rushed us into a wine-shop.[30]

Briefly, in the first passage only one sentence is compound, the last one. Except for it and the long complex sentence in the middle, the other sentences are simple and relatively short, averaging about ten words each. In all of the sentences except two, the subject is immediately followed by the verb. "Dancing-club" is repeated twice and is echoed by "danced" and "dancing-floor." The phrase "it was" is repeated three times, forms of "night" three times and "night" or "nights" repeated in combination with "a week" two times. "Proprietor" is mentioned twice. The function of the staccato style here is to emphasize the lifelessness and lack of purpose in the lives of the American and English expatriots. In the second passage, likewise, only one sentence is compound; one is complex; the rest are simple. The average sentence length is eight and one half words. In all the sentences, the subject is immediately followed by the verb. The pronoun "they" is repeated six times; forms of "dance" are repeated five times; "around" is repeated three times; and forms of "want" are repeated three times. In all the sentences except two, the first word is the noun or pronoun subject. The staccato style underlines the disorder of the fiesta. I have found five other passages in the novel, besides the description of the fight between Cohn and Jake, written in the staccato style that describe disorder in one form or another.[31] This style may also be used to describe scenes of lifeless-

ness,[32] the emptiness of life,[33] or scenes dramatizing other violations of the Hemingway code: such as, profiteering[34] ; the failure of
communication[35] ; and carelessness,[36] to cite a few examples.

To illustrate Hemingway's other style—a more rhythmical one—in
The Sun, I have chosen the following excerpt which describes the bus
ride to Burguete:

> After a while we came out of the mountains, and there were trees
> along both sides of the road, and a stream and ripe fields of grain, and the
> road went on, very white and straight ahead, and then lifted to a little rise,
> and off on the left was a hill with an old castle, with buildings close
> around it and a field of grain going right up to the walls and shifting in the
> wind. I was up in front with the driver and I turned around. Robert Cohn
> was asleep, but Bill looked and nodded his head. Then we crossed a wide
> plain, and there was a big river off on the right shining in the sun from
> between the line of trees, and away off you could see the plateau of
> Pamplona rising out of the plain, and the walls of the city, and the great
> brown cathedral, and the broken skyline of the other churches. In back of
> the plateau were the mountains, and every way you looked there were
> other mountains, and ahead the road stretched out white across the plain
> going toward Pamplona.[37]

We can easily detect the differences between this rhythmical
style and the staccato one. First, whereas in the staccato style, simple
and complex sentences are the predominant types, here compound
(and compound-complex) sentences are predominant. In fact, in this
excerpt, there are no simple or complex sentences. Secondly, the
sentences are on the whole much longer than those in the staccato
style, and average about forty words each, as compared with nine
and one half words in the first sample of the staccato style. This
length between pauses allows a continuous rhythm to develop. Of
the five sentences, only two begin with the subject as compared with
all sentences in the first staccato style excerpt, and in this rhythmical
passage the subjects vary among nouns, the expletive "there," and
among pronouns in the first person, both singular and plural, and
pronouns in the second person. Although in most of the sentences
the subject is followed immediately by the verb, in two cases this
pattern is varied by inversion, no instance of which appears in the
example of staccato style. There are five participial verbal transformations—"going," "shifting," "shining," "rising," and "going" again,
as compared with none in the staccato sample. Although the
rhythmical passage has only two compound verbs, as does the staccato one, the proportion in the rhythmical selection is much higher,
given the fewer number of sentences; the rhythmical excerpt also
contains two compound subjects and two compound objects, which

are completely absent in the staccato sample. Except for the words "mountains" and "there," one finds very little repetition proportionately in this passage, with the exception, of course, of "and." The absence of repetition gives a sense of freedom and movement as contrasted with the restriction which repetition creates in the staccato style. We can conclude that Hemingway's rhythmical style is marked essentially by the compound sentence with the conjunction "and," by the long sentence, by more varied sentence structure, and by longer phrases between pauses.

This rhythmical passage describes a certain beauty of nature which Hemingway's code heroes are supposed to appreciate. (It is significant that Robert Cohn falls asleep during the experience.) I have found three other important descriptions of beauty in nature or in human action which are written in this style.[38] Other instances in which the rhythmical style is used to indicate code values include seven descriptions of quiet order,[39] two interludes of sensuous comfort,[40] as well as three scenes of comradeship.[41] We can conclude that Hemingway consistently uses this style to describe character, action, or setting which dramatize his code of values. Again this stylistic device helps the reader to understand the moral world of the novel when Jake Barnes may not.

It seems to me that by the end of the novel Jake is still in the process of learning; he may at times understand the code but he is still not able to live up to it, as he has shown earlier by his fishing from the bank with worms, by his drunkenness, and by his violating Montoya's trust. He goes to Madrid to rescue Brett, gets drunk again, and drives away with her in a taxi, realizing, just as he had known before, that life with or without her is not going to be good for him.[42] The increasing disorder and failure in his life, which he had been able to control somewhat in Paris, is evident in the staccato style of the final descriptive paragraph:

> Down-stairs we came out through the first-floor dining-room to the street. A waiter went for a taxi. It was hot and bright. Up the street was a little square with trees and grass where there were taxis parked. A taxi came up the street, the waiter hanging out at the side. I tipped him and told the driver where to drive, and got in beside Brett. The driver started up the street. I settled back, Brett moved close to me. We sat close against each other. I put my arm around her and she rested against me comfortably. It was very hot and bright, and the houses looked sharply white. We turned out onto the Gran Via.[43]

Each sentence averages less than ten words. There are ten simple sentences, one complex one, and only two compound sentences. In all but one, the verb immediately follows the subject. The words "waiter," "taxi," and "close" are repeated, as are "driver" and the clause, "It was hot and bright." Jake seems to press close to Brett in defiance of the reality of their sexual separation. The scene recalls the earlier one in Paris when they kiss in the taxi and are just as aware of the tragic impossibility of their love.[44] So Brett, too, has degenerated, now more desperate in her search for happiness instead of accepting realistically her true nature. Thus, the novel ends in a mood of emptiness underlined by the staccato style. The policeman's baton, perhaps a symbol of Jake's sexual frustration, seems more properly to be a symbol of society's order, though ironically a restricted one, contrasted with the unfruitful disorder in Jake's and Brett's lives.[45] Style, among other factors, would lend support to Frohock's conclusion that the novel ends in the same mood of emptiness with which it began; the structure is circular rather than spiral.

Northern Illinois University
University of Nice

---

[1] Earl Rovit, *Ernest Hemingway* (New York: Twayne, 1963), p. 148.

[2] Mark Schorer, "The Background of a Style," *Kenyon Review,* III (1941), p. 103 (for the first view emphasizing Brett's "negative morality"); and Rovit, Op. cit., pp. 152-156 (for the second view pointing out her self-delusion).

[3] Arthur Scott, "In Defense of Cohn," *College English,* XVIII (1957), p. 314; William L. Vance, "Implications of Form in *The Sun Also Rises,"* *The Twenties: Poetry and Prose,* eds. Richard E. Langford and William E. Taylor (Deland, Florida: Everett/Edwards, 1966), p. 90. Vance finds a pyramidal plot corresponding with Cohn's conception of a romantic ending to his love for Brett. This pyramidal plot is superimposed on the episodic plot connected with the expatriots' world view. Vance suggests that Cohn's romantic view is the optimistic alternative to the sad reality of Jake's and Brett's failures.

[4] Mark Spilka, "The Death of Love in *The Sun Also Rises,"* *Hemingway and His Critics,* ed. Carlos Baker (New York: Hill and Wang, 1961), p. 92; reprinted from *Twelve Original Essays on Great American Novels,* ed. Charles Shapiro (Detroit: Wayne State University Press, 1958).

[5] John Rouch, "Jake Barnes as Narrator," *Modern Fiction Studies,* XI (1965-66), p. 366.

[6] Ibid., p. 369.

[7] Ernest Hemingway, *The Sun Also Rises* (New York: Scribners, 1926) p. 153; Claire Sprague, *"The Sun Also Rises*: Its 'Clear Financial Basis'," *American Quarterly,* XXI (1969), pp. 259-266 (discusses Jake's moral bankruptcy and the novel's ultimate ambiguity).

[8] E. M. Halliday, "Hemingway's Narrative Perspective," *Modern American Fiction,* ed. Walton Litz (New York: Oxford University Press, 1963), pp. 215-227; reprinted from *The Sewanee Review* (April-June 1952); R. W. Stallman, *"The Sun Also Rises*—But no Bells Ring," *The Houses That James Built* (East

Lansing: Michigan State University Press, 1961), pp. 184-185 (attributes the moral confusion of the book to Jake's weakness).

9 Saul Bellow, "Where Do We Go From Here: The Future of Fiction," *Saul Bellow and the Critics,* ed. Irving Malin (London: University of London Press, 1967), p. 220; reprinted from *To the Young Writer: Hopwood Lectures,* Second Series, ed. A. L. Bader (Ann Arbor: University of Michigan Press, 1965); also, Carlos Baker, *Hemingway: The Writer as Artist* (Princeton: Princeton University Press, 1963), pp. 74-75 (Hemingway's comments on the stylistic revisions of the loose first draft); and Mark Schorer, op. cit., pp. 101ff (remarks on the separation of style from content in *To Have and Have Not* and in later works).

10 Schorer, op. cit., p. 101.

11 Rovit, op. cit., p. 148.

12 Paul Ramsey, "Hemingway as a Moral Thinker: A Look at Two Novels," *The Twenties: Poetry and Prose,* eds. Richard E. Langford and William E. Taylor, p. 93, lists some of these qualities as stoicism, individualism, hedonism, friendship, and pessimism.

13 Rovit, op. cit., p. 158; Dewey Ganzel, *"Cabestro and Vaquilla:* The Symbolic Structure of *The Sun Also Rises,"* *The Sewanee Review,* LXXVI (Winter 1968), p. 48.

14 W. M. Frohock, "Violence and Discipline," *Ernest Hemingway: The Man and His Work,* ed. John K. M. McCaffery (Cleveland: World, 1950), p. 269; Philip Young, *Ernest Hemingway* (New York: Rinehart, 1952), p. 58; Robert O. Stephens, "Ernest Hemingway and the Rhetoric of Escape," *The Twenties: Poetry and Prose,* eds. Richard E. Langford and William E. Taylor, p. 85, notices a circular structure not only in the plot but also in paragraphs and sentences. Hemingway's own stated intentions would seem to agree with this last interpretation. As quoted in Baker, *Hemingway: Writer as Artist,* p. 81, a letter from Hemingway to Maxwell Perkins in 1926 states that *The Sun* was about the earth's endurance contrasted with the Lost Generation's ephemerality. For a different view, Robert Cochran, "Circularity in *The Sun Also Rises,"* *Modern Fiction Studies,* XIV (1968), pp. 299-305.

15 David Lodge, *Language of Fiction* (London: Routledge and Kegan Paul, 1966), p. 78.

16 Curtis Hayes, "A Study in Prose Styles: Edward Gibbon and Ernest Hemingway," *Texas Studies in Literature and Language,* VII (1966), 371-386.

17 Ibid., p. 382. A generalized transformation is the term applied to all types of changes, like substituting a gerund for a noun or a relative clause for an adjective, by which a matrix sentence—the simplest form to express the idea of the independent clause of a sentence—is modified to become the textual sentence—the sentence as ultimately written. Thus in the textual sentence—"The boy who is wearing the cap is my brother"—the matrix is "The boy is my brother" in which is embedded the constituent, "The boy is wearing the cap." The matrix sentence has been transformed by a relative clause.

18 Ibid., p. 382.

19 See, for example, John Graham, "Ernest Hemingway: The Meaning of Style," *Modern Fiction Studies,* VI (1960), 298-313; Raleigh Morgan, Jr., "Stylistics Devices and Levels of Speech in the Works of Hemingway," in *Sprache und Literatur Englands und Amerikas,* vol. III: *Die Wissenschaftliche Erschliessung*

der *Prosa* (Tubingen, 1959), pp. 145-154; and Robert Sykes, "Ernest Hemingway's Style: A Descriptive Analysis" (Unpublished dissertation, 1964).

[20] Charles R. Anderson, "Hemingway's Other Style," *Modern Language Notes,* LXXVI (1961), p. 442, identifies a lyrical style and illustrates it by analyzing a passage from *A Farewell to Arms* to conclude simply that this poetic manner provides a contrast to the spare style and is one of the reasons that Hemingway's work survives.

[21] Richard Bridgman, *The Colloquial Style in America* (New York: Oxford University Press, 1966), p. 222.

[22] Joseph Warren Beach, *American Fiction, 1920-1940* (New York: Russell and Russell, 1960), p. 100; reprinted from the original Macmillan edition (New York, 1941).

[23] Joseph Warren Beach, *The Twentieth Century Novel* (New York: Century, 1932), p. 536.

[24] Beach, *American Fiction,* pp. 101-102.

[25] Baker, *Hemingway: The Writer as Artist,* p. 83.

[26] Hemingway, op. cit., pp. 197-198.

[27] Schorer, op. cit., p. 103. Although Schorer is writing generally of Hemingway's early style, his description could apply to Hemingway's staccato style: "The directness and the brevity of its syntactical constructions, its muscularity, the sharpness of its staccato and repetitive effects . . . ."

[28] Frohock, op. cit., p. 269.

[29] Hemingway, op. cit., p. 19.

[30] Ibid., p. 160.

[31] Ibid., pp. 147-148, 152, 194, 203-204, 213 for passages describing disorder. No doubt, additional ones may be found.

[32] Ibid., p. 13.

[33] Ibid., pp. 31, 230-231, 247-248.

[34] Ibid., pp. 112-113.

[35] Ibid., pp. 162-163.

[36] Ibid., p. 207.

[37] Ibid., pp. 95-96.

[38] Ibid., pp. 111, 120, 224-225 for descriptions of beauty.

[39] Ibid., pp. 79, 92-93, 96, 98-99, 173-174, 206, 219 for passages describing order.

[40] Ibid., pp. 107, 129.

[41] Ibid., pp. 133-134, 156, 167.

[42] Ibid., p. 26, although Jake may indeed accept in the end the sterility of his relationship with Brett, his recognition of it is clearly anticipated in the earlier taxi scene when he says, "And there's not a damn thing we could do . . . ."

[43] Ibid., p. 258.

[44] Ibid., p. 25.

[45] Spilka, op. cit., p. 91, comments on this symbolism. Jackson J. Benson, *Hemingway: The Writer's Art of Self-Defense* (Minneapolis: University of Minnesota Press, 1969), p. 42, seems to be in agreement with my interpretation of the ending. Benson emphasizes Jake's recognition of his self-deception as contrasted with Brett's failure and adds that the novel is "a satire of sentimentality wherein contrasts of various levels of awareness are presented . . . ."

The Design of Heroism in
The Sun Also Rises

Bruce L. Grenberg

Perhaps because Jake Barnes of *The Sun Also Rises* is a writer rather than a soldier, athlete, or fisherman, because his activity of character is intellectual and perceptual in nature rather than physical, most critics have denied or confounded his essential heroism. They find him lacking in the positive, strenuous virtues by which Hemingway's "heroes" are to be recognized (viz. Frederic Henry, Harry Morgan, Robert Jordan, Santiago) and judge him, thus, to be a disappointingly passive protagonist who, emasculated by his own disillusionment, wanders aimlessly amid the lives of others until finding repose in a stoical resignation to the unpleasant reality of his own inabilities.[1]

Nothing, I contend, can be further from the truth of Jake's role in the novel. In fact, I should argue that in Jake's character we find the essence of Hemingway's conception of the hero, that the radical principles of Jake's vision, as they evolve in the narrative, provide the rationale for Hemingway's persistent conception of modern man and inform the substance and activity of all his heroes from Frederic Henry to Santiago.

To determine Jake's potentiality for heroism we must first examine the world in which he lives. As many have noted, that world viewed generally as post-war western civilization is basically sterile; and, more explicitly, the particular society of Brett, Cohn, Bill, and Mike is depicted as fragmented and directionless. As Edwin Berry Burgum observes, Brett, Mike, Cohn, and the others are "typically self-defeating and project their perversity upon their friends. Their *bonhommie* conceals a surly dislike of the very persons they pretend or desire to have as friends."[2] Indeed, of these characters it might be said that they do not seek each other's company so much as they, perforce, *are* each other's company. Uneasy as a society, the book's characters are just as unintegrated and inconsistent when considered individually.[3] Cohn is the Jewish boxing champion from Princeton who is at once timid and belligerent, cowed and aggressive. Brett, nominally an aristocrat, is a drunk and a near-nymphomaniac; and even within the bounds of her promiscuity she displays an incongruous affection for the impotent Jake and some anonymous homosexuals. Mike is the successfully bankrupt businessman, and Bill Gorton's well-adjusted exterior manner conceals, none too well, a compulsion to drink. Even Harvey Stone, who but drifts casually across the scene, is carefully described as a recent winner of two hundred francs who hasn't eaten in days.

The disorientation of this society is further revealed, or perhaps explained, by the inoperation of western culture's traditional values of patriotism, morality, honor, and religion. The ideal of patriotism is depicted as absurd in Jake's career as a soldier and especially in the nature of his wound; the grotesque speech by the Italian colonel but highlights the irony.[4] All the virtues of honor, glory, and heroism are presented as bogus in the otherwise digressive narrations of Mike's "war adventures" and medal attaining "heroics."[5] Also seen as illusory are the traditional values associated with "breeding" and social station; even the quasi-respectable validity of money and commerce are undermined by the image of Mike's bankruptcy and arrogant dependency.

With characteristic economy Hemingway in Book II succinctly mirrors the shattered conventions and traditions of western society: Mike hears music in the streets of Pamplona and asks, "Isn't that the procession?" " 'Nada,' some one said. 'It's nothing. Drink up. Lift the bottle.' "[6] The answer given is far reaching, for earlier Hemingway has stressed that "in the procession were all the dignitaries, civil and religious."[7,8] And Mike's conversation also reflects critically on Jake's statement early in Book I: "We would probably have gone on and discussed the war and agreed that it was in reality a calamity for civilization, and perhaps would have been better avoided. I was bored enough."[9] For in retrospect this observation is seen to be something other than mere irony and paradox; Jake expresses his pained conviction that the spurious ideals and misleading traditions of civilized society had led to their own dissolution in the chaos of World War I.

The essence of Jake's response to this deadened and deadening world is suggested in Chapter XIV, which serves as a prelude to the climactic action of the fiesta and bull-fight. In a quiet, introspective mood Jake observes, "There is no reason why because it is dark you should look at things differently from when it is light. The hell there isn't!",[10] and then continues, "Perhaps as you went along you did learn something. I did not care what it was all about. All I wanted to know was how to live in it. Maybe if you found out how to live in it you learned from that what it was all about."[11] The first statement reveals Jake's sense of past surety, now lost, and his present disability. And perhaps just as important the images of light and darkness metaphorically inform the second statement, which somewhat abstractly reflects Jake's aspirations for the future.

Amid the flurried dreamers and darkened dreams of the post-war western world, finding support neither in his society nor in its conventions and traditions, possessing no metaphysic upon which he can, or cares, to draw, Jake Barnes necessarily must seek enlightenment within himself.[12] And in the clean, well-lighted place which for Hemingway is the untrammeled self Jake finds the illuminating and cohering force of his seeing eye and mind. In this, man's most fundamental activity of ordering consciousness Jake finds the power not to dispel all the world's darkness nor to integrate all its fractured being, but to attain for himself a limited arena of meaningful, ordered activity. It is Jake's conscious discipline of this exertive though limited individualism that Hemingway depicts as the only force capable of providing meaning for man in the modern world. And it is Jake's hard-won apprehension of this truth which forms the pattern for heroism in all Hemingway's fiction from *The Sun Also Rises* to *The Old Man and The Sea.*

Since Jake's activity in the novel is that of primary consciousness, his participation in the events of Paris, Burguete, and Pamplona is essentially perceptual in nature; and consequently, the images of his narrative are of primary importance. Indeed, there are several integrated patterns of imagery in the novel which provide the clearest representation of Jake's progressive responses to the world, which reveal at once both the reality perceived and the mode of Jake's perception.[13] With the greatest cumulative effect Hemingway delineates the chaos and disorder of Jake's post-war world in pervasive image patterns of darkness and fragmentation and indicates through the converse image patterns of emergent light and coherence Jake's evolving capacity for creating meaning amid chaos through his ordering consciousness.[14] These images of light, expanding in force from the flares, arc-lights, and naked bulbs of Paris to the brilliance of the sun in the bull-ring and at San Sebastian, trace most emphatically for us Jake's growing awareness of what he can do, in spite of all that he cannot.

There are a number of instances in the first two books of the novel where single, intrusive images embody Jake's perception of fragmentation and disorder in the world. For example, in Jake's image-crowded mind, that which suggests the Greek Count Mippi-popolous is "an elk's tooth on his watchchain."[15] Certainly not in-explicable on a Parisian street, but nevertheless incongruous as images are "the man with the jumping frogs and the man with the boxer toys," who are pictured near by "a man who was pushing a roller that printed the name CINZANO on the sidewalk in damp letters."[16] Images just as intrusive are Bill Gorton's stuffed dogs and horse-cabs[17] and the statue of Marshall Ney, dramatically alien with purple wreath and gesturing sword amid the chestnut leaves.[18] Even the growing lightness of banter as Bill and Jake head for Spain does not remove the eye-jarring quality of the train waiter's purple armpits.[19] In the fashion of Poe, Hemingway seems to suggest, through image, the disjunctiveness lurking beneath the surface of apparent order; upon the cleanest hotel floor might be found a cock-roach three inches long.[20]

More emphatic in presenting to us Jake's fragmented vision of an incomplete world are the clusters, or collages, of disjunctive images which Hemingway employs at critical points in the narrative. For example, let us turn to the first picture of Jake and Brett alone, at the beginning of Chapter IV, which is particularly formative of our responses to Book I, since Jake's whole relationship to sophisticated, civilized Paris concentrates into the drama of his relationship with Brett:

> The taxi went up the hill, passed the lighted square, then on into the dark, still climbing, then levelled out onto a dark street behind St. Etienne du Mont, went smoothly down the asphalt, passed the trees and the standing bus at the Place de la Contrescarpe, then turned onto the cobbles of the Rue Mouffetard. There were lighted bars and late open shops on each side of the street. We were sitting apart and we jolted close together going down the old street. Brett's hat was off. Her head was back. I saw her face in the lights from the open shops, then it was dark, then I saw her face clearly as we came out on the Avenue des Gobelins. The street was torn up and men were working on the car-tracks by the light of acetylene flares. Brett's face was white and the long line of her neck showed in the bright light of the flares. The street was dark again and I kissed her. Our lips were tight together and then she turned away and pressed against the corner of the seat, as far away as she could get. Her head was down.[21]

This passage is not so much descriptive of the setting in the novel as it is an apocalyptic presentation of Jake's fractured world. This world's incoherence and divergence are reflected in the passage's ups and downs, in its contrasts of light with dark, of smooth with rough, in its jumbling of forms (square, line, "corner," "car-tracks") and in its conglomeration of objects—asphalt, trees, bus, cobbles, flares, etc. Although one can (and probably does) construct a coherent picture of the scene, it is necessary to do so by extrapolation from the shards of Jake's vision. The flares light up Jake's world only segments at a time, and he sees Brett serially, as it were—her hat, her head, her face, her face again, yet again, and her neck in a sequence like an old flickering movie. Consistent with this depicted mood, their communion is partial and transitory: only their "lips" are "tight together" and immediately Brett "turned away and pressed against the corner of the seat, as far away as she could get."[22]

Another significant instance of this imaged discord occurs at the end of Chapter IV. Jake has said good-night to Brett, and serving as an illustrated background to their relationship is another fragmented vision of stairs, a window, a car, curb, glasses, a sink, slippers, and a bed. At this early point in the narrative Jake's attempts to order his world are minimally successful; but symbolically the steady force of vision which he is to attain in the sun-lit ring of Pamplona has its flickering birth in the intermittent and restricted perspectives provided by the arc-lit streets of Paris.

The images of Book II at first continue the sense of discord. In contrast to the spuriously ordered Paris of the American tourist, where the purportedly authentic, "quaint restaurant" serves the standard, Midwestern American Sunday dinner of "roast chicken, new green beans, mashed potatoes, a salad, . . . apple-pie and cheese,"[23] Hemingway describes the real Paris, through the parallel image of a restaurant. Again the picture is of a "total" scene, but again it is described in fragments; what we are made to *see* literally in Hemingway's words are leaves, a square, an S bus, a bar, a pot, a ladle, a plate, an old man, a bottle of wine, and one hand.[24] And this scene, too, is lit up by "arc-light." Although one might argue that in this scene Hemingway is only being characteristically objective, he does go out of his way here to avoid the use of even simple conjunctions, merely placing perceptions side by side, in such a way that proximity does not stress coherent relationship.[25] And, I would add, the lack of immediate sequence and relationship in such a scene evokes the sense of fragmentation and disjunction that is the heart of Jake's apprehension of "civilized" Paris society.

As Jake, Bill, and Cohn leave Paris for Spain, Jake's experience and awareness shift from the world of man to that of nature. Significantly, the imaged views of the countryside around Bayonne, Pamplona, and, particularly, Burguete illustrate a completeness and coherence demonstrably lacking in Paris. Whereas in Paris Jake can scarcely see beyond the nearest corner or outside the range of the nearest light bulb, his outlook on the sun-drenched countryside is panoramic and integrated. As Jake approaches Spain his descriptions tend to become more and more generalized and encompassing: "We ate the sandwiches and drank the Chablis and watched the country out of the window. The grain was just beginning to ripen and the fields were full of poppies. The pastureland was green, and there were fine trees, and sometimes big rivers and chateaux off in the trees."[26] If the sweeping observation of this passage lacks distinctness and "objectivity," it nevertheless is strongly suggestive of wholeness and completion, and, for example, pasture, trees, rivers, and chateaux are seen to be related parts of a constituted whole. The qualities of fertility, order, and continuing life pervade Jake's vision of the Basque country: "the land all looks very rich and green and the houses and villages look well-off and clean. Every village had a pelota court and on some of them kids were playing in the hot sun."[27] Jake's sense of the unity in nature is further suggested by his directly sequential statements of image and action, for example, in the moment by moment description of the car's arrival in Pamplona.[28] This significant device is repeated most emphatically in the description of the trip to Burguete.[29]

As has often been pointed out, in his escape to the "simple" Spain of Burguete Jake attempts to flee the confusion and anguish brought upon him by the disordered world of Paris. In effect, Jake, with Bill Gorton as companion and "mirror," seeks to find through an almost conscious retrogression the echo of an earlier, more carefree and happy state of being—in this case, that of adolescence. Their trip up into the clear, cold air of Burguete, out of the "brown, heat-baked mountains"[30] is a backward soul-journey to the simplicity of youth; the boyishness of Jake and Bill, if somewhat hard to bear aesthetically, is meaningful on this psychological and philosophical plane, and the childlike Basques are fitting companions to their fun. The light-hearted fishing, make-believe,[31] and communion with nature are blessed by the absence of ignorance, disorder, and negativism —"There was no word from Robert Cohn nor from Brett and Mike."[32]

What Jake perceives in nature, of course, is an ideal of ordered values and spontaneous activity. But this order does not transfer directly to man's social and psychological world, and it is in that world that Jake must learn to survive. When Harris asks Jake and Bill to stay over in Burguete, Jake's reply is deceptively profound: "We have to go into Pamplona. We're meeting people there."[33] Jake recognizes that if he is not to withdraw permanently into a world of mere revery and isolation he must confront the complexities of human reality, even if it means risking annihilation. Unlike Nick Adams of "The Big Two-Hearted River," Jake does not postpone this meeting with a dangerous reality: he returns to Pamplona, the fiesta, and the bull-fight.

The fiesta is perhaps the novel's most explicit expression of the elemental disorder which lies at the heart of human existence. There is no meaning and no self-coherence in the fiesta: "The things that happened could only have happened during a fiesta. Everything became quite unreal finally and it seemed as though nothing could have any consequences. It seemed out of place to think of consequences during the fiesta."[34] The *riau-riau* dancers effectively form the kinetic image of the fiesta, and their self-effacing, wild gyrations, verging on frenzy, aptly signify the dissipated and pointless force of uncontrolled being: "In the crowd you saw only the heads and shoulders of the dancers going up and down"[35] ; "They all looked down while they danced. Their rope-soled shoes tapped and spatted on the pavement. The toes touched. The heels touched. The balls of the feet touched. Then the music broke wildly and the step was finished and they were all dancing on up the street."[36] The centrifugal dancers do attempt cohesion into a circle (with Bill and Jake) around Brett[37] ; but their "inspiration" is synthetically induced (through an alcoholic beverage suggestively named *Anis del Mono*) and proves to be forced and transitory.

The dancers' tentative choice of Brett as their goddess parallels Jake's own attraction to her throughout the book, and their worship proves to be no more stable than Jake's attempts to integrate himself with the world she represents. The dance breaks up with a precipitate rush to the wineshop, and there follows a disordered, self-effacing night of drinking, confusion (" 'What time is it do you suppose?' Cohn asked"[38]), and dimmed awareness ("Going down the dark streets to the hotel we saw the sky-rockets going up in the square"[39]).

Hemingway thus employs a coordinated sequence of light imagery to signify the relationship between the chaotic fiesta and the ritualistically ordered bull-fight. The rocket-lit night confusion of the fiesta gives way with the light of dawn to the running of the bulls, which in turn leads directly to the bull-fight, with Romero poised in the bright mid-day sun.[40]

Romero's heroic nature, manifest in his fighting of the bulls, is presented to Jake, Brett, and the others, and to us, essentially as an ideal. Named for Spain's legendary, most honored matador of the eighteenth century, and participating in the most traditionalized and ritualistic of "sports," Romero represents all the heroism that in the past had been possible for man. His mastery in the ring is a demonstration of "the old thing," and Jake's *afición* is a nostalgia for an era and a culture now gone in which courage, discipline, and faith were universal ideals—attainable by few perhaps, but recognized and revered by all.

Jake's pilgrimage to Pamplona in search of this ideal is quite analogous to his journey to Burguete. But in Burguete he had sought to recapture a natural ideal outside the social context, whereas in Pamplona he seeks an encompassing human ideal which would give order and meaning to a crumbling world. How else are we to consider his hopeful, excited encouragement of Bill, Brett, Mike, and even Cohn to apprehend for themselves the magic of the bull-ring, except to see that he hopes—perhaps prays—for their conversion from despair to belief. And Jake panders for Brett, as always the focal energy of the group, not to "test" Romero's heroism, but to discover, in effect, what rapprochement there might be between the old sureties and the nihilism of modern disbelief.

Past and present do reach out to each other, but tragically cannot touch; Romero cannot acquiesce to the shorn splendor of Brett, and Brett is, and can be, no madonna. Romero's heroism, hence, remains an ideal, incapable of being translated whole into the new world; and Brett's disillusionment proves to be all too real, incapable of being dissolved by old answers to other problems.

It is definitive of Jake's heroism in the novel to say that he succeeds in preserving the ideal in the actual, the past in the present, in maintaining the possibilities for heroism in an oppressively unheroic world. Through his *afición* for the integrated ritual of the bullfight Jake perceives a pattern of heroism which he can, and does, adapt to his own ends. That is, he sees in Romero not what it is to be a matador, but what it is to be a man.

Jake visits Romero in his room before the first fight. And here, in the only "private" scene we have of him in the entire book, it is clear that Romero, in spite of all his natural abilities, does not merely *assume* his heroic stance; he must achieve it in spite of, and because of, his common human frailty and vulnerability to panic in the presence of annihilation and death. Hemingway's presentation of Romero's anguished human predicament is parallel in method to the portrayal of Jake's agonized situation in the first half of the novel. The disorder surrounding Romero is manifest in Hemingway's description of the disarranged room, which is gloomy in itself, illumined only by "a little light coming in from the window on the narrow street."[41] All the accumulating values of light imagery in the novel inhere in this scene; the light not only illuminates the gloom, but also shines directly on Romero's "black hair." Romero reveals himself to Jake as an angel of light, wearing the usually termed "suit of lights," preparing himself to face the forces of darkness, and at this point it does not seem an exaggeration to say that the carefully wound sash that Romero dons suggests the ritualistic binding in of his fragile mortality, a mortality which must be controlled in order to face the bull in the center of the ring.

The implications of Romero's mastery in the bull-ring are heightened by Hemingway's contrasting presentation of the running of the bulls, which leads to the death of Vicente Girones. For it is critical to our understanding of Romero's value to recognize that his heroism maintains itself directly within the context of the turbid *corrida* and out of that confusion and fatality precipitates victory and enlightenment. The crowd, of which Girones is a part, and Romero face the same reality: "the bull who killed Vicente Girones was named Bocanegra[42] . . . and was killed by Pedro Romero as the third bull of that same afternoon."[43] And it is the milling, disordered fiesta mob that brings the bulls to the ring that they might be mastered:

> . . . the crowd was through the gate and into the ring with the bulls behind them. The red door of the ring went shut, the crowd on the outside balconies of the bull-ring were pressing through to the inside, there was a shout, then another shout.[44]

Ritualistically, then, the unbounded, pointless *corrida* leads directly to the ceremonious order of the bull-fight. And it is precisely this formalizing discipline which symbolizes for Jake, as it apparently did for Hemingway, man's ability to control his manifold experience through art, in order to defeat ritualistically what is inevitable in reality—that is, to "defeat" chaos and death.[45]

The bull-ring itself is, in a way that has not been fully recognized, one of the most effective symbolic images in the book. Important as the arena of Romero's performance, it is perhaps even more important as the focus of Jake's concentrated and fully developed awareness. Although Hemingway does not use the generic term "Plaza del Sol" in referring to the bull-ring of Pamplona, the ring does, in its roundness and brilliant yellow color, effectively symbolize the sun, source of all light and life. And reinforcing the symbolic image patterns mentioned above, this circle of light exists amid blood, chaos, and death. The blood red *barrera,* at the boundary of which Vicente Girones is killed during the *corrida,*[46] serves as a reminder to Romero and Jake alike of what force is to be subdued in the center of the ring. And in the ring on the afternoon of the climactic bullfight, the moment of truth for Jake, as well as for Romero and Bocanegra, occurs with the image of that morning's chaotic fiesta mob still fresh. In the morning the intensity of the shouts in the ring indicated "how bad a thing it was that was happening"; in the afternoon Romero displays his mastery over the bull and the disorder of the fiesta:

> He killed not as he had been forced to by the last bull, but as he wanted to. He profiled directly in front of the bull, drew the sword out of the folds of the muleta and sighted along the blade. The bull watched him. Romero spoke to the bull and tapped one of his feet. The bull charged and Romero waited for the charge, the muleta held low, sighting along the blade, his feet firm. Then without taking a step forward, he became one with the bull, the sword was in high between the shoulders, the bull had followed the low-swung flannel, that disappeared as Romero lurched clear to the left, and it was over.[47]

It is here that Romero, whose name signifies both pilgrim and "pilot fish," demonstrates to Jake the "old thing"—the thing that belonged to all heroic men of all past ages—the "holding of his purity of line through the maximum of exposure."[48] And the magnitude of Romero's office is clear:

> The bull lay heavy and black on the sand, his tongue out. Boys were running toward him from all parts of the arena, making a little circle around him. They were starting to dance around the bull.[49]
>
> . . . .
> The crowd wanted him [Romero] . . . . They were lifting him and all running toward the gate. He had his hand on somebody's shoulder. He looked around at us apologetically. The crowd, running, went out the gate with him.[50]

This crowd, Hemingway tells us, is "the boys, the dancers, and the drunks"[50]; and thus, analogically, Romero is presented as having resolved all of Jake's confused responses—his nostalgic innocence, his nihilism, his escapism. The doubts of Paris, the dreams of Burguete, the frenzy of Pamplona—all come to rest in Jake's recognition of Romero's example. In his firmness and grace, in his most controlled and stylized killing of Bocanegra, Romero provides for Jake an ideal exemplum of man's capacity for creating meaning through art out of the very elements of radical disorder.[51]

But Romero can give to Jake *merely* an ideal exemplum of the heroic. His heroism *per se* cannot be translated directly into the modern world Jake occupies. Jake, as all of Hemingway's later versions of the "modern hero," cannot canonize his beliefs in ritual, dogma, or institution. His struggle for meaning is necessarily a continuous process, and his success depends upon his persistent inner control of will and consciousness. In this sense Jake's faith is more difficult to maintain than Romero's, and his heroism is achieved against proportionately greater odds.

The actual proving of Jake's acquired orientation is depicted in Book III of the novel. The world, as revealed in imagery again, is no more coherent than it ever was. Book III opens with an imaged conglomeration of disjunctive objects—"rocket-sticks," "white wicker chairs," "marble-topped tables," "white-paper," "pillars," "a blue apron," "a bucket of water," "a cloth," and "strips" of paper.[52] And San Sebastian is taken over by a group of bicycle racers who "had raced among themselves so often that it did not make much difference who won. Especially in a foreign country."[53] The description given of one of these racers again consists of a group of fragmented images—"boils," "the small of his back," his "neck," "blond hairs," "his nose," and "handle-bars."[54]

But Jake amid this world has demonstrably changed; he basks in the truth of Romero's example in the bull-ring. Jake finds his arena on the beach of San Sebastian—which "was smooth and firm, and the sand yellow."[55] At San Sebastian, which holds the bitterest memories of his past defeats and impotence, where Brett has sojourned both with Cohn and with Mike, Jake tests in the surf his new found art of living. The rollers force him to "dive sometimes," and he finds it difficult "trying to keep in the trough and not have a wave break" over him.[56] But he takes pleasure in the "buoyant and cold" water, where "it felt as though you could never sink."[56] Eminently aware of his limitations in facing the world, Jake at San Sebastian lives with

284

his disabilities and exercises his capacity for what is possible. Jake's action on the beach, in a simple but poignant way, typifies his positive response to inevitable limitation:

> I thought I would like to swim across the bay but I was afraid of cramp.
>
> I sat in the sun and watched the bathers on the beach. They looked very small. After a while I stood up, gripped with my toes on the edge of the raft as it tipped with my weight, and dove cleanly and deeply, to come up through the lightening water, blew the salt water out of my head, and swam slowly and steadily in to shore.[57]

The most crucial event in Book III, however, is Jake's meeting with Brett in Madrid, for this meeting suggests Jake's controlled ability to get along in the world Brett consistently represents. The measured pleasure of the meal in Botin's contrasts sharply with the unordered eating and drinking of the fiesta; the taxi ride which ends the book forms a compelling contrast with the taxi ride of Book I, our first view of Jake and Brett alone. As Bickford Sylvester has observed, Jake's hearty meal at Botin's shows "that he can enjoy the good things of life even while faced with a reminder of all that he cannot have," and "here, as in his final remark when Brett is pressed against him in the taxi . . . Jake demonstrates precisely the ideal gift he has earlier observed in Romero. He, too, has acquired 'the old thing, the holding of his purity of line through the maximum of exposure.' "[58]

Jake has created his own "clean, well-lighted place" in the midst of "nothing, full of nothing." The fragmented world of darkness and disorder has yielded, at least in part, to Jake's self-assertion; "light was all it needed and a certain cleanness and order."[59] As Jake observes at the end of Book II, on the morning following the climactic bull-fight: "The world was not wheeling any more. It was just very clear and bright, and inclined to blur at the edges."[60] And though these blurred edges of vision remain a constant reminder to Jake of his merely partial victory over death and disorder, the clear brightness at the center of his world testifies to the absolute value of that partial victory.

University of British Columbia

¹ For a sampling of critics who view Jake as a passive figure see: James T. Farrell, "The Sun Also Rises," *The League of Frightened Philistines* (New York: Vanguard Press, 1945), reprinted in *Ernest Hemingway: The Man and His Work,* ed. John K. McCaffery (Cleveland: World, 1950), p. 224; Earl Rovit, *Ernest Hemingway* (New York: Twayne, 1963), p. 148; John S. Rouch, "Jake Barnes as Narrator," *Modern Fiction Studies* XI (1965-66), 364-65; Harold Kaplan, *The Passive Voice: An Approach to Modern Fiction* (Athens: Ohio University Press, 1966), p. 107. Critics like Kaplan (p. 110), Rovit (p. 148), and W. M. Frohock ("Ernest Hemingway: Violence and Discipline," *Southwest Review*, XXXII [1947], 92-3) seem to assume that stoicism is a necessary consequence of passivity. Mark Spilka, "The Death of Love in *The Sun Also Rises*," *Twelve Original Essays on Great American Novels*, ed. Charles Shapiro (Detroit: Wayne State University Press, 1958), reprinted in *Hemingway and His Critics*, ed. Carlos Baker (New York: Hill and Wang, 1961), pp. 89-92, goes so far as to discount Jake as the hero of the novel, seeing him as lacking in integrity and moral force.

² "Ernest Hemingway and the Psychology of the Lost Generation," *The Novel and the World's Dilemma* (New York: Oxford University Press, 1947), reprinted in McCaffery, p. 315.

³ Kaplan, p. 95, sees the characters of "the early scene" in Paris as "images of defacement" which do not project clearly because of self-contradiction.

⁴ Ernest Hemingway, *The Sun Also Rises* (New York: Scribners, 1926), p. 31.

⁵ Ibid., pp. 139-141.

⁶ Ibid., p. 163.

⁷ Ibid., p. 160.

⁸ Hemingway's description of the American pilgrims visiting the outworn shrines of Europe—Rome, Biarritz, and Lourdes (pp. 87-88)—demonstrates dramatically the deadness of the Church. The new, grotesque "shrines" of postwar Europe for Hemingway are Verdun, the Somme, Caporetto.

⁹ Hemingway, *The Sun*, pp. 16-17.

¹⁰ Ibid., p. 152.

¹¹ Ibid., p. 153.

¹² James B. Colvert, "Ernest Hemingway's Morality in Action," *American Literature*, XXVII (1955-56), 376, suggests that the pursuit of new values is the primary activity of all Hemingway's heroes: "Cut adrift from his moral moorings, the Hemingway hero appears in desperate struggle with the awful problem of finding a new value orientation, and . . . he attacks the problem with all the resources of his assertive individualism . . . . In completely isolating himself from a tradition in which he cannot believe, in rejecting altogether the value assumptions deriving from intellectual abstractions, he wipes clean in his profound skepticism the slate of his moral consciousness in order to record only those values which he discovers through personal experience."

¹³ Although critics of the novel have analyzed many of its images separately, I contend that there are discernible patterns of imagery which are central, not peripheral, to the book's statement and must be examined in a thorough manner. E. M. Halliday, "Hemingway's Narrative Perspective," *Sewanee Review*, IX (1952), 205, comes closest to seeing the rationale which underlies the function of these patterns: "Selecting his objective facts carefully, Hemingway manages to

convey accurately his hero's subjective states by implication: not only through what Jake does under given circumstances, but also through what, as narrator, Jake chooses to report from his perception of outward reality."

[14] One is compelled to think that Hemingway is projecting in Jake his own difficulties, aspirations, and accomplishments as an artist.

[15] Hemingway, *The Sun*, p. 28.

[16] Ibid., p. 36.

[17] Ibid., pp. 74-76.

[18] Ibid., pp. 29-30.

[19] Ibid., p. 90.

[20] Ibid., p. 93.

[21] Ibid., p. 25.

[22] See W. M. Frohock, p. 93, for a somewhat similar view of this crucial scene: "Substitute . . . the idea of emotion for light and you have Hemingway's guiding motive throughout the first part: he sees and says only what the abomination-of-desolation mood permits."

[23] Hemingway, *The Sun*, p. 78.

[24] Ibid., pp. 79-80.

[25] See Harry Levin, "Observations on the Style of Ernest Hemingway," *Kenyon Review*, XIII (Autumn 1951), reprinted in *Hemingway and His Critics*, ed. Baker, p. 109. Professor Levin sees as characteristic of Hemingway's style the presenting of "a succession of images, each of which has its brief moment when it commands the reader's individual attention"; I, of course, am suggesting that this stylistic quality has a basis in Hemingway's conception of man's fundamental perception of the world.

[26] Hemingway, *The Sun*, p. 89.

[27] Ibid., p. 93.

[28] Ibid., pp. 95-96.

[29] Ibid., pp. 108, 111-112.

[30] Ibid., p. 111.

[31] Ibid., e.g. pp. 125-127.

[32] Ibid., p. 129.

[33] Ibid., p. 131.

[34] Ibid., p. 159.

[35] Ibid., p. 158.

[36] Ibid., p. 171.

[37] Ibid., pp. 160ff.

[38] Ibid., p. 164.

[39] Ibid., p. 165.

[40] See Kaplan, p. 105: "The fight comes at the climax of the fiesta which is a riot of living with destructive forces set free. . . . But above it all stands the bullfighter, risking and taming chaos. In that formal beauty and ritual order, sport has become a religious service; it has given resolution to conflict." I agree essentially with Kaplan's explication of the fiesta and the bullfight, but I think it is critical to note in detail the narrative and symbolic process whereby fiesta *becomes* bullfight, disorder generates order. Since Kaplan, as suggested earlier, sees Jake as incapable of participating in Romero's heroism, his view of the ultimate value of the fiesta and bullfight is considerably different than mine.

[41] Hemingway, *The Sun*, p. 168.

[42] Hemingway's naming of the bull is most appropriate when one considers it as the embodiment of nihilistic force which opens the black mouth of the void to man's perception.

[43] Hemingway, *The Sun*, p. 206.

[44] Ibid., p. 204.

[45] See Nancy Hale, "Hemingway and the Courage to Be," *Virginia Quarterly Review*, XXXVIII (1962), 638: "Hemingway's preoccupation with the many arts of sport and killing . . . seems to me to suggest the preoccupation with art itself, of whatever kind. Art is what courage needs and summons, as a technique for meeting and defeating (or being defeated by) the bulls, the lions, the buffalo, the sea, whose meaning we know. In the world of art, it is possible for the flow of the river of life, that is to say of growth, to go on for a long time after it has been blocked in actual life." Kaplan, p. 106, and Kenneth Kinnamon, "Hemingway, *The Corrida*, and Spain," *Texas Studies in Literature and Language*, I (1959), 48, also see Romero's mastery in the ring as an expression of controlling art.

[46] Hemingway, *The Sun*, p. 204.

[47] Ibid., p. 229.

[48] Ibid., p. 174.

[49] Ibid., pp. 229-230.

[50] Ibid., p. 230.

[51] It is difficult to say whether Hemingway's conception of the nature and function of art was arrived at independently, for Paris in the 1920's was a breeding ground for countless artistic and philosophical theories. But in Dadaism, which Malcolm Cowley refers to in *Exile's Return* as "the very essence of Paris" in the 1920's, one finds analogous theories and practices which shed helpful light on the art of *The Sun Also Rises*.

Hemingway, of course, refers to Tzara in "The Snows of Kilimanjaro," and both writers published pieces in the April, 1924 issue of the *transatlantic* (Carlos Baker, *Hemingway: The Writer as Artist* [Princeton: Princeton Univ. Press, 1952], p. 23). Indeed, Hemingway's close association with Gertrude Stein between 1921 and 1926 would have made it almost impossible for him not to have encountered the ideas of Dada, for among Gertrude Stein's friends were Picabia, Duchamp, Mina Loy, Man Ray, and Tristan Tzara.

The Dada Movement was frequently considered to be a grand hoax and a sham—anti-aesthetic in its art, anti-intellectual in its thought. And certainly the Dadaists did little to alleviate this impression. However, their radical alienation from the "civilized" world and its conventions, their strident iconoclasm, and their frequently petulant and bizarre manifestations of rebellion did not eliminate their creations. And in their collages, photo-montages, and constructions may be discerned a certain desperate attempt to create order and meaning. Kurt Schwitters' definition of his "Merz" pictures (collages) suggests the nature of Dadaistic art and principle: "A picture consisting of *mutually incompatible parts united into a work of art* with the aid of paste, nails, hammer, paper, rags, machine-parts, oil-paint, lace, etc." (quoted in *Dada: Monograph of a Movement*, ed. Willy Verkauf [New York: Hastings-House, Publishers, 1961], p. 148; emphasis mine). Even more articulate of the aesthetic informing Dadaism is Georges Hugnet's comment on two leading artists of the movement: "Arp and . . . Max Ernst used pieces of newspaper, wallpaper, photographs, and vignettes at random and insisted on their *ready-made* qualities, *which they distorted, transposed and displaced, and by their facile treatment of the imponderable, they integrated these borrowed elements into a recreation of the object . . ."* ("The Dada Spirit in Painting," *The Dada Painters and Poets: An Anthology,* ed. Robert Motherwell [New York: Wittenborn, Schultz, 1951], p. 132; emphasis mine, except for "ready-made").

To put things most succinctly, the Dadaist in his most characteristic art form, the collage, attempted to effect unity and meaning through the artful ordering of mutually incompatible elements. And this ambivalent aesthetic seems based on his desire to demonstrate simultaneously his despair and his hope—to materialize his conviction that the world is essentially chaotic, his faith that man can impart order to this chaos.

The similarity between the basic aesthetic of Dadaism and the meaning and art of *The Sun Also Rises* is striking; neither the Dadaist in his art nor Hemingway in his novel conceived of art as providing an absolute solution to man's anguished existence. For both, art is merely a limiting, controlling force, which can subordinate chaotic elements within a consciously defined compass.

[52] Hemingway, *The Sun*, p. 237.

[53] Ibid., p. 246.

[54] Ibid., pp. 246-47.

[55] Ibid., p. 245.

[56] Ibid., p. 248.

[57] Ibid., p. 249.

[58] "Hemingway's Extended Vision: *The Old Man and The Sea*," unpubl. diss. (Washington, 1966), pp. 92-3. I am indebted to Mr. Sylvester for first convincing me of the importance of Book III in completing the picture of Jake's progress.

[59] "A Clean Well-Lighted Place," *The Short Stories of Ernest Hemingway* (New York: Scribners, 1938), p. 383. I suppose it is self-evident that I consider *The Sun Also Rises* a meaningful commentary on this later short story. If I am correct about Jake's activity of mind and will in forging a world for himself, it seems to me that the old waiter of the story should be appreciated more for his positive virtue of maintaining light and order than for the negative virtue of his mere "staying power."

[60] Hemingway, *The Sun*, p. 234.

FABER and GWYER Ltd.

PUBLISHERS

TELEPHONE: MUSEUM 9543.

24, Russell Square,
London, W.C.1.

31st December, 1925.

F. Scott Fitzgerald, Esqre.,
C/o Charles Scribners & Sons,
New York City.

Dear Mr Scott Fitzgerald,

"The Great Gatsby" with your charming and overpowering
inscription arrived the very morning that I was leaving in
some haste for a sea voyage advised by my doctor. I therefore
left it behind and only read it on my return a few days ago.
I have, however, now read it three times. I am not in the
least influenced by your remark about myself when I say that it
has interested and excited me more than any new novel I have
seen, either English or American, for a number of years.

When I have time I should like to write to you more fully
and tell you exactly why it seems to me such a remarkable book.
In fact it seems to me to be the first step that American
fiction has taken since Henry James.

I have recently become associated in the capacity of a
director with the publishing firm whose name you see above.
May I ask you, if you have not already committed yourself to
publish "The Great Gatsby" with some other publishing house in
London, to let us take the matter up with you? I think that
if we published the book we could do as well by you as anyone.

By the way, if you ever have any short stories which you
think would be suitable for the CRITERION I wish you would let
me see them.

With many thanks,

I am,

Yours very truly, *T. S. Eliot*

P.S. By a coincidence,
Gilbert Seldes in his New York
Chronicle in the CRITERION for January 14th has chosen
your book for particular mention.

Letter from T. S. Eliot to Fitzgerald praising *The Great Gatsby*. (With the
permission of Mrs. Eliot)

T. S. Eliot's Copy of *Gatsby*

Daniel G. Siegel

The day *The Great Gatsby* was published, on 10 April, 1925, F. Scott Fitzgerald was driving with Zelda in the south of France, traveling toward Paris. Arriving in Paris early in May, the Fitzgeralds rented an apartment, but continued touring throughout the summer, only returning to Paris in September. From Paris, sometime in October, Fitzgerald took courage and sent a copy of *The Great Gatsby* to T. S. Eliot in London.

Although sales of the book were decidedly modest, *The Great Gatsby* received a number of very good reviews, especially from Laurence Stallings and Gilbert Seldes. Also, Fitzgerald received complimentary personal letters from important literary figures, including Nathan, Cabell, Deems Taylor, Van Wyck Brooks, Willa Cather, and Edith Wharton.

Fitzgerald regarded T. S. Eliot as the greatest living poet, and the copy of *The Great Gatsby* he sent to Eliot—evidently after some months of hesitation—contained an appropriate inscription. It is reproduced here. Eliot's own response was impressive, surely more laudatory than Fitzgerald dared to hope. Eliot's letter to Fitzgerald, written on the last day of 1925, has been printed by Edmund Wilson in *The Crack-up* (1945). In part Eliot said:

> *The Great Gatsby* with your charming and overpowering inscription arrived the very morning that I was leaving in some haste for a sea voyage advised by my doctor. I therefore left it behind and only read it on my return a few days ago. I have, however, now read it three times. I am not in the least influenced by your remark about myself when I say that it has interested and excited me more than any new novel I have seen, either English or American, for a number of years. . . .
>
> . . . In fact it seems to me to be the first step that American fiction has taken since Henry James. . . .

The inscription which brought a self-consciousness to Eliot's response was penned boldly by Fitzgerald in dark ink on the free front endpaper of a copy of the first state. The inscription is a wonderful illustration of F. Scott Fitzgerald's most personable and winning traits: it is bold and exuberant, entirely unfeigning; and it is badly misspelled. Fitzgerald was a notorious bad speller; even here in what obviously is a most important inscription Fitzgerald does not break form. He misspells "Eliot" as he always does, and he misspells "enthusiastic."

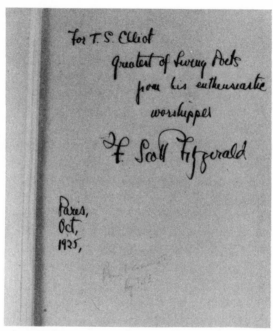

Inscription in the copy of *The Great Gatsby* Fitzgerald sent to T. S. Eliot. Collection of Daniel G. Siegel. (With the permission of Mrs. Eliot)

T. S. Eliot, fussy about detail, meticulous and circumspect in personal matters, evidently was not bothered by the misspelling of his own name by the young "worshipper." Eliot was not the sort of person who would want anyone to question the motivation of his responses, and he goes to some pains to assure Fitzgerald that the "charming and overpowering inscription" did not influence his critical estimation of *The Great Gatsby*.

Eliot's reply of course made Fitzgerald ecstatic. In Andrew Turnbull's edition of the Letters, there are printed two letters revealing Fitzgerald's extreme pleasure with Eliot's response. These letters, both written to Maxwell Perkins, one written in February 1926, the other in 1933, closely paraphrase Eliot's encomium, and Fitzgerald again refers to his evaluation of T. S. Eliot as the greatest of all living poets.

The copy of *The Great Gatsby* which Fitzgerald inscribed so winningly for T. S. Eliot shows some physical evidence of critical evaluation—criticism of a sort we can well imagine Eliot making.

In his famous letter of 31 December, 1925, Eliot declares he has read *The Great Gatsby* three times. Altogether there are penciled comments on fifteen pages, all of them brief and of a minor nature, written in black or blue pencil. I believe it is literally impossible to say for certain that T. S. Eliot wrote these comments. Simply, they are too brief. But they are typical of what one could expect from Eliot as critic-editor. (He was then an editor for Faber & Gwyer Ltd., reorganized in 1929 as Faber & Faber.) The pencilings deal with grammatical uses, choice of vocabulary, and observations of local or national characteristics. Interestingly enough, the two readings which most vexed Fitzgerald—"orgastic future" on the last page, and "eternal" for "external" on page 58—were not corrected by Eliot. Of a total of sixteen notes, eight consist simply of the insertion of a caret into the text, with an exclamative or the word "of" or "out" or "from" penciled in the margin (45:14, 70:12 & 19, 101:27, 110:7, 125:20, 140:25, 209:19). Commentary at 137:17 and at 142:7 consist only of alterations of spelling ("pyjama" and "moulding" in place of "pajama" and "molding"). For a meticulous editor these may be mere reflexive habits of work.

At 47:13 the use of "bug" is questioned, and in the margin is written, "i.e. insect." On page 195, line 11, the word "holocaust" is underlined, and in the margin appears "oh oh."

On pages 50, 107, and 212-13, vertical straight lines are penciled in the margins next to passages which consist of perhaps dubious characterizations: 50:19-25, the Englishmen dotted about; 107:9-11, the Americans eager to be serfs; 212-13:22-5, a night scene by El Greco.

The most extensive comment appears in the margin of page 27, and is the first to appear in the book. Unfortunately, I doubt anyone can decipher it; it contains seven or eight words and refers to the most famous Dr. T. J. Eckleburg, perhaps reading: "Some local ?(allusion not intelligible to me)."

It is a rare pleasure to be able to report upon the existence of this superb book, surely one of the most important association copies in the Fitzgerald realm.

Recollections of a Hemingway Collector

Fraser Drew

It was really Ernest Hemingway who turned me into a serious Hemingway collector. I had collected John Masefield while working on a Masefield doctoral dissertation and had a scattering of first editions by other modern writers, including several Hemingways. Then one spring a student in my modern literature class, a real Hemingway aficionado, pushed my interest in his hero to the point where I wrote to Hemingway and asked permission to send a couple of books for inscribing for the student and myself.

Hemingway's reply was so unexpectedly prompt, lengthy and cordial that I lost no time in sending him a package of all the first editions I had—the Boni and Liveright *In Our Time*, *The Torrents of Spring*, *The Sun Also Rises*, *A Farewell to Arms*, and a second copy of *Farewell* for my student. The package went out one June and returned the following May, with an intervening telegram from Havana of New Year's greetings and assurances that the books were safe. With my own five books in May came five others, sent by their author as "an act of contrition" for his long delay, and on the same day a delightful two-page, single-space, typed letter praising my patience and relating the various complications and misadventures that had delayed my books.

This unexpected gift, which I described in less detail several years ago in a letter to the *American Book Collector*,[1] included a 1931 Scribners *In Our Time*, German first editions of *The Sun Also Rises* and *For Whom the Bell Tolls*, the first Latvian edition of *A Farewell to Arms*, and an advance copy of Lee Samuels' *A Hemingway Check List*.

My own books were inscribed conventionally—"Best luck always" and "Sincere good wishes"—except for *The Torrents of Spring*, in which he wrote "For Fraser Drew, a man of great patience. May he never get boils as his illustrious predecessor did. Best always. Ernest Hemingway." In some of the books from his own shelves he wrote more. *Wem Die Stunde Schlägt*, the German *For Whom the Bell Tolls*, has the usual inscription plus "(Note how the Germans omitted the John Donne!) EH," as the writer points out the absence of the quotation from Donne's seventeenth meditation in the 1624 *Devotions Upon Emergent Occasions* which is found in American and English editions. A damp-spotted copy of *Fiesta*, the German *The Sun Also Rises*, has an inscription followed by "It's hard to keep books in mint condition in a country where they have hurricanes. These books are all survivors."

The Scribners *In Our Time*, which is a 1931 reprint, has only a brief note, but in the Latvian *A Farewell to Arms* which, he wrote, was in "one strange language you'll have to figure out for yourself (It looks like Icelandic to me)," he added "(Read this for home-work) EH."

The copy of *A Hemingway Check List* is a fine one. The letter of 22 May 1951, written the day he sent the books to me, calls it "a new check list book on what I have written (as yet unpublished but will be shortly by Scribners)." The book was published two months later in July. I have never collated the gift copy with one of the July printing of 750, but I did observe that the book from Hemingway does not contain the erratum slip tipped into the later copies after page 50. Hemingway inscribed it simply "For Fraser Bragg Drew from the subject Ernest Hemingway."

With such a windfall I could hardly have avoided becoming a serious Hemingway collector. Fortunately, competition was not lively at the Earle Bernheimer auction later in 1950, and mail bids brought me nine items in their beautiful Bernheimer green-labeled pigskin cases. One was No. 197 of the 300 numbered copies of *Today Is Friday* with its drawing by Jean Cocteau on the front cover. Cocteau later sent me from St. Jean Cap Ferrat an inscribed ink drawing for insertion in the envelope of the pamphlet.

Captain Louis Henry Cohn of The House of Books Limited, and his wife Marguerite, friends and collectors of Hemingway, gave me useful advice and found many Hemingways for me. From them I secured runs of *The Little Review, Der Querschnitt* and *The Transatlantic Review* and my excellent copies of *Three Stories and Ten Poems* and *In Our Time*, Hemingway's first two books. When I shuddered at the prices of these two scarce books, Captain Cohn was sympathetic to this young collector, then a low-salaried assistant professor. "If you really want to collect Hemingway, you must have these books above all others," he said as we three were eating sandwiches in the back room of the old House of Books on West 56th Street, and then he lowered the prices of the books which he had just acquired and which he could have sold promptly at the prices he had just marked in them.

Other acquisitions from the Cohns included No. 33 of the 300 copies of *God Rest You Merry Gentlemen* from the House of Books Crown Octavos series; No. 256 of the 525 Faulkner-Hemingway *Salmagundi*, and No. 2 of the 510 vellum-backed copies of the limited *A Farewell to Arms.* For several of these, Hemingway sent slips of paper with inscriptions for tipping into the books. I also have inscribed copies of Louis Cohn's pace-setting Hemingway bibliography, his note in the Summer 1935 *Colophon*, and No. 92 of his 93 "Bastard Notes."

When I visited Ernest and Mary Hemingway in 1955, I had with me no books from my collection in Buffalo. I had gone to Texas to give a series of lectures at Baylor University and had written Mrs. Hemingway for permission to telephone from New Orleans on my way home from Waco. A letter from her, awaiting my arrival at the Monteleone in New Orleans, gave the Havana telephone number which I called at once; an invitation to Finca Vigia followed.[2]

The next morning I could find nothing better than a second printing of *A Farewell to Arms* and some reading copies in New Orleans, but I took these along in the hope that Hemingway would inscribe them for my father, a faculty colleague, and three students. He did so most pleasantly at the end of our long talk.

Learning that my collection lacked a first issue of *The Spanish Earth*, he searched out and gave me his own copy, inscribing it "Author's copy. For Fraser Drew from his friend Ernest Hemingway. La Vigia 1955." This is perhaps the sentimental favorite of my collection. Then, taking several foreign editions from a shelf, he inscribed a French *L'Adieu aux Armes* "For Fraser Drew, hoping he has a good trip home," an illustrated Italian *Il Vecchio E Il Mare* " 'Il Novo Capolavoro' with pictures of no great value," and a two-volume paperback *Per Chi Suona La Campana* with lurid color illustrations on the covers; in Volume I he wrote "This corny edition" and in the other "Volumne (*sic*) two of For Whom the Bell Tolls with horrible cover. Best luck," signing my name and his, of course, in them all.

My only regrets were not having *Three Stories and Ten Poems* and *In Our Time* with me and not remembering to ask Hemingway to inscribe a little magazine I had picked up the day before in a pile of journals in a New Orleans bookshop. This was the May 1922 *Double Dealer* with the fable, "A Divine Gesture." I showed it to Hemingway and he read it quickly and smiled. "I haven't seen that in years," he said. I am very glad that I saw it in that pile of old magazines and took it along to Havana with me. It's in very good condition, too. But why could I not have had the wit to offer it for inscribing with the books?

State University College,
Buffalo

---

[1] Drew, "A Footnote to William White's 'On Collecting Ernest Hemingway,' " VII, (Dec. 1956), p. 2.

[2] "April 8, 1955 with Ernest Hemingway: Unedited Notes on a Visit to Finca Vigia," *Fitzgerald/Hemingway Annual*, 1970, pp. 108-116.

Collecting Hemingway

Archibald S. Alexander

The editor flattered me greatly when he asked me to write a piece about my Hemingway collection. I thought I had a good idea. I would write about the possible but imaginary sequel to an intriguing item in the collection, that is the copy of the "Address Delivered by Calvin Coolidge" on 4 July 1916, when he was Lt. Governor of Massachusetts. It was inscribed "To Ernest Hemingway, with regards, Calvin Coolidge." Hemingway was then not quite seventeen years old.[1]

However, after the flattery had worn thin, and with firmness somewhat disguised with tact, the editor made clear to me what I should write about. Naturally, I must bow to his judgment. I hope he feels that I have done so in what follows.

Two things came together to induce me to collect Hemingway. The first was that from a fairly early age I had become the recipient, at birthdays and Christmases, of presents of good books from my family. These were always accompanied by some conventional wisdom about the enduring quality of such presents, unlike candy, toys, etc. After some initial skepticism, as a child of my generation I went along with the conventional wisdom, and in due course was able to exert some influence on the kind of book given to me. Meanwhile, I followed the advice of one of the kindest men I have ever known, who happened also to be a bookseller and a person of excellent judgment in literature (the late Edgar H. Wells). He told me to buy whatever I wanted to read soon enough after its publication to obtain the first edition, at the original price. Then I lent it sparingly and used it lovingly. And so it was that by the time I went to college, I had a few good books, some of which possessed some pecuniary value and all of which I loved.

The second influence was reading, as my first exposure to Hemingway, *The Sun Also Rises*. That book needs no praise here. But its impact on me as a sophomore was very great. The results were twofold: I resolved to read whatever Hemingway published, of course in a first edition if obtainable; and such writing style as I then had, in prose fiction at any rate, underwent a metamorphosis which, as I read it now, gives evidence of some imitation of the Hemingway style, probably both conscious and unconscious.

I suppose this could end this particular piece of nonfiction. However, from the point of view of admirers of Hemingway and collectors of his works, there is more to be said.

Following the habit described above, I bought each successive Hemingway as it came out in the first edition, and hoarded it. I made a sustained effort to buy magazine articles by Hemingway or about him, and to keep book reviews and other items appearing in print. When I reached the point of becoming a partner in a New York city law firm, I bought some of the earlier items which I lacked. Because of friendship with members of the family which owned Charles Scribner's Sons, then and now Hemingway's publishers, I often had good luck.

But the bulk of the more unusual items in my collection I acquired in one supreme stroke of luck. David A. Randall, then the head of the Rare Books Department in Scribner's Book Store, led me into temptation by offering me a substantial collection of Hemingway items, including manuscripts, letters and presentation copies. The collection was probably the most complete then available. Of course I succumbed.

Among the things which makes collecting deeply interesting is the kind of by-product which comes from putting together something which you have acquired with something that is already in the public domain. I should like to cite an example, based on some of the items Dave Randall sold me.

It is reasonably well known to students of either Hemingway or F. Scott Fitzgerald that they knew each other and had the kind of relationship which one would perhaps expect when two such highly gifted temperaments suffered juxtaposition. In *A Moveable Feast*, published in 1964, there are over forty-five pages devoted to Fitzgerald. The total length of the book is 211 pages.

One may say that the picture of Fitzgerald which emerges from Hemingway's pages is not a product of hero worship. At times there is scorn, at other times pity and at other times clear admiration, perhaps more for what Fitzgerald could have written than for what he did write.

The prefatory note by Hemingway's widow, printed between Hemingway's preface dated 1960 and the beginning of *A Moveable Feast* itself, stated that the book "concerns the years 1921 to 1926 in Paris".

I have an apparently unpublished longhand letter from Fitzgerald to Boni and Liveright, signed "F. Scott Fitzg–". The letter was written from "14 Rue de Tilsitt Paris", and it is undated. At that time Boni and Liveright were Hemingway's publishers. The letter must have been written in December 1925, because I have Hemingway's letter from Paris to Mr. Liveright, dated December 7, 1925, on the same subject matter and saying "Scott Fitzgerald has read the manuscript and was very excited about it and said he was going to write you about it. I don't know whether he did or not." The manuscript was *The Torrents of Spring*. Hemingway explained to Mr. Liveright that this was not the long novel (*The Sun Also Rises*). Just in case the publisher didn't know it, Hemingway made clear that *The Torrents of Spring* is satirical.

My Fitzgerald longhand letter is evidently the one which he had told Hemingway he would write. The letter, written after "Ernest Hemminway showed me his new book", has high and unequivocal praise for *The Torrents of Spring*. In one sentence Fitzgerald writes, "I don't know how much value, if any, you attach to my opinion but it might interest you to know that to one rather snooty reader, at least, it seems about the best comic book ever written by an American."

Whatever Fitzgerald's other inadequacies, in his relations with Hemingway, this was a clear-cut act of perception and of generosity.

I also have a carbon copy of Mr. Liveright's answer, dated December 30, 1925. The Western Union cablegram of that day, addressed to Hemingway in the Vorarlberg, stated the matter more succinctly: "REJECTING TORRENTS OF SPRING PATIENTLY AWAITING MANUSCRIPT THE SUN ALSO RISES WRITING FULLY". Mr. Liveright's letter itself tells Hemingway that *The Torrents of Spring* was rejected, not because to publish it would be "horribly cruel" to Sherwood Anderson (whose publishers Boni and Liveright were), but "because we disagree with you and Scott Fitzgerald and Louis Bromfield and Dos Passos that it is a fine and humorous American satire." The balance of the Liveright letter makes it clear that the relations between author and publishers were such that it seems very natural that Hemingway ended up having Scribner's publish *The Torrents of Spring* and almost everything else subsequent thereto.

Of course after that you want to reread "The Torrents of Spring." Only then can you decide with whom to agree.

*   *   *

Looking back on it, it all seems very easy. I could not have planned it, because one cannot *plan* on good luck.

And now my problem is, how many years must I survive, in a state of solvency, until the last Hemingway manuscript is published?

---

[1] The William Faulkner Collection presented to The University of Virginia by Linton Reynolds Massey includes a copy of *Have Faith in Massachusetts* (1919) inscribed: "To William Faulkner, With Regards, Calvin Coolidge."

Fitzgerald Recommends Nathanael West For a Guggenheim

Jay Martin

For the April, 1934 issue of *The New Republic* Malcom Cowley surveyed contemporary writers for names of books which had been undeservedly neglected by the general public. Fitzgerald replied by naming Nathanael West's *Miss Lonelyhearts*. Planning his application for a Guggenheim Fellowship, West wrote to Fitzgerald on September 11, 1934:

> Ottsville,
> Bucks County
> Pennsylvania
> September 11th, '34

My dear Mr. Fitzgerald,

You have been kind enough to say that you liked my novel, Miss Lonelyhearts.

I am applying for a Guggenheim Fellowship and I need references for it. I wonder if you would be willing to let me use your name as a reference? It would be enormously valuable to me. I am writing to you, a stranger, because I know very few people, almost none whose names would mean anything to the committee, and apparently the references are the most important part of the application.

As you know, the committee will probably submit my plan for future work to you if you give me permission to use your name as reference. This will be a nuisance, of course, but the plan is a very brief one and you are only obliged to say whether you think it is good or not.

If you can see your way to do this, it will make me very happy.

Sincerely,

Nathanael West

Fitzgerald's letter of recommendation follows:

TO THE TRUSTEES OF THE GUGGENHEIM FELLOWSHIP.

Dear Sirs:

Today Nathanael West asked me for a letter of reference on behalf of his application for a Guggenheim fellowship.

—and, in the same post, came a consignment of a reprint by the Modern Library of a novel of mine, THE GREAT GATSBY, which had a new preface that included the statement that I thought young writers in America were being harmed now for the lack of a public, and I had mentioned specifically Nathanael West.

I don't know on what basis the Guggenheim fellowships are given but I know some of the people who have profited by them, and, while many of the men have been chosen worthily and well, such as Thomas Wolfe and Allen Tate, there have been others who have been sent to Europe who have not been worth their salt, and who—in the eventuality—have proved nothing.

I have sometimes felt that you have put especial emphasis on poetry while I think that the most living literary form in America at the moment is prose fiction. In my opinion Nathanael West is a potential leader in the field of prose fiction. He seems to me entirely equipped to go over on the fellowship.

With best wishes to the custodians of the great idea.

Sincerely yours,

F. Scott Fitzgerald

1307 Park Avenue
Baltimore, Maryland
September 25, 1934

To support his application for a grant to write "A novel about the moral ideas of the generation which graduated from college in 1924," West also solicited supporting letters from Malcolm Cowley, Edmund Wilson and George S. Kaufmann. Cowley declared that "West writes brilliantly," Wilson, that he was "a very finished writer," and Kaufmann, that he was "a writer of great promise."

Unfortunately, however, West's application proved unsuccessful.

Later, in Hollywood, after he and Fitzgerald had become close friends, in sending proof sheets of *The Day of the Locust* to Fitzgerald, West remarked: "I never thanked you for your kindness to me in the preface to the Modern Library edition of 'The Great Gatsby.' When I read it, I got a great lift just at a time when I needed one badly, if I was to go on writing" (April 5, 1939).

University of California, Irvine

Dialogue in Hemingway's "A Clean, Well-Lighted Place"

Nathaniel M. Ewell, III

There has been much discussion over the fractured dialogue in Ernest Hemingway's "A Clean, Well-Lighted Place."[1] The passage in question is the point in the story where the two waiters are discussing the matter of the old man's attempted suicide and the fact that his niece takes care of him since his wife is dead. The problem occurs at lines 4 and 5 of their dialogue where the waiters switch roles, and the reader is unsure which waiter has knowledge of the suicide attempt of the old man.

1. "He had a wife once too." (old waiter)
2. "A wife would be no good to him now." (young waiter)
3. "You can't tell. He might be better with a wife." (o.w.)
4. "His niece looks after him." (y.w.)
5. "I know. You said she cut him down." (o.w.)
6. "I wouldn't want to be that old. An old man is a nasty thing."[2] (y.w.)

Warren Bennett in his "Character, Irony, and Resolution in 'A Clean, Well-Lighted Place'" feels that he has solved the problem through his correspondence with L. H. Brague, Jr., of Charles Scribner's Sons and Professor Philip Young.[3] His explanation is acceptable but for the fact that he does not carry it far enough.

His conclusion is that a slug of type was "misplaced" in the first printing of the story in *Scribner's Magazine* in 1933 and that the error was perpetuated through *Winner Take Nothing* and *The Fifth Column and The First Forty-Nine Stories* until 1965 when an "editorial" correction was made by Charles Scribner's Sons. All of this is true. However, two slugs of type must have been misplaced—not just one. Obviously, the first omission occurs after line 3, "You can't tell. He might be better with a wife," and the second omission occurs after line 5, "I know. You said she cut him down." This solves the problem of which waiter has the information of the suicide attempt of the old man. It is the old waiter.

The June 1965 printing of *The Short Stories of Ernest Hemingway* alters the dialogue, presumably without any authorial sanction:

"He had a wife once too." (old waiter)
"A wife would be no good to him now." (young waiter)
"You can't tell. He might be better with a wife." (o.w.)
"His niece looks after him. You said she cut him down." (y.w.)
"I know."[4] (o.w.)

The only scholarly way to supply these lines would be from Hemingway's manuscript; but if a correction is made, it ought to be made by the addition of the two missing lines of dialogue, not by rearranging it, thus:

"He had a wife once too." (old waiter)
"A wife would be no good to him now." (young waiter)
"You can't tell. He might be better with a wife." (o.w.)
OMITTED LINE (young waiter)
"His niece looks after him." (o.w.)
"I know. You said she cut him down." (y.w.)
OMITTED LINE (old waiter)
"I wouldn't want to be that old. An old man is a nasty thing." (y.w.)

University of South Carolina

---

[1] See Robert Penn Warren, Introduction, *A Farewell To Arms* (New York: Scribners, 1949), pp. xv-xvi; Mark Schorer, ed., *The Story: A Critical Anthology* (New York: Prentice-Hall, 1950), p. 427; Carlos Baker, *Hemingway: The Writer as Artist* (Princeton: Princeton Univ. Press, 1952), p. 124; F. P. Kroeger, "The Dialogue in 'A Clean, Well-Lighted Place,'" *College English*, XX (Feb. 1959), 240-241; William E. Colburn, "Confusion in 'A Clean, Well-Lighted Place,'" *College English*, XX (Feb. 1959); pp. 241-242; Otto Reinert, "Hemingway's Waiters Once More," *College English*, XX (May 1959), 417-418; Edward Stone, "Hemingway's Waiters Yet Once More," *American Speech*, XXXVII (Oct. 1962), pp. 239-240; Joseph F. Gabriel, "The Logic of Confusion in Hemingway's 'Clean, Well-Lighted Place,'" *College English*, XXII (May 1961), pp. 539-546; John V. Hagopian, "Tidying Up Hemingway's 'Clean, Well-Lighted Place,'" *Studies in Short Fiction*, I (Winter 1964), pp. 140-146; Warren Bennett, "Character, Irony, and Resolution in 'A Clean, Well-Lighted Place,'" *American Literature*, XLII (March 1970), pp. 70-79.
[2] *The Fifth Column and The First Forty-Nine Stories* (New York: Scribners, 1938), p. 479.
[3] Warren Bennett, "Character, Irony, and Resolution in 'A Clean, Well-Lighted Place,'" *American Literature*, XLII (March 1970), p. 70.
[4] *The Short Stories of Ernest Hemingway* (New York: Scribners, 1965), p. 381. The Scribner code identifies this printing as H-6.65—i.e., the ninth printing of June 1965.

F. Scott Fitzgerald's Hollywood Assignments, 1937–1940

"A Yank at Oxford"	MGM	7 July-26 July 1937[1] (3 weeks)
"Three Comrades"	MGM	4 August, 1 September, 1 December 1937-1 February 1938 (6 months)
"Infidelity" (not made)	MGM	3 February, 9 and 19 March 1938 (4 months)
"Marie Antoinette"	MGM (Stromberg)	16 May 1938
"The Women" (with Donald Ogden Stewart)	MGM	27 May-8 October 1938 (6 months)
"Madame Curie"	MGM	7 November 1938-3 January 1939 (3 months)
"Gone With the Wind"	Selznick (on loan from MGM)	11-24 January 1939 $88,457 (Fitzgerald's earnings since 7 July, 1937)
"Winter Carnival"	United Artists (Wanger)	1-11 February 1939 $2,500
"Air Raid" (with Donald Ogden Stewart)	Paramount	14-31 March 1939 (1 month) $1,200

[1] These dates are taken from scripts in the MGM archives or the Fitzgerald Papers at Princeton University Library. —M. J. B. & J. McC. A.

"Open That Door" (based on the novel *Bull by the Horns*)	Universal	16-22 August 1939 (1 week) $1,500
"Everything Happens at Night"	20-Century Fox	September 1939 (1 day)
"Raffles"	Goldwyn	6-12 September 1939 (1 week) $1,500
"Cosmopolitan" ("Babylon Revisited")	Columbia (Cowan)	March-August 1940
"Brooklyn Bridge" (not made, no way of know- ing what Fitzgerald did on this script)	20-Century Fox	12 August 1940
Emlyn Williams's play *The Light of Heart* (made as *Life Begins at Eight-Thirty* by Nunnally Johnson, 1942)	20-Century Fox	11 October 1940

Not Hemingway But Spain

George Monteiro

In the midst of writing another piece on Ernest Hemingway's "A Clean, Well-Lighted Place," I became curious as to how the older waiter's famous prayers of *nada* would read in Spanish translation. Since Hemingway's classic story is itself set in Spain and actually contains a few Castilian expressions, I wanted to see what the effect would be, if any, of rendering the Lord's Prayer, along with the opening lines of the Prayer to the Virgin, into Spanish. I could not have anticipated the surprise that was in the offing.

At hand was a recently acquired copy of *Relatos,* a selection of Hemingway stories, published originally by Ediciones G. P. in Barcelona in 1957, and reissued in 1965. Checking *Relatos,* I was astonished to find, not that the *nada* prayers were inadequately or inaccurately translated, but that they were not even translated. In fact, the last 334 words of the story, including the two prayers, were unceremoniously lopped off—and with no indication whatsoever that the story as presented was incomplete.

"Un Lugar Limpio y Bien Iluminado," as the story is called in Spain, stops abruptly with the exchange of good-nights by the two waiters as they lock up the café for the night:

> —*Buenas noches—dijo el camarero más joven.*
> —*Buenas noches—dijo el otro.*

Thus ends the Castilian version of "A Clean, Well-Lighted Place." But in English the story continues with the older waiter:

Turning off the electric light he continued the conversation with himself. It is the light of course but it is necessary that the place be clean and pleasant. You do not want music. Certainly you do not want music. Nor can you stand before a bar with dignity although that is all that is provided for these hours. What did he fear? It was not fear or dread. It was a nothing that he knew too well. It was all a nothing and a man was nothing too. It was only that and light was all it needed and a certain cleanness and order. Some lived in it and never felt it but he knew it all was nada y pues nada y nada y pues nada. Our nada who art in nada, nada be thy name thy kingdom nada thy will be nada in nada as it is in nada. Give us this nada our daily nada and nada us our nada as we nada our nadas and nada us not into nada but deliver us from nada; pues nada. Hail nothing full of nothing, nothing is with thee. He smiled and stood before a bar with a shining steam pressure coffee machine.

There then follows a short exchange between the waiter and the barman. After the waiter has left the bar Hemingway sums up:

He disliked bars and bodegas. A clean, well-lighted café was a very different thing. Now, without thinking further, he would go home to his room. He would lie in his bed and finally, with daylight, he would go to sleep. After all, he said to himself, it is probably only insomnia. Many must have it.

Short of exact and authoritative information on the matter, we can only speculate as to the reason for truncating Hemingway's story to the point of its having no point at all. My guess is simple and rather obvious. The blasphemies which the author assigns to the older, disillusioned waiter were more than Hemingway's Castilian translator or publisher or both would (or could) risk in Franco's Catholic Spain.

Nor may it be anything more than a coincidence or a quirk of the editor's taste, moreover, that though he chooses to include no less than thirty-four of Hemingway's so-called "first forty-nine stories," he omits three of Hemingway's other "blasphemous" fictions: "The Light of the World" with its banal equation of an adulterous prizefighter with Jesus, "God Rest You Merry, Gentlemen" with its adolescent who fulfills the dictates of traditional Christian purity by attempting to castrate himself, and "Today is Friday," the playlet which recreates the naturalistic and worldly reactions to the Crucifixion on the part of the Roman soldiers who have executed Jesus as part of their quotidian duty.

In any case, whatever the reason for the omission of these three stories from *Relatos*, along with the silent truncation of "A Clean, Well-Lighted Place," the net result is that Hemingway's Spanish readers would never suspect that his stories, taken as a whole, contain this rather broad streak of what might be considered by many as

Christian blasphemy. Unfortunately—though the reason is entirely understandable—no publisher in Spain has ever brought out a translation of *For Whom the Bell Tolls*.[1] It remains purely academic to speculate on the liberties a Castilian, that is to say, Spanish, translator would out of necessity have to take with the history and politics of Hemingway's novel, particularly Pilar's virtuoso account of the ritualistic execution of village fascists and cowardly priests.

Brown University

---

[1] Audre Hanneman, *Ernest Hemingway, A Comprehensive Bibliography* (Princeton, 1967), pp. 199-201, lists only two Spanish translations of *For Whom the Bell Tolls,* both published in South America—Buenos Aires. Just as I write, there comes to hand a news report on book publication in present-day Spain. I translate the last paragraph, which is in Portuguese: "Spanish publishers, handicapped by censorship, are unable to bring out all the books they desire, even though on occasion the censors do practice a certain tolerance" (*O Estado de S. Paulo* [Brasil] , August 30, 1970). So much for Hemingway's Spanish Civil War novel.

Boulevardier Ghost

In his *Hemingway: An Old Friend Remembers* (New York: Hawthorn, 1965, p. 25) Jed Kiley states that the *The Boulevardier* published Fitzgerald. A search of all the issues yields nothing signed by Fitzgerald—or attributable to him. But there is something about Fitzgerald in the November 1928 issue on p. 14:

Peter Piffle

Mr. Carl Van Vechten, who wrote Nigger Heaven, was seen entering a bar on the Champs-Elysées the other day, in company of a young American author who writes about Flappers.

The young Author About Flappers suddenly felt violently ill. He turned white and fell to the floor. Waiters got around him and opened his collar, the barman made him smell salts and took him out in the air. The only person who paid no attention to him was Carl Van Vechten.

The trouble at the time was that no one around seemed to know where he lived, except Mr. Van Vechten, who, like Pontius Pilate, pouted his lips prettily, and said:

"I am not interested."

—M.J.B.

"A Bunch of Bananas"

January 4 1971

Dear Professor Bruccoli -

I was living in New York at the time of Hemingway's crash, and his words on his return from the jungle caught my ear. I wrote the words, beginning "A bunch of bananas and a bottle of gin/Lets the hunger out and the happiness in." Took them to Mack Goldman, then vice-president of Harms Inc, Madison Ave and 52nd St, who liked them, gave them to a composer, I think Dick Manning, who set them to a gay Calypso tune.[1] Took the song to Mitch Miller, then head of pop recordings for Columbia. He liked, but insisted on revisions, which I made but didn't like. It was recorded by Rosemary Clooney and José Ferrer, at that time felicitously married.[2] I heard it on the air twice, after which it was banned by the networks; I was told because its extolling of gin was taboo. It then vanished into oblivion. I have neither a copy of the song nor the record. I never heard anything from Hemingway, but have been told that it amused him.

Yours sincerely,

Ogden Nash

---

[1] "A Bunch of Bananas" (New York: Witmark, 1954).
[2] "A Bunch of Bananas (The Heming Way)," Columbia #4-40233.

"Babylon Revisited" Revisited

Kenneth McCollum

Bernth Lindfors, in the Winter 1962 issue of the *Fitzgerald News-letter*, pointed out the puzzling taxi ride taken by Charlie Wales in "Babylon Revisited," and indicated that Fitzgerald had made an ob-vious error in geography. There are, however, numerous other mistakes in time and logic throughout the story.

In the *Taps at Reveille* text,[1] Charlie remembers (382.10) that Mr. Schaeffer is part of "the long list of a year and a half ago." This implies that the list was from the period of good times. Yet Charlie states later (383.9) that he has been leading a reformed life for over a year and a half.

At 390.31, Charlie recalls that Duncan Schaeffer and Lorraine Quarrles were a part of a crowd from "the lavish times of three years ago."[2] Then at 395.8, Charlie states that "My drinking only lasted about a year and a half—from the time we came over until I—col-lapsed." Now, at 384.24, Charlie remembers: "but the days came along one after another, and then two years were gone, and I was gone" (he had collapsed). Let's recall that he had been sober for a year and a half, that he remembers the lavish times of three years ago, and that two years of his life had been wasted. There is an obvious inconsistency in the time frame. Even if two years of dissipa-tion were not mentioned, there would not have been enough time to party for a year and a half, have a breakdown, recover, straighten out personal affairs, find a job making more money than ever, and work for over a year (385.25).[3]

Another error is brought to mind in connection with Charlie's work. We know that Charlie's daughter, Honoria, has been residing in Paris. Charlie hasn't been in Paris for over a year, yet he says at 386.7 that he was "astonished how much she's [Honoria] grown in ten months."

Another mistake in events begins at 397.5 when Charlie states to the Peters' "I worked hard for ten years. . . ." Then at 400.15 Charlie states to Lincoln Peters "She's forgotten how hard I worked for seven years there. . . ."

We find the beginning of Fitzgerald's mistakes in logic once again in the opening scene in the bar. Charlie gives the bartender the Peters' address to give to Duncan Schaeffer, but later when the destructive scene occurs at the Peters' home he says (404.31), "They wormed your name out of somebody."[4] Also, it doesn't follow that Charlie would give the bartender the Peters' address rather than his own when the Peters' might associate him with bars—the last thing he wants. Also, he tells the bartender that he doesn't have an address when he enters the bar. Yet he must have. He had no luggage. He left the bar, got in a taxi, and drove to the Peters' home. Then (387.6), "He left soon after dinner, but not to go home." This definitely indicates that he had a place to stay.

During the recollection of the events surrounding the death of Charlie's wife, Helen, F writes of Charlie (399.3), "How could he know she would arrive an hour later alone, that there would be a snowstorm in which she wandered about in slippers, too confused to find a taxi?" Was Helen confused? She found their home by herself. She also found Marion's house when she couldn't get in her own (395.21).

In an incident described at 400.31, Charlie, after lunch, receives a note from Lorraine Quarrles. The note has been redirected by the bartender at the Ritz Bar where Charlie "left his address for the purpose of finding a certain man [Duncan Schaeffer]." Has he been back to the bar? Remember, he didn't give his address originally.[5] And on this day, he got up, called Lincoln Peters at the Bank, lunched with Lincoln, and went back to his hotel where he received the note. In the note, Lorraine states that Charlie was "so strange when we saw you the other day. . . ." Only one day has elapsed since their encounter. In connection with this same incident, Charlie says (401.27) "he was glad Alix had not given away his hotel address."[6] If Alix received Charlie's address, it was for the purpose of giving it to Duncan Schaeffer, and by now Charlie knows that Lorraine is with Duncan. He therefore has no reason to assume that Lorraine could not get the address through Duncan.

Fitzgerald was obviously satisfied with "Babylon Revisited," as the number of revisions to the *Post* story was small.[7] Primarily, the revisions were directed toward shortening the story and sharpening the verbiage. Fitzgerald made no effort to improve the logic in the sequence of events and made only one small attempt to adjust the faulty time periods. Fitzgerald was interested in words and their effect. He chose his words carefully and well. "Babylon Revisited" can survive regardless of its faults in logic and chronology.

University of South Carolina

---

[1] By this time Fitzgerald had supposedly edited out the inconsistencies in the original *Post* story; however, his efforts were not thorough.

[2] The time frame here was "two years ago" in the *Post* version. Fitzgerald attempted to correct the faulty reference but did not go far enough.

[3] The *Post* version did not mention time here. Charlie simply states that ". . . my income is bigger than it was when I had money."

[4] In the *Post*, this was "They wormed this address out of Paul at the bar." F corrected this in *Taps at Reveille* as the address had not been given to Paul but to Alix.

[5] Charlie had given the bartender the Peters' address and in the *Post* version Charlie got the note from Lincoln Peters who had received it at home from the Ritz Bar, a slightly more believable routing.

[6] In the *Post*, this was ". . . he was glad no one knew at what hotel he was staying."

[7] A collation of the *Post* story and the *Taps at Reveille* text reveals seventy-eight substantive changes and fourteen accidentals.

A Letter From Malcolm Cowley

October 13, 1970

Dear Bruccoli,

I haven't time to write an article about the Hemingway and the Faulkner Portables, but here is a letter off the top of my head. If it turns out to be interesting, you are free to use it in the Annual.

The original Viking Portables were pocket-sized books, as the name implies, printed in wartime during the paper shortage. At first they were informal anthologies; a good example (and perhaps the first title) was Alexander Woollcott's *As You Were,* which had a sale of more than 100,000 copies, largely to men in the armed forces (or their loving relatives). Then Pat Covici, God rest his soul, and Marshall Best, who together had charge of the series, began to commission anthologies of individual authors, beginning with those on the Viking list, such as Dorothy Parker and John Steinbeck. Introductions were short and editorial fees were low.

In 1944 they asked me to do a Portable Hemingway. They had obtained permission from Scribners, his publishers, but the licence was only for five years. Anyhow I went ahead with the job. It fitted in with my plans, since I was working—in a desultory fashion, I confess—on a history of American literature, and had found no way to proceed except by treating individual authors. An anthology with a fairly long introduction and editor's notes preceding the various sections seemed to me an effective critical form. Also I was financially independent for the time being, having received a subvention from the late Mary Mellon, a woman of great generosity. I was able to spend much more time on the project than the fee from Viking would have justified.

I was outraged by the critical judgment, then widespread in academic circles, that Hemingway was a Naturalist. I was interested in the prelogical elements in his work, the myth and ritual. At the time I hadn't read Jung, but much later I discovered that terms from Jungian psychology—persona, shadow, anima, the collective unconscious, etc.—apply better to Hemingway's work and his personality than Freudian concepts do.

In any case *The Portable Ernest Hemingway* turned out to be a much more carefully planned and executed book than the earlier Portables had been. It gave a new direction to the series, which, since that time, has become more scholarly and less directed toward the bookstore browser. The sale in hard cover, during the five years that the licence ran, was 45,000 copies. Then Scribners, alas, withdrew the licence, saying that they wanted to bring all of Hemingway's work under one roof.

As for *The Portable Faulkner,* it is a more complicated story, and I have told it at some length in the *The Faulkner-Cowley File.* I won't repeat it here, except to say that I had a hard time persuading Pat Covici and Marshall Best that Faulkner was a big enough author to justify giving him a Portable. It wasn't until I had written a long essay on Faulkner and cut it into chunks that appeared in several magazines that they finally told me to go ahead. In spite of favorable reviews, sales of *The Portable Faulkner* were rather modest for several years; I remember that it took a long time for the book to reach 20,000. Now, in paper, it sells about that many each year (though the total sales now stand at something like 50,000 in cloth and 160,000 in paper, not so big after twenty-five years).

Of course I was exchanging letters with Faulkner and continually asking his advice while preparing the Portable. When I sent him my introduction, I asked him in a letter (now lost; I didn't always make carbons, nor did Faulkner save many of the letters he received) whether I had put too much into it about the legend of the South. It was in answering that question that he said "I don't think there's too much Southern legend in it"—he was referring to my introduction, not to the Yoknapatawpha cycle, as some commentators assumed.

Cordially yours,

Malcolm Cowley

The Fitzgerald-Mencken Correspondence

Robert Emmet Long

An extremely large collection of H. L. Mencken's correspondence, housed at the New York Public Library (Manuscript Division), was made available to scholars for the first time on January 29, 1971. The collection contains an estimated total of 30,000 letters and has been kept under seal since Mencken's death fifteen years ago. There are copies of letters Mencken sent, and originals of letters he received from such prominent authors as Arnold Bennett, W. Somerset Maugham, Willa Cather, F. Scott and Zelda Fitzgerald, William Faulkner, John Dos Passos, Robert Frost, Sinclair Lewis, and Theodore Dreiser. The collection of letters which passed between Fitzgerald and Mencken is of special interest because of the important influence Mencken exerted on Fitzgerald's literary career.

The Fitzgerald-Mencken file contains 57 separate items, including—in addition to letters—telegrams and cards designed by Zelda. Many of the pieces are memoranda sent by Mencken to Fitzgerald when Mencken was editor of *The Smart Set* and *The American Mercury*. The most interesting letters in the collection were written by Fitzgerald (many of them handwritten); at the present time only a few letters from Fitzgerald to Mencken have been published. *The Letters of F. Scott Fitzgerald,* edited by Andrew Turnbull, contains only two letters to Mencken—both in 1925, and on the occasion of the publication of *The Great Gatsby.* The Fitzgerald letters in this collection do not alter one's understanding of the Fitzgerald-Mencken friendship, but they do add some new light.

Fitzgerald's early admiration of Mencken is already well-known and it is not surprising to find in a letter dated 5 September, 1920 that he regards Mencken "at the head and front of American letters." He mentions that he is writing George Jean Nathan into a novel on which he is at work—*The Beautiful and Damned,* a *roman à clef* of the *Smart Set* circle, reflecting many of Mencken's own attitudes.

The originals of the two 1925 letters printed in *The Letters of F. Scott Fitzgerald* are also contained in the file. In these letters Fitzgerald tends to pass diplomaticaly over Mencken's failure to appreciate *The Great Gatsby,* defending the novel by mentioning that it was written in the tradition of the novelist Mencken admired most —Joseph Conrad.

It is often believed that Fitzgerald became disillusioned with Mencken at this point in his career. Their estrangement in the thirties has been suggested in Sara Mayfield's biography *The Constant Circle: H. L. Mencken and his Friends* (1968). Yet letters in the Fitzgerald-Mencken file substantiate that the friendship continued. If they were rather distant, their correspondence was nevertheless cordial on both sides, without any trace of acrimony; and Fitzgerald continued to express his admiration. Just as Fitzgerald looked to Edmund Wilson as his "artistic conscience," he seems to have regarded Mencken as a father figure, or as he phrases it in one letter as "a man" in a "world of children."

There are two letters written in 1935 which are quite touching, in which Fitzgerald turns to Mencken as to one who would share and understand his sense of life as tragic. One of these letters, written in Asheville, North Carolina and dated 6 August, 1935,reads in part:

> Without any desire to begin a sleeveless correspondence I have found the urge to write you irresistable [sic]. In a world that in the last five years has become for me a world of children it was so damn nice to meet a man again, to know that one's shoulders weren't the only ones that were broken and bowed a bit trying to carry the awful burden of responsibility out of this dark cavern (Jesus, what a metaphor!). . . . We have both lived too deeply in our own generations to have much communication except with a mutual respect. . . but there are times when it is nice to think that there are other wheelhorses pulling the whole load of human grief and dispair [sic], and trying to the best of their ability to mould it into form—the thing that made Lincoln sit down in Jeff Davis' chair in Richmond and ask the guards to leave him alone there for a minute.

In another letter, written in Baltimore and dated 29 March, 1935, Fitzgerald praised Gertrude Stein and defended Hemingway; but most of all he wrote to express his sense of an "inconsolable gloom" and loneliness. In doing so, he reaches out to Mencken in a kind of kinship. The letter reads:

> I am particularly fond of the passages where Melanctha is "so blue" and I think by God that it is the best conveying of an inconsolable gloom that I have ever read. Please read some of it. . . .The very loneliness in which its

huge jump landed her is responsible for the crazy warping of her career and I hate to see you making generalities about her that made me definitely feel bad, just as when you jumped at conclusions about Hemingway's early work.

Got an odd reaction from seeing you the other night—of finding you, if I may be so bold as to say it, in a curious state of isolation neither sought for nor avoided. I suppose if one creates a world so wilfully effectually and completely as you have for instance, there is nothing much to do except to live in it. I find myself increasingly in a similar position, a barber who trusts only his own razors. At present everybody is too young for me or too old, too malleable or too set, and for my purposes there is really not a great selection of food at the intellectual banquet. This is too complicated to elaborate here. I simply want to say that I understand and respect your aloneness.

> Always cordially and admiringly,
>
> Scott Fitzg.

These two letters alone add to our sense of Fitzgerald's relations with Mencken in the thirties. Written with an informal grace, striking at times surprising and arresting images, they confirm one's sense of Fitzgerald's letters as one of the most personal and touching achievements of his literary career.

Queens College, CUNY

Jake and Bob and Huck and Tom: Hemingway's Use of *Huck Finn*

Earl Wilcox

Readers in American literature are well aware of Ernest Hemingway's high regard for Mark Twain's *Adventures of Huckleberry Finn.* The esteem is usually measured in reference to the remark Hemingway made in saying that "All modern American literature comes from one book by Mark Twain called Huckleberry Finn."[1] This accolade has been commented upon extensively, yet no one has noted a parallel in Hemingway's first novel, *The Sun Also Rises,* which verifies Hemingway's close reading and perhaps echoing Twain's novel.

In Chapter II of *The Sun Also Rises* Jake Barnes explores how he and Robert Cohn are essentially unlike: Cohn is a romantic and Barnes a realist. Hemingway's heroes, like Huck Finn and Tom Sawyer, are basically different in attitudes which they hold in response to books. In Twain's novel, "books" come to symbolize all the romantic, adventuresome spirit by which Tom Sawyer lives. In Chapter II of *Huck Finn* is an extended discussion of books and how Tom thinks he is expected to follow them explicitly, and the discussion is repeated at the Phelps' farm.

In very similar fashion—so similar as to remind us that Hemingway had read this Twain novel which superbly contrasts the romantic and the realist—Jake Barnes distinguishes between himself and Robert Cohn. One of the chief differences in the two personalities is accounted for by Barnes when he notes that Cohn, like Tom Sawyer, has also been reading books. Cohn, likewise, has believed too much of what they say. Barnes first thinks that Cohn is romantic because he has had very good luck in selling his first novel and in winning a large sum of money at bridge. Jake then turns to justifying Cohn's naive outlook by reflecting on Cohn's reading habits:

Then there was another thing. He had been reading W. H. Hudson. That sounds like an innocent occupation, but Cohn had read and reread "The Purple Land." "The Purple Land" is a very sinister book if read too late in life. It recounts splendid imaginary amorous adventures of a perfect English gentleman in an intensely romantic land, the scenery of which is very well described.... Cohn, I believe, took every word of "The Purple Land" as literally as though it had been an R. G. Dun report.[2]

An assessment by Huck Finn of Tom's readiness to believe quite literally all that he had read would scarcely be more accurate than this evaluation of Robert Cohn by Jake Barnes. Indeed, even the whimsical attitude taken by Barnes has a familiarity about it. One recalls that in the opening paragraph of his novel, Twain links *Adventures of Huckleberry Finn* with his earlier *Adventures of Tom Sawyer* by suggesting that on the whole the author [Twain] told the truth, with a few "stretchers" here and there. Similarly, Barnes says—about Cohn's accepting everything he has read as absolutely truthful—"You understand me, he made some reservations, but on the whole the book to him was sound."[3] Barnes sounds as if he has read Twain's novel, since he has adopted the same tone and rhythm in the sentence in which he describes Cohn's attitude toward Hudson.

But a more obvious and direct likeness between the two chapters in the two novels is seen in the advice Barnes gives Cohn about reading and romantically accepting at face value what one does read. Books again become the key to the frame of mind which Cohn displays. In comparing South America and Cohn's desire to go there with British East Africa, where he does not want to go, Barnes chides Cohn for his attitude. To prepare himself for a trip, Cohn need only to read a book about Africa. Barnes' analysis is: "That's because you never read a book about it. Go and read a book all full of love affairs with the beautiful shiny black princesses."[4] Again, this is precisely the kind of advice Huck might have given Tom had Tom not known what attitude to take toward some prospective adventure.

One final parallel in the two novels links Hemingway's and Twain's characters. The concluding and perhaps the most accurate evaluation of the differences between the romantic and realist is made in Jake Barnes' analysis of the sources of Cohn's ideas toward life. Cohn is sick of Paris, indeed sick of the entire world because it has not been as constantly and hedonistically satisfying as the books had told him it would be. Jake's conclusion to the matter is epitomized in this statement:

So there you were. I was sorry for him, but it was not a thing you could do anything about, because right away you ran up against the two stubbornnesses: South America could fix it and he did not like Paris. *He got the first idea out of a book, and I suppose the second came out of a book too.*[5]

In Huck's adventures during his trip down the Mississippi River, he sometimes wonders how Tom would have reacted in some of the situations in which Huck finds himself. The answer is that had Tom been along he likely would have quoted "books" as readily to Huck during the journey as he did before Huck left and when the two are reunited on the Phelps farm. Likewise, Cohn cannot resist having faith in—in fact, seems to believe in—the books he quotes to Barnes. Thus like Huck and Tom, Jake and Robert are radically different people: Cohn is a romantic who gets his first and his second (and I suppose his third) idea out of a book. Barnes is a realist who tries to come to grips with life as it is, not as it ought to be. In this important way, therefore, Chapter II of *The Sun Also Rises* in miniature reflects one of the major themes of the entire novel. But in its close similarity to Twain's *Huck Finn,* the chapter also gives further evidence of the exact ways in which Hemingway expressed his esteem for Mark Twain.

Winthrop College

---

[1] Ernest Hemingway,*Green Hills of Africa.* (New York: Scribners, 1935), p. 22.

[2] Ernest Hemingway, *The Sun Also Rises.* (New York: Scribners, 1926), p. 9.

[3] Ibid., p. 9.

[4] Ibid., p. 10.

[5] Ibid., p. 12, emphasis supplied.

East Egg, West Egg, All Around the Tower: The Geography of Fitzgerald's *Gatsby*

Kenneth T. Reed

In the opening chapter of F. Scott Fitzgerald's *The Great Gatsby*, Nick Carraway narrates a considerable quantity of background detail as a necessary prologue to what will soon transpire in the novel. Because the tone from passage to passage shifts between the earnest, the witty, and the matter-of-fact, we are perhaps tempted quickly to pass over Carraway's account of why he has left his home in the Middle West in favor of New York, and precisely where he has chosen to settle. The "where" of his relocation is of particular interest. "It was a matter of chance," he tells us, "that I should have rented a house in one of the strangest communities in North America." The strangeness that Carraway recognizes, it seems to me, has reference to more than the bizarre, meteoric nature of the social world he is about to characterize. His very geographical location is enough to invite, with good reason, a psychoanalytic reading. Suggestive in itself is the faint amusement in Carraway's tone when he observes that the "riotous" island on which he dwells has, "among other natural curiosities," a division into two testiculate eggs "identical in contour and separated only by a courtesy bay." So nearly identical are they, in fact, that "their physical resemblance must be a source of perpetual wonder to the gulls that fly overhead."

Furthermore, Carraway finds that his modest (by contrast) house in West Egg is dwarfed even more by the enormity of Jay Gatsby's mansion, "a colossal affair by any standard" replete with a "tower on one side, spanking new under a thin beard of raw ivy." To round out the urogenital imagery is "the great wet barnyard of Long Island Sound" and the marble swimming pool that graces Gatsby's estate. Given the easy, near whimsicality of the two paragraphs that describe the geography of East Egg, West Egg, and the Gatsby mansion,[1] the ambiguity of the imagery would seem to be hardly a subconscious accident on Fitzgerald's part.

Miami University

---

[1] F. Scott Fitzgerald, *The Great Gatsby*. (New York: Scribners, 1925), pp. 5-6.

Islands in the Stream—
The Initial Reception

William R. Anderson, Jr.

Hemingway's much-discussed "big book" manuscript was finally published on October 6, 1970. By the end of the year, *Islands* had received attention from most of the popular review organs of the American and British press. The following is a résumé of opinions expressed during that initial three months of the novel's life. American newspaper reviews are represented only selectively, with an eye toward geographic distribution. British reviews are from publications readily accessible in the United States.

Thirty reviews are digested. They constitute a reception which can only be described by the classic term "mixed." The reviews fall more or less conveniently into three categories, with a roughly equal number in each category. Thirteen notices are basically unfavorable; nine can be categorized as favorable; and eight express ambivalent or neutral judgments. Within the text, reviews are identified as briefly as possible. The appended checklist provides full publication data.

As might be foreseen, the worst pannings came generally from local reviewers in regional American cities. The *Houston Chronicle* described the book as a dud; dull, pompous and unreadable. The reviewer for the *Atlanta Journal and Constitution* concurred, with the statement that he had to force himself through the novel. Despite some rather cynical observations about the dialogue in the "Cuba" section—"not very far removed from the Hardy Boys and Tom Swift in intellectual content. . ."—he was able to salvage some respect for Hemingway by deciding that *Islands* as published represents a very early, rough, draft. This is an opinion frequently expressed elsewhere in criticism of the novel. The *San Francisco Examiner and Chronicle* reviewer discovered a few good stylistic passages, such as the opening description of the house on Bimini, but then dismissed the overall novel as lightly-fictionalized autobiography, full of bad writing. His evaluation was shared by the writer for the *New Orleans Times-Picayune*, who described Honest Lil, the Havana whore, as "one of the most forgettable characters in American literature."

The popular American newsmagazines presented a united front in panning *Islands*. Their approach seems almost according to prearranged formula—two parts glibness, one part condescension. *Time* found the book acceptable as a curio, publishable only as a sort of literary counterpart of the nostalgic sales of cinematic properties which had recently occurred in Hollywood. *Newsweek,* similarly, recognized some sort of historical or pietistic rationale for publication, but ridiculed Thomas Hudson's emotional excesses. *Life* found *Islands* full of rhetoric and meaningless action, but did credit Hudson with a sense of the necessity for continuing the struggle to endure. Any affirmative touches the *Life* reviewer had to offer, however, were negated by his finding that Hemingway did not understnad people. *National Review* described Hemingway as a sort of tough Walter Pater, whose muscular aestheticism made *Islands* a study in the beauty of violence, and, as such, undesirable for publication.

Not all the unfavorable reviews were so superficial or arbitrary. Louis D. Rubin, writing for the *Washington Sunday Star,* went to considerable pains to support his criticisms. He felt that the lack of editing and cutting, and the embarrassingly obvious autobiographical parallels made *Islands* mediocre, at best. Nevertheless, he felt it deserved publication, although he would have preferred its appearance as identifiable working papers. Essentially similar evaluations were offered by Irving Howe in *Harper's,* by John Updike in the *New Statesman,* and by Bernard Oldsey in the *Nation.* These three extensive reviews were free of the air of facile or hasty judgment sometimes apparent elsewhere. They all found the book lacking a controlling theme or pattern. Howe and Oldsey objected to its autobiographical aspect, and Updike wished for some sort of introductory editorial apparatus and for tighter editorial controls. In agreeing with Rubin that the manuscript should have reached print only as a portion of the posthumous literary papers, Oldsey felt that Hemingway's "...built-in, shock-proof shit detector" would have precluded publication without serious and substantial rewriting.

The final entry in this negative category appeared in the *New York Review.* Although it was long and evidently much-labored, full of allusions to Eliot, Edmund Wilson, C. S. Lewis, and other literati, its principal objections to the book were not wholly clear. The review seemed to write *Islands* off as a study in suicidal morbidity, indicative of Hemingway's terminal artistic disintegration.

The objections raised by the more seriously-considered of the unfavorable reviews are not easily dismissable. Even the favorable reviews generally were careful to avoid unlimited approval. For the most part, American reviews in this category were succinct and unemotional. Hemingway scholars Charles Mann and Matthew J. Bruccoli, predictably, found *Islands* important and worthy, but admitted it is flawed in spots. Mann's notice, in *Library Journal*, termed it a "big, impressive, haunting book." Bruccoli's, in the *Fitzgerald/Hemingway Annual 1970*, stressed its expressions of manliness and courage, values similarly stressed in the *Virginia Quarterly Review* notice. The *Milwaukee Journal*'s review, while expressing some reservations about the lack of brevity, termed the book mature and powerful.

Interestingly, with the exception of Updike's *New Statesman* review, all the British notices were favorable. Malcolm Bradbury in the *Manchester Guardian* and John Wain in the London *Observer* joined the *TLS* reviewer in ranking *Islands* solidly at the middle level of Hemingway's accomplishment, below books such as *The Sun Also Rises* and *A Farewell to Arms,* but generally above *Across the River and Into the Trees* or *The Old Man and the Sea.* While faulting its loose structure, they generally credited it with solid, if uninventive, accomplishment. Bradbury was particularly enthusiastic over the sense of Hudson's loneliness the book communicated, and joined Updike in lamenting the absence of editorial commentary. *TLS* carried this interest in the editorial policies which governed the book's publication even further by attacking Mrs. Hemingway and Charles Scribner, Jr., for textual irresponsibility in making *any* unidentified cuts and emendations, a rather marked contrast with the attitudes of most U. S. reviewers.

Among U. S. popular literary periodicals only two offered approval. Malcolm Cowley's long review for *Atlantic Monthly,* dealing extensively with the composition history of *Islands,* was basically favorable, with some qualifications about the strong autobiographical tendency of the book. Cowley felt that the book was an affirmation of Hemingway's struggle to maintain his level of craftsmanship in the face of mounting problems toward the end of his career.

The New York Times Book Review featured Robie Macauley's evaluation as its leading article, fittingly, since it was the most unreservedly enthusiastic review the book received. Macauley termed *Islands* "a complete, well-rounded novel, a contender with [Hemingway's] very best," and found it much better than the products of any of the current crop of young writers.

Those who disliked the novel, and those who liked it, are relatively easy to classify, although there are degrees of intensity within each category. The remaining eight reviews were much more complex, reflecting judgments so qualified, or so tentative, that they must be placed in a separate, middle-ground classification. Generally, these reviews found *Islands* to contain some very fine writing, marred in places by various factors, but not so seriously that it deserved rejection from the ranks of literary worth. Thus the *Washington Post Book World* review (also published in the *Chicago Tribune* of the same date) found particular merit in the "Bimini" section, and predicted that *Islands* will help shore up Hemingway's flagging reputation. A syndicated review distributed by the Media General News Service, and seen in the *Richmond Times-Dispatch*, took a carefully neutral stance, offering very little evaluation of the book, and stressing "newsy" autobiographical parallels. It found *Islands* "wiser" than some of Hemingway's other works, in that he was able to be self-deprecatory in it. *The Christian Science Monitor* balanced the book's excesses of emotion against its value in reaffirming Hemingway's sense of duty in the face of pain, and joined in the general reservations about the value of the autobiographical aspects in a fictional work.

In the October issue of *Esquire,* which introduced the "Bimini" section of the novel to the public, Arnold Gingrich offered a tentative editorial evaluation, finding that section very fine, but expressing doubts about the other two segments.

Probing to a deeper level, reviewers for several of the popular literary journals struggled to arrive at some qualified evaluation. Perhaps least convinced of the book's merit was Jonathan Yardley in *The New Republic.* He accused Hemingway of becoming too absorbed in himself, and his own "Papa" legend, in the later fiction. Thus *Islands* is marred because its author had allowed autobiography and fiction to merge in his life to a degree which got in the way of his ability to create fresh fiction. Nevertheless, *Islands* benefitted from Hemingway's ability to use the *machismo* legend as a protective shield to permit him to continue writing. Somewhat less critical, the *Commonweal* reviewer faulted the book for lack of organization and theme, but found it worth reading for Hemingway's mastery of style.

In a long *Saturday Review* article, John Aldridge found the book neither very good nor very bad, but vacillating between real accomplishment and sad self-indulgence. He particularly praised its descriptions of physical action, but found it too episodic and fragmented. Aldridge was one of the few reviewers to find the Havana Bar scene worthy of praise, for its humor. He joined the majority, however, in finding the autobiographical elements too disruptive, causing a confusion of Thomas Hudson and Hemingway which tends to devitalize the fiction.

Finally, there is Edmund Wilson's long, carefully-written *New Yorker* review. In the process of giving a detailed plot summary, Wilson also described a stimulating tension he felt had been established between the hero and his environment, a tension which had been missing from much of Hemingway's later work. He praised the descriptions of nature, but faulted the wordiness and lack of organization in the book. In an implicit slap at those who oppose editorial tampering, he defended Mrs. Hemingway and Scribner for their emendations. In the end, Wilson concluded that *Islands* has a much more important future than was readily apparent to its first readers.

The initial critical reception of *Islands in the Stream* was not wildly enthusiastic. Some interesting observations can be made, however, concerning that reception. First, it should be remembered that the completely negative reviews were primarily from sources on the periphery of the literary world. Secondly, on a percentage basis, the novel received a far more appreciative reading in England that it did in the United States, although there were some fine notices here too. Thirdly, a great many of the reviewers seem to have become so preoccupied with the heavily autobiographical nature of *Islands* that they were unable to separate Thomas Hudson and Hemingway, a failing they persisted in attributing to the author, too. Frequently this confusion prevented reviewers from providing more fruitful insights into the meaning of the novel. Rather than condemning thinly-fictionalized autobiography (rightly or wrongly), many of the most influential reviewers might have been better occupied had they attempted to comprehend and explain what Hudson, and thus Hemingway, was saying about the loneliness of the tough-minded first rate professional artist.

A CHECKLIST OF REVIEWS

Part I: British Reviews

Anonymous. "Hemingway's Unstill Waters," *Times Literary Supplement* (16 October 1970), pp. 1193–1194.

Bradbury, Malcolm. "Broken Stoic," *The Manchester Guardian Weekly* —North American Edition (24 October 1970), p. 18.

Updike, John. "Papa's Sad Testament," *New Statesman,* LXXX (16 October 1970), p. 489.

Wain, John. "No Surprises," *The London Observer Review* (11 October 1970), p. 33.

Part II: American Reviews

Aldridge, John W. "Hemingway Between Triumph and Disaster," *Saturday Review,* LIII (16 October 1970), pp. 23-26, 39.

Anonymous. Review, *Virginia Quarterly Review,* XLVII (Winter 1971), p. viii.

Broyard, Anatole. "Papa's Disappointing 'Big One,' " *Life,* LXIX (9 October 1970), p. 10.

Bruccoli, Matthew J. Review, *Fitzgerald/Hemingway Annual 1970,* (Washington: NCR/Microcard Editions, 1970), p. 245.

Cowley, Malcolm. "A Double Life, Half Told," *The Atlantic Monthly,* CCXXVI (December 1970), pp. 105-106, 108.

Davenport, Guy. "Hemingway As Walter Pater," *National Review,* XXII (17 November 1970), pp. 1214-1215.

Doerner, Joan Bennett. "Hemingway's Scrap Heap Hardly Does Him Justice—Another Novel Scrounged." *Houston Chronicle* (4 October 1970), p. 18.

Epstein, Joseph. "The Sun Also Sets: Starring Papa," *The Washington Post Book World* (11 October 1970), pp. 1, 3.

Ferguson, Charles A. "Hemingway 'Novel' Has Three Unrelated Parts," *The New Orleans Times-Picayune* (11 October 1970), Section 2, p. 6.

Foote, Timothy. "Papa Watching," *Time,* XCVI (5 October 1970), pp. 90, 92.

Gingrich, Arnold. "Publisher's Page: Notes on *Bimini,"* *Esquire,* LXXIV (October 1970), pp. 6, 12.

Hall, Jeffrey. "Papa: Portrait of Author Emerges in 'Islands in the Stream,' " *The Richmond Times-Dispatch* (4 October 1970), Section F, p. 4.

Hogan, William. "Hemingway's Unfinished Novel," *San Francisco Examiner and Chronicle,* "This World" Section (4 October 1970), pp. 34, 40.

Howe, Irving, "Great Man Going Down," *Harper's Magazine,* CCXLI (October 1970), pp. 120-125.

Long, Robert Emmet. Review, *Commonweal,* XCIII (23 October 1970), pp. 99-100.

Macauley, Robie, Review, *The New York Times Book Review* (4 October 1970), Section 7, pp. 1, 51.

Mann, Charles W., Jr. "Once Again the Familiar Hemingway Is With Us," *Library Journal*, XCV (1 September 1970), p. 2827.

Nordell, Roderick. "The Sea As a Mirror: Hemingway's View of Himself," *The Christian Science Monitor* (8 October 1970), p. 13.

Oldsey, Bernard. "The Novel in the Drawer," *The Nation*, CCXI (19 October 1970), pp. 376, 378.

Porterfield, Walton D. "In A Big Novel, Ernest Hemingway Returns 'In All His Magnificence,'" *The Milwaukee Journal* (4 October 1970), Part 5, p. 4.

Raymond, John. "Hemingway: Papa's Sea Epic Is Merely a Draft," *The Atlanta Journal and Constitution* (11 October 1970), p. 8-D.

Ricks, Christopher. "At Sea with Ernest Hemingway," *The New York Review of Books*, XV (8 October 1970), pp. 17-19.

Rubin, Louis D., Jr. "New Hemingway Novel Poses Questions," *The Washington Sunday Star* (4 October 1970), p. E-1.

Wilson, Edmund. "An Effort at Self-Revelation," *The New Yorker*, XLVI (2 January 1971), pp. 59-62.

Wolff, Geoffrey. "Out of the Desk," *Newsweek*, LXXVI (12 October 1970), pp. 118, 120.

Yardley, Jonathan. "How Papa Grew," *The New Republic*, CLXIII (10 October 1970), pp. 25-26, 30.

University of South Carolina

Color in Fitzgerald's Novels

Anne R. Gere

In his book on the art and technique of Fitzgerald, James Miller describes *The Great Gatsby* as "A superb impressionistic painting, vivid in color and sparkling with meaning."[1] There can be no doubt that color does play a major role in this novel and moreover that Fitzgerald's use of color is directly related to the meaning of *The Great Gatsby*. A number of interesting studies of this relationship have been made, among them Richard Burleson's discussion of Fitzgerald's "somewhat damning commentary on the American dream and the red white and blue,"[2] through his use of color. However, it is the contention of this discussion that Fitzgerald uses color in a significant way in all of his novels and that color imagery of *The Great Gatsby* takes on new dimension in light of the other novels.

It is in conjunction with his moralistic stance that Fitzgerald uses color imagery most effectively. His novels are permeated with an absolute moral code, which is concerned with faithfulness to one's fundamental self and the necessity of overcoming the forces which seek to destroy one's intrinisic virtue. The tragedies of Anthony, Gatsby, and Dick Diver are all related in this sense because each of them allowed a subtle corruption to rule his life. Although Amory's life does not become tragic, he must come to terms with the corruptions of life and accept the resulting disillusionment. Color is used in a significant way to heighten the plight of each of these men. Westbrook, in writing about color imagery in *The Great Gatsby* asserts that color is frequently used to show nature crossed or distorted.[3] This idea can be extended however, to include Fitzgerald's other novels as well. Because he believes that man is born good and becomes corrupted by forces of life, Fitzgerald sees this corruption as a distortion of nature and his use of color emphasizes distortion by employing individual colors in a context opposite from their usual associations. And it is this very distortion which gives Fitzgerald's color imagery its strength.

Green, one of the most prominent colors in *The Great Gatsby*, appears constantly in unnatural and distorted context; instead of appearing in association with fertility, naturalness, and immortality, it highlights sterility, contrivance and death. The green dock light which becomes an object of worship for Gatsby is an electric light, as removed from the natural green world as Gatsby's apple-green shirts and the "green leather conservatory"[4] that is the inside of his car. The fertility implied by green is distorted by the green tickets Daisy hands out at Gatsby's party, saying that she will exchange them for kisses. This quasi-prostitution of affection aptly illustrates Daisy's willingness to sell herself for security rather than enjoy real love. Wilson's unnaturally green face after learning of his wife's unfaithfulness and the confusion about the color of the car which killed Myrtle: "Mavro-michalis . . . told the first policeman that it was light green,"[5] are further examples of the distortions emphasized by the color green. In concluding his discussion of color in *The Great Gatsby*, Burleson suggests that the hope of the book may lie in the cyclical life of vegetation, but this is difficult to accept when one considers the "thin beard of raw ivy"[6] which struggles to exist on Gatsby's rented house, "the scarcely created grass"[7] around the house, and the description of Gatsby's gardens as blue rather than the natural green.

The genesis of this use of green to point out inversion of natural order is found in *This Side of Paradise*. Amory is disillusioned by a show of affection without genuine feeling and sees it as a perversion of natural love. Green enters to heighten this disillusionment and disgust as Amory is necking in a car with a girl with green combs and begins to question what they are really doing. A similar use of green is made when Amory's partner in sexual initiation has "eyes glittering green as emeralds."[8] Fitzgerald uses green to highlight the lack of real affection between Amory and Eleanor. Daisy's green tickets may be a more subtle representation of this same idea. Death caused by an automobile is directly associated with green—perhaps serving as precursor for Myrtle's death scene—when "tragedy's emerald eye"[9] heralds Dick Humbird's demise. That Amory himself has green eyes is made increasingly significant as he realizes the staleness and futility of his life, discovering "with a sense of shock that someone else had discovered the path he might have followed."[10]

Another primary color of *The Great Gatsby* is yellow, which like green is used in an inverted way. Instead of being associated with the life-giving qualities of the sun, yellow appears strongly in scenes of death and disaster. Gatsby's cream-colored car is referred to as yellow when it becomes an instrument of death. Gatsby's own death scene is surrounded by the "yellowing trees,"[7] and yellow is the color which borders both sides of the valley of ashes. Two of the most prominent names in the novel—Daisy and Egg (whether east or west)—imply a center of yellow, and both represent distortion. Daisy compromised herself for security in marriage to Tom (the straw man) and is never capable of realizing what she has missed; and both East and West Egg have been transformed from their natural green state to showplaces of social snobbery.[11]

This Side of Paradise, The Beautiful and Damned and *Tender is the Night* all use yellow to heighten distortion or disaster and show a consistency in Fitzgerald's color imagery. *This Side of Paradise* uses the traditional sun color in two scenes of Amory's sudden revulsion with physical expressions of affection. Both Myra and Axia put their yellow heads on Amory's shoulder to produce a strongly negative response in him. Dick Humbird's death is preceded by a composition in which yellow is the dominant color. In *The Beautiful and Damned* the travesty of settling for little (as Daisy does) is earlier illustrated by Richard Caramel, who is described as having yellowish eyes, and like Daisy, he never realizes what he has missed in compromising himself. The meaningless quality of the Patches' marriage is constantly emphasized by yellow. Their physical and mental distance when Anthony leaves with the army is described as an area of "yellow sobbing."[12] Anthony's affair with Dorothy, described as "an inevitable result of his increasing carelessness about himself"[13] is frequently illuminated by yellow light. And when the Patches have finally won their inheritance and are on a cruise, a girl in yellow describes Gloria as "sort of dyed and unclean"[14] while Anthony congratulates himself on his victory—failing to realize that "the victor belongs to the spoils" as Fitzgerald reminds us in the subtitle.

Throughout *Tender is the Night* yellow is strongly emphasized in scenes of Nicole's breakdowns. She impulsively gives a yellow evening bag, stuffed with all the yellow articles she can find, to a guest who admires it, and shortly thereafter is found in the bathroom in a schizophrenic breakdown. This is more dramatically repeated at the Agiri Fair when Nicole, in a yellow dress, runs away from Dick and later in the same day, after commenting on a yellow house, grabs the steering wheel of the car in an attempt to kill the whole family. The yellow glint in Baby Warren's eyes foretells Dick's destruction—the Warren family has no interest in him personally; they are just interested in what he can do for Nicole. And as Dick's disaster approaches he is seen with yellow accessories such as gloves and cane.

335

A. E. Elmore has written in his article "Color and Cosmos in *The Great Gatsby*" that Fitzgerald's use of color imagery in this novel does not end with ironic inversion.[15] To illustrate his point, Mr. Elmore points to the color white which, according to him, moves from symbolizing purity to corruption and then back to purity again. Mr. Elmore sees the traditional symbolic value of white heightening the faithfulness of Gatsby's vision of Daisy before their reunion and then reinforcing the positive qualities of Gatsby after his death. However, Mr. Elmore fails to consider the white card which Gatsby waves in the face of the policeman who stops him for speeding. This overt corruption associated with white comes when Gatsby still worships the white Daisy of East Egg. In addition, Nick's nightmare about West Egg, which after Gatsby's death should represent his positive qualities, features a drunken woman in white who is always being taken to the wrong house because no one has bothered to learn her name. Therefore, it would seem that the ironic inversion of white is sustained throughtout the book. The implicit white surrounding the yellow of Daisy and Egg is developed in the Buchanan house, described as one of the "white palaces of fashionable East Egg"[16] and the constant mentions of white in reference to Daisy. It is in keeping with this pattern that the place where Tom and Myrtle carry on their illicit affair is described as "one slice in a long white cake of apartment houses."[17] And as Nick looks at Gatsby's house for the last time he sees "on the white steps an obscene word scrawled by some boy with a piece of brick."[18]

Both *This Side of Paradise* and *The Great Gatsby* have terrifying views of New York city as hauntingly white. Although Amory's view is more terrifying as he sees the white walls as living things, Nick's trip down the "White chasms of lower New York"[19] is also frightening by its very contradictory nature. Another terrifying use of white is found in Amory's view of Dick Humbird's dead body which became "this heavy white mass."[20] This quality associated with white reappears in *Tender is the Night*. In her sickness Nicole is frequently surrounded by white, but when she is recovering at Dick's expense, they are both pictured in white, signifying the transference of Nicole's mental illness to Dick. It is during this same time of recovery at Dick's expense that Tommy Barban, Nicole's new lover, notices her "white crook's eyes"[21] for the first time. Nicole's "new white eyes"[22] represent her new strength but a negative quality intrudes because the strength is derived from Dick, reducing him to an empty shell. As he has done in *The Great Gatsby*, Fitzgerald uses white in all of these novels when goodness or innocence is lost.

In speaking of the use of pink in *The Great Gatsby*, Westbrook asserts that this bright hue colors some of the most unhappy events in the novel and in addition gives an atmosphere of plentitude and overripeness to the book. While this seems basically true, it is possible to see pink in more specific terms, relating directly to the theme. The potential and new life usually associated with pink is rejected in favor of a false and elusive quality as Fitzgerald develops his use of the color. In an artificial burst of emotion Daisy exclaims over some pink clouds saying that she'd like to put Gatbsy in one and push him around, and it is the pink-suited Gatsby who faithfully watches the pink light of Daisy's bedroom while she is actually downstairs with Tom planning their getaway after Myrtle's death. This use of pink heightens the tragedy of Gatsby's allowing the girl with money in her voice to rule his life.

A similar use of pink is made with Rosalind in *This Side of Paradise*. The pink in Rosalind's life is almost overpowering, but once the color is established, Fitzgerald quickly shows that the youth which she represents is an elusive quality unattainable by Amory. Rosemary in *Tender is the Night* is an echo of Rosalind and she, too, is surrounded by pink in her early appearances; while she remains in this state she is totally unattainable to Dick Diver. (It is only when she reappears surrounded by the color black that their affair develops.) There is a further implication in the pink associated with Rosemary. During her early appearances in the book, Nicole is often described as a pink rose and when Nicole no longer has this quality, Dick is attracted to Rosemary who, in an equally elusive way, suggests what Nicole once was. The elusive quality in both cases results from Dick's seeing each woman through the glow of his own illusions.

The color gray provides one exception to Fitzgerald's consistent pattern of employing color in a context opposite to its usual connotation. This may be explained by the fact that in every other case the author uses color to point up negative qualities. Since gray connotes lifelessness, indifference and meaninglessness, there is no need for him to distort the associations of the color. Instead he fully uses the existing negative implications of gray. *The Great Gatsby*'s valley of ashes, existing under the faded eyes of Dr. T. J. Eckleburg, is a study in gray, an all-pervading gray ("ashen dust. . .veiled everything in the vicinity")[23] which causes a loss of vitality in the lives of all who enter it. Significantly, it is from the valley that the "ashen fantastic figure" comes to take Gatsby's life. In another vein, Jordan Baker's gray eyes point toward the meaninglessness of her affair with Nick, just as the "gray names"[24]—recorded on an outdated timetable—of those who accepted Gatsby's hospitality suggest their ephemeral quality.

It is in *The Beautiful and Damned* that Fitzgerald first makes a similar use of gray. The once desired and then despised little gray house saps the Patches of their limited vitality. It was "as though they heard the gray house, drably malevolent at last, licking its white chops and waiting to devour them."[25] Even when they leave the gray house the quality of it follows them, "Before they had been two months in the little apartment in 57th Street, it had assumed for both of them the same indefinable but almost material taint that had impregnated the gray house in Marietta."[26]

The emptiness of the Patches' lives is shown in Gloria's obsessive desire for a gray squirrel coat. She states, "I could think of nothing except how I wanted a gray squirrel coat—and how we can't afford one."[27] The personal deterioration of both Anthony and Gloria is reflected in gray. Gloria muses, "Youth has come into this room in palest blue and left it in the gray cerements of despair."[28] Anthony's eyes which were once a deep clear blue fade into gray as his expectations of life are progressively limited and his later nervous collapse is merely another manifestation of what has already been indicated by the gray.

As we have seen, the color imagery of *The Great Gatsby* is developed and amplified in Fitzgerald's other completed novels. Of itself this use of color would have little significance beyond being a manifestation of Fitzgerald's aim of expressing the totality of experience in visual terms. However, the distortion suggested by Westbrook points toward the underlying negative qualities which Fitzgerald wishes to present. No further preaching is necessary because the vacuity, sterility and disaster accompanied by colors of opposite or reinforcing connotation speak for themselves.

University of Michigan

---

[1] James E. Miller, *F. Scott Fitzgerald, His Art and His Technique* (New York: University Press, 1964), p. 77.

[2] Richard A. Burleson, "Color Imagery in *The Great Gatsby*," *Fitzgerald Newsletter* XXXIX (Fall 1967), p. 290.

[3] J. S. Westbrook, "Nature and Optics in *The Great Gatsby*," *American Literature* XXX (March 1960), p. 78.

[4] F. Scott Fitzgerald, *The Great Gatsby* (New York: Scribners, 1925), p. 77.

[5] Ibid., p. 165.

[6] Ibid., p. 6.

[7] Ibid., p. 194.

[8] F. Scott Fitzgerald, *This Side of Paradise* (New York: Scribners, 1920), p. 243.

[9] Ibid., p. 94.

[10] Ibid., p. 136.

[11] Burleson, op. cit., p. 291.

[12] F. Scott Fitzgerald, *The Beautiful and Damned* (New York: Scribners, 1922), p. 309.

[13] Ibid., p. 324.

[14] Ibid., p. 448.

[15] A. E. Elmore, "Color and Cosmos in *The Great Gatsby*," *Sewanee Review*, LXXVIII (Summer 1970), p. 441.

[16] Fitzgerald, *Gatsby*, pp. 6-7.

[17] Ibid., pp. 33-34.

[18] Ibid., p. 217.

[19] Ibid., p. 68.

[20] Fitzgerald, *Paradise*, p. 95.

[21] F. Scott Fitzgerald, *Tender is the Night* (New York: Scribners, 1934), p. 377.

[22] Ibid., p. 380.

[23] Fitzgerald, *Gatsby*, p. 30.

[24] Ibid., p. 73.

[25] Fitzgerald, *Beautiful*, p. 232.

[26] Ibid., p. 295.

[27] Ibid., p. 374.

[28] Ibid., p. 234.

From F. Scott Fitzgerald's scrapbook.

Ole Anderson, Ole Andreson,
and Carl Andreson

In *Papa Hemingway*, A. E. Hotchner reports these Hemingway statements: "Mr. Gene Tunney, the Shakespearean pugilist, once asked me if the Swede of the story ("The Killers") wasn't actually Carl Andreson. . . .I told him yes. . . . But that's all I told him because the Chicago mob that sent the Killers was and, as far as I know, is still very much in business."[1]

On 28 June 1920 Tunney knocked out Ole Anderson in the third round. I have been unable to learn anything about Ole Anderson's subsequent career and possible murder. A little help from the mob, please.

—M.J.B.

---

[1] A.E. Hotchner, *Papa Hemingway* (New York: Random House, 1966), p. 163.

1942

Enlisted in U. S. Coast Guard and was commissioned a Lieut. Commander.

GENE TUNNEY
(James Joseph Tunney)

Born, May 25, 1898, New York City. Weight, 190 lbs. Height, 6 ft. ½ in. Managed by Sammy Kelly, Billy Roche, Frank (Doc) Bagley and Billy Gibson.

1915

July	2—Bobby Dawson, New York	KO	7
Dec.	15—Young Sharkey, New York	KO	6
Dec.	29—Sailor Wolfe, New York	KO	2

GENE TUNNEY, New York, N. Y.

1916

—Billy Rowe, New York	ND	6
—George Lahey, New York	ND	6
—Young Guarini, New York	WF	3
—George Lahey, New York	KO	3

1917

Feb.	9—Victor Dahl, New York	ND	10
Oct.	2—K. O. Jaffe, New York	ND	10
Dec.	21—Yg. Joe Borrell, New York	KO	2

1918

Jan.	15—Hughey Weir, New York	KO	2
July	8—Young Guarini, Jersey City	KO	1
May	2—Enlisted in U. S. Marine Corps.		
Dec.	—Tommy Gavigan, Romorantin	D	12
Dec.	—Howard Morrow, Romorantin	KO	6
Dec.	—Marchand, Paris	KO	2

1919

Won A. E. F. light-heavyweight championship in France, defeating K. O. Sullivan and Ted Jamieson in final rounds after defeating 20 opponents in elimination series, staged throughout France. Also defeated A. E. F. heavyweight champion, Bob Martin, in special 4-round bout.

Nov.	14—Dan Dowd, Bayonne, N. J.	ND	8
Dec.	15—Bob Pierce, Jersey City	KO	2

1920

Jan.	1—Whitey Allen, Jersey City	KO	2
Jan.	10—Bud Nelson, Bayonne	KO	1
Feb.	4—K. O. Sullivan, Newark	KO	1
Jan.	26—Jim Monahan, Jersey City	KO	1
Mar.	4—Ed Kinley, Jersey City	KO	5

Nat Fleischer's Ring Record Book

Apr.	5—Al Roberts, Newark	KO	7
June	7—Jeff Madden, Jersey City	KO	2
June	28—Ole Anderson, Jersey City	KO	3
Oct.	7—Paul Sampson, Paterson	ND	8
Oct.	22—Sgt. Ray Smith, Camden	KO	2
Nov.	25—Leo Houck, Philadelphia	ND	6
Dec.	7—Leo Houck, Jersey City	ND	10

1921

June	30—Young Ambrose, N. Y. C.	KO	1
July	2—Soldier Jones, Jersey City	KO	7
Aug.	16—Martin Burke, N. Y. C.	W	10
Aug.	29—Eddie Joseph, N. Y. C.	W	12
Sept.	15—Herbert Crossley, N. Y. C.	W	7
Oct.	15—Jack Burke, N. Y. C.	KO	2
Nov.	22—Wolf Larsen, N. Y. C.	KO	7
Dec.	22—Eddie O'Hare, N. Y. C.	KO	6

1922

Jan.	13—Battling Levinsky, N. Y. C.	W	12

Won American light heavyweight title.

Feb.	11—Jack Clifford, N. Y. C.	KO	6
Feb.	14—Whitey Wenzel, Philadelphia	KO	4
Mar.	3—Fay Keiser, Grand Rapids	ND	10
Apr.	10—Jack Burke, Pittsburgh	KO	9
May	23—Harry Greb, N. Y. C.	L	15

(Lost American light-heavyweight title)

July	7—Fay Keiser, Rockaway	W	12
Aug.	4—Ray Thompson, Long Branch	KO	3
Aug.	17—Charlie Weinert, Newark	ND	12
Aug.	24—Tommy Loughran, Phila.	ND	8
Oct.	25—Chuck Wiggins, Boston	W	10
Nov.	3—Jack Hanlon, N. Y. C.	KO	1
Nov.	29—Charlie Weinert, N. Y. C.	KO	4

1923

Jan.	29—Jack Renault, Philadelphia	NC	4
Feb.	3—Chuck Wiggins, N. Y. C.	W	12
Feb.	23—Harry Greb, N. Y. C.	W	15

(Regained American light-heavyweight title)

May	7—Jack Clifford, Detroit	KO	8
May	16—Jimmy Delaney, Chicago	ND	10
July	31—Dan O'Dowd, Long Island	W	12
Dec.	10—Harry Greb, N. Y. C.	W	15

(American Light-heavyweight title)

1924

Jan.	15—Harry Foley, Grand Rapids	ND	10
Jan.	16—Harry Foley, Grand Rapids	ND	10
Jan.	24—Ray Thompson. Lakeworth, Fla.	KO	2
Feb.	15—Martin Burke, New Orleans	W	15
Mar.	17—Jimmy Delaney, St. Paul	ND	10
June	26—Erminio Spalla, N. Y. C.	KO	7
July	24—Georges Carpentier, N. Y. C.	KO	15
Aug.	18—Joe Lohman, Columbus, O.	W	8
Sept.	17—Harry Greb, Cleveland	ND	10
Oct.	27—Harry Foley, Memphis	KO	1
Nov.	10—Buddy McHale, Memphis	KO	2
Dec.	8—Jeff Smith, New Orleans	ND	15

1925

Mar.	27—Harry Greb, St. Paul	ND	10
June	5—Tommy Gibbons, N. Y. C.	KO	12
July	3—Ital. Jack Herman, Kan. City	KO	2
Sept.	25—Bartley Madden, Minneapolis	KO	3
Nov.	18—Johnny Risko, Cleveland	W	12

1926

Sept.	23—*Jack Dempsey, Philadelphia	W	10

*Tunney won world heavyweight title.

1927

Sept.	22—Jack Dempsey, Chicago	W	10

(Heavyweight title bout)

Referee: Dave Barry; receipts, $2,658,660; Tunney's share, $990,000; Dempsey's share, $447,500. Attendance: 104,943.

1928

July	26—Tom Heeney, N. Y. C.	KO	11

(Heavyweight title bout)

1941

Appointed Commander, U. S. Naval Aviation and Commissioned Chief Recreation Officer in U. S. Navy.

MAX SCHMELING

Born, Sept. 28, 1905, Klein Luckaw (Brandenburg) Germany. Weight, 196 lbs. Height, 6 ft. 1 in. Managed by Arthur von Bulow and Joe Jacobs.

1924

Aug.	2—Czapp, Dusseldorf	KO	6
Sept.	19—Vanderryver, Kolnege	KO	3
Sept.	20—Louis Dyłsburg, Bichum	KO	1
Oct.	4—Rocky Knight, Kolnege	W	8

Nat Fleischer's Ring Record Book

Hanneman Addenda*

Audre Hanneman

RECENTLY PUBLISHED WORK BY HEMINGWAY

Books and Pamphlets

Two-volume French edition: *Oeuvres romanesques: Poèmes de guerre et d'après-guerre.* Tome I. Paris: Gallimard, 1966. 1,472 pages. [Bibliothèque de la Pléiade, v. 189.] Edited by Roger Asselineau. With a Foreword, Preface, Chronology, and Notes by the editor. Contents: *TOS, FTA, SAR, AMF, DIA*, short stories and interchapters from *First 49*, and poems from the *Collected Poems.* By various translators.

Note: In reviewing the first volume, the *Times Literary Supplement* noted: "The 'Bibliothèque de la Pléiade' is well-known as one of the most attractive and compendious series of texts ever to have appeared. The works chosen for it have all a good reason for being called 'classic'. . . . Ernest Hemingway is the only writer in English to be included. There is not a single British writer in the list.

"Hemingway's inclusion is a remarkable tribute to his standing in France, and this edition 'de la Pléiade' is bound to enhance his reputation. . . ." *TLS* (June 22, 1967), p. 557.

Qeuvres romanesques: Reportages de guerre Poèmes à Mary. Tome II. Paris: Gallimard, 1969. 1,760 pages. [Bibliothèque de la Pléiade, v. 207.] Edited by Roger Asselineau. With a Foreword, Notes, and Bibliography by the editor. Contents: *GHOA, THAHN, FWBT, TFC, ARIT, OMATS*, short stories from *First 49*, the previously uncollected short stories "A Man of the World" and "Get a Seeing-Eyed Dog," articles from *By-Line*, "Two Poems to Mary," and EH's Nobel prize acceptance speech. By various translators.

*Miss Hanneman was unable to compile a complete Checklist for this issue.

343

First hard-cover edition: *The Collected Poems of Ernest Hemingway.* Published by Haskell House Publishers Ltd., New York, in 1970, at $3.95. ii + 28 + 1 blank leaf. 8-3/8 × 5-1/2. Issued in pink-violet boards, lettered in gold on the backstrip. White endpapers. Note: This edition differs from the fourth pirated edition in several respects: the publisher's imprint appears on the title page (p. [1]); p. [2] gives date of first publication, publisher's imprint, LCC and SBN numbers, and note of origin; p. [3] is blank.

First paperback edition: *Men Without Women.* Published by Charles Scribner's Sons, New York, August 5, 1970, as No. SL217 of the Contemporary Classics of the Scribner Library series. viii + 232 pages. 8 × 5-3/8. $1.95. See A7.[1]

First paperback edition: *The Fifth Column and Four Stories of the Spanish Civil War.* Published by Bantam Books, New York, October 1970, at $1.25. No. Q5645. viii + 216 pages. 7 × 4-3/16.

First edition: *Islands in the Stream.* Published by Charles Scribner's Sons, New York, Oct. 6, 1970, at $10.00. x + 466 + 2 blank leaves. 8-7/8 × 6. The first printing consisted of 75,000 copies. "Note" by Mary Hemingway regarding preparation of the manuscript, on p. [7]. Note: See publication of Part One in *Esquire* below. Note: *Islands* was the special fall 1970 selection of the Book-of-the-Month Club. Note: *Islands* was Number One on the "Best sellers" list in *Publishers' Weekly* (Jan. 4, 1971), p. 82, with the comment: "New leader of fiction best sellers. Has sold over 100,000 copies."

Pamphlet. *Will You Let These Kiddies Miss Santa Claus?* Facsimile of the cover and EH's article in the *Co-operative Commonwealth,* II (Dec. 1920). 4 pages. 9 × 6. Issued in December 1970, in light brown paper covers, lettered in dark brown. 125 copies were printed by Matthew J. Bruccoli and C. E. Frazer Clark, Jr. as a keepsake for friends of the *Fitzgerald/Hemingway Annual.* Collation: Facsimile of the cover on p. [1]; EH's article on pp. [2]-[3]; note by M. J. B. and C. E. F. C. on p. [3]; colophon on p. [4]. See C52.

---

[1] All references refer to *Ernest Hemingway: A Comprehensive Bibliography* by Audre Hanneman (Princeton: Princeton University Press, 1967).

Periodical contributions

Italian translation of *DIA*: *Morte nel pomeriggio, Tempo* [Milan], XXVIII, No. 3 (Jan. 19, 1966) *to* No. 13 (March 30, 1966).

Serialized in eleven installments. Illustrated by Picasso. Translated by Fernanda Pivano. Cover photograph of EH on the first installment.

Article reprinted: "The Best Rainbow Trout Fishing," *Sports Afield*, CLXIV (Sept. 1970), 56-57, 138. Drawing of EH by Bob Abbott. Reprinted from the *Toronto Star Weekly* (Aug. 28, 1920). See C47. Note: Heading: "YOUNG HEMINGWAY—OUTDOOR WRITER Before he was Papa he was Ernie—and he wrote about fishing like no 21-year-old you ever read."

Excerpt: "Bimini," *Esquire*, LXXIV (Oct. 1970), 122-137, 190, 192, 194, 196, 198, 200, 202. First publication of a 34,000-word episode from Part One of *Islands in the Stream*. This excerpt "bridges various passages" in the book (p. 122). Cover photograph of EH, over-printed with a page from the holograph manuscript. See also Publisher's Page: "Notes on Bimini" by A. G. [Arnold Gingrich], pp. 6, 12; Backstage with Esquire, p. 30; and Editor's Note, p. 121.

Article reprinted: "Will You Let These Kiddies Miss Santa Claus?" *Fitzgerald/Hemingway Annual 1970*, pp. 105-107. Reprinted from the *Co-operative Commonwealth*, II (Dec. 1920). See C52. See also keepsake above.

Miscellanea

First publication of a Hemingway translation: White, William. "Hemingway as Translator: Kiki's Grandmother," *English Language Notes*, IV (Dec. 1966), 128-132. EH's translation of Chapter 12 of *Kiki's Memoirs* (Paris, 1930) is printed in parallel columns, on pp. 130-132, with Samuel Putnam's translation. (See B7.) The three-page holograph manuscript is in the collection of the University of Texas.

Previously unpublished work by EH in *Ernest Hemingway: A Life Story* by Carlos Baker (Scribner's, 1969).

p. 12: "My First Sea Vouge" [sic]. A four-paragraph short story, written April 17, 1911 for his sixth-grade English class. "EH's first extant short story" (p. 568).

p. 15: "The Opening Game." Six lines from a poem, written April 12, 1912.

p. 35: Character sketch of Lionel Moise, "from an undated, unpublished holograph MS" (p. 570).

p. 60: "The Passing of Pickles McCarty." The lead paragraph of a short story, probably written in "the spring of 1919" (p. 574).

pp. 65-66: "Wolves and Doughnuts." Fragment of a short story, written in Petoskey on the back of a letter dated Dec. 20, 1919 (p. 575).

p. 88: "Blood is thicker than water." Five-line poem, "composed ca. Feb., 1922" (p. 577).

pp. 90-91: "Paris 1922." Six "one-sentence sketches, probably composed ca. late May, 1922" (p. 578).

p. 101: Character sketch of Dave O'Neil, "composed probably spring, 1923" (p. 579).

pp. 120-121: Sketch of Robert Reade and Gregory Clark, written in the "fall, 1923" (p. 582).

pp. 131-132: "Some observations on esthetic principles" from the deleted conclusion of "Big Two-Hearted River," "composed Aug., 1924" (p. 585).

p. 261: "List of earthly pleasures." Deleted passage from holograph manuscript of *Green Hills of Africa* (p. 611).

p. 263: "Dialogue on courage and allied powers." Deleted passage from holograph manuscript of *Green Hills of Africa* (p. 611).

p. 428: Three lines of a poem "on battle in forest," written Sept. 24, 1944 (p. 642).

p. 563: Deleted passage about "the rich" from the manuscript version of the last chapter of *A Moveable Feast*, "composed ca. 1958" (p. 592).

p. 609: Canceled passage "about courage and cowardice" from the holograph manuscript of *Green Hills of Africa*.

Reviews

George R. Minkoff. *A Bibliography of the Black Sun Press.*
Introduction by Caresse Crosby. Great Neck, New York:
Minkoff, 1970. $17.50.

By Charles Mann

Let it be said immediately that the Crosbys' achievement looks
better each year, and discerning collectors who, in still recent years,
picked up Black Sun Press books at bargain rates can congratulate
themselves. The content of the press is impressive, the printing itself
attractive, and although the gold and silvery paper of the boxes is easily nicked or marred, the bright colors make a brave show. It took
work, as Caresse Crosby makes plain in her valuable, and now sadly,
posthumous, preface. For Harry and Caresse, printing was not a dil-
letante exercise. Their collaboration with *Maître Imprimeur* Lescaret
was a genuine endeavor to get the very best material available, and to
present it in an appropriate format. Of interest to readers of the
Fitzgerald/Hemingway Annual (May we hope for a suitable acronym
from our editors? I'm old enough to balk at FHA.) is Caresse's note
that the Fitzgeralds were as elusive as eels, and that after Scott and
Zelda failed to show for a dinner given by the MacLeishes, the
Crosbys didn't quite dare approach them for a contribution. Their
seeing the Fitzgeralds as "aloof and formidable figures" seems a faint
echo of Morley Callaghan's first reaction to Scott and Zelda's "Olym-
pian profiles." Hemingway came late to the press, and then only in
1932 reprints in the low-priced Crosby Continental Editions of *The
Torrents of Spring,* and *In Our Time.* However, Joyce, MacLeish, D.
H. Lawrence, Eugene Jolas, and Pound all published one or more
works under the Black Sun imprint; and what modern private press
can match the first appearance of Hart Crane's *The Bridge*, splendidly
made and printed in 1930 with illustrations by Walker Evans. In the
end, the production of the press spanned twenty-seven years (1924-
1951), and numbered sixty-five items, much of it first-edition material. In her preface, Caresse Crosby is rather modest about the Black
Sun Press. She needn't have been.

Mr. Minkoff of Great Neck, New York, is a bookseller specializing in modern letters. This handsome and useful work is a labor of love. I have already reviewed it in a general way for the *American Reference Books Annual* 1970 wherein my review calls attention to some faults; predominantly, a confusing use of brackets, and a careless editorial and proofing job which allowed a sheaf of minor errors to stand. However, rather than place Mr. Minkoff in double jeopardy, let me refer the reader to the listed errors in my other review, and to another note of cavil by Robert S. Fraser in *Library Journal,* August, 1970, p. 2653.

Pennsylvania State University Library

Sara Mayfield. *Exiles from Paradise.* New York: Delacorte Press, 1971.

By Arlyn Firkins

Sara Mayfield, most recent of the biographers of F. Scott and Zelda Fitzgerald, comes to her task armed with the conviction that "derivative" researched biographies are less reliable than "portraits from life." That is a false position (and no one could be more vehement than Miss Mayfield in denying the validity of Fitzgerald's own fictionalized "portraits from life" of his wife), but it can have its own integrity, and Miss Mayfield should have carried it to its logical conclusion. She ought to have written a memoir, and not to have attempted a biography. Her research is amateurish, and as a biography *Exiles from Paradise* seems, in fact, entirely derivative.

Fitzgerald's novels are tragedies of which he is the victim; Nancy Winston Milford, in her exhaustively researched but by no means derivative biography, proved that the Fitzgeralds' story was a tragedy of which Zelda was the victim. Miss Mayfield, in exaggerating Zelda's achievements, minimizing her insanity, and glorifying her return to Montgomery, repudiates the tragedy.

Exiles from Paradise is an openly—and an irritatingly—biased biography. Whether she is denying the probability of premarital sexual intimacy between Scott and Zelda, minimizing Zelda's attraction to Jozan, or insisting that the insanity was not Zelda's but her husband's, Miss Mayfield staunchly misinterprets anecdotes and suppresses evidence—or dismisses it as uncharacteristic, referring her readers always to that final authority, "those who knew both Scott and Zelda well." At times she becomes angry: Fitzgerald, "a blond Adonis in a Brooks Brothers uniform," on page 14, is "a shavetail lieutenant in a nearby army camp" on page 192. But Miss Mayfield grew up with Zelda Sayre, and loved her; her point of view is understandable, and so openly acknowledged as to forewarn the reader, and preclude deceit. Her literary style, moreover, alternately pedestrian and overwritten, is not persuasive. Only once does she write movingly: "Few women have ever been placed in such a painful position as that in which Scott placed Zelda. She bore it so loyally, with such proud dignity and Spartan fortitude that it should have won her more respect and admiration than she has received from the critics" (p. 292). But Miss Mayfield immediately and unfortunately abandons her eloquence, continuing: "Almost without exception they represent Zelda in her last years as an eccentric recluse, leading an aimless, vegetative life. But their reports do not tally with those of her family and friends." The reports of her family and friends that follow range from the touching (Zelda's compassion for the spastic child of a neighbor) to the ludicrous (her delivery of "an inspired discussion of religion" to a meeting of "the Bluestockings, the top-flight study club"), but they tend to reinforce the picture of an eccentric recluse.

The acceptable argument that of the Fitzgeralds Zelda was the superior person—more loyal, more loving, more imposed upon—is not, however, the thesis of *Exiles from Paradise*. Miss Mayfield demands nothing less of her readers than an acknowledgment that Zelda was the superior artist:

> . . .very few [of the Fitzgeralds' friends] will disagree as to which of the Fitzgeralds had genius and which of them talent and a knowledge of a writer's craft (p. 295).

(Miss Mayfield does not define genius, but apparently believes that it entirely consists of a certain brilliant originality of imagination.)

> Both [Fitzgerald] and Hemingway were jealous of the fact that Zelda was the born 'natural' and the 'original' that neither of them, for all their skill in construction and craftsmanship, would ever be (p. 196).

Miss Mayfield calls upon "any fair-minded critic, who can divest himself of the prejudices that accrue from Scott's reputation" to recognize the superiority of *Save Me the Waltz* to *Tender is the Night* (p. 197). Her estimations of both books (*Tender is the Night* was written with "one eye on the Book of the Month Club and the other on the divorce court" [p. 220]) seem to be the result of an inability to distinguish between fiction and autobiography. She is distressed by the differences between the details of Nicole Diver's and Zelda's illnesses, and reinforces her praise of *Save Me the Waltz* with a dull critique of its accuracy by Zelda's sister Rosalind.

Earlier in *Exiles from Paradise* Miss Mayfield had bracketted the Fitzgeralds' literary endeavors (p. 100): "Zelda's articles in the *Metropolitan* and Scott's stories in the *Post* kept them in the public eye" (p. 100). And she resents, on Zelda's behalf, the addition or substitution of Fitzgerald's own name to some of his wife's stories and articles. It is impossible not to suspect Miss Mayfield of some deliberate misinterpretation here; she must be aware that Fitzgerald's name was used because Zelda's pieces were hard to sell without it.

But the most outrageous of Miss Mayfield's claims is that all of Fitzgerald's finished books were in fact collaborations: "In her obituary in *The Montgomery Advertiser,* Grover Hall, Sr., the Pulitzer prize-winning editor of the paper, came forth with a fact that Scott's biographers have omitted to mention, but Zelda's friends have long known: 'Mrs. Fitzgerald had collaborated with her husband on some of his books. . .' in fact, on all of them except the unfinished fragment of *The Last Tycoon*" (p. 295). Miss Mayfield's evidence is well-known to Fitzgerald's biographers, and consists of the uses he made of Zelda's diaries and letters (by no means the best things in his work, as Miss Mayfield would have it) and of his long-acknowledged respect for her judgment. Nowhere among the Fitzgerald manuscripts at Princeton is there any evidence that Zelda worked over her husband's drafts, or that he appropriated and worked over hers. Miss Mayfield makes much of the assertion that Fitzgerald "had published nothing commercially before he met her and very little after he left her—a hard fact for Fitzgerald's biographers to admit—and one that has been sedulously avoided by them—but common knowledge among her friends" (p. 157).

Before Fitzgerald met Zelda, he had completed *The Romantic Egoist* and had published six stories and two one-act plays in the *Nassau Lit*—including "Babes in the Woods" and "The Debutante." (Because they appeared commercially in *The Smart Set* in 1919, Miss Mayfield attributes their inspiration to Zelda, but they were about Ginevra King. Miss Mayfield also overemphasizes Zelda's importance to *This Side of Paradise* by moving forward Fitzgerald's use of her diaries—in *The Beautiful and Damned*—that prompted her "plagiarism begins at home" remark.)

By 1917, Fitzgerald had also written books and lyrics for three Princeton Triangle Club shows, had been an editor of the *Tiger* and of the *Nassau Lit*, and had written four plays performed in St. Paul by the Elizabethan Dramatic Club. What, one wonders, *would* Miss Mayfield accept as a literary output sufficient to prove the artistic independence of a twenty-two-year-old man?

Fitzgerald regarded Zelda as his "material" and did use her, sometimes with selfish disregard for her well-being. That fact, avoided by none of Fitzgerald's biographers, does not constitute collaboration.

Sara Mayfield, staunch friend that she is, is an unlikely writers' biographer, for she is completely without literary sensibility. There is nothing in *Exiles from Paradise* to indicate that she is aware of a qualitative distinction between the writings of (for example) Ernest Hemingway and Donald Ogden Stewart. It is a failing which seriously and frequently undercuts her intentions. Contrasting Zelda's religious sincerity with Fitzgerald's heartless impatience, Miss Mayfield follows two paragraphs—of purely biographical interest—from one of Zelda's religious letters with a phrase of Fitzgerald's, calling people like Zelda "mere guests on earth, eternal strangers carrying around broken decalogues they cannot read" (p. 285). As a description of Zelda it may be unjust—but she never wrote a line so good.

Miss Mayfield, in her conclusion, notes evidence that Zelda is finally beginning to get the artistic recognition that is her due. An enthusiastic letter to the editor of *Esquire* is anonymously cited, and there are instances of various friends' unwillingness to part with any of her paintings. Miss Mayfield describes a memorial set up by the Montgomery Museum of Fine Arts: (p. 291) "a glass case. . .filled with reminders of her—a soft scarf, a copy of *Save Me the Waltz,* a gold-beaded bag, a perfume atomizer, an overturned wine glass, and a pair of white gloves." My admiration for Zelda Fitzgerald is less extravagant than Miss Mayfield's, but I think she deserves a better tribute than that brand of hometown patronage. Zelda Fitzgerald was not an artist, but she had taste. She would, I hope, have preferred as a monument her husband's least flattering "portrait from life."

Jay Martin. *Nathanael West: The Art of His Life.* New York: Farrar, Straus & Giroux, 1970. $10.

By R. L. Samsell

Grateful for the new biography of Nathanael West, and hearing that the biographer was teaching at the nearby Irvine campus of the University of California, I reached for the phone and arranged to

meet with Prof. Jay Martin. A week or so later we lunched in New-
port Beach, discussing his book, mutual friends, favorite writers, literature in general. At this meeting, I had only found time to browse
through some of the Fitzgerald sections of Prof. Martin's biography,
and, always responsive to new Fitzgerald material, I was enthusiastic
about the professor's book. Now, having meticulously read the full
biography, and having reread and studied each of Nathanael West's
four short novels, my enthusiasm is no more.

The book's preface is comprised of several lists acknowledging
those who aided Prof. Martin with documents, manuscripts, letters,
tapes, interviews, and correspondence. Covering eight pages, these
lists bear impressive names in the literary world, and, quite naturally,
the length and breadth of such lists do have an intimidating effect.
Further, the preface reveals that Prof. Martin's biography was subsi-
dized by a Guggenheim grant. Also, West's brother-in-law and sister,
Sidney and Laura Perelman, cooperated with Prof. Martin throughout the fashioning of the biography. Good enough. We have thorough research, impressive colleagues and authorities—the credentials
for a major contribution to American letters. For all this, Nathanael
West does not come alive in this book. The structure, too, is ill-
planned. The book's emphases or shadings or both seem to derive
more from the availability of materials than from the functional use
of those materials. Surprisingly, too, Prof. Martin adds little to
his predecessors' analyses of West's novels. But perhaps the biography is most seriously flawed by prosy indulgences of the profoundly
philosophical sort—"With Leonard Fields at Los Banos he [West]
had been doomed to live; and with Eileen at El Centro, doomed to
die." Finally, as we shall see, exacting research is not demonstrated
by the compilation of impressive lists.

Disappointed, I turned to the prose of Nathanael West for solace,
and, to my chagrin, and surprise, I found no solace. West, in years
past, had been among my favorites. His inscribed first editions reside
on my shelves. Surely, I must be wrong. I tried again. It was curious, this experience. Perhaps my reading of West had been affected
by my disappointment with Prof. Martin's biography. So I looked
to other authorities: Edmund Wilson, Stanley Edgar Hyman, L. E.
Sissman. Wilson declared *Miss Lonelyhearts* to be a remarkable
book. Hyman placed the story of *Miss Lonelyhearts* at the summit
with *The Great Gatsby* and *The Sun Also Rises*. Sissman, reviewing
Prof. Martin's biography for *The New Yorker,* expanded Hyman's select group to include *The Day of the Locust.* While Prof. Martin had

avoided evaluations, he did emerge from his viscosity with this flag—
"He [West] had moved beyond the Dada satire and rebelliousness of *Balso Snell* to moral indignation. The wit and satire of Sinclair Lewis and George S. Kaufman, the anger of James T. Farrell and Dos Passos, the pity and sympathy of Dreiser and O'Neill, the stoicism of Hemingway—compared to these, West's work shows a power of beauty and bitterness which places him in Yeats' 'great tradition'. His true peers were writers like Sherwood Anderson, Fitzgerald, Eliot, Faulkner, and Williams."

Thus humbled, I tried West still another time. Perhaps, I thought, it is a mood, a passing churlishness. Then I turned to Hemingway. With churlishness, perhaps, at last, I could deal firmly with even Papa. No, no, it didn't work. Jake Barnes was as sparkly as ever—as indeed was Nick Carraway. In truth, each of these gentlemen improves through the years. Then, after all, it might be Nathanael West. In *Miss Lonelyhearts*, I could not lose the feeling that the prose is tense, constrained, sometimes torturously unrhythmical. Often, one senses the exhaustion of West's task. When the prose should zing, it wilts; while when it should ease off, it becomes nervously shy, self-conscious, taut. Soon enough, *Miss Lonelyhearts* becomes mere mental exercise—an imagerial obstacle course which delights Westian harriers.

While *The Day of the Locust* lacks *Miss Lonelyhearts'* cohesion, West's last novel displays a richer, surer prose, highlighted by the potency of Chapter 14 (Cowboy Shoup and the Mexican). The beginning chapters, too, are fashioned gracefully, and there is a blend of heart and head which surpasses *Miss Lonelyhearts'* anesthesia. In *Locust*, however, a valid, unifying meaning, or concept, is missing. While there is reason to believe that West saw his midwestern hayseeds as capable of feeling cheated—betrayed by the emptiness of the American Dream—I doubt that Nathanael West, the thinker, held this view throughout the four years he worked on *Locust*. And, however cheated the hayseeds may or may not have felt, it is doubtful that their love and envy of movie stars camouflaged the kind of seething hostilities which would give rise to Tod Hackett's "The Burning of Los Angeles." This latter rationale, or notion, is sheer balderdash. Those who tout Nathanael West as a great writer have also envisioned him as something of a prophet, pointing to the Watts riot as a Westian prophecy, and, more, signifying Watts as the precursor of things to come in America. Nonsense. Today's pyrotechnics are ignited by groups and individuals with complex and highly conceptualized grievances, more elemental and inflamatory than those felt by West's locusts. In point of fact, the rioters in West's novel have never rioted—not at Grauman's Chinese, nor anywhere else—but, instead, they have penned prosaic letters to the midwestern plains, rallying relatives and anybody else who would listen, "Come West. Why, it's just grand out here," etc. Should a premiere be held at Grauman's tomorrow, the crowd would be barely distinguishable from those which buzzed there some thirty years ago.

Moreover, *Locust* barely qualifies as a Hollywood novel. Hollywood, in full scale, is at least a three-ring circus. *Locust*, on or off Hollywood Boulevard, is only a bold stare inside a sad sideshow. It is Hollywood's subculture, the lunatic fringe about which local citizens felt the same curiosity and revulsion as did West. Faye Greener would not be recognized by the studio crowd as a starlet, or even an extra, but as merely one of the star-struck kids from God-knows-where, who hangs around with popped eyeballs and autograph books. Homer Simpson, despite his hands, is strenuously dull. Faye's father, Harry, is the prototypical Show Biz bore. The celebrated trek by Tod Hackett through the Dream Dump is just an overbaked anecdote. No, taken as a piece, *Locust* is a fragmented glimpse of a few offbeat, so-called Hollywood characters (immigrants), a novel of vignettes held together by good writing.

Prof. Martin's biography, not unlike his subject's novels, is unsubtly structured, block on block—the method being to cover one site at a time, then move on, and on. For example, in the section on West's personality, the observations of West's friends and acquaintances are collaged into place. The effect is to render an essential West who remains rather uncomplicatedly changeless, albeit eccentric, throughout the full course of his life. This is biographically convenient, but gives Prof. Martin's characterization of West the sense of facile insubstantiality, and, despite the biographer's editorializing profundities, West, rather than deep, comes off only egocentrically young and superficial. In truth, West may have been just those things—young, superficial—despite Prof. Martin's determined intrusions to the contrary. This paradox in the book—the clash between reporting and editorializing—renders West nebulous rather than complex. In a word, it would seem Prof. Martin's preconceptions were not neutralized by his research.

I have found that West's local friends agree he was a warm, gentle man, characteristically quiet, but intensely verbal should the subject interest him; that he was clothes-conscious, about six feet tall, dressing in the English manner (called Brooks Brothers by Hollywood friends); that he was a broad reader, a book collector, a hunter, fisherman, a dog lover; that women found him attractive (Leonard Fields: "There were always a lot of pretty girls around. Pep had some basic strength, warmth, that women liked."); that his hair was reddish-brown, complexion pale; that his eyes were soft, broodingly watchful; that he was lethargic, tentative, sometimes shy, guardedly amiable. His lethargy (thus the name, Pep) would be lost in an instant when discussing books or authors. He was a great one for thrusting a discovery on a friend—B. Traven's *Treasure of the Sierra Madre* excited him greatly. It is interesting to note that Jo Conway, West's secretary, is emphatic when she says: "Pep had commenced to love Hollywood." She goes on to tell of an afternoon, when, returning from Lucy's, a famed local restaurant, Pep came charging into the office, declaring—"I just saw Ginger Rogers! She said hello to me!" This glimpse of West is in contrast to the bigger-than-Hollywood characterization offered by Prof. Martin. Leonard Fields, West's first producer at Republic, is a singularly perceptive and articulate gentleman. Accordingly, his remark that West did not like to rub elbows with the hoi polloi is a remark worth pondering when evaluating West's temperament, for the novelist was, after all, an Ivy Leaguer, European traveled, a published novelist, decidedly class-conscious—Nathaniel von Wallenstein Weinstein. Prof. Martin suggests his subject was at home in any company, virtually an elbow rubber. A little research, too, informs us that West lived in fine homes and apartments in Hollywood for those several years after his stay at the Pa-Va-Sed on Ivar. What Prof. Martin does not realize is that Hollywood, in the thirties, was, north of Hollywood Boulevard, a fashionable residential area. It was not until World War II that Hollywood and its famous Boulevard deteriorated to its present seaminess. Categorically, West never resided in anything or anywhere —in Hollywood—which in any way could be construed as Prof. Martin's "seamy." Finally, it was in Hollywood he met the Golden Girl, My Sister Eileen, and, in love with his surroundings, making money by the ton, he purchased a frond-fringed hacienda—with a separate, chimneyed dwelling for writing—on two acres in North Hollywood. In 1937, in the car episode with Leonard Fields which gave rise to Prof. Martin's portentous "doomed to live," West was beginning to make a work of art of his life. A few brief years later, West was stunningly successful. Nathanael West had not been betrayed by the American Dream.

In other matters of research, it does seem that our biographer extends himself to make the very most of the leanest facts. He employs the technique of linking in one way or another—obscurely or tangentially, but assertively—his subject's name with those of the immortals: Einstein, Humphrey Bogart, Pound, Joyce, Edmund Wilson, Faulkner, F. Scott Fitzgerald. This latter linkage is strained to the breaking point. Fitzgerald and West are labeled close friends. Throughout the biography, as early as Chapter 1, the Fitzgerald-West alliance is strongly thrust at us. In explaining West's fatal car crash (pp. 6 and 7): "Perhaps West was hurrying back from Mexicali—he did not usually leave so early—preoccupied with the news of the death of his friend F. Scott Fitzgerald, who had died on 21 December at 5:30 of a heart attack . . . his death was made known on the twenty-second." But did West know of Fitzgerald's death? It seems unlikely. Calexico is a world removed from Hollywood.

My talks with Frances Kroll Ring reveal that Fitzgerald did not see much of West: "I remember perhaps a couple of occasions; but it simply wasn't the time to start up a friendship. He was a loner, mostly, in those days. I know he thought highly of Sid Perelman." Although Frances Kroll Ring was Scott Fitzgerald's secretary for the last twenty-one months of the author's life, she was not interviewed by Prof. Martin. We should remember that 1939 was Fitzgerald's difficult, even desperate year. His relationship with Sheilah Graham was stormy. His fiscal problems were becoming insurmountable. Not until December, 1939, did Fitzgerald take hold of himself, and, on the wagon, work consistently at his novel, stories, and screen plays. Meanwhile, West was squiring Eileen McKenney, a courtship ending in marriage. It would seem the two authors had few opportunities to form a close bond. Fitzgerald did attend a West party on 13 December 1940, while, too, coincidentally, their respective deaths occurred shortly thereafter, and one day apart, i.e., 21 December and 22 December. These proximities achieve an effect, but do not establish a friendship.

I feel Prof. Martin's book aims for effects which must be challenged. Perhaps, as so often happens in the biographical weal, a little hero worship fires the professor's kiln. Flesh and blood come out cold statuary—to be appraised and viewed, rather than to be sensed, felt, heard, understood. In literary criticism, too, we frequently see a tidy dichotomy drawn between the greats and the hacks. Somewhere, surely, there must be room for the many good writers who ply their trade, occasionally exciting us with flashes, even chapters, peculiar to themselves. Nathanael West falls somewhere in this realm. True, he strove for higher ground. His novels have large meanings. His themes are entertaining. He exercised laboriously delicate care over each word. But the means by which he achieved his meanings were too spare, too simple, only rudimentary. His novels are, in truth, only gaudy necklaces of short stories. He was no prophet. No martyr, either. He was a fine writer. But to bronze such moderate stature can only be pretentious.

Hans Günter Schitter. *Die drei letzten Romane F. Scott Fitzgeralds: Untersuchungen zur Spiegelung von zeitgeschichtlichem und mythischem Bewusstsein im literarischen Kunstwerk.* Bonn: H. Bouvier, 1968. (Abhandlungen zur Kunst-, Musik- und Literaturwissenschaft, Band 69) 254 pp. DM 33.oo.

By Horst H. Kruse

Though the reading public in Germany has never taken Fitzgerald to its heart in quite the same manner as his American readers have, his novels and stories have long been standard fare for the German student of American literature, satisfying a curiosity about American society more frequently than about its literature. Hans Günter Schitter's study of Fitzgerald's last three novels—originally a University of Freiburg dissertation—strikes an even balance between these two interests. In investigating contemporary and mythic consciousness as reflected in *The Great Gatsby, Tender is the Night* and *The Last Tycoon*, it picks up where previous studies—both American and German—have left off. Excluding all biographical material, Schitter concentrates on the text of the three novels, taking them not primarily as expressions of the author's individuality, but rather as evidence of the working of a collective unconsciousness that Fitzgerald encountered in his surroundings and in which he himself shared. In the terms of C. G. Jung: The agents, the situations and the events as described in the works of Fitzgerald are archetypal expressions of their times and of the fundamental experiences that these times provided, a reflection and an illumination of the existential condition of the American of the 1920's and the 1930's. Archetypes, in Jung's sense of the word, are pictorial representations of the collective unconsciousness, and as such they constitute myth. Jay Gatsby, Dick Diver and Monroe Stahr as well as some of the minor characters, thus, are seen as mythical heroes who embody different but closely related stages in the development of a specifically American as well as a universal human consciousness. Gatsby emerges as an embodiment of the myth of the beginning, the initial stage of an American consciousness. A naive, optimistic dreamer, he ignores reality, escapes reality, and thus saves the dream. But the inevitable confrontation of dream and reality has only been postponed. Dick Diver, caught between ethic and aesthetic aspirations, trying out various roles until he loses his identity, is a "psychological" rather than a "mythic" hero, but he nevertheless becomes a representative character. A "spoiled priest," he fails to communicate his message to a disoriented world because he has lost faith in himself. The American dream of a new beginning has reached its end. In Monroe Stahr, however, a new mythic figure arises, a figure whose ethics are based on "tolerance, kindness, forbearance, and even affection" and who succeeds in realizing these traditional virtues in an exemplary ascetic life:—the prophecy of a new, a utopian myth?

What keeps this study from becoming a speculative inquiry into the collective psyche of the American is the author's explicit aim not merely to consider myth as such, but to examine—in the light of Fitzgerald's novels—the operation of myth in history, and, most importantly, the way in which myth has found its artistic expression. The approach—needless to say—works best for *The Great Gatsby*, a novel whose "mythic quality" has long been recognized and whose "ideographic method" has been commented on by Lionel Trilling. Schitter convincingly demonstrates how all aspects of the novel combine to establish the "mythic character" of Gatsby, paying due attention to the function of narrative technique, to legendizing qualities, to mythic properties in the use of symbols, to symbolism in the handling of atmosphere, to the magic of Gatsby's personality, to the loneliness of the mythic hero, to the archetypal symbolism of the fable itself, to mythic dimensions in the handling of time, and to the static quality of Gatsby's mythic existence.

The treatment of *Tender is the Night* strikes me as less successful, partly because the novel does not quite as readily lend itself to this approach, partly also because Schitter fails to follow the pattern adopted for *The Great Gatsby*. Still sound as literary criticism, his reading of the second novel does not seem to aim at a *systematic* investigation of its mythic qualities. Nonetheless, the basic thesis that

Gatsby and Diver represent successive stages in the development of a specifically American collective (un)consciousness can be allowed to stand, and Schitter is careful enough not to push it much further: *The Last Tycoon*, certainly better suited to his purposes than *Tender is the Night,* receives but a sketchy treatment. His diffidence toward an unfinished text precludes a thorough exploration of much of the overt symbolism, and it seems only appropriate that he should use a question mark when speaking of Monroe Stahr as the embodiment of a "future-oriented myth."

University of Kiel

Bruce Kellner. *Carl Van Vechten and the Irreverent Decades,* Norman: University of Oklahoma Press, 1968. $7.95.

By Paul Padgette

Recent accounts of the Lost Generation abound in biographies of the literary lions of the Twenties. Future historians will be able to trace every moment of the literary life of our most sophisticated decade. In this period American writers emerged and joined the mainstream of world literature as American books gained critical attention abroad.

Nineteenth Century America had had her giants: Irving, Emerson, Twain, James—all familiar to readers in England and on the Continent. They were our earliest literary expatriates. Poe and Whitman had to wait for wide recognition both at home and abroad; Melville, alas, didn't gain acceptance until well into this century.

The more recent movement began in 1903 when Gertrude Stein took up residence in Paris. She has been followed in the ensuing decades by many persons whose names first blossomed in the Twenties. Not the least of these, of course, were Fitzgerald and Hemingway. However, not all who came to Paris remained. Sherwood Anderson preferred America. Carl Van Vechten was another who came, saw and returned.

Carl Van Vechten was born in Iowa in 1880, studied at the University of Chicago, began writing as a reporter on Hearst's *Chicago American* and graduated to New York and fame in 1906. He joined the *New York Times* as assistant to music critic Richard Aldrich.

Following the tradition, he tried Europe, and was the *Times* correspondent. His expatriate days were short and he returned to live in New York until his death in 1964. The Atlantic crossings were numerous, but he never entertained the idea of a foreign residence. Alice B. Toklas said in *What Is Remembered*, "Avery Hopwood and Carl Van Vechten together created modern New York." (Playwright Hopwood is remembered with Mary Roberts Rinehart as co-author of the play, "The Bat," based on Rinehart's novel, *The Circular Staircase*, which ran for 867 performances in 1920.) Although the Toklas statement is an exaggeration, it conveys the spirit of Van Vechten's New York life-style. His enthusiasm illuminates the pages of his critical writings on dance, music and theatre, and it reaches its zenith in the series of the New York novels: *Peter Whiffle, The Blind Bow Boy, Firecrackers* and *Parties.*

No novel more than *Parties* (1930), the sub-title is "Scenes From Contemporary New York Life," savors the last years of the decade more succulently. Van Vechten called them the Splendid Drunken Twenties, an epitaph both Hemingway and Fitzgerald could second. It is a modern black comedy of manners, the central characters fashioned after Scott and Zelda Fitzgerald. Bruce Kellner in his recent biography on Van Vechten comments, ". . . years after those lights have been extinguished, there is a strong flavor of bitters." David and Rilda Westlake (Scott and Zelda) and their drunken friends personify "jagged sophistication" as they move in a repeating circle of parties, sleep, eat, drink. Fitzgerald's flappers invented the decade and Van Vechten's inebriates ended it—from innocence to decadence in ten years. Beneath the veneer of high life, the strong and basic moral values of Middle America are implied by Van Vechten.

Kellner's study, *Carl Van Vechten And The Irreverent Decades*, University of Oklahoma Press (1968), details Van Vechten's life in what is the definitive study until sealed letters, diaries and other documents are opened for inspection several years in the future at the New York Public Library and Yale University Library, both depositories of Van Vechten Collections. Kellner was fortunate in his friendship with his subject for more than a decade before CVV's death, which allowed first hand interpretation not always available to a biographer. However, this is the strength as well as the weakness of the book. Many developments in CVV's life, particularly in the early years, are casually discussed or avoided. Certain questions form in the reader's mind. For example, the situation around Van Vechten's first marriage and divorce are veiled in bland statements of public fact as in the celebrated incident of Van Vechten's time in jail for failure to pay alimony. The reader wants to know why they divorced or, indeed, why they ever married since the only obvious attraction was a childhood in Iowa in common. In today's vernacular: She was "straight," Van Vechten was "hip" or, at least, "mod."

On the other hand, Kellner's chapter on CVV's second wife, the actress Fania Marinoff, is his most winning one. With keen insight he draws a vivid portrait of her early struggles and climb to prominence on the New York stage. Van Vechten's devotion to her is manifest.

The accumulation of detail during the productive years of writing is carefully drawn and engagingly presented. The number and variety of people who entered, remained and passed through Van Vechten's eighty-four years is probably unequalled among American writers. These incidents are re-created with clarity and are the greatest asset of the biography as literary history. A bibliography on the subject and secondary sources is scholarly in content and extensive enough to entice F/H fans. The bibliography alone is worth the price of the book. To add to this delight are sixty-four pages of fascinating illustrations. In today's market, only a university press can put this kind of volume together for $7.95!

Van Vechten's output was not limited to the writing of his seven novels; he was a respected voice on music and theatre. In the early years of this century he became America's first dance critic. A total of nine volumes of criticism, selected and expanded from newspaper and magazine origins, were published between 1915 and 1926. His detailed history of the cat, *Tiger In The House* (1920), remains in print after fifty years. In 1932 he published his *Sacred And Profane Memories*, and in 1955 Yale Library issued two small volumes of *Fragments From An Unwritten Autobiography* culled from Yale *Gazette* pieces over the years.

Only four years after his own first book, Van Vechten wrote an introduction to another's work. In the following years, and into his last year, he continued to write prefaces, introductions, edit books and worked to help other writers. As literary executor and long-time friend, he edited eight volumes of Gertrude Stein's writings for Yale in the 1950s. As sponsor and promoter, Van Vechten furthered the careers of others and created collections to house their works in appropriate institutions.

A new career dominating the last three decades of his life was portrait photography. Fifteen thousand persons from the performing and creative arts sat for him at his invitation. Van Vechten's two celebrated photographs of Scott Fitzgerald in 1937 have been widely reproduced. One or the other illustrated the FSF *Letters*, both Andrew Turnbull's and Arthur Mizener's biographies, and the Bodley Head dust jacket of *Afternoon Of An Author*. Kellner's book includes a sampling list of the sitters in a "Photographic Catalogue" in addition to thirty-two pages of photographs by Van Vechten.

The personal relationship between CVV and FSF was casual and literary in character. Turnbull's *Letters* include five from FSF to CVV. Mizener, Turnbull and Kellner all include references to both writers and recall the many parties (including the famed Theodore Dreiser fiasco) at which both were guests or hosts. The same friendly relationship is not in evidence where Hemingway is concerned. According to Van Vechten, in conversation with this reviewer several years ago, he only met Hemingway once. Neither one wished to repeat the experience. Hemingway's falling out with Gertrude Stein is implied since Van Vechten was devoted to her. There are sixteen references to FSF in the Kellner index, and, of course, one of the FSF photographs is reproduced. Only one reference to Hemingway is in the index, and that only in a passing reference to Paris.

Perhaps the core value of this book is as literary history. Because of Van Vechten's extremely wide influence and personal acquaintance with so many people for so many years, his life, in essence, is an account of more than a half century of literature in America, and to a lesser extent, England and Europe. Kellner's biography portrays this era from a viewpoint that is intellectual, penetrating, and not without good humor. What more can be expected from a book, or, indeed, from a man?

Aaron Latham. *Crazy Sundays: F. Scott Fitzgerald in Hollywood.* New York: Viking, 1971. $7.95

By Alan Margolies

Among the many books about Hollywood written during the past few years, a good number, including Bob Thomas's *Thalberg* and *King Cohn* and Bosley Crowther's *The Lion's Share,* have been intended for both the general moviegoer as well as the expert. Both Thomas and Crowther are aware of the value of a good yarn and they include many in their books. On the other hand, both writers have done at least some original research. The experts know of the distortions in these books and they approach them with wariness, but they use them because they do contain some valuable material.

Crazy Sundays, at least in part, belongs to this category. Its author has interviewed many people and has done much reading. He has repeated a good many stories about Fitzgerald and Hollywood and has introduced more than a few new ones. He has told his story in such a way that, after a while, the reader begins to feel that Hollywood really was like this during the time that Fitzgerald was there. In addition, he has done much research both in the Fitzgerald Papers at Princeton and in the Hollywood studio archives, and he has come up with some material previously unavailable. The scholar will find a good deal in this book that is interesting, but he will have to tread with care.

Mr. Latham demonstrates how the formative years of Fitzgerald's life parallel the formative years of the movies. In addition, by pointing out numerous examples from the novelist's fiction, he demonstrates Fitzgerald's use of film subjects and imagery. He tells us much about the writer's life in Hollywood, contributing such new material as Fitzgerald's relationship with Bill Warren, his friendship with George Oppenheimer and Frances and Albert Hackett, and his meeting with Maureen O'Sullivan. Most importantly, he discusses in detail the writer's film scripts.

For example, he describes Fitzgerald's treatment for a silent version of *This Side of Paradise* that never was produced and demonstrates how it differed from the novel so as to conform to the conventions of the movies. He describes Fitzgerald's collaboration with Bill Warren on a treatment of *Tender is the Night* and how that, too, differed from the original. In his analysis of Fitzgerald's later scripts, Mr. Latham not only specifically shows us what the author wrote, but he attempts to draw parallels between this work and his fiction. Especially interesting and invaluable are the conference notes and the script material obtained in Hollywood.

But the book has many defects. Mr. Latham's prose, at times, is extremely slick, an effect that may satisfy the general reader but only annoy the scholar. Fitzgerald is described, while sitting at an MGM writer's table, as having a "presence as bland as the potato soup." Of Shirley Temple's mother Mr. Latham writes, "The Captain of the Good Ship Lollypop had something of a pirate for a mother." Of the novelist's final work he writes, "The prose in the new novel, *The Last Tycoon,* was so alive that it almost seemed to get up and walk, and yet Scott wrote most of it lying flat on his back."

Mr. Latham's taste is not much more acceptable, but again this probably will appeal to the popular audience. In describing the novelist's first meeting with Sheilah Graham, Mr. Latham parallels it with Monroe Stahr's glimpse of Kathleen (who resembles the producer's late wife), and writes of Fitzgerald, ". . . of course the author's own wife was not really dead, only crazy." Other stories involving Mrs. Fitzgerald and Miss Graham will probably amuse the average reader even more, but others may find them completely inappropriate.

Also disturbing are the author's many tortured comparisons. "In September of 1917, his senior year," he writes, for example, "Fitzgerald achieved the rank of professional author, making his first sale—a poem for which *Poet Lore* paid two dollars. The same year Charlie Chaplin, twenty-seven, made a sale also: he signed a contract with First National for one million dollars a year. Appropriately, one of Chaplin's first pictures, filmed in 1914, had been called *Making a Living*." The relationship seems strained. And does Mr. Latham know that *Making a Living* was not a representative tramp film, and that it was about a shrewd, nervy swindler?

In his interviews, Mr. Latham has relied on the memories of those who must recall events of thirty years ago and more. People do forget, or, at the least, they unconsciously distort, and this is especially true in Hollywood. Are the stories with their seemingly imagined descriptions as accurate as they purport to be? Of "Broken Soil," for example, Mr. Latham says that Edwin H. Knopf "proudly sent his screenplay to Scott." But Knopf wrote me in early 1970 that he did not know how Fitzgerald obtained his copy of the work.

Finally, there are many factual and interpretative errors and many omissions in *Crazy Sundays*. Two of Fitzgerald's St. Paul plays, "The Girl from 'Lazy J' " and *Assorted Spirits*, for example, are not mentioned. There is no discussion of the scenario that Fitzgerald was supposedly writing for Dorothy Gish in 1920; nor is there any mention of his poor 1923 screenplay for the Film Guild's silent gangster film *Grit*, and of his titles for Allan Dwan's 1923 film *The Glimpses of the Moon*. Mr. Latham omits any discussion of Fitzgerald's plans for a ballet film and his treatment "Gracie at Sea," both written during the middle 1930s and omits as well a few of the films, including *Brooklyn Bridge* (for Twentieth Century-Fox), worked on during the last Hollywood visit.

George Hannaford's name ("Magnetism"), Tony Barrett's name (the hero in Knopf's *The Wedding Night*), and Ursula Parrott's name (author of the short story "Infidelity") are all misspelled. Did *This Side of Paradise* really sell 26,000 copies during its first week? Notwithstanding the statement that Fitzgerald did little in 1926, he did produce the first drafts of what eventually would be *Tender is the Night.* "An Alcoholic Case" was published *prior* to Fitzgerald's last trip to Hollywood. The *Winter Carnival* treatment is *eleven* pages long, and a three-page sequence outline also exists. Mrs. Edwin Jarrett *and* Kate Ogelbay wrote the stage version of *Tender is the Night.* Carl Dreyer's *The Passion of Joan of Arc* was not a spectacular, and in no way can Fitzgerald's introduction of a magic lipstick in *Lipstick* be comparable to the many great effects of Georges Méliès. Finally, Mr. Latham believes that *Infidelity* and *Cosmopolitan* were good scripts; not everyone who has read them is of the same opinion—and not everyone sees *Infidelity* as *'The Great Gatsby* revisited."

But those interested in Fitzgerald and film will have to read *Crazy Sundays* because of the previously unavailable material dealing with the scripts.

John Jay College of Criminal Justice, CUNY.

Fitzgerald Checklist

Anon. "A Positive Postscript," *The Johns Hopkins Magazine*, XXI (October 1970), 9. Concerning Fitzgerald's gravestone.

———. Proof of biographical article on Fitzgerald in *The Standard American Encyclopedia*. *Fine Books and Manuscripts,* Parke-Bernet Galleries, 13 October 1970, Sale number 3088.

Astro, Richard. "*Vandover and the Brute* and *The Beautiful and Damned*: A Search for Thematic and Stylistic Reinterpretations," *Modern Fiction Studies*, XIV, 4 (Winter 1968), 397-413.

Benson, Sally. "The Young and the Beautiful." Play based on the Josephine stories, produced by The Company Wing. 15, 16, 22 and 23 January 1970 in New York City; directed by Sal Allocco.

Blake, Nelson M. *Novelist's America: Fiction as History, 1910-1940*. Syracuse: Syracuse University Press, 1969. Chapters on Fitzgerald, Wolfe, Lewis, Faulkner, Steinbeck, Dos Passos, Farrell, Wright.

Boyle, Thomas E. "Unreliable Narration in *The Great Gatsby*," *Bulletin of the Rocky Mountain Modern Language Association,* XXIII (1969) 21-26.

Bready, James H. "Reading Mencken's Mail," *Baltimore Sun Magazine* (24 January 1971), 4-5, 7.

Bruccoli, Matthew J., ed. *Profile of F. Scott Fitzgerald.* Columbus, Ohio: Merrill Publishing, 1971. Contents: "My Generation," F. Scott Fitzgerald; "Introduction to *The Portable F. Scott Fitzgerald*," John O'Hara; "Scott Fitzgerald's Critical Opinions," and "Scott Fitzgerald's Reading," John Kuehl; "*The Great Gatsby*—A Study in Literary Reputation," G. Thomas Tanselle and Jackson R. Bryer; "*Tender is the Night*—Reception and Reputation," Matthew J. Bruccoli; and "Fitzgerald Attends My Fitzgerald Seminar," Vance Bourjailly.

Bufkin, E. C. "A Pattern of Parallel and Double: The Function of Myrtle in *The Great Gatsby*," *Modern Fiction Studies*, XV (Winter 1969-70), 517-524.

Burhans, Clinton S., Jr. " 'Magnificently Attune to Life': The Value of 'Winter Dreams,' " *Studies in Short Fiction*, VI (Summer 1969), 401-412.

_____ . "Structure and Theme in *This Side of Paradise*," *Journal of English and Germanic Philology*, LXVIII (October 1969), 605-624.

Elmore, Albert E. "An Interpretation of *The Great Gatsby*," *Dissertation Abstracts*, XXIX (1969), 2706A (Vanderbilt).

_____ . "Color and Cosmos in *The Great Gatsby*." *Sewanee Review*, LXXVIII (Summer 1970), 427-443.

Finney, Ben. *Feet First*. New York: Crown, 1971. Includes reminiscences of Fitzgerald and Hemingway.

Fitzgerald, F. Scott. *"—and a few missing words would destroy so much"*. Columbia, S.C.: 1970. A keepsake of 200 numbered copies, privately printed for distribution by the Center for Editions of American Authors at the conference on Editing and American Literature, Embassy of the United States of America, London, England, 1 July 1970. Facsimile of typescript of the first page of "My Generation," with a note from Fitzgerald to his secretary.

_____ . *As Ever, Scott Fitz*—ed. Matthew J. Bruccoli with Jennifer McCabe Atkinson. New York: Lippincott, 1971. "Foreword" by Scottie Fitzgerald Smith.

_____ . *All The Sad Young Men*. New York, 1926. Inscribed: "For Dorothy Hale Litchfield from hers faithfully F. Scott Fitzgerald. Villa St. Louis. Juan-les Pins, France. June, 1926." #306, *Paul Richards, Autographs*, No. 56.

_____ . Autograph Letter Signed to Marya Mannes, Paris, 21 October 1925: "Thank you for writing me about *Gatsby*—I especially appreciate your letter because women, and even intelligent women, haven't generally cared for it. . . . America's greatest promise is that something is going to happen, and after a while you get tired of waiting because nothing ever happens to American people except that they grow old, and nothing happens to American art because America is the story of the moon that never rose. . . . My new novel is marvellous. I'm in the first chapter. . . . Can you name a single American artist except James G. Whistler (who lived in England) who didn't die of drink? . . ." #44, *An Auction of Literary and Artistic Materials for the Benefit of Antiwar Congressional Candidates*, Gotham Book Mart Gallery, 8 October 1970.

_____. *Dear Scott/Dear Max,* ed. John Kuehl and Jackson F. Bryer. New York: Scribners, 1971.

_____. *F. Scott Fitzgerald in His Own Time: A Miscellany,* ed. Matthew J. Bruccoli and Jackson R. Bryer. Kent, Ohio: Kent State University Press, 1971. Collected material, most of which has not appeared in book form. Part one consisting of introductions, poems, parodies, essays, blurbs, and book reviews by Fitzgerald; the second, of interviews, parodies, editorials, and reviews about Fitzgerald.

_____. *Taps at Reveille.* New York, 1935. Inscribed: "For Sylvia Lewis in memory of those days when she translated *A Rebours* for me in my cork-lined converted Pullman F. Scott ("Huysmans") Fitzgerald The Flood—1938." #55, *Miscellanea Mainly Literary and Historical Including a Large Selection of Californiana and Other Western Americana,* Bennett and Marshall, No. 9.

_____. *Tender is the Night.* Scribner Library printing 0-5.70. The Cowley text, apparently reprinted by accident: the Scribner Library normally uses the 1934 text.

_____. *This Side of Paradise.* New York, 1920. Inscribed to Bert Cohn. #39, *English and American First Editions,* Parke-Bernet Galleries, Sale Number 3130, 8 December 1970.

Rimbaud/Fitzgerald/Schmidt. "Documentary: 'Voyelles,' by Arthur Rimbaud; 'Translation,' by F. Scott Fitzgerald; 'Notes.' by Paul Schmidt," *Delos: A Journal on and of Translation,* II (1968), 100-104.

Foster, Richard. "Mailer and the Fitzgerald Tradition," *Novel: A Forum on Fiction,* I (1968), 219-230.

French, Warren. "Fiction: A Handful of Survivors," in *The Forties: Fiction, Poetry, Drama.* DeLand, Fla.: Everett/Edwards, 1969, pp. 7-32.

Gindin, James. "Gods and Fathers in F. Scott Fitzgerald's Novels," *Modern Language Quarterly*, XXX (March 1969), 64-85.

Goodwin, Donald W., M.D. "The Alcoholism of F. Scott Fitzgerald," *Journal of the American Medical Association*, CCXII (6 April 1970), 86-90. Prints part of a 1931 letter Fitzgerald sent to an American psychiatrist describing a dream.

"I am in an upstairs apartment where I live with my Mother, old, white-haired, clumsy and in mourning. On another floor are a group of handsome and rich young men, whom I seem to have known slightly as a child and now want to know better, but they look at me suspiciously. I talk to one who is agreeable and not at all snobbish, but obviously he does not encourage my acquaintance. . . . During this time I discover that there is a dance downstairs to which I am not invited, I feel that if they knew better how important I was, I should be invited.

Mother and I have been quarreling . . . I go downstairs again, wander into the doorway of a sort of ballroom, see caterers at work and then am suddenly shamed by realizing this is the party to which I am not invited. Meeting one of the young men in the hall, I lose all poise and stammer something absurd. I leave the house, but as I leave Mother calls something to me in a too audible voice from an upper story. I don't know whether I am angry with her for clinging to me, or because I am ashamed of her for not being young and chic, or for disgracing my conventional sense by calling out, or because she might guess I'd been hurt and pity me, which would have been unendurable, or all those things. Anyhow I call back at her some terse and furious reproach. . . .

Mother and I were hungry. We wanted bacon and eggs, but mother was only given bacon and I was only given eggs. On being reminded that she'd only just had a collation a little before, my mother objected that the portion had been small, and was met with an austere, characteristic snub.

We returned home. On entering the house mother gave me a book, asking me pathetically (but remember her patheticness almost always repelled me) if it wasn't a particular book I'd loved and lost in my childhood. It was almost that book but not quite. . . . The dream now became an onimous night mare. . . ."

Graham, Sheilah. *The Garden of Allah*. New York: Crown, 1970.

Gross, Barry. "The Dark Side of Twenty-five: Fitzgerald and *The Beautiful and Damned*," Bucknell Review, XVI (Winter 1968), 40-52.

_____. "*This Side of Paradise:* The Dominating Intention," *Studies in the Novel*, I (Spring 1969), 51-59.

Gross, T.L. "F. Scott Fitzgerald: The Hero in Retrospect," *South Atlantic Quarterly* (Winter 1968), 64-77.

Hamblen, A.A. "The Fitzgerlads' Coming of Age," *University Review*, XXXV (Winter 1968), 157-160.

Hoenisch, Michael. "Die Werke F. Scott Fitzgeralds: Entwurf einer Chronologie der Entstehungsdaten," *Jarhbuch für Amerikastudien*, XIV (1969), 185-218.

Kenyon, Nina N. "Self-Hatred as a Basis for Criticism of American Society," *Dissertation Abstracts*, XXIX (1969), 2713A (St. Louis University).

Klise, Thomas S. *Gatsby—The Great American Myth.* Peoria, Ill.: Klise Co., n.d. Phonograph narration, with reading script, for filmstrip.

Kopf, Josephine Z. "Meyer Wolfsheim and Robert Cohn: A Study of a Jewish Type and Stereotype," *Tradition: A Journal of Orthodox Jewish Thought*, X (1969), 93-104.

Kruse, Horst. " 'April Is the Cruellest Month . . .'—Natudarstellung und die Selbsterkenntnis des Erzahlers in F. Scott Fitzgeralds *The Great Gatsby,*" *Literatur in Wissenschaft und Unterricht,* I (1968), 28-40.

_____. "F. Scott Fitzgerald: *The Pat Hobby Stories,*" in *Amerikanische Erzählunge von Hawthorne bis Salinger: Interpretationen. Kieler Beiträge zur Anglistik und Amerikanistik, Band 6,* ed. Paul G. Buchloh. Neumünster: Karl Wachloltz, 1968, pp. 155-186.

Latham, John Aaron. *Crazy Sundays.* New York: Viking, 1971. Excerpt: "Performing Arts/A Day at the Studio—Scott Fitzgerald in Hollywood," *Harper's Magazine*, CCXLI (November 1970), 38-39, 41-43, 46, 48, 50.

Lee, Lynn A. "The Significant Popular Novel as American Literature, 1920-1930; 1950-1960," *Dissertation Abstracts*, XXX (1969), 329A (Minnesota).

Long, Robert E. "The Hero and Society in the Earlier Novels of F. Scott Fitzgerald: A Study in Literary Milieu," *Dissertation Abstracts*, XXIX (1969), 2715A-16A (Columbia).

Mayfield, Sara. *Exiles from Paradise*. New York: Delacorte Press, 1971.

McCall, Dan. " 'The Self-Same Song that Found a Path': Keats and *The Great Gatsby*," *American Literature*, XLII (January 1971), 521-530.

McCarthy, Paul. "Daisy's Voice in The Great Gatsby," *Lock Haven Review*, XI (1969), 51-56.

Millani, Sister Mary E., M.Z.S.H. "Irony and Symbolism: An Examination of the Longer Fiction of F. Scott Fitzgerald," *Dissertation Abstracts*, XXIX (1969), 2718A (St. Louis University).

Miller, James E., Jr. *"The Great Gatsby" (F. Scott Fitzgerald)*. DeLand, Florida: Everett/Edwards, n.d. In The Twentieth Century American Novel series of recorded lectures in the Cassette Curriculum.

Murari, Timeri. "Bricktop: In Her Corner," *The Washington Post* (21 December 1970), C1, C3. Unreliable account of Fitzgerald hesitating to enter Bricktop's club because he had no money.

Perelman, S.J. "The Machismo Mystique, or Some Various Aspects of Masculinity, as Demonstrated by Ernest Hemingway, Mike Todd, F. Scott Fitzgerald, and a Sensuous Shrimp from Providence, Rhode Island," *McCall's*, XCVIII (February 1971), 88-89, 168-169.

Rao, Nageswara. "The Structure of *Tender is the Night*," *Literary Criterion*, VIII (Summer 1969), 54-62.

Rodda, Peter. *"The Great Gatsby*," *English Studies in Africa*, XI (1968), 96-126.

Rouge, Peter. "F. Scott Fitzgerald: La Femme et la mort," *Etudes Anglaises*, XXI (1968), 160-167.

Rylander, Edith. "Two Minnesota Boys," *Sinclair Lewis Newsletter*, II (Spring 1970), 5-6.

Stafford, W.T. "Fitzgerald's *The Great Gatsby*," *Explicator*, XXVIII (March 1970), #57.

371

Stern, Milton R. *The Golden Moment The Novels of F. Scott Fitzgerald.* Urbana: University of Illinois Press, 1970.

Tamke, Alexander R. "The 'Gat' in Gatsby: Neglected Aspect of a Novel," *Modern Fiction Studies*, XIV (Winter 1968/69), 443-445.

White, William. "Hemingway and Fitzgerald," in *American Literary Scholarship: An Annual: 1967*, ed. James Woodress. Durham: Duke University Press, 1969, 97-112.

Winter, Keith. "Artistic Tensions: The Enigma of F. Scott Fitzgerald," *Research Studies, A Quarterly Publication of Washington State*, XXXVII (December 1969), 285-297.

The publication of Fitzgerald's letter to Hemingway in the 1970 *Annual* was reported in an AP article by Rob Wood. This article was printed in the following newspapers:

Anonymous. "Letter Casts Fitzgerald as 'Critic,' " *Worcester Telegram* (5 January 1971), 20.

———. "Hemingway Help," *The Washington Post* (5 January 1971), C6.

———. "Fitzgerald Letter to 'Poppa' Bared," *Durham Morning Herald* (5 January 1971), 4B.

———. "Letter Sheds Light on Polishing of 'Sun Also Rises,' " *Newark Evening News* (5 January 1971).

———. "Fitzgerald Letter to Hemingway Published," *Toronto Daily Star* (5 January 1971), 18.

———. *Philadelphia Inquirer* (6 January 1971).

———. "Fitzgerald Letter to Hemingway Printed: Urged Changes in Novel," *Los Angeles Times* (5 January 1971), 16.

———. "Hemingway Cut Novel on Fitzgerald's Advice," *Kansas City Times* (11 January 1971), 3B.

———. "Professor Says Scott Fitzgerald Influenced Hemingway's 'The Sun': Criticism Affected First Four Chapters," *Arizona Daily Star* (5 January 1971).

———. "Scott to Ernest," *Atlanta Constitution* (5 January 1971).

_____. "Fitzgerald Was Critical of Hemingway Novel," *Omaha World-Herald* (5 January 1971).

_____. "F. Scott Fitzgerald Letter Found: Prompted 'Sun Also Rises' Revision," *Peoria Journal Star* (6 January 1971).

_____. "Publish Fitzgerald Letter of Advice to Hemingway," *The Des Moines Register* (5 January 1971).

_____. "Conspiring to Improve a Plot," *Newsday* (6 January 1971).

Wood, Rob. "Letter Shows Hemingway Took Fitzgerald's Advice," *Miami News* (6 January 1971).

_____. "Letter Published Urging Famous Book Revision," *Mobile Register* (5 January 1971).

Zelda Sayre Fitzgerald

Fitzgerald, Zelda Sayre. "Miss Ella," *Ladies' Home Journal,* LXXXVIII (January 1971), 78-79, 106-107. Reprinted from *Scribner's Magazine*, XC (December 1931).

Milford, Nancy. *Ladies' Home Journal,* LXXXVII (June 1970), 117-121. Excerpts from *Zelda.*

_____ . "Scott and Zelda: Their Wild Years Near Wilmington," *Philadelphia Inquirer Magazine* (13 December 1970), 10-16. Excerpts from *Zelda.*

Reviews of *Zelda:*

Anon. *Time*, XCV (13 June 1970), 99.

_____ . "Putting Zelda Back Centre of Stage," *Times Literary Supplement* (1 January 1971), 8.

Bryer, Jackson R. " 'A Pair Whose Fantasies Matched'," *Baltimore Sun* (14 June 1970), D5.

Donadio, S. *Commentary*, L (August 1970), 54 ff.

Janeway, Elizabeth. *Saturday Review*, LIII (13 June 1970), 30-31.

Long, Robert Emmet. "The Beautiful and the Damned," *Commonweal*, XCII (24 July 1970), 370-371.

Mannes, Marya. "Book of the Week: Biography as Fever Chart," *New York*, III (25 May 1970), 53.

McPherson, William. " 'Zelda,' " *Washington Post* (12 June 1970), B1, B4.

Martin, Judith. " 'Zelda' Life and Legacy," *Washington Post* (7 July 1970), 24.

Mizener, Arthur. "F. Scott's Doomed Princess," *Life*, LXVIII (12 June 1970), 24.

Moore, Harry T. "Zelda," *New York Times Book Review* (14 June 1970), section 7, pp. 1, 10ff.

Reeve, F.D. "The Rise and Fall of a Love Affair," *Washington Post Book World* (28 June 1970).

Samuels, Charles Thomas. "A Woman's Place," *New Republic,* CLXII, 26 (27 June 1970), 24-17.

Schorer, Mark. *Atlantic,* CCXXVI (August 1970), 104-106.

Shapiro, Morton. "Zelda: The Golden Girl of the Flapper Age," *Charlotte Observer* (14 June 1970), 7F.

Sklar, R. *Nation*, CCXI (17 August 1970), 123-124.

Yardley, Jonathan. "About Books," *Greensboro Daily News* (7 June 1970), B3.

Zimmerman, P.D. *Newsweek*, LXXV (15 June 1970), 102ff.

General

Andrist, Ralph K. *et. al. The American Heritage History of the '20s and '30s.* New York: American Heritage, 1970.

Arlen, Michael J. *Exiles*, New York: Farrar, Strauss and Giroux, 1970.

Browne, Ray B. and Donald Pizer. *Themes and Directions in American Literature, Essays in Honor of Leon Howard.* Lafayette, Indiana: Purdue University Studies, 1969.

Frank, Charles P. *Edmund Wilson.* New York: Twayne, 1970.

Gent, George. "Mencken's Letters Displayed Today," *The New York Times* (29 January 1971), 20.

Genthe, Charles V. *American War Narratives 1917-1918: A Study and Bibliography.* New York: David Lewis, 1969.

Gilmer, Walker. *Horace Liveright Publisher of the Twenties.* New York: David Lewis, 1970.

Hilfer, Anthony Channell. *The Revolt from the Village, 1915-1930.* Chapel Hill: University of North Carolina Press, 1969. Review by Clayton A. Holaday in *American Literature*, XLII (May 1970), 261-263.

Keats, John. *You Might as Well Live The Life and Times of Dorothy Parker.* New York: Simon and Schuster, 1970.

Klise, Thomas S. *Thomas Wolfe.* Peoria, Ill.: Klise, n.d. Phonograph narration, with reading script, for filmstrip.

Martin, Jay. *Nathanael West The Art of His Life.* New York: Farrar, Straus & Giroux, 1970.

May, Ernest R. and the Editors of *Life. The "Life" History of the United States, Volume 10: 1917-1932, War, Boom and Bust.* New York: Time, 1964.

Minkoff, George. *A Bibliography of The Black Sun Press.* Great Neck, New York: Minkoff, 1970.

Parker, Dorothy. *Constant Reader.* New York: Viking, 1970.

Sklar, Robert, ed. *The Plastic Age (1917-1930).* New York: Braziller, 1970.

Yates, Norris W. *Robert Benchley.* New York: Twayne, 1968.

News Briefs

Rocky Mountain Modern Language Association. The twenty-fourth annual RMMLA Meeting was held at Sun Valley, Idaho 8-10 October 1970 and had a Hemingway emphasis. Mary Hemingway and John Hemingway spoke, and there were papers by G. H. Jones ("Indian Camp: A Latter-Day Descent to the Dead"), Gerry Brenner ("Epic Machinery in *For Whom the Bell Tolls*"), and Philip Young (on the Nick Adams stories). Mrs. Hemingway described her editorial principles for *Islands in the Stream*: 1) Nothing added; 2) Cut repetition; 3) No improvements. The Winter 1970 issue of *Rendezvous,* distributed at this meeting, had 6 articles on Hemingway.

Anais Nin Journal. Under the Sign of Pisces: Anais Nin and Her Circle is edited by Richard Centing and Benjamin Franklin and can be ordered from The Ohio State University Libraries, Columbus, Ohio 43210—$2.00 per year.

American Literary Manuscripts. This valuable 1960 volume is being revised. Please send corrigenda and addenda to Professor J. A. Robbins, Department of English, Indiana University, Bloomington, Indiana 47401.

Shakespeare & Co. Sculpture.
Michael de Lisio, the New York sculptor, showed at the Minneapolis Institute of Arts in January 1971 many of his 29 portraits of literary figures: Gertrude Stein, Proust, James, Wilde, Auden, Baudelaire, *et al.* Readers of the *F/H Annual* will be interested to learn that among the exhibited portraiture was a terra cotta James Joyce, seated by a table "awaiting proofs of *Ulysses*." Joyce is the first completed study from de Lisio's work-in-progress: an environmental sculpture of Sylvia Beach's Shakespeare and Company bookshop. That re-creation is now expected to be four feet long and three feet deep. De Lisio reports "I haven't figured the height yet, but there will be several tables and the walls will suggest books, etc. In addition to Sylvia Beach, there will be the seated figure of Joyce which is nine inches high, a standing figure of Eliot which is about twelve inches high; also there will be Hemingway, Fitzgerald, Pound, Valery, Gide and Antheil." De Lisio expects to complete the project by

autumn, 1971, and hopes a grant will enable him to have it cast properly in patinated bronze. "Just in case I cannot go on with the project, I am modeling the pieces so that they can live independent of the bookshop."

Photographs of the work-in-progress, as well as an earlier patinated bronze of Pound "Leaving St. Elizabeth's Hospital (1958)," appeared in *Life*, 29 January 1971, p. 10, and in a handsome catalogue issued by the Minneapolis Institute of Arts.—Lawrence D. Stewart, San Fernando Valley State College.

The Great Gatsby Galleys

On 18 May 1971 at Parke-Bernet Galleries a previously unknown set of the uncorrected galleys for the original version of *The Great Gatsby* ("Trimalchio") was sold. The successful bidder was Seven Gables Bookshop at $2,600 acting for the Bruccoli Collection.

Fitzgerald Bibliography Queries

For his F. Scott Fitzgerald bibliography, Matthew J. Bruccoli is seeking locations for Canadian and Australian issues (editions?) of these titles:

This Side of Paradise
    Canada: Copp, Clark, 1920?
    Australia: Hodder & Stoughton, 1921?

Flappers and Philosophers
    Canada: Copp, Clark, 1920?
    Australia: Hodder & Stoughton, 1921?

The Beautiful and Damned
    Australia: Collins, 1922?

Also, can anyone supply information about a Fitzgerald blurb for *The Enormous Room* by e. e. cummings? The blurb seems to have appeared on a dustjacket for another Boni & Liveright book.

Harold Ober

The Fitzgerald/Ober Correspondence

In 1919 after Scribners accepted *This Side of Paradise,* F. Scott Fitzgerald turned his attention to the business of a professional writing career. To earn his living as a writer, he knew he would need the services of a good literary agent, and at the suggestion of the St. Paul writer Grace Flandrau, he approached the Paul Revere Reynolds agency in New York. Within six weeks of Fitzgerald's introduction to the Reynolds agency, he became the special client of Harold Ober, and they began a relationship which lasted for twenty years—the span of Fitzgerald's career.

As Ever, Scott Fitz—, (New York: Lippincott, 1971), edited by Matthew J. Bruccoli with the assistance of Jennifer McCabe Atkinson, with a Foreword by Scottie Fitzgerald Smith, is the first published record of a major American author's relations with his agent. The letters—which include both ends of the correspondence—offer evidence about stories, articles, movie and radio scripts by Fitzgerald, as well as information about contracts Ober negotiated for Fitzgerald and an accounting of Fitzgerald's financial obligations to Ober. The letters tell the story of Fitzgerald's repeated efforts to improve stories, his delight when the prices for his stories were increased by Ober, and the frustrations he knew when his stories were rejected. This collection provides information about Fitzgerald's writing habits; the processes Ober followed in selling Fitzgerald's material; their shared confidence as Fitzgerald unhesitatingly joined Ober when he started his own agency in 1929; Ober's concern for the entire Fitzgerald family during the bad years of the 1930's; the pain both men felt at the 1939 break in their relationship.

Fitzgerald best summed up his reliance on Ober in a letter to Maxwell Perkins after the Fizgerald-Ober break had taken place: "When Harold withdrew from the questionable honor of being my banker, I felt completely numb financially and I suddenly wondered what money was and where it came from. There had always seemed a little more somewhere and now there wasn't."

Dear Scott/Dear Max (New York: Scribners) The F. Scott Fitzgerald-Maxwell E. Perkins correspondence will be reviewed in the next *Annual.* The editors, Jackson R. Bryer and John Kuehl, provided us with a set of the galleys; but it is not right to review such an important work from working proofs. In any case, serious Fitzgerald readers will have to buy this volume. The Fitzgerald-Perkins relationship as seen through this correspondence is too important to be overlooked.

F. Scott Fitzgerald In His Own Time: A Miscellany (Kent, Ohio: Kent State University Press. $12.50) is a volume of uncollected writings by and about Fitzgerald. The by-Fitzgerald section, edited by Matthew J. Bruccoli, includes poems, all the Triangle Club lyrics, *Tiger* and *Nassau Lit* humor, reviews by Fitzgerald, introductions and blurbs, public letters and statements, articles, autobiographical pieces, and Fitzgeraldana. The about-Fitzgerald section, edited by Jackson R. Bryer, includes interviews, reviews of Fitzgerald's work, essays and editorials, parodies, and obituaries.

FITZGERALD/HEMINGWAY ANNUAL

Edited by Matthew J. Bruccoli and C. E. Frazer Clark, Jr.

An annual publication devoted to writings by and about F. Scott Fitzgerald and Ernest Hemingway. The first volume (1969) contains "Dearly Beloved," a recently discovered short story by Fitzgerald, plus a lost Hemingway review of Sherwood Anderson's, "A Story-Teller's Story." The second volume (1970) contains Fitzgerald's letter to Hemingway commenting on *The Sun Also Rises* and suggesting cuts that Hemingway subsequently made, notes and comments on the letter by Philip Young and Charles Mann, and an unsigned, and previously unidentified article by Hemingway written in 1920. Each issue contains interviews, reminiscences, and reviews of recently published books by and about both authors.

1969 volume *$10.00*
1970 volume. ISBN 0-910972-03-6 . . . . *$12.00*

FITZGERALD NEWSLETTER

Edited by Matthew J. Bruccoli.

A corrected and revised edition of a newsletter issued in processed form between 1958 and 1968 as a focal point for information about F. Scott Fitzgerald, his life and writings. *327 pp.*

If billed *$10.95*
Payment with order . . . . *$ 9.95*

ERNEST HEMINGWAY'S APPRENTICESHIP, OAK PARK 1916–1917

Edited by Matthew J. Bruccoli.

Hemingway's uncollected early writings in the Oak Park High School *Tabula* and *Trapeze*. Illustrated. *ISBN 0-910972-05-2*.

Trade Edition . . . . *$ 6.95*
Extra-Illustrated Collector's Edition, limited to 200 copies *$12.50*

HEMINGWAY AND *THE SUN* SET

Edited by Bertram D. Sarason.

A collection by and about the persons who were prototypes for the characters in *The Sun Also Rises*. Illustrated. *ISBN 0-910972-06-0*.

In production.

"CHILDREN OF THE SEA" AND THREE OTHER UNPUBLISHED PLAYS BY EUGENE O'NEILL

Edited by Jennifer McCabe Atkinson.

Two one-act and two full-length plays by Eugene O'Neill now printed for the first time and presented in accurate texts from O'Neill's typescripts. *ISBN 0-910972-14-1*.

In production.

 NCR Microcard Editions

THE NATHANIEL HAWTHORNE JOURNAL

C. E. Frazer Clark, Jr., Editor

Consulting Editor: Matthew J. Bruccoli
University of South Carolina

The first issue of this annual includes previously unpublished Hawthorne letters to Longfellow and Caleb Foote ❀ the first census of Hawthorne letters ❀ "A Week's Vagabondage with Hawthorne," a previously unpublished recollection by Francis Bennoch ❀ the first printing of the complete text of a biographical sketch of Hawthorne by his publisher, James T. Fields ❀ previously unpublished recollections of her brother, by Elizabeth Hawthorne ❀ "The Interrupted Nuptials," a lost tale ❀ and articles by Arlin Turner, Lillian Gilkes, B. Bernard Cohen, Edward Stone, Leo B. Levy, and John M. Dorsey. ❀ $13.00..

The Nathaniel Hawthorne Journal
is a 308-page, hard-cover annual,
published by:

 NCR Microcard Editions

To Scott with
affection and esteem

Ernest/

For Whom the Bell Tolls—Collection of Matthew J. Bruccoli